The Sociology of Education

The Sociology of Education

P. W. MUSGRAVE

THIRD EDITION

METHUEN

LONDON AND NEW YORK

First published in 1965 by
Methuen & Co. Ltd
11 New Fetter Lane, London EC4P 4EE
Second edition, and first published as
a University Paperback, 1972
Third edition 1979
Reprinted 1983

Published in the USA by
Methuen & Co.
in association with Methuen, Inc.
733 Third Avenue, New York, NY 10017

Printed in Great Britain by
Richard Clay (The Chaucer Press) Ltd
Bungay, Suffolk

British Library Cataloguing in Publication Data
Musgrave, Peter William
The sociology of education.—3rd ed.
1. Educational sociology
I. Title
301.5'6   LC191   79-41112

ISBN 0–416–73030–2
ISBN 0–416–73040–X Pbk

Contents

Acknowledgements

A book of this kind naturally owes much to a great many people, but I wish particularly to thank the following:

My teachers at the Institute of Education, the University London, Dr G. Baron and Mrs J. E. Floud (now of Nuffield College, Oxford).

My students on the postgraduate and certificate courses at Homerton College, Cambridge during 1962–4, who left little unquestioned.

My colleagues at Homerton, who gave much assistance, often without knowing it, and particularly Dr N. K. Willson, who gave a great deal of her time to read and comment on the final draft.

My wife, for the typing of this book and much else besides.

Aberdeen, 1965   PWM

Preface to the Second Edition

Since 1965 when this book first went to press the reorganization of secondary education on a comprehensive basis has continued and the results of much new research have been published. I have taken account of both the structural changes and the new findings in this second edition in order that it may continue to serve as an introduction to this part of sociology for intending teachers. At the same time I have taken the opportunity of making some alterations suggested by various critics and by my own changing views of the whole field of sociology. Put briefly, the results of this rewriting are that Part I now focuses on the position of the child in society; much of the general introductory sociology that was included in the first edition has been omitted and chapters have been added on the school, the peer group and the mass media. Part II consists of the former Part III and deals with the sociology of the school; there is one new chapter here on the curriculum. The former Part II now forms Part III and this consideration of the social functions of education has been changed least of all.

I wish to add to the former list of acknowledgements: the staff and students of the Department of Sociology in the University of Aberdeen during the period 1965–9, who made me a rather better sociologist; the staff and students of the Faculty of Education in Monash University during 1970–1 who reminded me that I was also an educationist; my secretary, Mrs C. Stuart, who amongst other skills converts odd drafts into neat typescript.

Monash University, Melbourne, 1971   PWM

Preface to the Third Edition

Since 1965 when the first edition of this book was published and even since 1972 when the second edition appeared, not only has there been much change in the administrative structure of British education, especially at the secondary level, but some of the directions in which advanced industrial societies are moving seem to have become clearer. As a result, particularly of the latter development, sociological theory, both at the societal and at the inter-personal levels, has been in turmoil, and education has been one of the institutional areas in which sociologists have been most keen to try out their new ideas.

I thought it right, therefore, that this book should be considerably revised if it was to remain a useful introduction to its subject, especially for teachers in training. The general framework remains much as it was for the second edition and fewest changes have been made to Part I, but in Part II the mass of recent work on classrooms and in Part III much of the general thinking done of late about social institutions have led me to do a great deal of rewriting.

I wish to make a number of acknowledgements: to my students on the course, 'Introduction to the Sociology of Education', in the southern summers of 1978 and 1979, who showed me some of the ways in which the second edition was out-of-date; to the Master and Fellows of Corpus Christi College, Cambridge, who provided accommodation in the northern summer of 1978 for me to write in peace; and to Mrs V. Newson, Mrs E Sinclair and Mrs C. Stuart, all of whom helped to type the manuscript in the midst of much other work.

Monash University, Melbourne, 1979   PWM

I

Introduction

Sociology is a social science. This implies that sociology is an attempt to build up a set of logical and consistent theories about the society in which we live. Because of the primitive state of sociology as a subject, however, theories are not yet available over wide areas of the field and what we have are really well-developed frameworks within which logical analysis of social phenomena is possible. The subject matter of sociology includes the institutions which mark our society; such are the family, the class system and the economy. One important institution in a modern society is the educational system. The increasing concern with education has led to a specialism within the larger field of sociology which deals with the sociology of education. In this branch of the subject a study is made both of the relationships between education and society as a whole and of the interpersonal relationships that are characteristic within educational organizations. This book is an introduction to this specialized field and, since it is intended for British readers, it will mainly be concerned with conditions in Britain, though comparative examples from other countries are useful for indicating more clearly what is happening in this country.

A science should contain no prejudice. Therefore, polemics must be avoided, though very often decisions on educational policy are the very stuff of politics. On the whole we shall be concerned with means and not ends, but sometimes we shall be brought to the point beyond which a sociologist can no longer go without taking a moral position. This must and will be made clear. All teachers should realize when they are arguing from evidence and when their position is based on political or other beliefs.

There are two parts to our subject – society and education. To understand the sociology of education the student must learn something both of sociology itself and of education. Sociology often, but not always, demands statistics to demonstrate a truth, to indicate an order of magnitude, to make a point clear. These figures are not to be learnt parrotwise nor are they to be feared. They are only used where essential to the argument. Technical terms are used sparsely and are shown in italics on first use, being defined in the text at the same point. Footnotes have also been kept to a minimum. After each chapter there is a reading list to which references are made in the text by adding the date of publication to the author's name. (The place of publication is London, unless otherwise stated.) Many of these books now exist in paperback editions. Readers may like to note that nine of the books in the series 'Contemporary Sociology of the School' (Methuen) are cited and more than half the papers in S. J. Eggleston (ed.), *Contemporary Research in the Sociology of Education*, 1974.

The book has been divided into three parts. The first concentrates upon the way in which children become members of society. This process (Chapter 2) takes place to a great extent under the influence of their families (Chapter 3), though there are marked differences in the ways in which they develop according to the social class from which they come (Chapter 4). When considering the influence of the family and of social class some basic general sociology has been included upon which a sound sociology of education can be built. Finally, in the first part of the book two chapters analyse other important influences on the development of the child: the group of friends with whom he mixes (Chapter 5) and the mass media (Chapter 6).

In the second part the position of teachers in the schools is considered on the grounds that teachers who have thoroughly examined the forces operating on themselves will be more effective in their work. Four facets of a teacher's position are considered. A teacher serves in a school where he is at the centre of a complex web of forces which act upon him both from outside and from inside the school (Chapter 7). He is a member of an occupation usually referred to as a profession (Chapter 8). Before continuing the examination of the teacher there is a consideration of what he teaches, namely of the curriculum (Chapter 9). Next, those processes that influence the teacher which are school-based (Chapter

10) and finally those which are restricted to the classroom (Chapter, 11) are examined.

The final part examines the relationship of the contemporary British educational system to other social institutions. The main concern here is with the schools, though higher education and other forms of education are mentioned. The functions of education in relation to certain important fields are analysed. An attempt is made to answer four questions. What part does education play in relation to the political system (Chapter 12), in ensuring the workings of the economic system (Chapter 13), in selecting those with different capabilities to fill different positions in society (Chapter 14) and, finally, in the balance between social stability and social change (Chapter 15)?

Though much work has now been done in this field there are still areas where the research that the topics warrant has not been done. An introductory textbook should avoid controversy and, therefore, an indication is given where facts are sparse. But a reasonably uncontroversial narrative has always been provided on the grounds that it is of overriding importance to give teachers and all others interested in education the analytical framework within which to view children, schools and teachers.

PART I

The Child and Society

2

Socialization

The members of any social group, whether it is as large as a nation or as small as a village darts club, have expectations of how those who join it should behave. If the group is to survive in its present form, they must somehow or other ensure that those who join their group learn the behaviour expected of them when they fill the new positions that they occupy as nationals or as darts club members. In the case of a nation, in the first place parents teach their children, often without conscious thought, how to be good Englishmen, Scotswomen or Australians, whilst in a formal organization such as a sports club, frequently only those likely to conform are allowed to join, training prior to membership may be compulsory and clear rules specify what behaviour is normal for those filling the position of member. In all these cases where a situation is being defined or clarified to the newcomers to any group or where social arrangements exist to ensure that mutual behavioural expectations or *roles* are learnt, sociologists give to the process of induction the name of *socialization* (Clausen, 1968).

A. The Structural Perspective

In this chapter the process of socialization will be analysed from two points of view. Firstly, we shall look at the process as it takes place through time to see what roles are learnt as individuals during their life pass through the various positions available to them. Secondly, we shall examine the social process whereby individuals at any one moment learn through interaction with others how they are expected to behave. To the latter process we shall give the name of the *interpersonal perspective* and the former will be called the *structural perspective*.

Any group may be seen as made up of a number of *social*

positions which interlock in a patterned way because the members have mutual expectations of each other. This is most clearly seen in military units where clear-cut expectations of behaviour based on accepted patterns of authority are known to all members, but similar patterns exist in all groups with any elements of permanence. This idea has been extended beyond such simple groups to whole societies, so that sociologists speak of the *social structure*. On this large scale there are numbers of positions that form possible routes or pathways through the social structure. These positions may cluster around similar activities. For example, around the family there are such positions as father, mother, son or daughter; within education there are the positions of teacher, inspector, pupil or school caretaker; in the economy the positions of manager, worker, doctor or plumber; and, finally, within political institutions such positions as prime minister, civil servant, mayor or voter. Any child may be expected to prepare himself so that when he is older he can play the roles successively of pupil, worker, father and voter. Any adult may be expected to behave at more or less the same time as a father, a worker and a voter. One very important effect of having to play successions of roles and several roles concurrently is that the social structure holds together in a more or less cohesive manner, since individuals have many connections with many different parts of the society of which they are members.

1. *The Life Cycle*

Anthropologists have given much attention to the ways in which different societies have divided up the succession of roles that are particularly associated with the family. In simple societies, and even in the rural sectors of more advanced societies, where the family forms the unit of subsistence, these roles are central to much of social life. This succession of divisions has been called the *life cycle*. Thus, in a study of a French village in the Vaucluse the following eight major positions with specific expectations of behaviour existed: baby, child, lad/maiden, newly married, father/mother, widow(er), old person, and, finally, that role for which we are all destined, deceased person.[1] To anyone who has been socialized into a Westernized urban society there is one obvious omission here, the role of a mother or father whose family has left home. This omission highlights the fact that the rural cycle differs both between and within societies. There are rural and urban versions of the role which a boy or a girl in the USA must learn, but there are also differences in what is considered normal behaviour for an adult woman in the USA and in Britain.

2. *Age Grades*

These recognized divisions in the life cycle are sometimes known as *age grades* and very often important ceremonies mark the transition from one age grade to the next. The rites that mark the passage from being seen as a child to being seen as a young man or woman have been investigated by anthropologists in many societies. Such rites are very visible and often marked by physical scarring or the subsequent wearing of different clothes. In this way all will know just how anyone may be expected to behave and how in turn they should behave towards those they meet. In our own society there is much difficulty in knowing when transitions from one age grade to the next do occur. When those in mourning wore black for a year after their bereavement all knew who were to be treated with consideration as widows. Today it is very easy to cause distress by saying in good faith to the recently bereaved that her husband has not been in the local pub for a drink for a week or two.

The problem of knowing just what role a person is playing is particularly difficult in the case of the transition from childhood to adolescence and from adolescence to adulthood. Thus, children become adults at different ages along different dimensions. In Britain a child ceases to pay half fare on the railways at fourteen, is an adult as far as driving a car is concerned at seventeen, but may not vote till eighteen, or marry without parental consent till eighteen. In the last case, however, the age of adulthood is sixteen in Scotland, which once again points up the differences that exist between societies in the ages at which a child becomes an adult. Other examples may be quoted; in the state of Victoria in Australia a child becomes an adult on the railway at fifteen and may not yet vote till eighteen, but in New Zealand a person of fifteen may drive a car. There are big differences in the social definition of the word 'precocious' between societies and in its application to various dimensions of behaviour.

3. Ascribed and Achieved Roles

There are some positions and roles which cannot, or cannot easily, be refused. Those filling these positions must behave as is expected of them. A very clear example is provided by the sex role. In every known society members must either be male or female and for physiological reasons it is difficult, though not impossible, to pass from one sex to the other. Another example, based on social rather than physical considerations, is that in a capitalist society a baby cannot avoid being born to parents who belong either to the middle or to the working class. In societies where social strata have other foundations than class a somewhat similar situation exists and babies are born to be sons of a ruling class or daughters of peasants and so on. Early, or indeed any, movement away from this inherited position is rare, though possible through the process of adoption. A final example, increasingly of importance in Britain, relates to roles associated with colour of skin; one is born black, yellow or white and in contemporary British society, though not in all societies or even perhaps in all parts of British society, certain implications of this accident of birth are hard to escape. Such roles are termed *ascribed* by sociologists. They may be contrasted with roles which are not socially compulsory, but which may be *achieved* if one is able and so desires. Thus a man is ascribed maleness, but achieves the position of husband.

There is an important link between ascribed and achieved roles that is crucial in the context of this chapter. The future opportunities in life, or in the terms used here, the possible pathways through the social structure open to an individual, are largely determined by the nature of the social positions into which he is put willy-nilly. In other words the roles that he may achieve are in many cases constrained by his ascribed roles. In our society, though this is perhaps not so true of socialist societies, boys have more chance of becoming engineers or bus drivers than do girls, who in their turn are more likely to work as librarians or typists. There is also a greater probability that children born into the middle class will achieve an occupation of higher status than boys and girls of working-class parents. Basically these two examples draw our attention to the manner in which the social structure may be seen as providing tracks or pathways through life from which it is very difficult, though not impossible, to deviate.

4. *The Dimensions of Socialization*
Some behaviour is expected of us in all the settings into which we enter whilst we are expected to behave in certain other ways only in one specific position. The roles that we play all the time, for example those concerning sex or social class, will be referred to here as *primary roles* and will be examined in more detail in the next two chapters. There are patterns of behaviour relating to such roles as that of a church sidesman at morning service on Sunday that are played in only one setting. These will be called *tertiary roles*. In addition there is a large number of roles that are played in some, but not all settings. These *secondary roles* form a large and important part of what we learn whilst being socialized. Some examples will be mentioned very briefly here, though further consideration will be given to such secondary roles in later chapters.

The way in which we analyse secondary socialization is determined by the nature of the social system with which we are concerned. Thus, in advanced urban societies such as Britain or Australia, there are clusters of closely interrelated roles that centre on economic and on political institutions, but members of these societies do not play these roles constantly. Such roles may, therefore, be considered as secondary roles, and much secondary socialization takes place in childhood. By the age at which adolescents leave school they already have learnt, partly at home and partly at school, an incomplete, but wide, knowledge of the occupational structure. In other words, their economic socialization as producers is well under way. At an earlier age they have learnt something of their national role, knowing who to support, for example, in a war or in an international sporting event. Similarly, children gradually learn their political roles so that they know not only such details of their own particular political system as how to vote, but also feel that they are part of it and have a greater or lesser degree of power to take part in and to influence political decisions that concern them.

5. *Anticipatory Socialization*

Clearly socialization is a forward-looking process. In the political and economic examples that have just been given the child was enabled to learn more efficiently the behaviour that was later expected of him because, whether consciously or not, prior preparation had been given to him. This preparation has been termed *anticipatory socialization*. The teaching of social studies at school is often a very relevant part of the child's preparation for the economic and political roles that he will play in the future. The engaged couple rehearse together prior to marriage many of the behavioural patterns that they will later play as husband and wife. Likewise, the pregnant woman, at least mentally, prepares herself for her future as a mother.

This process of anticipatory socialization is important in that, if it is apt, it eases the transition into future positions. The young person who has been taught at school to study in the more independent way expected of him at a university or college will more easily move from the role of secondary pupil to that of tertiary student. Discontinuities in behavioural expectations are to some degree eliminated. However, anticipatory socialization may be misplaced and thereby discontinuities may remain or even be increased. The child who does not achieve the particular occupation to which he has been led to aspire because either his parents or his school have unduly raised his hopes will have greater difficulties in moving into his economic role than might otherwise have been the case.

One final point must be made before completing this examination of socialization from the structural perspective. Since we can talk of a life cycle of roles through which individuals move, socialization must clearly be a lifelong process. In recent years, as sociologists have realized that this concept and the analytical tools associated with it are equally applicable to the learning of adult roles, much work on adult socialization has been done (Brim and Wheeler, 1966). Socialization is not something that happens only in childhood. New roles must be learnt, and often old behaviour must be forgotten because it is no longer apt for the new positions that are assumed or the new groups that are joined. This is particularly true as persons grow older. They are no longer expected to behave as young folk do. This is attested by the existence of such phrases as 'mutton dressed as lamb'. Adult socialization, however, builds greatly on the foundations laid in childhood mainly because, as psychologists have shown us, what we learn as children is more permanent in nature than what we learn in later life.

B. The Interpersonal Perspective

Behavioural expectations or, in the language of the sociologist, roles may be laid out in an interlocking pattern which can be conceptualized as the social structure, but how are they actually learnt? Learning has been seen very much as a part of the province of the psychologist. What has the sociologist to say about learning that is of help to the teacher (Boocock, 1972)? In beginning to answer these questions the focus of this chapter must be switched from looking at social structure to an examination of the manner in which people interact at a face-to-face or interpersonal level. Once something has been understood of the way in which learning takes place in a model situation where two people interact, then the possibility exists of extending this process to socialization in all parts of the social structure and at all stages of the life cycle. Basically, what has to be explained is how an individual indicates to another his definition of what social reality is in such a way that the other learns this version and makes it his own (Berger and Luckmann, 1967).

1. *Mutual Steering*

One useful model for examining the way in which socialization takes place at the interpersonal level is to use the idea of 'feed-back'. This concept may be applied to the way in which two persons steer each other as they interact with one another. Let us take as an example a teacher in a primary school. She has expectations of herself in her role as teacher and of the behaviour of the children aged, say, seven in her class. Her pupils likewise have expectations of their teacher and are willing to imitate or to obey her in order to learn what they take to be socially acceptable behaviour. They may be willing, and this is important, either because they value their teacher or because they see her as powerful enough to insist that they do as she wishes. In either case they interpret the cues that the teacher feeds back to them consequent upon any action that she observes or knows them to have made. The teacher signals to them by a nod or a smile that to throw papers into the waste paper basket is valued behaviour; it meets the value of tidiness which she wishes to teach to her pupils. But she may also indicate to them by a frown or by words of disapproval that to throw paper darts even into the waste paper basket is not acceptable; it contradicts the value of orderliness upon which she puts great emphasis and which she hopes will become a valued part of the social reality that she will recreate in her pupils.

A point worth noting is that the range of behaviour tolerated in any role is usually quite wide. There are strict and less strict, tidy and less tidy teachers. Because of this each individual has some chance to make, rather than just to take, his own role. When one remembers the very large number of positions that any one person has to fill at any point in his life – for example, son, customer, holiday-maker, adolescent and so on – it is clear that there is considerable room for individuality in the way in which interpretations of each role are combined. Social devices do, however, exist to restrict the range of tolerated behaviour in certain positions. Thus, many schools insist that their pupils wear uniforms that ensure that they are highly visible and cannot, therefore, easily deviate from the behaviour desired by the school authorities.

2. Sanctions

The process of mutual steering may indicate to the learner how he is to behave, but what has still not really been explained is why he behaves as is desired. In any teaching situation, whether formal, as in a school, or informal, as in a family or small group, the sanctions used by the teacher or parent are crucial to the whole process since it is because of them that he can make his definition of the role stick. The term *sanction* is being used here in a non-emotional sense to cover all measures used to ensure that an individual behaves as is desired. Sanctions may be positive in the form of rewards or negative in the form of punishments. They may take a physical form, e.g. corporal punishment, or be material, e.g. prizes or fines, or immaterial, e.g. the giving or withholding of love. The system of sanctions that a teacher or parent selects from the wide battery available depends very much upon his own background, and the age and the sex of the child that is being socialized. English evidence seems to show that corporal punishment is more frequently used by working-class parents with young children, whilst middle-class parents in their turn more often use the threat that they will withdraw love. In all social classes girls are treated somewhat differently from boys, but their fathers are more indulgent of them than their mothers (J. and E. Newson, 1963). In somewhat stark contrast to these tendencies, prefects in independent schools for upper middle-class boys apparently still use corporal punishment more frequently as a sanction than their equivalents do in state schools for boys of the same age.

3. *Consensus or Conflict?*

The need to use sanctions to make a role stick has raised the question that has already been hinted at, namely the nature of the relationship between the teacher and the learner. Very often, particularly in the case of young children, the system of values held by the parent or the primary school teacher is absolutely unquestioned by the child. There is in effect a common system of values. The child wants to behave as the parent wishes him to do or to learn what the teacher has in mind for him. The sanctions, whether in the form of rewards or punishments, that the parent or teacher uses are seen as such by the child. The goals implicit in the behaviour are jointly held and the authority of the adult is accepted.

Suppose this were not the case. Immediately, important questions of control are raised. Where there is no consensus on values, then some form of power must be used to make the child do as is expected of him. A middle-class child will accept the threat 'Mummy won't love you any more if you do that again' as a sanction because he values his mother, but a teacher may have to deal with children who do not either want to behave as he feels right or hold the same values as he does. In such a case, where immediate obedience is required, coercion or the use of power or at least the threat of it will often be used. Thus, parents deprive their children of pocket money or physically force them to do what they want and teachers use systems of detention or in some cases, even where supposedly this action is not permitted, such physical punishment as blows with a ruler to force children to do what the teachers value highly.

In these latter cases the situation is one of conflict as opposed to those described beforehand where there was agreement. Recently there has been much more emphasis put in sociological writing on explaining situations in terms of conflict, since, especially perhaps in the field of the sociology of education, there has been a tendency to assume consensus. For this reason, the model of mutual steering that has been outlined here as a way of analysing the process of socialization at an interpersonal level, has been developed in such a way that it may be used to examine situations that have the characteristic either of conflict or of consensus. This is apt, since situations of both types exist in whatever socialization takes place, whether in childhood or amongst adults.

4. *The Growth of Self*

(i) *Natural and Personal Powers*. All children are born with some natural powers, but as they grow and as a result of their own particular experiences they develop personal powers. An individual's natural ability, therefore, as worked on by past experience enables him to cope with the present, but his past does not determine only *one* future. Rather there are a number of possible futures open to him and as soon as the individual brings one of these alternatives into being he has excluded the others. The concept of choice must, therefore, be central to any consideration of socialization. Parents and others responsible for children try to teach them to make deliberate and rational choices so that they appreciate the consequence of their actions for themselves and for others. The power to make choices is not, however, taught in a vacuum, but parents teach their children to operate within a system of rules and to aim for a set of targets. Both these constraints vary according to the setting concerned. Thus, the aims given to children from each social class are different, or again the rules on holiday are not the same as those at home. These rules set the guidelines for interaction between persons and within groups. As long as we choose to maintain such rules, the groups are maintained as they are. Our intentions or, perhaps more accurately, our lack of any other intentions prevent the collapse of the social *status quo*.

(ii) *Choice*. Rules, therefore, are always open to renegotiation and we must ask at what stage a child has the power to influence the present system of rules under which he is operating. Most actions by children depend upon recipes for behaviour learnt in the past, usually from their parents. They know that they must take nightclothes off in the morning and put outdoor things on to go to school; they know what to eat and how to move peas from plate to mouth; and they know, though do not always remember, how to behave when near to roads.

Since the ultimate aim of parents is that their children shall be able to make rational choices and particularly to cope with crises and unpredicted problems, 'recipe knowledge' (Berger and Luckmann, 1967, p. 56) is not enough. Children must be taught to make reflective decisions (Musgrave, 1978). Such decisions are very complex in nature. Take as an example a teenager who must decide whether to go out with his parents to the theatre on his mother's birthday or to accept an invitation to a party with his friends. Four elements are crucial to the making of decisions of this type: knowledge about the specific events concerned, e.g. the drama; factors relevant to the situation, e.g. the cost of tickets, perhaps already bought; the actual and likely interpretations of his possible behaviour by the others involved; and, finally, a process whereby he balances the first three elements to make a decision, e.g. 'I think Mum will be hurt whilst my friends will hardly notice I'm not there.' In passing, it should be noted that every such choice to interact with one person or group rather than with another expresses something about the personal characteristics of the chooser.

(iii) *Stages*. Rules, then, are learnt, but can, if the initiative is taken, be renegotiated between individuals. What may be asked is how early in their lives can children take part in this process of negotiation. When a baby is born he is culturally neuter. At this stage the mother in the main has the task of providing rules and targets for her child. Shotter (1974) has called this initial stage 'psychological symbiosis'. The baby uses his mother to do the thinking that is necessary to realize his intentions. He is attached to her by her loving behaviour towards him whilst, for example, feeding him, but he can very early in life influence his mother by cries or other sounds. She, in turn, acts as if she understands him. Analysis of the crying of infants as young as three weeks has shown that babies exhibit what many mothers call 'faking'. Even such individual physiological differences as the rate at which the stomach digests milk can ensure that an infant gains more attention from his mother than might otherwise be the case.

This early stage ends when at around the age of fifteen months the child becomes more capable of reflective behaviour. The child comes to see himself as apart from the mother. One index of this is that when using a spoon the baby no longer feeds himself and his mother indiscriminately, but rather uses the spoon merely for his own feeding. He then goes a stage further in the process of achieving independence and learns to deny his mother by saying 'no' to her.

The period of social games can now begin. Play is a crucial part of the socialization process. By play is meant activity that is not seen as necessary for the conduct of life. In play the child learns the difference between people and things. One of the earliest of social skills learnt is how to open and close at will his social links with others. Much of his early play is imaginary. Such behaviour is no longer solely dependent upon his present context but upon the larger social structure. An interesting example, reported by the Russian psychologist, Vygotsky, concerned two sisters whom he saw playing at being sisters. In play children, while released from serious immediate consequences, build personal powers which enable them to make later reflective choices.

5. *Deviance*

There is one last point before the main agents of socialization are considered very briefly. Some children act in ways that are seen by others involved in a particular social situation to be breaking the rules in operation at the time. Such behaviour is referred to as *deviant*. As used by sociologists this term has no overtones of condemnation, but merely covers behaviour falling outside the tolerated range along whatever dimension is being considered. Thus, a boy may be normal in respect of his familial roles and be seen as a good son, but may be deviant at school and, therefore, seen as a bad pupil. Furthermore, deviance may be due to behaviour that falls outside either end of the range of tolerated behaviour. In, for example, the playing of religious roles, one may be a saint or a sinner. To a sociologist in his role of sociologist, whatever his view as a moral person, neither is good or bad; both are deviant.

Behaviour that is seen as deviant can arise in a number of ways. Firstly, a child may have learnt wrongly or never been told how to behave in a given circumstance; he acts in ignorance and exhibits what to others is deviant behaviour. But, secondly, he may intend to be deviant; he may set out 'to be a naughty boy'. Indeed, some children are socialized into behaviour that most others see as deviant. A vivid example of this process is found in Dickens' description of Fagin trying to make Oliver Twist into an efficient thief. This example also indicates the distinction between deviance and delinquency; the latter term relates to acts that break the law and these, e.g. exceeding the speed limit, may not necessarily be seen as deviant.

These two cases are straightforward. However, recently sociologists have given much attention to a third situation where, once the label of deviant has been attached to a child, he comes to see himself more permanently in the light of that label. An example of this process would be where a child comes to see himself as slow because his teacher constantly tells him that he is so.

Finally, a fourth way in which deviance may arise must be noted. Rules are often very general and rely for interpretation on 'common sense' so that all specific possible actions are not covered. Thus, even where a child knows all the rules, he may still, whilst behaving in good faith, do something which may never have been done before in the particular circumstances and which his parents or teachers decide is unacceptable and, hence, deviant behaviour. From such instances new rules often emerge.

What can be clearly seen is that deviance is a complex concept. It can be a result of a failure in the process of socialization, but it need not necessarily be caused in this way. All acts of deviance must be seen in their particular social contexts and judged as far as possible from a sociological perspective, although in life a parent or a teacher may have to consider moral principles prior to determining how to deal with acts defined as deviant.

C. The Main Agents of Socialization

For the sake of completeness the main agents of socialization will be considered briefly as a conclusion to this chapter. In advanced, urban societies four agents seem crucial, namely the family, the school, the peer group and the mass media. The remainder of the first part of this book will be given over to a consideration of three of these agents, whilst the whole of the second part will be concerned with various aspects of the fourth, namely the school. Through these agents a version of social reality is created in the minds of the next generation which may match that of adults or may, along some dimensions, be deviant by their criteria

1. *The Family*

In the past, and still in most simple societies, the family provided the main setting where roles of all types were learnt. As a result of experiences gained largely within the family the child became a loyal member of his tribe which was a political system in itself, a worker within the subsistence unit of his own family, and, in addition to this secondary socialization, he learnt from the members of his large, multi-generational family such primary roles as his sex role. In our contemporary society the family still acts as a powerful agent of socialization, especially for primary roles and for much of the knowledge of routine activities that has been called recipe knowledge.

With the growth of the capitalist economy the social class system has developed and different styles of life have evolved in various social groupings. These have been and are passed on from one generation to the next. One result of this is that whereas in simple societies most people knew very much the same, the stock of knowledge is now distributed differentially amongst the groupings within any complex society. This clearly will have important implications for education, and a separate chapter must be set aside in which the differences between the manner of socialization in the main social classes will be considered. Whatever the social class, much of what is taught is passed to the next generation without any conscious thought. Often the main method of socializing the child would seem to be the regular presence of a role model to be imitated who has power or is highly valued and who persistently behaves in a consistent manner. Inconsistency, particularly with regard to sanctioning behaviour, muddles the child, who often feels insecure since he does not know which actions are approved and which are not.

Unusual family structure has an effect on the way in which children are socialized. Thus, children in families where owing to bereavement or divorce there is only one parent undergo anomalous upbringings. Evidence shows that children of both sexes brought up by a mother alone tend to take more of a woman's view of the world than is usual, and that in the more rare case where a man brings up his family alone the children interpret reality more from a man's viewpoint than is normally the case.[2] In this connection it could be of interest to study the children of fathers who have such occupations as trawlerman, commercial traveller or long-distance lorry driver.

2. *The School*

Not only does the way in which families differ in their life-style distribute certain kinds of knowledge differentially throughout society, but the very complex and specialized nature of contemporary economic roles also implies a further distribution of the stock of social knowledge. In addition, the educational demands of many occupations are such that very few parents are today capable of teaching their children what they need to know to play such roles. Many parents have difficulty helping their children with simple algebra or elementary science when set as homework, and would not know where to begin if asked to teach them quadratic equations or advanced physics.

Because families from different social classes differ in their values there is the likelihood that some children may come to school with values that clash with those held by their teachers. This can lead to a discontinuity between school and home. A clear and perhaps extreme case will indicate the nature of the problem. In Northwest Canada children from the Kwakiutl tribe of Eskimos are brought up so that the reality of time is very different for them from that of most Canadian children. For them the working day is longer in summer than in winter. Therefore, they find it hard to fit into a regular school routine that lasts from 9.00 to 4.00 all the year round regardless of the length of daylight. Furthermore, their fathers teach them to catch salmon, a main part of their traditional diet, by example rather than by verbal explanation, so that school seems to provide a very artificial way of learning. Also aggression is not punished at home, but is found to be most unacceptable at school.[3] This may seem to be an unreal case in the context of contemporary Britain, but we shall see that the differences between Kwakiutl and working-class children are not so great as may be thought.

Though the school can be a powerful agent of socialization, it is such constraints as those just mentioned that must be examined if the success or failure of socialization within formal educational organizations is to be assessed. Frequently counter-influences are encouraged by the presence within the school of groups of young persons who support each other in negating the influence of the school.

3. *The Peer Group*

Strictly, the term *peer group* should describe any group of equals according to some stated criterion, but sociologists usually apply it to groups made up of persons who are of the same age and most often to groups of children or of adolescents. A recent study (Willmott, 1969) has shown that in East London all the boys and most of the girls in this survey were in groups of two or more and that the average size of these groups was around five. Such small cliques should not be confused with gangs, which are frequently associated with deviance or even delinquency. The groups with which we are here concerned play a normal part in the process of socialization in most societies. They provide experiences to those who are growing up of a type that are not available in their own families.

From children's point of view families are hierarchical since their parents are superior in power to them. Before children leave their families of origin to go to work and eventually to set up families of their own, they need to have certain experiences that they cannot undergo in their own homes, but which will provide skills required in adult life. For example, they should mix in groups that do not have great differences in rank and where individuals may achieve status on their own behalf rather than be ascribed the status of an inferior member. Discontinuities between the role of child and that of adult will also be lessened by mixing with those of the appropriate sex who are not members of one's own family. Many adults look back with amused embarrassment on their first date, but they should remember that their awkwardness in meeting the opposite sex became less because of their membership of various peer groups.

Once again a social mechanism can be seen to function as an agent of socialization, though equally clearly no one doubts the spontaneous and real joy that individuals experience during the times that they spend with their young friends. There is something of a paradox here. The family, to which many people ascribe the duty of socializing the next generation, often does so without parents or other members of the family giving much thought to the process. Schools were established as formal organizations to socialize children because the task of recreating social reality was thought to have passed beyond the capability of the family, but nevertheless they are for one reason or another only partially successful. Yet the peer group, by nature a spontaneous group dedicated to leisure, is a powerful agent for socializing the young both by its own lights and even by some socially acceptable criteria.

4. *The Mass Media*

Over the last century the circulation of newspapers, magazines, comics and books has risen to match the rising spread of literacy. More recently films and the radio have become available to the majority of the population in advanced, urban societies. However, during the last twenty years the phrase 'the mass media' has become increasingly associated with one particular medium, namely television. This medium penetrates into almost every home in contemporary Britain and provides information, entertainment and role models of great apparent power to children. Examples are the currently fashionable pop stars and aggressive heroes, whose speech, habits and clothes are widely imitated, particularly by teenagers. What has to be considered in a later chapter is how and in what way television and other mass media influence the socialization of children.

D. Conclusion

The aim of this chapter has been to build up a theoretical framework which may be used to examine socialization in some detail. The process of socialization has been considered in two ways. Firstly, the passage of the child through the social structure was described and attention given to the various dimensions of behaviour which a member of a given society must learn as he becomes an adult. Secondly, the idea of a sociology of learning was introduced and attention was switched to the interpersonal level. At this level the important point was made that situations where learning occurred could be divided into, firstly, those which were characterized by consensus and an agreed set of values and, secondly, those in which conflict was present so that coercive sanctions were often necessary to ensure that the desired behaviour took place. In this latter situation negotiation is found from an early age so that the child begins to choose for himself, to develop personal powers and to have some initiative over what he does and what he becomes. He acts for himself, though inevitably constrained by his social circumstances. These theoretical ideas will be used in the rest of this part of the book and in the next part in a more detailed consideration of the four main agents of socialization which were introduced in this chapter, in order to discover what is the nature of the social reality that they pass on to the next generation.

BIBLIOGRAPHY

P. L. Berger and T. Luckmann, *The Social Construction of Reality*, 1967.
S. S. Boocock, *Towards a Sociology of Learning*, New York, 1972.
O. G. Brim and S. Wheeler, *Socialization After Childhood. Two Essays*, New York, 1966.
J. A. Clausen (ed.), *Socialization and Society*, Boston, 1968.
P. W. Musgrave, *The Moral Curriculum: A Sociological Analysis*, 1978.
J. and E. Newson, *Infant Care in an Urban Community*, 1963.
J. Shotter, 'The Development of Personal Powers', in M. P. M.

Richards (ed.), *The Integration of a Child into a Social World*, 1974.

P. Willmott, *Adolescent Boys of East London*, 1969.

NOTES

1 L. Wylie, *Village in the Vaucluse*, New York, 1964.
2 For some examples see E. Z. Dager, 'Socialization and Personality Development in the Child', in H. T. Christensen (ed.), *Handbook of Marriage and the Family*, Chicago, 1964.
3 R. P. Rohner, 'Factors Influencing the Academic Performance of Kwakiutl Children in Canada', *Comparative Education Review*, October 1965.

3

The Family,
Socialization and Education

In the first part of this chapter the family will be considered as a social institution. The aim will be to indicate the nature of family structures in Britain today (Harris, 1969). In the second part of the chapter the interpersonal perspective will be emphasized, so that the learning of the roles provided by the structure already described will be the focus, and, more particularly, the learning of those roles that tend to influence how children will later fare at school. Social class differences will be mentioned occasionally here, but this is so important a topic that the whole of the next chapter will be given over to its consideration.

A. The Family as a Social Institution

How can we define the word *family*? To a sociologist the family is one of the many small face-to-face groups that he calls *primary groups*. It has certain peculiar characteristics that differentiate it from other common primary groups such as groups that work together or meet together regularly for some leisure pursuit. Firstly, it gives special recognition to the relationship between one male and one or more females or between one female and one or more males. The former case covers the common Western European or American family; the latter covers the case found in Tibet where one woman and a group of brothers form the family unit. This definition is influenced by the findings of anthropologists among primitive peoples, but it serves to remind us that the typical family pattern found in Britain is not the only one nor even the universal one in this country. The purposes that the family serves can be fulfilled in several ways. Temporary liaisons and men with several spouses, more frequently in succession than at the same time, are found in all social classes in the so-called civilized countries. These forms of family will give their offspring an up-bringing of a quality very different from that given to children born into families of the more usual Western European pattern.

Anthropologists have found that some pattern of family organiza-tion is a common social institution even amongst peoples who do not understand the connection between the sex act and the birth of children. The theory held quite commonly in the nineteenth cen-tury that sexual communism was to be found amongst lower civiliza-tions has not been substantiated. Even amongst those peoples who are ignorant of the significance of the sex act, there is a strong feel-ing between mother and child. The position of the father is less definite, as the part of the father in the family may be played by a 'social' father rather than by the biological father. However, here can be seen the second peculiar characteristic of the family, namely the stress given to kinship in the way that the family is organized.

1. *The Functions of the Family*

One of the ways in which sociologists analyse any institution is by asking what the consequences for it are of society being organized as it is or, in other words, what *functions* it is fulfilling. The concept of function is descriptive, not explanatory, and has to be used with some care. There are three types of danger. Firstly, the argument developed can easily become teleological, that is, the effect observed may be treated as a cause. Thus, one may move from saying that one consequence of the present family system is the socialization of the young to a position where the claim is made that families exist to socialize the young. Secondly, because functional analysis starts from the *status quo* the assumption can be made that no change will occur and, furthermore, that there is general agreement with the present situation. Yet, as already indicated briefly in the last chap-ter, family systems have changed quite radically over the last two centuries. Finally, where an analysis underestimates social change, an ideological stance of a conservative nature may be adopted. How-ever, if all these difficulties are avoided, and they can be, the use of the concept, function, can provide an analytical entry into many sociological problems and, hence, it will be used in this book.

The first question that must be answered here is, therefore, what are the chief functions of the family? Traditionally, answers to this question have been given under three headings. Consideration has been given to the way that the family first fulfils the satisfaction of sex needs, secondly acts as an economic unit, and thirdly cares for the young and old. Each of these functions will be examined in turn, though it is to the way that the family cares for the young that most attention will be given because of its greater relevance to education.

(i) *Sex Needs*. There are very powerful impulses to sexual behaviour in most humans, and any organized society will wish to place this area of conduct under a form of control. Whatever family system is chosen, sex can be met in some way within the family. Today, amongst the more developed societies this function of the family has become more complex. In a modern industrial society marked by many impersonal contacts the individual could feel isolated and develop a personality insufficient to meet his problems, if he had not some secure base from which to venture forth and to which he might return. The family provides this security, giving the individual the affection and interest which are needed to sustain him in the many brief and temporary contacts with the world at large. A person can often manage his psychological tensions if he can take his troubles home.

The institution of marriage has changed greatly over the last century; it is coming to be viewed today more as a partnership of equals than, as was the case, as a relationship between a dominant male and an almost servile female (Young and Willmott, 1973). The family has ceased to provide all the meals and most of the clothes, since many meals and clothes are now bought outside the family. The family has come to be used as a very specialized agency for providing the affection that helps to ensure the emotional stability needed if men and women are to manage their lives successfully under modern conditions.

(ii) *Economic*. The primitive family was a subsistence unit that organized the raising and getting of food. The family held and farmed the land. In countries where hunting and fishing were important means of food supply the family organized the labour for these purposes. Today, production of most goods and services is carried out in factories or outside the household, and members of the family are employed as individuals, not as one unit. Rewards in the form of money wages are paid to individuals who are often adolescents. Work and home or family have become separated. Different codes of values may rule in both, with the result that there is a loss of emotional unity within the family.

There is a further economic function that the family used to fulfil. Before the industrial revolution it was normal for the child, whether boy or girl, to learn his future occupation with the family; son usually followed father. This continuity is now no longer common, though in some of the professions there is evidence that this 'self-recruitment' of occupations still occurs;[1] the case may be cited of the sons of doctors following their fathers. Today the child does not learn the technical skills of a job from his father, but picks up the social skills and the background to the job. Again, in areas where one industry is predominant, such as in a mining village, the possibility that a son can do other than follow his father is remote. But the majority of children live today in urban areas that contain a diversity of industries and occupations. In these conditions the family cannot fulfil its former function. Most parents can give neither the specialized training necessary nor the advice that a child needs if he is to match his abilities and aptitudes to the local opportunities for employment in the best possible way.

(iii) *Socialization*. Just as those who become members of any group must learn its ways, so must new members of the family be socialized into the roles relating to that stage of the life cycle through which they are passing. However, the family has a crucial position in the social structure since it is mainly through the family that society at large initiates its new recruits. It will be noticed that no consideration is here being given to one part of the third function of the family, namely the care of the old. This is of no less importance in itself, but the socialization of the young has a more direct relevance to education. Therefore in the context of this book this aspect must be given the main emphasis.

Although any group must initiate its recruits, the family socializes its young in a different way because of its peculiar structure. This

ensures that there is a difference in age between the older members – the parents, and the new recruits – the children. Thus, particularly where the children are young, the parents can exert great
power over them. Secondly, except in the case of one-parent families, families are bound to contain members of both sexes, unlike
such groups as men's clubs. The family provides not only physical
care, but also teaches to the children the parents' interpretation of
social reality around them, and it is within the family that the child's
personality is developed in the early and the formative years.

The family is not a necessary social institution from the biological
point of view, since reproduction of the species does not demand
such an organization. But within the limits set by hereditary poten-
tiality the personality is formed, and in most contemporary societies this development takes place best through the socialization of
the young within a small group such as the family (Parsons, 1956).
The child learns the patterns of behaviour needed to exist in his
environment. The young learn not just how to subsist but how to
exist socially. Boys learn what to wear and how to treat other boys
and girls. They learn what behaviour to expect from other children
of the same and the other sex. They notice how their parents behave, often internalizing these patterns through their play, as, for
example, when children dress up to play at weddings. It is important to note the complementary nature of any role, since it includes
both the expected behaviour of that role and also the behaviour
expected in others towards that role. Furthermore, to be fully competent in their social existence, children must ultimately learn the
relevance of third parties to themselves and to the others with whom
they interact. It is only by knowing each other's roles that we can
cooperate with one another.

Children may play at roles like actors in the theatre, but ultimately they become these roles. The girl playing at mother takes
on the characteristics of personality associated with women in that
society; the personality expected in an American woman is different
from that expected in an English woman. In their earliest years
children are egocentric, but as they grow older they gradually
achieve the capacity to put themselves in the positions of others.
This process takes place mainly within the family. For example,
the child comes to know that his mother may be too busy to attend

to his immediate needs. In sociological terms he has begun to appreciate that roles are complementary. The child learns that age governs behaviour as he watches his mother and father. He comes to have a wider view of adult roles as he makes visits with his parents and observes other adults. He also learns from his parents and other adults the many occupational and leisure roles that are current in his environment.

As the child grows older the process becomes more complex. The older child or adolescent comes into contact at school or at work with values that may be very different from those held within his own family. His parents, as members of an older generation, may not change their values as quickly as the younger generation. There can, therefore, be discontinuities between the values of the family and its young. This becomes more possible after the adolescent has left school, as he meets an even wider range of values. The young worker can have encountered three different and conflicting codes of honesty, that of the home, of the school and of the factory. Thus it is that the process of socialization often ends in conflict and sometimes in rebellion by the adolescent. The educational problems that are inherent in this situation will be discussed later in this chapter.

2. *Family Systems*

Anthropologists have described many primitive societies which have very complex family structures so as to carry out the above functions. Some family units combine closely more than two generations, namely of adults and children stretching vertically over three or more generations. These families may also cover several degrees of kinship, stretching horizontally to include cousins and in-laws. The technical term given to this system of organization is the *extended family*. A form of this system was found in Britain before the industrial revolution, but under the impact of industrialization the extended family has gradually changed in character. Today in most industrial countries the family is thought of as a small unit consisting of parents and perhaps two children. To such a unit the name of the *nuclear family* has been given.

In the 1870s the average number of children in completed families in Britain was around six; by the 1900s it had dropped to three and by the 1920s to two (Fletcher, 1962). There were differences between the social classes, as can be seen from the following table:

Family size for women married in:	1900–9	1920–4
Non-manual husbands	2·81	1·90
Manual husbands	3·96	2·72
Average	3·53	2·42

The last column represents the size of families that must have been complete since the women concerned were past childbearing age. These figures clearly show both the decline in family size and the differences between the social classes.

Many advertisements show the nuclear family of 'mum, dad and the kids'. This type of family has come to be considered as the norm by many, particularly perhaps among the middle-class occupations which include teachers and social workers. Hence, much of what is implied in the organization of the modern family and assumed to be a usual part of family life by many teachers may be peculiar to the middle class. A good example of this tendency is the value placed on the exclusive mother–child relationship, which is considered to have almost the universality of a biological law, but which may well be a local and temporary pattern. Those brought up in a nuclear family must beware of the parochialism that considers the extended family as a deviation from the norm.

Bott (1957) has pointed out that when considering the modern urban family the whole network of social relationships maintained by the family must be taken into account. She suggests the hypothesis that the closeness of the relationship between the husband and wife varies with the closeness of the tie between the family and its own social network. As a concrete case one may think of the working-class husband who goes out to the pub and leaves his wife at home with her relations. Here there is separation in the family of marriage directly offset by a close relationship by both husband and wife with the surrounding environment. But Bott points out that such a situation is not purely a matter of social class. In professional families also the relationship between husband and wife may be marked by distance. Though close-knit family systems are more likely in the social conditions under which the working class lives, they are not universal or peculiar to those conditions.

Industrial societies allow various types of family system. Within Britain several ways of organizing the family have been reported, varying according to such factors as whether the environment is rural or urban, in Scotland or England, and what the prevailing local industry is.[2] However, the nuclear family does have some advantages in an industrialized society. Movement, both of a geographical nature and up or down the social class system, is probably easier for a small family with few local connections than for members of an extended family. These two types of movement, known as *geographical* and *social mobility*, are very necessary in the rapidly changing conditions of a modern industrial society.

We have taken the view of Talcott Parsons and his followers that the family is one particular type of small group. Parsons (1956) tried to go further and proposed a general theory of the family applicable to all family structures and covering the local differences found by anthropologists. Briefly, the theory is that the father's role is especially concerned with tasks and can be termed *instrumental*, whilst the mother's role is considered to be centred on the emotions and can be termed *expressive*. This theory did seem to deal with most of the evidence relating to family structures in Western societies, but recent trends towards one-parent and communal families are not easily accounted for. However, Parsons' work did indicate the immense difficulties in any attempt to develop widely applicable theories or conceptual frameworks in sociology.

3. *Conclusion*

Prior to 1960 a number of studies of the British family showed clearly that, although there was a greater applicability of the nuclear family, especially when analysing middle-class families and those living on housing estates, yet the links between generations and the patterns of help associated with the extended family were still commonly found. In general, the results of these studies (Young and Willmott, 1957; Willmott and Young, 1960) still probably hold, but there do seem to be some changes occurring in family structure that could spread and that have important implications for education. There is, firstly, an increase in the frequency of one-parent families either due to the fact that divorce is now more common in all social classes than before the war or due to the greater number of single mothers. Secondly, there is, especially perhaps amongst the middle class, a growth of communal families, many of which are somewhat impermanent in composition.

In addition to these structural changes, the functions of the family in contemporary Britain seem to have altered somewhat. Although the family remains the main agent of early socialization, this process has come to be seen as very complex. In much the same way as the function of providing literacy and numeracy is now beyond the family and has been handed to the school, the process of socialization has been complicated by the work of psychologists, sociologists and other so-called experts, whose advice has taken the place of that of Granny and is regularly available to young parents in the mass-circulation dailies and weeklies. In order to make up for the apparent inadequacies in the socialization provided by the contemporary family, there has been a great expansion in the personal-service professions, both at the fully professional level, e.g. educational psychologists, and at the semi-professional level, e.g. social workers, many of whom work in the educational system. Medical experts have made many young women afraid of having a baby; social experts are now making parents feel guilty about the ways in which they bring up their children. As a result of this latter tendency, the familial functions of the school have widened.

However, the socializing function of the family is still very crucial and has an important relationship with the educational system. At the simplest level, before the child starts his formal education he has already learnt much in the family that the school takes for granted. Even when the child goes to school he spends more time in the family than with his teachers. It is for these reasons that knowledge of the family is important to the teacher, especially if the teacher's experience is of a different type of family structure from that of his pupils. We shall, therefore, now pass from examining family structure to the ways in which parents socialize their children.

B. Socialization within the Family and Education

Not all the analysis and information contained in the last section has direct implications for education. Some is essential background and some will be used in later parts of this book. If we consider the three functions of the family from the standpoint of the educational system, the first, the sex function, has little direct relevance. The economic function is of some importance though still in an indirect way. Since the nuclear family has lost this function in its pre-industrial form, some other social institution has had to take over. The teaching of the basic skills necessary to earn a living in a modern community has been handed to the educational system. Literacy is one such skill. In the same way schools can undertake much of the vocational guidance that is essential to steer a child into the job for which he is most suited. This task is unnecessary in a primitive village. These educational problems will be considered more fully later, particularly in the third part of this book. There remains the process of socialization. The interrelation between education and socialization will be discussed under three headings – early socialization, personality development and the control of the adolescent. Finally, to cover some of the contemporary changes in family structure, a brief consideration of socialization in communes will be added.

1. *Early Socialization*

The patterns of behaviour that a society has to pass on to its new recruits are referred to as its *culture*. It must be stressed that this term will always be used in this its anthropological sense and never with any aesthetic connotation. In a primitive society the transmission of the culture was a major part of education. One of the most famous of recent anthropologists, Margaret Mead, studied the way children grew up in Samoa (Mead, 1928) and in New Guinea (Mead, 1930). Her accounts are based on life in one form of extended family and describe how the children of these peoples were given what we should call their primary education in the family without ever entering a school. The extended family did not need to hive off part of its function of socializing the child to a special educational institution. In our culture there are many patterns of living that are passed on in the same way, but the traditional peoples that Margaret Mead was describing did not yet have to cope with the rapidly changing culture that our children must do. The nuclear family can teach a child when to shake hands or how to eat a meal, but it cannot easily teach the child how to read or to do complicated mathematics, particularly if both parents go out to earn a living.

Two problems are at once raised. At what age should education outside the family begin and what alternatives should be available both at the start and later? These are administrative decisions and here the important point is that, by the age of five or six when children in most European countries start at school, the family has already done a great deal of an educational nature. Much of the culture has by this age been transmitted. Also, during the next few years when the majority of children are very malleable the school works alongside the family which still has a very potent influence. There is the possibility of a partnership of or a clash between the two institutions that are socializing the child. The danger of conflict is probably lessened by the fact that the school tends to stress the instrumental learning needed for future life in a complex industrial community, whilst the family on the whole stresses the expressive development of the personality and the emotions. However, certainly in Britain, the schools have come to consider that they have a pastoral care for their pupils. Therefore the values that the school tries to inculcate may be at odds with those that the family attempts to teach the child. For example, stealing may be thought very wrong by the teacher, but no one may prevent a country child from taking apples from an orchard or a city child from taking fruit from a lorry moving through his playground, the streets.

The children in Samoa and New Guinea, whose upbringing was described by Margaret Mead, could learn all the roles that they had to play from the education that they received as they were socialized within the extended family. But the roles that an adult in contemporary Britain needs to learn cannot all be taught within the nuclear family. A very simple example will show this to be true. A nuclear family is of one social class and mainly meets members of the same or almost the same social class. In industry, however, a manager or a workman must meet all social classes and know how he is expected to behave in each different social situation. The school can provide experience of a wider range of adult roles in a less emotional frame of reference than the family. This opening of the world to the child is one important function of the school that is often forgotten by teachers in their stress on sheer knowledge and on the inculcation of moral virtues.

Yet though the family cannot do everything and may clash with the school it does much more than teachers are sometimes prepared to admit. Children come to learn what is expected of them and of others. 'You're a big boy now, you mustn't cry.' 'You don't do that to smaller children, do you?' They begin to learn how their family views adults of other social classes that impinge on them; the middle-class child who imitates his mother's telephone voice when she orders from the local grocer has begun to learn something of the social class system. Vocational aspirations may be mainly of an unrealistic type in very young children. 'I want to be a fireman.' But, when the child is older, the family has been found to have a very strong influence on occupational choice, and often this power is exercised without the more precise knowledge that the school could give. Sex roles are learnt, as are views on modesty, the latter often in the process of toilet training. The nursery rhymes that are sung, first at home and then in early schooling, begin to stress the moral virtues. Bo-Peep found the lost sheep and the Knave of Hearts was punished for stealing the tarts. In the type of single-class environment common in suburbia or on housing estates, differences in cultures between social classes are reinforced, since the children's playgroups are homogeneous. 'I wouldn't play with that Tommy if I were you, he's not a nice boy', or 'he's stuck up'.

There are, however, more subtle forces at work. Several large-scale and thorough investigations have shown that measured intelligence (IQ) varies directly with the size of the family. This tendency operates at each social class level. In 1947 a survey was made of all children born in Scotland in 1936, out of which a smaller and representative sample was chosen containing the 7,380 children born in the first three days of each of the twelve months in the year. The evidence from this survey showed the connection between family size and IQ at all social class levels very clearly, as can be seen in the following table. Furthermore, it should be noted that ordinal position within any size of family apparently plays no part in these differences in IQ.[3] More recently Douglas' work (1964) has given evidence of the same trend. His sample consisted of 5,362 children living in England, Scotland and Wales born in the first week of

March 1946. As in the Scottish survey, some details from which are shown in the table, he found that there was not a dramatic fall in IQ in middle-class families until the family contained four or more children, but there was no group of middle-class families where size did not have some influence on the IQ score of the children.

Mean test score by occupational class by size of family

Occupation	Size of family				
	1	2	3	4	5
Professional and large employers	52·5	52·3	53·7	51·3	43·1
Skilled manual workers	41·7	40·7	39·4	35·8	33·4
Unskilled manual workers	34·6	36·1	33·1	32·8	29·4
	(Maximum score possible = 76)				

There has been much speculation as to the exact reason for this connection between size of family and IQ. The argument has usually run that parents of low IQ have large families and that, since there is a correlation (of about 0·5) between the IQ of parent and child, the children of these larger families will tend to have a low IQ. Yet this does not account for the incidence of this effect at all social class levels. Recently it has been argued that the causation runs in the opposite direction. The large family results in the low IQ, mainly because the younger infants in a large family, in which the children are closely spaced in age, are not given sufficient time and attention by their mother so that their inherited intellectual capabilities can be developed to the full.

There is some evidence to back this view. In the Scottish Mental Survey the 974 pairs of twins were found to have an IQ on average five points lower than that of only children. A French investigation has shown that the IQ of children in families whose ages are well-spaced is on average higher than in closely spaced families. But an additional factor must be taken into account, namely that variations in both family size and in IQ may be affected by a common causative factor. Thus it is known that there are certain important differences in values between those who have large and those who have small families. The ability to defer present pleasures into the future is one such value that is differentially held. The hypothesis that there is a common cause, namely the pattern of values held by parents, that influences both family size and the IQ of children, has been tested and appears to be true.[4] It would seem that, whatever the cause, the quality of life in large families does influence measured intelligence and perhaps even attitudes towards school. These tendencies in their turn will have a vital bearing on success at school, more especially in the process of selection for secondary education, where this is still relevant.

The family teaches the child a great deal, both consciously and unconsciously, during the first few years. Later the school takes over part of the task, but few teachers come to influence a child as deeply as his parents do. This deep influence does not only extend to the transmission of the outward signs of the culture. It has already been pointed out that the child tends to become the roles that he plays. The connection between the family and personality therefore requires examination.

2. *Personality*

There are inherited determinants of personality which put limits on the moulding that society can do. These, if anything, form the core of individuality in a person. But how is it that individuals show their singularity against a basic personality that is common to their own culture and different from other cultures? Why is it that a Cockney or a Scot is credited with a certain type of personality?

Anthropologists have reported some of the most significant cases of such differences. Margaret Mead described two tribes in New Guinea who lived in relatively close physical proximity, but who did not meet owing to the impenetrable nature of the intervening country. In one tribe the men cared for the children, whilst the women did the hunting and the food-gathering. Each sex had the personality characteristics that one would associate with the tasks allocated to it. In the neighbouring tribe the pattern of tasks and of personalities was more akin to that in our own culture. As in these two cases, each society ensures that its members have a substantial degree of conformity in this respect, so that individual personalities fall within the permitted range. In this process the link between the community and the personality is the family.

There is a basic psychological need for the child to attach himself to others, especially to adults. The nature of such attachments is very general. The child loves its mother, not any of her specific acts. The loved adult becomes a model that the child will imitate. He will attempt to imitate all the different roles that the adult plays. These roles are structured differently in each individual, and the emphases put on different parts of the role structure are different from those in other individuals. The child internalizes these systems of roles to lay the foundation of his own personality. Personalities come to differ because of varying inherited potentialities and because the experiences that are met, even in early life, are not common to all members of society. But the traits of personality that are common to any one country can be understood to have their beginnings within the family. It is worth adding here that evidence will be produced in the next chapter to show that such inter-cultural differences in personality exist between social classes as well as between nationalities.

There exist very few technically sound empirical studies by sociologists of the ways in which children in early childhood learn. This is probably because of the great difficulties of employing the usual sociological methods with subjects of this age. However, recently the results of research done in an underprivileged area of Sydney have supported the aptness of applying the model of mutual steering to the socialization of very young children.[5] A sample of 108 mothers and their children aged three to five, some of whom were at nursery school, completed a number of tests to discover whether the children learnt certain values that their mothers held. The mothers were found to hold an integrated cluster of values that emphasized self-reliance, cooperation and compliance, as did the nursery school teachers concerned. The children also held these same values in a similarly integrated way, but where their mothers held these values more strongly, and where the child went to nursery school, the values were held more firmly. In addition, the more accepting of her child the mother was, the more fully did the child appear to learn the appropriate values. It seemed also that the children developed a personality paralleling this cluster of values that they had learnt by conforming to the expectations of the valued others with whom they interacted. Here the personality of the pre-school child was being formed through a process of mutual steering.

Although the development of personality is a process that continues throughout life, the foundations are laid before the child goes to school. By the age of five or six the child has begun to learn within the family how to cope with the many tensions and frustrations that are inescapable in life with others; how, for example, to control his anger or how to postpone his immediate desires. After the child goes to school, his teacher may become the model that is imitated and hence a potent influence upon the development of the child's personality. In this respect teachers and the school once again can reinforce or conflict with the foundations laid in the family. Under modern conditions, however, there is one particular way in which the educational system can be of great assistance in the development of personality.

Smaller families and the physical isolation inherent in living in for example, high-rise flats or semi-detached suburban houses can cut children off from other adults and more particularly from an ample experience of other children. This can result in an exclusive and over-intense relationship between the adults in the nuclear family, especially the mother, and the children, who may develop over-dependent personalities. This tendency can be corrected by sending the children to nursery schools, where they must learn to live with other children who conflict with them. Today in Britain the supply of nursery schools does not meet the demand for them. The contemporary demand appears to have two sources. There are middle-class parents who realize that they cannot give their children the best environment in which to develop their personalities. Secondly, there is a demand from the working class for a place to leave their children when mother goes out to work. Inasmuch as this demand is met, the mothers are unconsciously allowing their children a fuller chance of developing the personality through coming into contact with the wider range of children who attend the nursery school.[6]

3. *Control of the Adolescent*

The nuclear family offers enough scope for the young child, but at he grows older he needs to go outside this narrow circle, not juss to learn the social skills that he will need as an adult, but to fulfil the psychological needs that come with adolescence. The most obvious need is to experiment with sexual roles amongst those of the same age. By convention this is impossible within the family. However, as soon as the child becomes attached to a group of his own age outside the family, his conduct, which was relatively easy to determine within the family, becomes far less capable of control. Such groups of adolescents have, or rapidly evolve, codes of values and of behaviour of their own which, as will be seen in Chapter 5, will in all probability be very different from those of either the family or the school. This makes for conflict, but when social change is rapid there is a further cause of difficulty. The code of values evolved in the group may not only be at odds with the home and the school, but will also almost certainly differ from the code that was common amongst the adolescent groups of twenty-five years ago, when the parents and teachers of today's adolescents were young. There are various reasons for this gap in values. The major causes are that there have been big changes in the generally held moral code over the last generation and that there are very different ways open to the young today to spend their spare time in our wealthier society.

One of the most important attitudes involved in this problem is that towards authority. A fully developed adult personality will be able to obey those in authority, cooperate easily with equals and, if necessary, assume some authority. To a certain extent these three abilities can be learnt within the family, though the stress put on each will change as the child grows older. The ready obedience expected from a five-year-old cannot be exacted from a fourteen-year-old. Schools are supposedly arranged to achieve this same purpose as the chances of assuming authority rise as the child nears leaving age. In the past there were social institutions organized so that there was a smooth transition in this respect from childhood to full adult status. The training to become a medieval knight or the apprenticeship system in pre-industrial days are good examples.

Where there is not a smooth transition from family to school, or from either of these social institutions to work or to adult life, a discontinuity is said to exist and there is the possibility of conflict. Where this occurs, possibly because the family or school does not fully meet the needs of the adolescent, children will create or find the spontaneous type of youth group that is often called 'a gang'.

Youth organizations, such as Youth Clubs, may be started by educational authorities or by adults interested in the welfare of the young, such as religious bodies, but they are often rejected by the adolescents for whom they are intended because of their connection with adults and with authority.

This latter tendency raises a problem inherent in the notion of the continuity of socialization. Continuity implies that the roles of the growing child are fairly rigidly defined at each stage and that this knowledge is widespread. In the primitive tribes described by the anthropologists there was no doubt about this, as the movement from stage to stage was marked by such 'rites of passage' as initiation ceremonies. In contemporary Britain no one is clear when a child becomes an adolescent. Even the word 'teenager' does not mean what it would seem to indicate. There is no clear universal agreement as to what the rights and privileges of an adolescent are. In different families, social classes and schools, and at different times, childhood has had a different duration (Gillis, 1974). This lack of clarity in defining the role of the adolescent is bound to lead to conflict both within the family and at school as the child grows up. Sex will often be the centre of this conflict because of the strength of the biological forces involved, though to the family the difficulty may seem to be the hour at which the child must return home, or to the school how much homework is to be done.

The spirit of rebellion implicit here can have the result that these spontaneous gangs become totally dissociated from school and even feel themselves to be against all that school stands for. Under these conditions culture transmission in the school is very difficult. One of the more serious effects may be that the rebellion is expressed in actual crime. The peak rate for juvenile delinquency amongst boys is in the last year at school, and the incidence, though the gap appears to be narrowing slightly, is far greater amongst boys than girls. At the age of fourteen, formerly the minimum legal age for leaving school, the number of crimes, excluding motoring and other non-indictable offences, is double that committed by those between seventeen and twenty-one and almost three times that for those between twenty-one and thirty.[7] Whilst this problem must not be minimized, it can be seen as a passing phase of adolescence.

That this problem of discontinuity in the process of socialization is peculiar to contemporary urban communities can be seen clearly by comparing a rural community. In Gosforth,[8] an isolated village in Cumberland, the young, especially if brought up on a farm, were found to be members of families that provided for their psychological needs as they grew older. There was no great discontinuity. The children gradually learnt more of their future adult roles; in the school holidays and the long summer evenings there were plenty of interesting odd jobs around the farm to hold their attention and at the same time prepare them for adult life. The result was that, though there were groups of youths who met together, there was nothing equivalent to the urban youth culture. The same point was shown to be true in Israel in an investigation that is about as near to laboratory conditions as the social scientist is likely to come. In Israel there are two types of cooperative farm, both of which have approximately the same school system, but which have very different family organizations. In the Moshavim the family is the basic unit of production, whilst in the Kibbutzim this is not so and living is on a more communal basis. The very different family systems seem to be the reason for the comparative lack of youth activity in the Moshavim and the intense youth activity in the Kibbutzim.[9]

4. *Socialization in Communes*

Though the family is still seen as the main socializing agency in Western capitalist societies, particularly at the infant level, there is growing criticism of it, mainly because of the belief that individuality and spontaneity are crushed by this manner of upbringing. For this and many other reasons unconnected with childbearing, experiments in, for example, temporary liaisons or in communes have been initiated. The question can, therefore, be asked: what results upon the socialization of children do such ways of living have?

There is little evidence as yet based on research. Most communes in the USA or Europe have been started by middle-class radicals, and their main aim for the children involved seems to be to avoid teaching them the values of capitalist society. One result seems to be that there is often no clear alternative set of behavioural expectations to offer to the young. The hope is that these children will become autonomous, independent persons able to choose for themselves their own self-identity. Two processes may be identified. Firstly, there are effects due to an upbringing in a group more akin to the traditional extended family. Thus, the children no longer necessarily identify strongly with one male and one female who are usually their biological parents. But, secondly, much will depend upon the context of the particular commune concerned, which may be credal or non-credal, rural or urban, large or small, isolated or not. However, because of the radical beliefs of most persons involved in such experiments two ideological strands seem to be commonly found, namely the already noted priority given to freedom and choice. In addition, and in many ways connected with the dismissal of bourgeois values, there exists an orientation to the future such that ambition for an occupation of high status is not valued and a short time-perspective of days or weeks rather than of years is learnt.

The ultimate effect upon individuals of these new socializing experiences is problematic for various reasons. Many communes are short-lived; others have a transient membership. One sympathetic observer has suggested that in such circumstances the withdrawal of the firm links through parents to external social reality may 'lead to a progressive disintegration of the psychic structure rather than help develop personalities that are autonomous and resistant to social manipulation'.[10] Certainly, though such innovations in family structure are now more acceptable, the behaviour of children coming from such settings is still likely to be considered deviant in major respects by many and to be subjected to sanctions.

5. *Conclusion*

From the individual's point of view the way that the family is organized and the direction in which the family system is changing are important. The family moulds the personality of the child before he goes to school and is a potent influence on the child throughout his school life. Culture is transmitted within the family, and this helps to form national character within the limits imposed by biological inheritance. From the point of view of the state and the school, one of the most important functions of the family is to assist in taking the child through the stage of adolescence with the minimum possible anti-social behaviour and yet in such a way that the child's personality is not warped by any undue repression.

BIBLIOGRAPHY

E. Bott, *Family and Social Network*, 1957.

J. W. B. Douglas, *The Home and The School*, 1964.

R. Fletcher, *The Family and Marriage*, 1962.

J. R. Gillis, *Youth and History*, New York, 1974.

C. Harris, *The Family*, 1969.

M. Mead, *Coming of Age in Samoa*, 1928.

M. Mead, *Growing Up in New Guinea*, 1930.

T. Parsons, *Family, Socialization and Interaction Process*, 1956.

P. Willmott and M. Young, *Family and Class in a London Suburb*, 1960.

M. Young and P. Willmott, *Family and Kinship in East London*, 1957.

M. Young and P. Willmott, *The Symmetrical Family*, 1973.

NOTES

1 R. K. Kelsall, 'Self-recruitment in Four Professions', in D. V. Glass (ed.), *Social Mobility in Britain*, 1954.

2 Compare W. M. Williams, *The Sociology of an English Village: Gosforth*, 1956 (rural); W. Littlejohn, *Westrigg*, 1963 (Scottish rural); N. Dennis, F. Henriques and C. Slaughter, *Coal is our Life*, 1956 (a one-industry town). Also see the next section of this chapter.

3 From *Social Implications of the 1947 Scottish Mental Survey*, 1953, p. 49, Table XXIV; R. Illsley, 'Family Growth and its Effect on the Relationship between Obstetric Factors and Child Functioning', in R. Platt and J. S. Parkes (eds.), *Social and Genetic Influences on Life and Death*, Edinburgh, 1967, p. 39.

4 For an account of this problem see J. McV. Hunt, *Intelligence and Experience*, New York, 1961, pp. 337–43. For Scottish evidence see J. Nisbet, 'Family Environment and Intelligence', in A. H. Halsey, J. E. Floud and C. A. Anderson (eds.), *Education, Economy and Society*, New York, 1961. For the hypothesis of a common causative factor, see D. Oldman, B. Bytheway and G. Horobin, 'Family Structure and Educational achievement', *Journal of Biosocial Science*, Supplement 3, 1971, pp. 81–91.

5 E. Scott, 'Social Value Acquisition in Pre-school Aged Children', I,

II and III, *Sociological Quarterly*, Summer and Fall 1969, and Winter 1970.

6 For some doubts as to whether children who go to kindergarten ultimately have any social and intellectual advantage over those who do not, see J. W. B. Douglas and J. M. Ross, 'The Later Educational Progress and Emotional Adjustment of Children who went to Nursery School or Classes', *Educational Research*, November 1964.

7 D. J. West, *The Young Offender*, 1967, pp. 14 and 19–24.

8 Williams, *The Sociology of an English Village, op. cit.*

9 S. N. Eisenstadt, 'Youth, Culture and Social Structure in Israel', *British Journal of Sociology*, June 1951. For supporting evidence from the USA see R. I. Hough, G. F. Summers and J. O'Meara, 'Parental Influences, Youth Contraculture and Rural Adolescent Attitudes towards Minority Groups', *Rural Sociology*, September 1969.

10 C. Bookhagan, E. Hemmer, J. Raspe and E. Schultz, 'Kommune 2: Child-rearing in the Commune', in H. P. Dreitzel (ed.), *Childhood and Socialization: Recent Sociology No. 5*, New York, 1973, p. 147. For communes see also G. Zicklin, 'Communal Child-rearing: A Report on Three Cases', ibid., pp. 176–208, and B. M. Berger, B. M. Hackett and R. M. Millar, 'Child-rearing Practices in the Communal Family', in H. P. Dreitzel (ed.), *Recent Sociology No. 4: Family, Marriage and the Struggle of the Sexes*, New York, 1972, pp. 271–300.

4

Social Class and Socialization

Already social class[1] has been mentioned on several occasions, but in the interests of simplicity no detailed attention was given to the differences between the social classes either in family structure or in their ways of socializing children. However, so important are these differences, particularly in their effect on the chances that children have of benefiting from educational opportunities, that a separate chapter must be devoted to this topic. The procedure will be as in the last chapter. A brief introduction to the sociological work on social class will precede a consideration of the ways in which differences between the social classes affect the socialization of children.

A. Social Class

The idea of social class is a relatively simple one. There are many common forces influencing the behaviour of all who fill the same social position in any society. A rather extreme example was the medieval monk. So similar were the lives of monks throughout Christian Europe that they were probably more like each other, regardless of their place of birth, than they were like the peasants who came from their own home districts. Under contemporary conditions the social constraints at work on any person as he fills his economic role as a producer are of crucial importance because this position gives him his livelihood and, in any society above the subsistence level, his standard of life. In a capitalist society the majority are workers with little property other than their own capacity to work, whilst the minority are either owners of businesses or salaried employees, often of professional status, both categories having considerable security and often much property. Since the time of Karl Marx much has been written of the effects, implicit in a capitalist society, on those filling such positions. In a rather similar fashion to the example of the monk, capitalists in, for example, the United Kingdom, Australia and Germany are probably more alike in many of their attitudes and in their style of life because of the similarity of their economic roles than they are like the workers whom they employ in their own national communities. This idea of classes based on the similarity of social experience is relatively easily understood, but it has proved very difficult to isolate such categories in statistical terms or, to express this in a different way, to put the concept of social class into operation in sociological research.

1. Indices of Social Class

Many attempts have been made to discover what proportion of the population are in the different social classes. In any such investigation indices must be defined and used to represent the concept under examination. Several have been employed. Firstly, the investigator may ask a question of the following type, 'To what social class do you belong?' The answer will be purely subjective. Answers to such questions vary according to the wording of the question. Thus, a higher proportion of respondents will say that they are members of 'the working class' than will admit to belonging to 'the lower class'. The timing of the question also seems to influence the answers. An American survey conducted immediately after the accession to power of the British Labour Party in 1945 found that a higher proportion claimed to be working class than in a strictly comparable survey a few months earlier. Again, to ask a person's friends to what social class he belongs may bring a number of different answers. When people ascribe others to social classes they take account of many imponderable details, typical of which is accent. In different parts of Britain varying weight will be placed upon whether a person speaks with or without an accent.[2] It is probably true to say that in the south of England someone with a well-educated Scottish accent will be put into a higher social class than will a person with a well-educated Yorkshire or Lancashire accent.

Because of the obvious difficulties in attempts based on

subjective measures of social class, sociologists have tended to use objective indices more frequently, particularly where statistical work is necessary. Since social class rests primarily on economic foundations, the objective indices most often used are of an economic nature. Occupation is perhaps the commonest, though there are problems even here. Children can be included with their parents. The retired may be allocated to the occupation that they followed last, though this may not have been their life's career. But the thorniest problem is how to allocate women, many of whom work at occupations which are of a lower social class than that to which they clearly belong. In fact, wives are usually included in their husband's class regardless of their own occupations; the position of spinsters is, however, difficult to solve. Another possible objective index is income; the problem here is to decide whether it is individual or family income that is the more important determinant of social class.

An index that is rarely used is the pattern of consumption. How is the income spent? Many people earn £7,000, but they may spend it in very different ways. To be specific, some dockers and some teachers earn the same income, but their expenditure follows different patterns, and these consumption patterns are the outward signs of their different social class position. Each individual expresses the pattern of values that he holds in the way that he spends his money. The teacher may be buying his house and even spending a considerable amount on his children's education, whilst the docker lives in a council house and owns a car. These different patterns of values are vital in determining social class. Aggregates of individuals with the same or nearly the same income are clearly not necessarily of the same social class, though it must also be stressed that even groups consisting of individuals who hold the same values are not a class until they are conscious of having important common values and interests. Class consciousness makes a mere aggregate into a social class.

The ownership of wealth plays an important part in determining social class, since an unequal distribution of wealth leads to the unequal incomes that make it possible to give children a more advantageous start in life. Despite the very high rates at which death duties are levied, there are still big inequalities of inherited wealth. Thus, whereas in 1911–13 the wealthiest 1 per cent of the population owned about 65·5 per cent of personal net capital, by 1951–6 this proportion had been reduced to 42·0 per cent. However, income does seem to be less unevenly distributed than fifty years ago, although this is an area of investigation in which economists are far from reaching complete agreement. A policy aimed at achieving a fairer distribution of incomes has been pursued over recent decades by means of measures affecting the extremes of the income structure. High incomes have been taxed heavily and part of the proceeds transferred to the lower income groups, often in the form of social services and welfare benefits. By 1939 this had levelled out some inequality. During the 1939–45 war there seems to have been a rise in the proportion of the national income that went to wage earners as opposed to salary earners and those living on unearned income. In the years since the war the percentage share of wages in the net national income has declined from 48·4 in 1946 to 40·0 in 1968; over the same period the proportion going to salaries has risen from 23·4 to 35·4 per cent and that going to self-employment has fallen from 14·0 to 8·4 per cent.[3] The situation is, however, further complicated by the fact that the *real income* (the amount of goods and services that the money income will buy) of the working class has undoubtedly risen (Westergaard and Resler, 1976).

There have been a number of attempts to construct measures of social class using one or a combination of the indices mentioned above (Marsh, 1965). Probably the most used divisions of social class in Britain are those employed by the Registrar General in the government's decennial Census of Population. The five broad categories (I to V) are socio-economic in character and may be termed: I – Professional and similar occupations, e.g. lawyers, doctors, professional engineers; II – Intermediate occupations, e.g. farmers, retailers, teachers; III – Skilled and clerical workers, e.g. most factory workers, shop assistants, most clerical workers; IV – Semi-skilled occupations, e.g. bus conductors, domestic servants, window cleaners; V – Unskilled occupations, e.g. dock labourers, watchmen and most kinds of labourer. Slight changes in the allocation of occupations to the five categories have been made from one Census to the next so that the results are not quite comparable. However, using the data gathered it is possible to give, as in the table below, a rough indication of the distribution of the population by socio-economic status or, to speak less accurately, by social class, both through time and at the most recent Census.

The careful reader will have noticed that as yet no definition of 'social class' has been made. Throughout the discussion of class a number of interlocking strands have been traced. To summarize

Social class of occupied and retired males in England and Wales

		1931	*1951*	*1961*	*1971*
I	(Professional)	2	3	4	5
II	(Intermediate)	13	14	15	17
III	(Skilled and clerical)	49	52	51	48
IV	(Semi-skilled)	18	16	21	17
V	(Unskilled)	18	15	9	8
	Not classified	—	—	—	5
		100	100	100	100

Sources: Marsh, 1965, p. 198, and *Social Trends*, No.6, 1975, p. 12.

briefly, the first of these is economic. Occupation is vital here, mainly in that it yields an income, though wealth can also provide this. Different sizes of income lead to differences in life chances. The second strand is that of status, which measures the prestige accorded to an individual. Status tends to vary with economic criteria such as occupation or income, but this is not always the case. The status of a professional footballer or a popular singer may not be measured directly by his income. Thirdly, there is the underlying strand of power, which can be defined as the ability to control the behaviour of others. This usually varies directly with economic criteria, but there are again awkward exceptions; top civil servants or the leaders of trade unions have much greater power as defined above than their incomes might lead one to expect.

It is, therefore, very difficult to know just what is meant by the term 'social class'. It would perhaps be best to use the term 'class' only in the strict Marxian sense, that is to refer to social conflict and to analyse both the groups involved in such conflict and the attendant social change. Today in Britain the conflict between these groups is not over property ownership or economic conditions as Marx assumed, but is rather over the exercise of power. As pointed out above, these groups only become social classes when they realize that they hold interests in common. Thus the working class has come to acknowledge a common set of interests and values, and works for power so as to preserve and extend these values through such institutions as the Labour Party and the trade unions. In this sense 'class' remains, as with Marx, a tool for the analysis of social change (Giddens, 1973).

However, for convenience we continue to talk about the upper, the middle and the working classes (and even of sub-divisions within these classes) in contexts other than a strictly Marxian one. In this book the main relevant problem will concern the relationship between social class and education. The focus will, therefore, be on the ways in which membership of social classes can influence the likelihood of benefiting from education and how success or otherwise in education can affect membership of particular social classes. Much of the work quoted will be based on indices of social class and it must be remembered that any such index is being used to represent the quality of a lived situation in which persons have experienced similar social realities because they are filling similar social positions.

2. Social Mobility

When assigning an individual to a social class, stress has come to be put on what he has achieved rather than the position to which he was ascribed by birth into his family. Naturally his family will influence what he achieves, but the vital difference between the social class system and such other modes of stratification as the Hindu caste system is that relatively greater movement is possible between the strata. This movement between social classes is termed *social mobility* and can be in either an upward or a downward direction. In the context of this book social mobility assumes great importance since under modern conditions it is thought to be mainly through education that movement up the social class system is possible. In general it is difficult today to be considered a member of the middle class unless one has an occupation for which a relatively high level of education is the prerequisite.

The more movement between the social classes there is, the more socially mobile that society is said to be. Comparisons are made between social mobility in, for instance, the USA and Britain. The generally held beliefs about these two societies are opposite ones. The American system is reputed to provide ample opportunity for upward mobility, whereas in Britain it is supposed to be difficult to 'get on'. However, recent research shows that, 'despite large differences in educational systems, the role of educational attainment in occupational mobility is highly similar in the two countries'. There is less mobility between the generations in Britain, but this seems to be due to the stronger effect of father's occupational status on that of his son in Britain than in the USA.[4] Certainly it is part of the contemporary democratic ideal that there should be as much social mobility as possible. Today in Britain a large measure of equality has been gained in many fields, for example between the sexes or before the law. Yet, though it is probably true that over the last century upward social mobility has become more possible for the lower classes, it will be shown that for various reasons there are not equal chances to gain political power or access to occupations carrying the higher incomes. One of the root causes of this inequality is to be found in the way that the educational system works.

The accurate measurement of social mobility is difficult. It is not sufficient merely to know how many individuals move up and down the social class system. For a true picture the changes in the numbers of the available positions at each class level must be known. For instance, it has been said that there is a permanent tendency to upward social mobility under contemporary conditions, since in a modern economy there is a growing number of managerial and administrative positions that carry high social status and whose occupants are considered middle-class. Some indication of this process can be seen in the changing proportion of the various classes in the table on page 64 above. As these new middle-class positions are filled, it may be said that upward social mobility has increased. But before a true account can be given as to whether the actual chances of social mobility have become greater or less than at some former date, allowance must be made for those changes in the occupational structure of a country that alter the relative numbers of the available positions at each social class level (Glass, 1954).

For women one possible avenue of upward social mobility is to marry a husband of a higher social class than themselves. The role of a woman in our contemporary society contains skills that are very 'portable'. Such are the skills of housekeeping and child-rearing. The role of a man is more heavily weighted towards occupational skill, and upward social mobility must usually be achieved through success in a man's occupation. It has been shown that women do marry 'above themselves' significantly more often than men (Glass, 1954, p. 327). This fact must be remembered when mothers' attitudes towards their children's education are discussed.

Another important concept is that of *social distance*. This refers to the imagined distance between the social classes. It is generally held that over the last century the classes have moved much closer together. Greater wealth has been distributed somewhat more evenly. Many material possessions which even twenty years ago were symbols of status are now too common to bring the prestige associated with scarcity. A good example is the spread in ownership of cars. Again, the clothes worn by all classes are now much more uniform and do not provide a reliable guide to membership of social class unless one has a very detailed and up-to-date knowledge of fashion, and even then there may be difficulties.

Taken together these two tendencies, the lessening in social distance and the increase in social mobility, can combine to bring for some a heightened awareness of social class. The upper strata see themselves more threatened by the lower classes and feel the need to defend their social position. Since the change in the chances of upward social mobility are in the main due to the increase in provision of education and to the more egalitarian ways of entry to secondary education, middle-class defensiveness can take the form of opposition to educational reform (Runciman, 1966). This was certainly the case in Germany around 1900, as in that country then there was a very strong sense, particularly among the middle class, of '*Stand*', which can roughly be translated as 'social position'.

3. *Social Class in Britain Today*
The combination of a growing national income and its somewhat more equal distribution has enabled the British working class to lead a more affluent way of life in recent years. Some writers have

held that this has brought a change in attitudes towards social class. It is said that the worker now considers himself to be middle-class. This trend has been called the *embourgeoisement* of the worker. The main basis upon which this analysis has rested is economic. Statistics can be quoted to show that many members of the working class must own expensive pieces of household equipment. Thus by the middle of 1962 eight out of every ten households in Britain had a television set, three out of five a vacuum cleaner, and two out of five a washing machine. In 1961 there were about six million private cars on the roads, a fair proportion of which must have been owned by members of the working class. The government report that gave these figures was entitled *Social Changes in Britain*. It concluded that this country could not lapse back into the working-class poverty of the 1930s and that the average man had made a great investment in his future 'as a middle-class citizen'.[5]

It has been convincingly argued (Goldthorpe *et al.*, 1969) that this is not in fact a true picture of what has taken place. The economic fact of greater wealth cannot be disputed and a more even distribution of incomes can be accepted. But interpretations of these developments can differ. The teacher and the docker may earn the same income and perhaps even own the same household equipment, but the teacher has a higher degree of security of employment and a much greater chance of promotion during his career. A study through time of the pattern of a typical middle-class career would yield a very different picture from that of a member of the working class. The latter usually reaches his maximum income early and, despite changes in his job, will rarely raise his real income after the age of twenty-one. This is a very different picture from the normal step-like progression of the member of the middle class. In fact the chances of rising above the supervisory level, for example above the job of foreman, are actually declining in contemporary British industry and, if upward social mobility through the educational system increases, the traditional 'hard way up' is bound to assume less importance, since the more able members of the working class will have already achieved middle-class status through the educational system.

However, the main criticism of the thesis of the embourgeoisement of the worker is not on economic grounds. If the worker has become middle-class, he should have taken on the norms or the pattern of values and beliefs of that class. There is no doubt that most members of the working class now own possessions of the type that economists have christened consumer capital. Yet this need not make them into capitalists. They may still be distrustful of property as a basis of the social system. Thus, the authors of a recent British study, based on a random sample of those living on certain council estates in 1972-3, commented on two facets of working-class attitudes that are often overlooked, namely 'a series of oppositional and, often, aggressive attitudes . . . to the premise on which the present structure of British society is built . . . that the ownership, use and rights of property should be allocated on the basis of market forces', and, secondly, 'a glimmering of another principle . . . that stresses the satisfaction of need rather than ability to pay'. It is such 'feelings of subordination, discrimination, unfairness and hostility which are the essence of class opposition'. Furthermore, they can 'be expressed in terms in which the word "class" is never used'.[6]

To summarize, it seems doubtful that the working class has in fact assumed middle-class attitudes. Statistical evidence of the poll type has also been used to support the thesis of embourgeoisement; between ten and forty per cent of manual workers in various recent studies have claimed themselves to be middle-class. It has been indicated above that there is great difficulty in accepting such subjective estimates of social class position. However, evidence from a very carefully designed survey of the poll type made in 1961-2 has been used to back Goldthorpe and others' refutation of the thesis of embourgeoisement.[7] In this investigation an examination was made of the type of definition given to the term 'middle class' by the thirty-three per cent of the men or their wives who by an objective index were in manual occupations but who claimed to be middle-class. It was found that, though the majority may have been conscious of being in some sense different from the traditional working class, yet their definitions of middle class seemed to show no definite sense of belonging to the non-manual category of occupations that is here termed middle-class.

There is a further point to consider. Even if the working class has taken over middle-class norms, has the middle class accepted these new recruits to its own social class? It has already been suggested that a lessening of social distance may have led to an increase in middle-class defensiveness. Certainly there has been great difficulty in creating socially mixed communities on new housing estates. The middle class will not remain in predominantly working-class communities. This same tendency can be seen more clearly in industry; the status distinctions between managers and workers are as rigid as any in contemporary Britain and are institutionalized by separate canteens which may number as many as four of descending status in some large-scale factories. Yet it must be pointed out that there are also changes amongst the middle class. The professional part of the middle class seems to have left the extremely individualistic stance usually associated with this class in Britain and to be readier than formerly to use cooperative action almost of a trade-union type. Recent actions by many teachers seem to provide evidence of this process.

It is this last point that leads us to a truer interpretation of what may be happening. The two classes are changing independently under the impact of the same social and economic forces. At a time of full employment the working class may have become more individualistic, whilst the growth in the size of industrial units may have made middle-class professional men more willing to band together. Both classes are changing. It is not a true picture to concentrate only on the changes that affect one class, the working class.

B. Socialization and the Social Class System

I. *Children and Social Class*
Wealth can be inherited and, despite death duties, some inequality of income perpetuated. A high income enables parents to give to their children the advantages that money can buy. It is a great help to a child to live in pleasant surroundings, be provided with educational toys,[8] to go to a private school with a high staffing ratio, to receive stimulating experiences such as foreign travel in adolescence, and to have the entry into the 'right circle'. In the words of the German sociologist, Max Weber, such children are receiving better 'life chances' than the children of poorer parents. The family

not only transmits material benefits to its offspring, but also passes on some of the more indefinable and immaterial aspects of social class. The child undergoes social experiences of power and prestige upon which his ideas of class are built. The way in which his parents treat others and are treated by them give him the cues as to how he should later deal with his superiors and inferiors in class position.

Children of primary school age seem to mix very freely with children who to adults appear to be obviously of another social class. In rather the same way they ignore such adult caste boundaries as colour in choosing their playmates. In both cases, however, it appears that they recognize that there are differences but do not know the social customs associated with these differences. An interesting experiment was carried out with 179 children between six and ten years of age in Glasgow. Drawings were prepared that showed adults of obviously different social classes in incongruous circumstances. The children usually spotted this. For instance, when a picture of a workman wearing overalls and shaking hands with a man in a suit carrying a briefcase was shown to a child he commented that men dressed in that way do not shake each other's hands.[9]

A study has also been made of the views of British adolescents on social class. This survey was carried out in the early 1950s amongst boys from both grammar and secondary modern schools. When asked if they knew what social class meant, 60 per cent (49 per cent grammar, 74 per cent secondary modern school) said that they did not know, but it was found that they had already acquired a thorough understanding of our social class system. Their views were very like those of adults and had been picked up unconsciously in their ordinary day-to-day life. Amongst those who understood the term 'social class' the usual frame of reference was wealth or consumption pattern, unlike adults, for almost three-quarters of whom the frame of reference seems to be occupation. A third of these boys were aware of the importance of status symbols; they appreciated that a man may be judged by how he dresses or by his accent. They also had an understanding of the idea of social mobility; 60 per cent considered that upward mobility was associated with achievement, intelligence and personality, though those middle-class boys who were in secondary modern schools laid more stress on manners, dress and speech. Adults of all classes stressed education much more and manners hardly at all. Boys of below-average intelligence spoke just as easily about social class.[10]

Evidence gathered in Sydney late in the 1960s has shown something of how children learn their social class roles. Though the content of the Australian social class system is somewhat different from that of Britain, yet the process of socialization, being influenced by similar psychological constraints, is probably very much the same. Between the ages of about five and eight, these Australian children saw social class in terms of dramatic contrast; an uncle was a 'millionaire', but Mum was 'poor'. In the next stage up to the age of around twelve the structure of the class system was grasped, but in very concrete terms; the garbageman earned very little money, whilst others had luxuries, clothes and cars. By sixteen, children seemed to hold detailed, complex and more abstract versions of the class structure with all its attendant subtle nuances related to areas of residence, types of school and snobbery. They were now able to relate individuals to this system, particularly in terms of careers, through the various pathways of positions that it made available. It would seem that a knowledge of class is gained mainly through the process of familial socialization, one more indication of the important social role played by the family.[11]

2. *Social Class Learning*

Each social class has its own particular way of life. Many examples could be given of the differences between the middle and the working class. What is considered right behaviour varies; for example, each social class treats its womenfolk in a different way. Table manners and what is eaten and drunk vary greatly. It is possible to view each class as having a culture of its own. Strictly these ways of life can be seen as sub-cultures of the overall British culture. Each sub-culture will entail a separate pattern of socialization very different in some respects from that undergone by the children in the families of another social class. These sub-cultures are characterized most obviously by the differing outward behaviour, such as the drinking of tea at the evening meal instead of water, or the watching of a game of soccer instead of the playing of a game of golf. But it will be shown in this section that at a deeper level there are differences even in the basic personality patterns and modes of thought found in the social classes. The transmission of all these differences is a special case of the process of socialization described earlier in this book, but in view of its importance and the interest that it has raised it has come to be analysed separately and has been given the name of 'social class learning'.

One of the pioneer investigations in the field of social class learning was that of the American, Allison Davis, carried out in the early 1940s.[12] Conclusions from American evidence cannot be transferred directly to British situations, but they can be guides in examining our own similar problems. Davis showed that there were great differences between the social classes in the child's learning in such basic areas of behaviour as eating, aggression and sex. He traced these social class variations in behaviour and personality to very different patterns of mothering in infancy. More particularly he analysed the social class patterns of breast feeding and toilet training.

A longitudinal survey (J. and E. Newson, 1963, 1968 and 1976) is being made of how some 700 mothers bring up their children in the city of Nottingham. The object is to investigate contemporary ways of caring for children as they grow older, and the survey provides evidence that is comparable with that of Davis. It was found that although middle-class mothers were definitely more progressive in their attitude to child care, the influence of more enlightened methods was spreading down the social scale. But there were some major differences in approach. For example, the idea of what was meant by 'a spoilt child' varied. Basically the answer depended upon what each social class would indulge. The middle-class mother would put up with tantrums but would not feed an endless supply of sweets to her child; the working-class mother would not indulge her child's tantrums but would give him sweets when he wanted them. The middle-class mother put up with more crying at night before going to comfort her child or giving him a feed. The question of sanctions has also been considered. How were the parents to ensure conformity? When a child offended, the working-class mother tended to use smacking immediately, though particularly in the case of mothers in unskilled workers' families, not very consistently, whilst the middle-class mother preferred to try 'to love her child out of it'.

By the time the children are seven the Newsons (1976) have shown that in a whole variety of ways the daily experience of the different social classes, in terms of where they are allowed to go, how they spend their time and to what extent they are kept under surveillance, is markedly different. They refer to the common thread through such experiences as 'the chaperonage factor' and found this to fall off in strength as one considers progressively lower social class groups. Furthermore, and important for the argument here, this effect is not related in a statistically significant way to such geographical factors as accessibility to play areas or dangerous roads. It seems 'due more to a difference in basic attitudes than to the circumstances in which families are constrained to live'.

Discontinuities can be built into the process of socialization and this is especially true in the matter of discipline. It is probable that authority is wielded in a working-class family in a very different way from that in a middle-class family. The working-class parent will often make his child do what he wants more by a gesture than by a verbal command backed by the reason for the order argued at the child's level of understanding. Punishment in the working-class home is probably more often based on the consequence of the wrong done rather than on the intent of the action. Thus, in a very detailed study Wootton examined the speech patterns of twenty children aged about four and their mothers whilst at home together in Aberdeen. He noted differences in the ways in which middle- and working-class mothers controlled their children – that is, in what the Newsons (1976) called their 'artillery of words'. The middle-class mothers more often enquired about their child's intention or feelings. They also more frequently used oblique suggestions and less often employed threats. In addition middle-class mothers tended to give justifications for their requests or orders. It seemed also as if more discretion was given to the middle- than to the working-class children. As has been noted elsewhere the middle-class child is 'accorded discretion to *achieve* his social role', while 'his role is *assigned* to the working-class child'.[13] The child who is brought up with a working-class notion of authority will note great discontinuity when he enters the world of school which tends to be governed by middle-class attitudes. The more formal the atmosphere of the school becomes, more particularly when he reaches secondary school, the greater will the discontinuity become between the idea of authority learnt at home and that which he meets at school. The child can react in a number of defensive ways. Wrongdoing may be automatically denied. Feelings of guilt may in these circumstances become dissociated from many anti-social acts.

The Newsons also found that feeding habits differed greatly. All the children had ample chance to suck, but in different ways according to their social class. The middle-class child was more often breast fed, but was weaned earlier; the working-class child was bottle fed for longer and was allowed a dummy. There was little thumbsucking amongst the children (only eight per cent) but, as may be expected, it was more pronounced amongst the earliest weaned middle-class babies. The middle class began potty training earlier and were more successful at it; unskilled workers' wives were very much later than others. Genital play was stopped by working-class mothers, but permitted or diverted by the middle class.

3. Personality Differences

The overall impression of the Newsons' evidence, though not all the details, is much the same as that of Davis. The working-class mode of infant care was characterized by a pattern of indulgence that in Davis' view led to a lack of self-discipline in older working-class children and adults. These very different ways of socialization led to markedly different patterns of personality. Davis noted that the working class did not control their basic psychological drives in the same way as the middle class did. The working class tended to extremes. When money was available, they over-ate and overheated their rooms. They used aggressive action much more often, and this was particularly so with regard to sex. These ways of behaviour were approved as normal among the working class, whereas the middle class directed the identical drives into channels that were socially approved in their sub-culture. Working-class aggression became middle-class initiative; the same psychological drive could take the form in a working-class child of actually striking a teacher and in the middle-class child of hard work leading to good school marks that would earn him the name of 'teacher's pet'.

What evidence is there for similar personality differences in Britain? The Nottingham sample used by the Newsons was fairly representative of the general population and the two broad patterns of indulgence which they noted might be expected to lead to the two opposing personality types found by Davis. The initiative and self-discipline typical of the middle class can be traced back to the pattern of middle-class infant care found by the Newsons. Its foundations lay partly in the early patterns imposed with regard to feeding habits and toilet training and in the way the mother tried to love her child out of wrongdoing. The opposite personality traits typical of the working class, have their counterpart in the opposite habits of infant care found in the working-class part of the Newsons' sample. Furthermore, the differences by social class that were noted in the techniques of socialization used in early childhood were reinforced by the changed methods that were suitable for the child at the age of seven. The Newsons (1976) devised an index of child-centredness covering, for example, parental attitudes to their child's play, his complaints about school and the expression of sorrow after being angry towards him. They found that, statistically, significantly more middle- than working-class mothers scored as highly child-centred – about a half of the former as against only a quarter of the latter.

Therefore, although extremes in type of personality cannot be assigned outright to the broad bands that make up the working and the middle classes, yet it seems likely that Davis' two types are approximate descriptions of the basic personality found among many in the middle class and among certainly a large proportion of the lower working class. In between these social classes it seems likely that there is a continuum with the basic personality tending towards one or other of the extremes according to the social class being considered. The teacher, who is more often than not from the middle class, has to deal mainly with children from the working class and may well find that one of the main demands put upon him, if he is to achieve success, is the adjustment that he must make in order to teach children, the majority of whom have a very different pattern of personality from his own. Neither pattern is deviant in any moral sense; both were formed through the normal process of social class learning, and within each broad pattern there are very many individual differences of personality.

There is one dimension of personality that is much more directly related to success in education than the important, but general characteristics so far discussed. This is the need felt by an individual for achievement (Swift, 1966). One tradition of research, stemming from the work of McClelland,[14] has shown that the need for achievement is learnt very early during the process of socialization. Parents put before the child frames of reference defining what is thought to be excellent and encourage the child to refer to these standards in all he does. Children who have already been found by other tests to have a high need for achievement tend to take calculated risks when given games to play in which there is the chance of failure; they neither take the easy way nor trust to luck. The parents of such children tend to set problems for them that are not too difficult, but that are just beyond their present capabilities, and to encourage them warmly without actually interfering whilst their children are seeking solutions.

McClelland's work links with another tradition of research, namely that on the achievement syndrome. This latter work has been closely related to social class. It has suggested that there is a cluster of attitudes relating to achievement. Especial attention is given in this syndrome to three sets of opposing viewpoints. There is, firstly, the priority that the individual gives to himself as opposed to the groups with whom he interacts and particularly his own family. Next, there is the belief held about how much control over his immediate environment an individual sees himself to have as opposed to the view that things just happen to him because of luck or chance. Lastly, there is the willingness that a person has, to put off present satisfaction to the future in preference to living for the immediate moment. Clearly the child who has been taught the syndrome that has been shown to be a middle-class characteristic, namely to defer present gratification, to believe that his present efforts or lack of them will be rewarded or punished in the future and to rate his own interest above that of the group, is more likely to do well at school.

Much research in this tradition has been done in the USA, but studies have shown that this syndrome apparently also exists in Britain. Thus, in a study of children aged eleven or twelve undertaken in Aberdeen, boys seemed to hold to the middle-class syndrome more strongly than girls. At the time that they were questioned these children already knew which of them had been chosen to go to selective secondary school and those with a high IQ displayed the middle-class version of the achievement syndrome more strongly than those with an IQ of less than 115. A similar finding for children aged fifteen has been reported in the London area. However, differences between the social classes were not as clear in Aberdeen as expected, except on the dimension of looking to the future. Questions may, therefore, be raised concerning the age at which these roles are learnt and about whether a traditional and relatively staunch Presbyterian city such as Aberdeen is typical in this respect.[15]

A crucial determinant in this respect seems to be the extent to which the family religion stresses individual, as against ritual, contact with the deity. The Protestant ethic with its emphasis on an individual approach to God can be seen as a special case of the general law here, since McClelland's work has shown that certain pre-literate, non-Christian societies fit this same pattern. Self-reliance appears to be an essential trait. This and such Protestant economic virtues as hard work are character traits that can be stressed either in church or at home and in both cases are likely to influence the way in which children fare at school.

4. *Attitudes towards Education*

So far it has been shown that social class learning can result in children with a personality type that is not sympathetic towards school. Clearly the attitudes that parents show towards their children's schooling can offset or reinforce this tendency. Though there are exceptions middle-class parents have again and again been found to have more favourable attitudes to schooling than those from the working class. Studies have found that middle-class parents claim to have thought more about the education of their children and more often to want them to go to selective secondary schools. Douglas found comparable results in his national sample. But in addition he found that the mother's interest in her child's school progress varied by social class and seemed to be of great 'importance' in deciding chances of entry to a grammar school. Thus, if measured intelligence is held constant, children with mothers who are undecided get eight per cent fewer places than expected, whilst the children of mothers wanting them to go to a secondary modern school and leave at the minimum legal age have sixty per cent fewer grammar school places than expected.[16]

Some children from the working class against whom the educational cards seem to be stacked do better in the educational system than might be expected. Why are some children so different in this respect? Work in both the USA and Britain gives one possible structural explanation of the source of these deviants. In Huddersfield (Jackson and Marsden, 1962) there was a strong connection between success in the eleven-plus examination amongst working-class children and whether or not their mothers were downwardly socially mobile. These 'sunken middle class' mothers held values different from the social class in which they were now located, and therefore, to pass to the interpersonal perspective, were likely to socialize their children into deviant values. Other work, this time done in Lancashire, supported findings from the USA that the children of fathers who were foremen or mothers who had been secretaries had a more than proportionate share of children who passed the eleven-plus. Such parents seemed by virtue of their closeness to the middle-class role models that they met at work to be able, for example, to look further into the future than the parents of children who did not manage to go to selective secondary schools.[17] The implication is that certain children located in the working class are socialized into a set of values deviant for that class, but which enable them to succeed at school, and that this occurs because the experiences of their parents are atypical of the working class. Sometimes, for apparently idiosyncratic reasons, a child comes to be seen by his teachers and parents as clever. It may be as Jackson and Marsden found in one or two cases that he is 'literary early'. There is evidence to support the view that in such cases this success leads to the parents subsequently forming aspirations for their child that support him in his deviant role.[18] In this perhaps relatively infrequent case the direction of causation is reversed. It is not the child who is caused to succeed because of his parents' aspirations, but rather the parents change their values because of their child's success.

Once a child gained entry to a grammar school his success there could be much influenced by his parents' attitudes towards education. Himmelweit found in 1951 that working-class boys were less successful in certain London grammar schools than were middle-class boys, despite the fact that they realized that their present efforts at achool were related to their probable future success in life. A major contributory cause seemed to be lack of parental support for working-class boys. Middle-class parents visited the school more often and came to watch school games or plays more frequently. The middle-class boys themselves thought that their parents were more interested in their progress at school. Their parents more often supervised homework.[19] Douglas reported that the possession of a separate room for homework varied directly with social class. This is partly, but not entirely, a matter of the type of house that can be afforded, and in this connection overcrowding is much more common under working-class than middle-class housing conditions. Homework in a crowded room with a television set turned on is very difficult.

Compared with the inter-war years a far higher proportion of children stay on at school after the legal minimum leaving age – now sixteen. This must to a large extent be due to parental encouragement. Douglas found that there was no real difference between older and younger parents in this respect and concluded that the change must be a general one that affected parents of all ages. It is commonly held that this trend is due to the growing numbers of parents who have themselves undergone higher education and secondary education beyond the minimum legal leaving age. If such educational experience is 'infective' one would expect a growing number of the children of these parents to stay on longer in the educational system. This impression is reinforced by the following figures, which cover the Robbins Committee sample of children born in 1940–1. If children of parents of whom one or both have had selective education are compared with those of parents of whom neither has had selective education, it is found that 5·9 times as many achieved entry to degree-level courses, 5·2 times as many two

'A' levels, 3·5 times as many five 'O' levels, and 2·4 times as many entered selective secondary schools.[20]

This last tendency is only indirectly related to social class in that in the past selective education has been more of a middle-class prerogative, and therefore the infective process did not spread far. It had more the nature of a feedback system. However, it can be seen that attitudes towards education are an important determinant of chances of success in secondary education.

As might be expected social class learning leads to a differential ability to benefit from formal education. This is less so amongst really able children, but becomes more the case as one considers children of lower measured intelligence. Likewise this differential tendency becomes of more importance the higher up the educational system one goes, and is therefore more pronounced at university level than in the sixth form and at eighteen than at sixteen years of age. This can be seen clearly from the following table, which refers to the large sample of children born in 1940–1 in England and Wales that was investigated by the Robbins Committee on Higher Education.

Academic achievement of children at maintained grammar schools (percentages)

IQ at eleven plus	Father's occupation	Degree-level course	At least 2 'A' levels	At least 5 'O' levels
130+	A. Non-manual	37	43	73
	B. Manual	18	30	75
	A divided by B	2·06	1·43	0·97
115–129	A. Non-manual	17	23	56
	B. Manual	8	14	45
	A divided by B	2·12	1·64	1·24
100–114	A. Non-manual	6	9	37
	B. Manual	2	2	22
	A divided by B	3·00	1·50	1·68

Source: Higher Education, 1963, Appendix One, from Table 5, p. 43.

If one considers the relative *social class chances* as measured here by the line 'A divided by B', it is clear that the children of non-manual fathers have better chances than those of manual workers of gaining a given standard of education as successively lower IQ bands are taken, for example 3·00 times as against 2·06 in the case of university courses. Again, holding IQ constant, the middle class, as measured here, has a greater chance of reaching each level of education than the working class, for example in the lowest IQ category 3·00 times as against 1·68. The exception to this last generalization is the expected one, namely that the class chances for the ablest category of gaining five 'O' levels are more or less equal.

In interpreting these figures it must be remembered that they only refer to those already at a grammar school. Entrance to these schools is also linked to social class. Thus Douglas (1964) found that below the children who were in the top 2 per cent of measured intelligence, social background was an important factor in entrance to the grammar school. Thus, for those with an IQ level of between 107·5 and 110·5 at eight years of age, the rate of entry to grammar school at eleven that was achieved by the different social class divisions was as follows: the upper middle class 51 per cent, the lower middle class 34 per cent, the upper working class 21 per cent and the lower working class 22 per cent. It must be realized that the minimum IQ for entry to grammar school is in the region of 114, though great regional differences occur. The results quoted are in an IQ band well below the top 2 per cent of ability and hence much influenced by differences in social class learning.

5. *Thinking*

So far in this chapter we have been considering the effect of different social class patterns of learning on the personality of children and thereby on their chances of success in school. But over the last twenty years the additional possibility has been raised that social class learning may have an important effect on the actual development of intelligence. In recent years the generally accepted notion of intelligence has changed greatly (Vernon, 1969). The work of two psychologists, namely the Swiss Jean Piaget and the American D. O. Hebb, has been particularly influential.[21] Piaget has stressed the developmental aspects of intelligence, and Hebb has made the valuable distinction between inherited potential and present mental efficiency. The new analysis to be considered here is based on the importance of language learning in the development of intelligence and of ways of thinking. Most thinking entails the use of language. Much of the work of Bernstein and his associates (1971, 1973 and 1975) has attempted to show that sub-cultures transmit different modes of speech and hence different modes of thinking.

The analysis of the vocabulary and grammatical structure of any language uncovers much of the social reality that we normally take for granted. Thus, where in English there is one word for snow the Eskimos have and need some twenty words. Again in English the pronoun 'you' is used in addressing both familiar friends and relations and also those met for the first time, whereas in German and many other languages separate pronouns, e.g. *du* and *Sie*, exist to cover these two eventualities. Knowing a language not only entails a knowledge of words and how to use them, but knowing the right thing to say and the correct style to use in any situation. A child has to learn that offence can be given by using four-letter words when addressing Granny, the teacher or a clergyman, whilst his friends will often think it odd if he does not use them. Thus, in growing up we all become capable of using several styles of language and of choosing which to use as we negotiate different social situations.

Bernstein worked with middle- and working-class boys in London and found that in the working-class sub-culture there is on the whole a particular mode of speech that is characterized by its very restricted nature. Sentences are short, dependent clauses are rare, vocabulary is small, adjectives few and not used with fine discrimination, abstract ideas are infrequent, and, finally, gesture is commonly used in addition to or in place of speech. This syntactically simple language may be called 'restricted code' and those who are brought up to speak this code will automatically be brought to think in the same uncomplicated way regardless of whether they are genetically capable of far more complex thought. To those who can use a more complex code of speech there will not be the same limit to mental development. In the middle-class sub-culture children hear the speech of their parents who put a very high value on verbalization (J. and E. Newson, 1968) and on answering their children's questions.[22] Since they are encouraged by adequate rewards, children in the middle class imitate their parents' linguistic code. This tends to be a more elaborate mode of speech; sentences are long and contain a complicated structure of dependent clauses, many subtly chosen adjectives are used, the words 'it' and 'one' are common, abstract nouns are found, and gesture assumes a much less important place in communication. This is termed 'elaborated code' by Bernstein and gives its speakers the possibility of thinking of a much more complex and abstract quality than is open to those who speak in restricted code. The middle-class child can understand both codes, but the working-class child is brought up to a restricted code and finds great difficulty in translating elaborated code into something that he can understand. It should perhaps again be added that the account given here for ease of exposition covers limiting cases. Between these limits there will exist combinations of the two extremes.

Evidence for this theory is provided by examining the results of members of the working and middle classes in intelligence tests. Typically the working-class scored far lower than the middle-class child on verbal tests and somewhat lower even on non-verbal tests. This result was interpreted as evidence that the mental operations necessary to do non-verbal tests are nearly equally available to both the working and the middle classes, but that the mental operations necessary for understanding the more complex parts of verbal tests are only available to the middle class and do not become part of the mental equipment of the working class. However, other research workers have not always replicated this result. Douglas, for example, found a slight tendency for the middle class to do better in verbal and the working class in non-verbal tests, but for his very large national sample these results were not statistically significant.

As a result of these doubts Bernstein's work in relation to language, though not his work in more general aspects of social class learning, has come under criticism. Firstly, a number of studies in more than one country have disputed the direct correlation between language code and social class. Thus, an analysis of data gathered in Bristol in the 1970s yielded the conclusion that there is 'no clearcut relationship between language use and either social class or educational success after one year of schooling'.[23] Such differences can be due to the technical difficulties of this type of research such as, for example, the problems implicit in defining social class groupings. But there are more basic flaws in the argument. These may be summarized by saying that any analysis by codes tends to take no account of the fact that language is used in interpersonal interaction in social contexts. One must examine what language is brought to what situation and with what intent.

This problem is highlighted by work done by Labov (1973) in the USA on the type of non-standard English spoken by blacks in ghetto areas. Labov has shown that the language used by such blacks, usually seen by middle-class people, and particularly by teachers, to be of a low level and poor quality, is logical and complex, and can be used to express subtle meanings. This work might only be seen as having direct relevance to black inhabitants of Britain, but a recent report of research now in progress in Belfast, Glasgow and Reading indicates that a very similar analysis can be applied to the language used by the working class (Stubbs, 1977).

The language used at home by many working-class children can be seen as an English-based creole, an extreme dialect of standard English. When the working-class child arrives at school he is more or less unintelligible to his teacher and perhaps the teacher is also unintelligible to him. But by early in the primary school the child has become capable of understanding both dialects, his creole and standard English. Creole does not seem to interfere so that oral communication normally proceeds easily. However, what has to be explained is why these children who can to a greater or lesser extent use both dialects frequently choose not to apply their knowledge of standard English to tasks at school when they know both that success at school could be important to their future and that their teacher values their use of standard English.

What has to be examined is the assumptions of those involved in such situations about how and when it is appropriate to use different dialects to different audiences. Certain questions by teachers are, for example, seen by middle-class children as part of the learning process ('have you not got one of those at home?'), but by working-class children as the prying of bureaucratic welfare agencies and by black children as attempts to bring them into the white culture. Clearly two points can be made as a result of this sociological analysis: firstly, the speaking of non-standard English must lessen a child's chance of success in the present educational system, but secondly, such a dialect is neither good nor bad in itself, but is merely an integral part of certain social contexts.

Therefore, the working-class child may well bring a twofold handicap to school. Firstly, his personality is so structured that he is unlikely to exhibit the qualities that are needed if he is to do well in today's schools, but secondly, he is likely to be attached to a language which is seen as inappropriate by his teachers and which is not used in books or other methods of learning at school. But, what is worse, he is probably less ready for school in that he has had little experience of negotiating meaning through using language. Though such experience can be found amongst speakers of all dialects it does seem less available to working- than to middle-class children. Thus, in his study of young children in Aberdeen Wootton found that both the frequency and the nature of speech between mothers and their children was different for each social class. From his data he thought 'it likely that some middle class boys speak to their parents more than twice as much as some working class boys in any given day'. More of this speech related to situations that did not involve control. Furthermore, the middle-class parents tried to extend dialogues to encourage their child to think in terms of 'validity, causality and conceptual hierarchy'. Whilst working-class parents switched their style of talk when with their children, middle-class parents treated 'conversations with their children with a level of seriousness and critical appraisal more similar to adult conversations'.[24]

However, it is to a fuller examination of the personality structure of the child that we must turn to try to explain why the child perceives the school situation in a way that entails restricting his use of standard English, thereby hindering his chances of educational success.[25] The working-class child has not had his spare time carefully organized for him, as is often the case with middle-class children. He has a very general notion of the future and is less capable of pursuing long-term goals. This reinforces the already mentioned difficulty of postponing his present whims. To such children arbitrary luck rather than rigorously planned work appears to be the reason for success. On the other hand, the middle-class child comes to school with his intelligence developed in the direction required for success. In addition his personality has been moulded in a very different social setting so that he sees the importance of long-term goals and perceives that he himself, rather than good fortune, is the main influence on his chances of achieving such goals. The working-class child largely has his social role assigned to him, whilst the middle-class child is accorded discretion to achieve his social role.[26] These two ways of perceiving the school situation that are due to personality differences may explain the previously quoted paradoxical finding of Himmelweit, in her survey of London grammar schools, where working-class boys did not do as well as middle-class boys despite the fact that they knew that their success at school could influence their long-term chances in life.

The description of social class learning that has been given here has stressed limiting cases. It can be appreciated that such cases are useful tools of sociological analysis, yielding results from which it is possible to work. But in the world of the school all is not so clear-cut. The situation is blurred by the existence of 'illiterate' middle-class parents, who care little for their children and do not provide an environment favourable to their full development, and also of working-class parents who, perhaps through extensive further education, have come to value education and who can speak in both codes. It can, however, be appreciated that a knowledge of the extreme effects of differential social class learning on the personality and intellect of children will be of great assistance to all who work in schools.

Perhaps the most succinct summary to most of what has been said here concerning social class learning is provided by some answers given by respondents in a survey amongst mothers of American five-year-olds who were about to go to school.[27] They were asked: 'Suppose your child was starting school tomorrow for the first time. What would you tell him? How would you prepare him for school?' One middle-class mother replied: 'First of all, I would remind her that she was going to school to learn, that her teacher would take my place, and that she would be expected to follow instructions. Also, that her time was to be spent mostly in the classroom with other children, and that any questions or any problems that she might have she could consult with her teacher for assistance.' When prompted, 'Anything else?', she replied: 'No.

Anything else would probably be confusing for her at her particular age.' Here the message given to the child is assured and informative; school is shown as paralleling the home and as a place involving the personal relationships of almost near-equals, the teacher and the pupil; and the classroom is defined as a place of learning.

A working-class mother replied to the same question in the following way: 'Well, John, it's time to go to school now. You must know how to behave. The first day at school you should be a good boy and should do just what the teacher tells you to do.' In marked contrast to the middle-class case this child is being socialized in anticipation of his going to school in such a way that his role is defined as passive rather than active; the roles central to the situation are seen as about authority and instruction rather than about help and near-equality; the relationships in the school are presented as impersonal rather than close and friendly; and, lastly, the message given to the child is restricted and vague rather than ample and specific.

C. Conclusion

Social class is a topic to which sociologists have given much attention. Yet to define the term is very difficult, and for our purposes here the important point is that those ascribed at birth to different social classes are largely socialized into different subcultures within which there are different patterns of learning. Social class learning affects three psychological concepts – personality, perception and thinking – and, perhaps of more importance, it implies a differential distribution of knowledge, skills and competence that varies by social class. The transmission of the different styles of life associated within each class takes place in the main, especially in early childhood, through the family. In this way social class position is normally passed from generation to generation and whole classes may be seen as self-recruiting.

Yet the key to the class system in comparison to such other modes of social differentiation as, for example, the caste system, is the relative ease of social mobility between the various levels. Such mobility in Britain today takes place in large part by means of the educational system. This must be the case in an industrial system with a strong egalitarian tradition. The political outcomes of this democratic philosophy in the form, for example, of the welfare state, together with certain economic developments such as the growth of a wealthy group of salaried employees, have helped to temper capitalism so that the prediction made by Marx that the divide between rich and poor would grow so great that a socialist revolution would occur has not yet proved true.

Yet the process of social class learning outlined here, which is implicit in the contemporary structure of society, clearly prevents children brought up in the working class from achieving their full potential in the school at a time when success at school is almost a necessity for entry into many occupations. In an egalitarian age this tendency raises the problem of whether it is possible to diminish these social class differences. The educational problems implicit in this issue will be raised again in Chapter 14, when the way in which the educational system acts as a selective agency is considered.

BIBLIOGRAPHY

B. Bernstein, *Class, Codes and Control*, Vol. I, 1971; Vol. II, 1973; Vol. III, 1975.

J. W. B. Douglas, *The Home and The School*, 1964.

A. Giddens, *The Class Structure of the Advanced Societies*, 1973.

D. V. Glass (ed.), *Social Mobility in Britain*, 1954.

J. H. Goldthorpe, D. Lockwood, F. Bechhofer and J. Platt, *The Affluent Worker in the Class Structure*, 1969.

B. Jackson and D. Marsden, *Education and the Working Class*, 1962.

W. Labov, 'The Logic of Non-standard English', in N. Keddie (ed.), *Tinker, Tailor: the Myth of Cultural Deprivation*, 1973.

D. C. Marsh, *The Changing Social Structure of England and Wales, 1871–1961*, 2nd edn, 1965, Ch. VII, 'Social Classes and Educational Opportunities'.

J. and E. Newson, *Infant Care in an Urban Community*, 1963.

J. and E. Newson, *Four Years Old in an Urban Community*, 1968.

J. and E. Newson, *Seven Years Old in the Home Environment*, 1976.

W. G. Runciman, *Relative Deprivation and Social Justice*, 1966.

M. Stubbs, *Language, Schools and Classrooms*, 1977.

D. F. Swift, 'Social Class and Achievement Motivation', *Educational Research*, February 1966.

P. E. Vernon, *Intelligence and Cultural Environment*, 1969.

J. H. Westergaard and H. Resler, *Class in a Capitalist Society: a Study of Contemporary Britain*, 1976.

NOTES

1 In this book the full term 'social class' will be used in this connection except where the context is clear, in order to avoid any confusion with the educational term, 'the school class', i.e. a group of children taught together.

2 H. Giles, 'Our Reaction to Accent', *New Society*, 14 October 1971.

3 A. H. Halsey (ed.), *Trends in British Society since 1900*, 1972, Tables 3.2 and 3.19.

4 D. J. Treiman and K. Terrell, 'The Process of Status Attainment in the United States and Great Britain, *American Journal of Sociology*, November 1975, p. 579.

5 This report was never published officially, but is reproduced in *New Society*, 27 December 1962.

6 H. F. Moorehouse and C. W. Chamberlain, 'Lower Class Attitudes to Property: Aspects of the Counter-Ideology', *Sociology*, September 1974.

7 W. G. Runciman, 'Embourgeoisement: Self-rated Class and Party Preference', *Sociological Review*, July 1964.

8 B. Bernstein and D. Young, 'Social Class Differences in Conceptions of the Use of Toys', *Sociology*, May 1967.

9 G. Jahoda, 'Development of the Perception of Social Differences in Children from Six to Ten', *British Journal of Psychology*, May 1959.

10 H. T. Himmelweit, A. H. Halsey and A. N. Oppenheim, 'The Views of Adolescents on Some Aspects of the Social Class Structure', *British Journal of Sociology*, June 1962; F. M. Martin, in Glass, 1954, pp. 59–61 and 74.

11 R. W. Connell, 'Class Consciousness in Childhood', *Australian and New Zealand Journal of Sociology*, October 1970.

12 A. Davis, *Social Class Influences on Learning*, Cambridge, Mass., 1948.

13 A. J. Wootton, 'Talk in the Homes of Young Children', *Sociology*, May 1974; B. Bernstein and D. Henderson, 'Social Class Differences in the Relevance of Language to Socialisation', in Bernstein, 1973.

14 D. C. McClelland, *The Achieving Society*, Princeton, N.J., 1961; for a concise, but complete, account of relevant work see D. C. McClelland, 'The Achievement Motive in Economic Growth', in B. F. Hoselitz and W. E. Moore (eds.), *Industrialization and Society*, Unesco, 1963.

15 P. W. Musgrave and G. R. B. Reid, 'Some Measures of Children's Values', *Social Science Information*, March 1971, especially pp. 147–9.

16 F. M. Martin, in Glass, 1954, pp. 162–3, and Douglas, 1964, pp. 21–2 and 45.

17 D. F. Swift, 'Social Class, Mobility-ideology and Eleven Plus Success', *British Journal of Sociology*, June 1967.

18 D. M. Toomey, 'Home-centred Working Class Parents' Attitudes towards their Sons' Education and Careers', *Sociology*, September 1969, p. 314.

19 See H. T. Himmelweit, 'Social Status and Secondary Education since the 1944 Act: Some Data for London', in Glass, 1954.

20 Douglas, 1964, pp. 50–1; *Higher Education* (Robbins Report), 1963, Appendix One, p. 57.

21 For Piaget see J. H. Flavell, *The Developmental Psychology of Jean Piaget*, Princeton, N.J., 1963; see also D. O. Hebb, *The Organization of Behavior*, New York, 1961.

22 W. P. Robinson and S. J. Rackstraw, 'Variations in Mothers' Answers to Children's Questions, as a Function of Social Class, Verbal Intelligence Test Scores, and Sex', *Sociology*, September 1967.

23 G. Wells, 'Language Use and Educational Success: an Empirical Response to Joan Tough's *The Development of Meaning* (1977)', *Research in Education*, November 1977.

24 Wootton, 'Talk in the Homes of Young Children', *op. cit.* (see n. 13).

25 B. Bernstein, 'Some Sociological Determinants of Perception', in Bernstein, 1971.

26 B. Bernstein and D. Henderson, 'Social Class Differences in the Relevance of Language to Socialization', in Bernstein, 1973.

27 R. D. Hess and V. C. Shipman, 'Early Experience and the Socialization of Cognitive Modes in Children', *Child Development*, September 1965, pp. 876–7.

5

Youth Cultures and Peer Groups

This chapter is concerned solely with the influence of groups of equals upon children and adolescents, though such groups do affect the behaviour of such subsequent age grades as university students or old age pensioners. The actual process of socialization is the same in the peer group as it is in the family and the analysis must, therefore, be carried out in much the same way, that is by focusing first on structural aspects and then turning to the interpersonal level. The justification for giving so much space to this topic is that children spend much time both in and out of school hours mixing in groups which have been shown to have considerable influence on their behaviour and attitudes in general, as well as on their capacity for education. In addition, as children grow older they move away from their families and begin to relate more to their peers. Furthermore, in most contemporary societies the time allowed to the young to pass through the stages of preparation for adulthood seems to be lengthening. For an increasing number today the age of starting work has been postponed until at least twenty-one. This longer preparation for adulthood has become possible largely because of the greater wealth in such societies as the USA, Britain and Australia. However, this same increase has made the influence of peer groups more complex, since affluence allows more choice to the contemporary young than was possible for previous generations. Conflict over the way in which these choices are made is therefore likely between the representatives of older generations, namely parents and teachers, and those moving away from the influence of the family and the school into the ambit of various groups of peers.

A. The Structural Perspective

A key analytical concept here is that of *generation*, an aggregate of similarly aged persons. The different generations are made up of peer groups of very varied types and serving different functions for their members, though the types and the functions do change through time.

1. *Generations*

Most structurally based sociological thinking about the problem of the generations is influenced by Mannheim (1952). He began his analysis by comparing generations to social classes. In each case those occupying a similar social position are constrained by a similar set of social forces. In the case of social class these are related to the position filled in the economy; in the case of generations the forces are related to the age structure of the society. Generations, in Mannheim's words, are 'based on the existence of biological rhythms in human existence'. But it is to the sociological, not physiological relevance of such rhythms that attention must be given.

New members are constantly being born into any society; these provide a fresh contact with the current state of the culture and thereby allow the possibility of change. In addition, the old disappear and in this way some social amnesia can occur. The members of any one generation can only participate in a limited part of history, so that it becomes necessary to try to transmit the heritage of the past to newcomers to the society. But each generation views the present differently because each does so from a different accumulation of knowledge and experience. So reality is constructed differently by each generation. However, this process of transmission is continuous so that big jumps in generational styles are rare. Rather the change allowed for, indeed in part created by, the constant interaction between the generations tends to be smooth in nature.

Mannheim saw the ages from seventeen to twenty-five as a crucial period in the formation of cultural consciousness. By seventeen young people have the knowledge and confidence to take decisions on many matters; by twenty-five, or perhaps somewhat later under contemporary conditions, many individuals have become so rooted in the social structure through marriage or the ties of a job that any major break with their present style of life is difficult. It is during this relatively rootless period that many hope that the young will at least try to initiate cultural changes of all types.

Within any one generation there can exist 'generation units'. As Mannheim put it, 'Youth experiencing the same concrete historical problems may be said to be part of the same actual generation, while those groups within the same actual generation who work up the material of their common experiences in different specific ways, constitute generation units.' There are, for example, conservative and radical groups within the older and younger generations, and there are conformist and anti-social groups in each generation. Amongst youth, in particular, there are many styles of expressing the values of the present young generation. What has to be examined is how and why these forms have arisen now.

2. *Changes in Generations*

There is some doubt about the date around which adolescence came to be a recognized status in the Western life cycle. But certainly the modern image of adolescence owes much to the Victorian middle class. Sometime in the middle of the last century two important themes in the contemporary view of adolescence became prominent: dependence and separation. In the public schools, increasing then in number and popularity, boys and, later, girls were allowed a dependent, but separate prolonged preparation for adulthood. Soon, books and magazines were produced to meet this new market and these were in nature suited to strengthen the new image of adolescence. Examples could be *Tom Brown's School Days* (1857) and the *Boys Own Paper*, founded in 1855 (Murdock and McCron, in Hall and Jefferson, 1976). This image of adolescence could not easily spread widely into the working class because of the hard economic circumstances of the times.

After the start of the war in 1939, however, the status of youth changed greatly. The scarcity of labour ensured that their wages rose more rapidly than those of adults and after the war full employment maintained their changed bargaining position in the labour market. Many other important social changes affected youth, including now working-class youth. Firstly, their command over purchasing power had risen and this, taken together with the increase in the birth rate in the immediate post-war years, meant that by the 1960s there was an opportunity, eagerly accepted by manufacturers, to develop special consumer goods for a mass teenage market, particularly for clothes, records and other products for use in leisure time.

This increased wealth and a consequent drive to express independence from the family came at the same time as certain educational changes that worked in the opposite direction. The population of the young in school rose because the minimum school-leaving age was raised to fifteen in 1947 and sixteen in 1973, and also because increasing numbers stayed voluntarily at school, largely since this alternative seemed likely to pay off in better job opportunities. Furthermore, greater general wealth and better social conditions, both at home and at school, led to sounder health and earlier physical maturity which implied earlier sexual maturity.

Intergenerational conflict, as was indicated in the last section, is normal, but in the circumstances since 1939 youth has become very much more independent and generation-conscious. Furthermore, these changes now affect not only the family, but most pupils in secondary schools and many persons who come into contact with youth in their leisure hours. Many have written of contemporary youth as if it were totally segregated from the rest of society. Certainly, the great scope for choice amongst many different alternative styles of life and ways of spending money has proved a visible and ready source of conflict between the generations. Many of the resulting activities, whether relating to dress or music or to the behaviour exhibited by young people, have been seen by their elders as deviant. This is an almost inevitable result of the apparent spurning by youth of the traditional agents of respectability – parents, teachers and clergy – and the choosing by the young on their own initiative of new models of behaviour, often from the world of the mass media.

The concept of a 'youth culture' has been used to isolate the values and behaviour exhibited by many young people today. This is a somewhat misleading phrase as there are so many sub-cultures available to or created by contemporary youth, some of which are accepted and some condemned by those with power in contemporary society. The values involved are no longer imposed by or accepted from the older generation, but are now more or less freely chosen by the young concerned, although in many cases young persons may still have a very narrow range of choices available to them – for example, between joining a group centred on a badly equipped church youth club, hanging around the streets without breaking the law or behaving in an illegal manner.

Those in power in any society have always been concerned that the young shall not become alienated from the norms of contemporary society. Such a change has been seen as likely to cause social instability. Therefore, various organizations have been created, either officially or with official blessing, which have the aims, whether conscious or not, of preserving the ideological *status quo*. Bodies like the Scouts, the Guides, the Boys' Brigade or the Cadet Corps have endeavoured to harness the energies of youth to nationally approved causes. Likewise, youth clubs have been run by secular or religious bodies with similar aims. The different social classes have reacted differently to these organizations. Clearly the social predicament of each social class is different. The working class, going to work early, achieves some economic independence before middle-class youth, who tend to stay longer within the educational system, thus remaining separate, but without much economic or other independence. These social class differences will be taken up again when considering the interpersonal perspective.

3. *The Functions of the Peer Group*
So far, the analysis has moved from a consideration of generations to generation units and thence to the smaller groups that make up such units. These groups serve important functions, both for society and for the individuals who are their members. However, here the main focus will be upon the functions of peer groups for individuals. In both cases the nature of these functions changes through time consequent upon changes in the social structure.

In the family or at school the child is in a situation of subservience, where power can be exercised over him. In both situations the child is in a heterogeneous age group (Eisenstadt, 1956) where some, by virtue of a position based largely on their age, are more powerful than others. However, a peer group is a homogeneous age group. All the members are of the same or very similar age. Therefore, in such a group a child can gain certain experiences that he cannot possibly have in the normal family, particularly in the small-sized nuclear family usual in contemporary industrialized societies. The experience of mixing with equals is an essential preparation for adult life, since at work or at leisure much time must be spent and many important actions must be undertaken in company with one's peers. He who during adolescence does not master the social skills of mixing with his peers will not be able to lead a normal adult life.

Perhaps the most important set of social roles that cannot be learnt completely within the family are those concerning sex. Young persons may learn something of their sex role if they have one or more siblings of the opposite sex in their families, but they must mix with boys and girls other than their close relations if they are to learn how to treat the opposite sex in the socially approved manner so that they have the social skills needed for courtship and a stable marriage. Despite contemporary changes in the nature of marriage, continuing relationship based on love still seems to be the normally approved system in most Western societies. However, the age of marriage is tending to fall whilst there is a tendency for the time spent at school to lengthen, so that parents and teachers are more likely to come into conflict with adolescents over the matter of their relationship with the opposite sex. It is while amongst their peers and usually away from the control of their elders that adolescent boys and girls can try out the behaviour expected of them towards the opposite sex and move from apparent gaucherie to greater sophistication. They learn how to approach and to talk with those of the opposite sex and how much of themselves to invest emotionally in each other so that they have some chance of becoming more able to make a reasonable choice of marriage partner by early adulthood.

Another important consequence of the existence of peer groups is that the individual learns to achieve and accept status in a group on his own account rather than because of his ascribed position in his family. In a society where social and geographical mobility is common, in taking up a new job or at holiday times, movement away from the family is frequent and individuals must mix with others who do not know them. The social skills involved in 'keeping one's end up', learnt in the peer group, enable the achievement of social ease outside the circle of normal acquaintance.

There are, as noted above, social, as well as individual, functions of peer groups, though these are of familial and political, rather than direct educational, importance. The way in which membership of certain approved organizations may help to support the ideological *status quo* has already been mentioned. There are other social functions. For example, the family, even in the extended form, does not usually provide marriage partners, whereas the peer group mixes those from many family groupings and thereby spreads the possible scope of friendship. This same process, particularly in small-scale societies, facilitates the integration of social systems since the network of those who know each other becomes very complex through mixing in groups at school, church, work and in clubs or societies. An important example of this process is the way in which the old boys' clubs of British and Australian public schools, cross-cutting profession and occupation, political party and often national boundary, help to integrate the upper middle classes within those two countries.

B. The Interpersonal Perspective

Young people make their choices and live their generational lives largely with their friends. Within these groups of peers, individuals create the sub-cultural diversity which offsets the apparently strong contemporary pressures for cultural uniformity. As peer groups form, their members bring to them their past experiences and the effects of the pressures acting upon them in other social positions that they fill. Sociologists have analysed such effects by using the concept of latent role to cover the behavioural expectations brought to a situation from outside it. In the second part of this section we shall examine the latent roles that young persons bring to their peer groups. Finally, some attempt must be made to judge the relative power of the three agents of socialization that have been considered so far.

1. *The Formation of Peer Groups*

Various types of grouping amongst youth are normal, not pathological, social phenomena. Some groups create styles that older generations tolerate or even praise; the behaviour of Boy Scouts doing 'bob a job' week is not labelled as outside the boundaries of tolerated behaviour in young persons. Other groups clearly take part in breaking the law; the behaviour of those who take a bob rather than earn it is seen officially as juvenile delinquency. Between these two extremes there is a wide range within which young people can choose to create or adjust to very different sub-cultural styles of life.

The importance to the contemporary young of such sub-cultures is largely based on the fact that adolescents have extremely restricted choices for action at work or at school so that a major part of their response to their social class location can be made in the sphere of consumption and leisure. These spheres of action provide 'a more negotiable space than the tightly disciplined and controlled work (or school) situation' (Clark *et al.*, in Hall and Jefferson, 1976). Within this space the young can create what Mannheim called 'concrete groups', the members of each of which can adopt or interpret or create a style of life that meets the needs of their position. Levi-Strauss' concept of *bricolage* is relevant here: 'the reordering and re-contextualization of objects to communicate fresh meanings, within a total system of significations, which already includes prior and sedimented meanings attached to the objects used'.

In this process groups draw upon the cultural sources around them to create new styles and to express generational meanings. The parent culture can provide materials. Thus, working-class youth can draw upon, for example, a tradition of collective activities, an emphasis on territoriality and a concept of masculinity, or middle-class youth upon the tradition of displaying individual initiative, the feeling of the importance of high art and on an apparently more casual role for the two sexes. But whatever materials are chosen there are certain focal concerns for the young generation of any historical moment and these now seem to centre on dress, music, ritual, slang and, perhaps, various means of transport. Ethnographic studies of the Mods and the Rockers (Cohen, 1972) in the 1960s show this process clearly and also indicate how each of these styles was adapted and adopted by different social groupings. Furthermore, the reaction, so violent in its nature that it has been called a moral panic, that ensued has also been described; the older generation and such agents of respectability as the police, the magistrates and the daily press all attempted to bring the actions of the young back within what they saw as the boundaries of tolerable behaviour.

To many adults, including teachers, the subtleties of sub-cultural styles are lost and merged into a stereotype of youth as long-haired ('unkempt'), casually ('sloppily') dressed and ill-spoken ('swears all the time'). What must, therefore, now be examined is the way in which normal young people form peer groups, choose a style and negotiate a leisure-time life of their own in the interstices of the culture of the older generations. Two studies, both written in the 1960s, provide evidence in the light of which this process of normal peer group formation in adolescence can be studied.

In the first study, Willmott (1966) looked at the life of 279 adolescent boys aged between fourteen and twenty in Bethnal Green (London) during 1964, and in the second Dunphy (1969) examined the structure and formation of adolescent groups, made up of both sexes, in Sydney, Australia, during the period between 1958 and 1960. In both projects the research workers relied rather more on participant observation than on the use of questionnaires and were able to come very close to the teenagers whom they were studying. Dunphy found that in his sample of 303 boys and girls aged thirteen to eighteen there were forty-four 'cliques', containing between three and nine members, but with an average size of 6·2 persons. Similar groups of about five boys were found in Bethnal Green. These cliques were linked into twelve 'crowds' of between fifteen and thirty members, and averaged 20·2 teenagers. 'The crowd [was] essentially an association of cliques', as there were between two and four (average 3·1) cliques per crowd. Only four of the forty-four cliques were not linked with any crowd.

One common misconception is that such crowds are 'gangs'. This was the case neither in Sydney nor in Bethnal Green. Although these cliques and crowds persisted over a number of years, most of the other features usually associated with a gang were absent.

There was, for example, no pronounced division of labour within the groups such that roles with specific tasks were allocated to members. There were no signs of warfare over territory or of organized law-breaking, although a certain amount of minor law-breaking, and especially in Bethnal Green of theft among the younger boys, was a sub-cultural norm. Above all there was no hierarchy; on the contrary the members of the groups saw each other as true equals. However, the larger groups in Bethnal Green and the crowds in Sydney were known by the names of a prominent member, although the members claimed that he was not really a leader. In order to understand his position and function, the life history of the system of cliques and crowds must be described.

During the early teens peer groups are made up entirely of boys or of girls and these small single-sex groups are isolated from one another. At about fifteen, though to specify an exact age is impossible, the members of the single-sex cliques begin to interact with each other and the leaders in each group seem to be the first to intermingle with the opposite sex. There is, therefore, a period during which the isolated single-sex cliques are being transferred into a linked system, the crowd, made up of cliques, now containing both sexes. However, by the late teens the process of disintegration is likely to have begun as the members of the new cliques become engaged or married and tend to drift away from the very loosely organized activities of the crowd.

The crowd is the focus, especially at weekends, for the more organized social activities such as parties or visits in large numbers to beaches or entertainments, whilst the cliques in both Sydney and Bethnal Green were mainly used by their members for 'hanging around' or for conversation, particularly in weekday evenings, when no activity was organized for the crowd as a whole but when there was the need, normally felt by these adolescents, to be away from their families. Though, as noted above, the members of all these groups claimed that there were no leaders, each group was structured around one member, who was the best-known outside the group. In Sydney it was through him that the clique was linked to the crowd. As is usually the case in any type of group, this leader displayed the norms of the group in their clearest form. In Sydney this meant that leaders 'were invariably more advanced in their relationship with the opposite sex than were their fellows'. 'Going steady', for instance, was more common amongst leaders than followers. In Bethnal Green leaders appeared to be the toughest member of the group, though this implied the adoption of a style of bravado rather than the use of physical violence. It is worth noting that members of all these groups had to live up to the norms expected of group members. The reward for such behaviour was acceptance and the punishment for a falling away was exclusion, a severe sanction when an entrée to the culture of the teenage group is as strongly desired as is usually the case today.

Another aspect of leadership in the groups in Sydney might also have been predicted from what is known about the structure of small groups. There were often two leaders, though it is possible that one person could have done the work of both. The one on whom the discussion has so far turned is termed the instrumental rather than the expressive leader, and he tends to be responsible for seeing that the group achieves its main purpose. In the case of the Sydney groups this implied the arranging of occasions when boys and girls could meet and in the case of the groups in Bethnal Green the organizing of entertainment or sports, and by sixteen, the age after which in Britain motorcycles may legally be ridden, the organization of group cycle activities.

Though in both studies the adolescents used youth clubs, more attention was given to this aspect by Willmott. At the time of his survey two-fifths of the boys were members of a club, but the greatest incidence was at about sixteen or seventeen, whilst by the age of twenty only one in seven were still members. By that age 90 per cent of the boys had been members of a youth club at some time.

In his large sample, representative of Britain, Douglas found that only 16 per cent of the boys and 15 per cent of the girls never joined a club, though there were differences by social class with the lower working-class adolescents showing the highest percentage, namely 21 for boys and 19 for girls.[1] Although these clubs were run by adults and were criticized as 'strict' by the adolescents in this sample, they did seem to fill the necessary purpose of being 'meeting places' or 'somewhere to go' outside the family. In fact Willmott says that 'every youth club – and for that matter, every Scout Group or Cadet Corps – is really a federation of peer

groups'. In other words, the older generation has provided an institution where adolescents may organize 'a crowd'. Ultimately
members left these clubs as they grew older and began to go steady,
or because they 'lost interest'. In neither case had the clubs failed.
They had helped in the process of socialization by easing the
transition to adulthood.

C. Latent Roles

Those who join any group may be expected to conform to the norms
of that particular group, but they also play other roles elsewhere in
the social structure. There are certain behavioural expectations
such as those relating to sex roles that have a very powerful influence on how persons act in whatever social setting they find
themselves. These primary roles, as they were called in Chapter 2,
are brought from outside the groups and, though apparently latent,
may to some extent constrain how an individual acts whilst a member of a group. Clearly, different behaviour is expected from a boy
and from a girl as members of the peer groups that have so far
been considered in this chapter. Here we shall examine four important roles. In addition to the sex role, those concerned with age,
social class and colour will be discussed.

1. *Age*

The older a child grows, the more he seeks group activity outside
the family and also the more likely it is that he is influenced by
groups that are outside the full control of those in charge of the
school, even though the activities of the group may take place
largely within the boundaries of the school. Exact ages are hard to
link to types of group structure, but in view of the progression from
family-based activity through school to peer group-based activity,
age roles will be considered here according to the three broad stages
of schooling.

(i) *Pre-schooling*. Very young children tend to play by themselves
a great deal and when they start to relate to other children they
rarely form groups, but tend to play usually in pairs. Though deep
and lasting friendships can be found between pairs of children,
temporary pairings seem more common except where the social

situation is such that the availability of possible playmates is limited, as may be the case in such remote country areas as the Scottish highlands and islands or the Australian outback. At this age friendships and those small groups of shifting membership that do temporarily exist are based on both sexes. Boys and girls intermingle without thought or restriction. Spontaneous group activity as such is rare, with one possible exception. Young children may gang up on one child and temporarily cast him in the role of scapegoat, though even this form of group activity is rare and not very lasting. Children at this age are learning how to behave towards others and hence seem to be experimenting with their relationships towards their peers. Thus, the characteristics of all groups at this early stage are their small scale, impermanence and cross-sex nature. John is friends with Ian today, Jenny tomorrow and Ian again next week.

(ii) *The Primary Stage.* There is some evidence concerning the nature of groups amongst children as they pass through the primary age range. This is based on a number of studies done in English primary schools (Blyth, 1960). Around the age of seven, peer groups seem to be rather unstructured and still unstable in that membership changes quite substantially even within a school year. There is, however, the beginning of the division that has already been noted into single-sex groups. By the age of eight or nine this division is more marked and after nine quite separate groups of boys and girls appear. Boys by this stage will not be seen dead playing with girls and vice versa, and powerful sanctions operate within the peer group so that each sex conforms to the behaviour expected of it. The groups of boys are larger and more closely structured than those of the girls, who have a tendency to form pairs or trios. These small groups of girls are less closely linked together compared with the bigger groups of boys. The latter gather around a leader who may have one or more henchmen. The leader is often the captain of a class team or an able child, so that the informal structure of the class is paralleling the formal structure that has been organized by the teachers. Furthermore, the peer groups in the primary school classroom seem, sometimes unbeknown to the teacher, to be based on relationships made outside the school, at home or in the local neighbourhood. The fact that many children who are in the same class also live close to each other, perhaps regularly going each day from their homes to school together in a group, provides the opportunity for building relatively permanent relationships. Thus, by eleven, when children pass to secondary school their peer groups seem to have become larger, especially in the case of boys, more permanent and based on one sex only. John is never a friend of Jenny's but has been a friend of Ian's for a long time.

(iii) *The Secondary Stage*. So far no differentiation has been made amongst the peer groups that have been considered, but recent work by Sugarman [2] makes clear that certainly by the secondary stage different types of peer groups exist within the school. In this study Sugarman interviewed a sample of eighty boys in the fourth form who were drawn from a grammar, two modern and a comprehensive school in the London area. No evidence was found even in the grammar school to show that prestige was given for academic success. Groups formed around different activities to which status was given within each category of group. The peer groups found amongst these adolescent boys could be divided into three categories. There were, firstly, those based on playing games in the school playground. In these groups the norms centred on the rules of the games and on being a 'good sport'. The sanctions used against deviants were, for example, rough play, refusing to pass the ball to them, or even leaving them out of the teams. Secondly, there were those groups who just talked. Topics were very varied, but sport and television were common subjects and some groups focused on such specific interests as motorcycles or pop music. Evidence will be cited in the next chapter to show that sometimes each peer group may specialize by favouring one type of music or one pop star, and sanctions are used to ensure that all members are followers of the speciality of their chosen peer group. In general, however, these groups of talkers tend to generate very specific systems of norms and sanctions that relate to their own particular interests. Thirdly, there were groups of 'hard boys'. Status was gained by being successful in fights.

These findings reported by Sugarman make it seem likely that peer groups in secondary schools centre on interests and hobbies which by this stage of adolescence are starting to be relatively specialized. How true this generalization is for groups outside the school is uncertain, mainly because, as Sugarman himself has shown in other work relating to the same study, teenagers in general have a high level of commitment to a mass youth culture based on pop music, fashion, dancing and discos. Furthermore, the higher the commitment to the teenage role, the lower seems to be an adolescent's commitment to the role of pupil that is associated with the school.[3] Whilst at secondary school, John might be in a group with Ian that was based on a common interest which was probably totally unconnected with school, and out of school he and John might well meet Jenny and another girl to play some part in the teenage scene. In sum, the very fact that children grow older has clear implications for their behaviour in peer groups. For example, as they become more confident of their ability to choose friends, their groups become more permanent and more structured. In addition, as their interests become more stable, groups in school seem to become differentiated, specialist and less centred on the school, although outside the school the power of the teenage culture may well have an homogenizing effect. However, clearly the changing nature of the sex roles is a powerful latent influence and must be given further consideration.

2. Sex

As boys and girls grow towards adult status, their sex roles increasingly govern the nature and activities of their peer groups. In earlier years Blyth's results indicate that in the primary stage girls form smaller and less structured groups than boys do. In the USA, Coleman (1961) has reported similar findings for the secondary stage, since girls in high schools were members of small cliques more often than boys. They also seemed to have more intense friendships than did the boys. In addition, girls in the American high school conformed more readily to school and local norms than did boys.

It is when examining groups outside school that a crucial difference between the sexes appears. In many peer groups, for example those associated with the Teddy Boy sub-culture of the 1950s, girls have been more or less absent. However, since the late 1960s, particularly amongst groups associated with the largely middle-class Hippies, girls have had a place, and more recently the unisex sub-culture by definition allows them a role. One unique reaction to the predicament of girls in our society has been the emergence of the teeny-bopper. This sub-culture depends heavily upon commercial pressures, but nevertheless allows girls of between ten and fifteen to negotiate a role for themselves. Their only needs are a bedroom, some posters, a record-player and permission to invite friends. Anyone can achieve this style; there is little chance of personal humiliation or of being labelled as deviant (McRobbie and Garber, in Hall and Jefferson, 1976).

Yet even for those taking the unisex role the subservient status of women in our society is not overcome. When the two sexes joined together in mixed groups, Dunphy noted that it was a boy who took the role of instrumental leader. Likewise in Bethnal Green, girls were 'picked up' or 'dated'; the boys had to be seen to take the initiative. In general, as is only to be expected, peer groups reflect the social scene in which they exist, so that they are influenced throughout adolescence by the gradual development of the sex roles. More particularly, mixed groups reflect the inferior status of women compared with men in contemporary Western society.

3. *Social Class*

It is only recently that much research has been done that is relevant to the latent role of social class in peer groups. For the working class in particular, youth sub-cultures provide chances to break the weak links in the socialization process in the family or the schools and, therefore, to create discontinuities in the transmission of culture to the next generation. Within the constraints of time and money working-class boys strive during their brief adolescence to fulfil their longing to be the daring, tough and fun-loving men that they see as the ideal for males. Within the space, by convention still somewhat more restricted, available to them girls try to create a style that will win them their man and found a secure family of procreation. Ironically, the attempt to create discontinuity often does little more than overemphasize characteristics of the culture of the older generation and, even if a small measure of discontinuity is achieved, this is a temporary situation that works to ease later movement of the younger generation into its inevitable position as the next parental generation. When at the end of this chapter we examine the relative power of the peer group and the family, we shall see that such temporary but functional discontinuity is probably a rather common occurrence.

As Willmott has shown, in these efforts several distinct sub-cultures may emerge within one geographical area. By the stage of adolescence it may well be that the social class of aspiration rather than that of origin largely influences behaviour. Willmott divides his sample into three groups: the 'middle class', the 'working class' and the 'rebels'. Each group had very different attitudes, learnt at home and at school, which governed their response to their environment and particularly the sort of life to which they aspired. Members of each category seemed to have a different style of leisure activity. Those with middle-class aspirations had a best friend who more often lived outside Bethnal Green, visited the West End more often and expected to marry later than those in the other two categories. The 'rebels' had low occupational aspirations, related more closely to the local area, and were more approving than the other adolescents of fighting. Some young people, however, may not be deeply involved in any of these local sub-cultures and they are more likely to opt for official youth clubs or for some aspects of the commercially provided national teenage culture.

Middle-class youth sub-cultures seem more diffuse and individualistic and, hence, less centred in well-articulated groups. Evidence for this can be found in Douglas' sample. Thus, 36 per cent of upper middle-class boys as opposed to 16 per cent of those from the lower working class had academic hobbies; the situation for girls was very similar. Again, 28 per cent of upper middle-class boys, but 52 per cent of lower working-class boys were interested only in sports; the results for girls did not show a difference by social class.[4] However, many hobbies, particularly those attractive to middle-class youth, are of a type that can be practised alone or with close friends rather than in peer groups. When middle-class youths do join groups they are more likely to become members of such approved groups as Scouts or Guides.

Just as much expected behaviour may differ by social class, so may misbehaviour, and the very different social situations of the social classes do seem to result in differing types of deviance. Willmott indicates that stealing and pilfering are quite usual activities in

Bethnal Green, a working-class area, though adolescents are fully aware that this behaviour is seen to be wrong by those with authority. The deviant behaviour of middle-class adolescents is more often associated with the two characteristic differences in their structural position, namely their greater wealth – for example drug taking; and their lengthier exposure to the educational system – for example 'dropping out'. Similar arguments can be used to explain the fact that most politically radical students have been middle-class. In all these cases, whether amongst the working or middle class, such deviance is seen by agents of respectability as part of the current crisis in authority and, since youth is seen in this respect as the source of possible social breakdown, repression is often felt necessary.

4. Colour

The huge influx of immigrants into Britain since the war from the West Indies, Africa, India and Pakistan poses questions of cultural and individual integration. Both these processes have been hard to achieve when, as is often the case, the immigrants have in the main settled in residentially segregated areas. Some manifestations of black sub-cultures, particularly connected with jazz, have had an influence in white teenage cultures, but this apart, mixing between coloured and white youth outside school has not been pronounced.

Within the separate coloured groups the processes at work are the same as amongst whites. Labov, for example, has shown how amongst pre-adolescent black boys in New York the type of language used is a very sensitive index of their involvement in the street culture. Core members used a totally different language system from marginal members.[5] It must be remembered that prejudice also exists amongst coloured immigrants both towards the British and towards each other. Thus, in work done in 1963 Kawwa found that, though there was more negative prejudice against coloured persons amongst children in London than in Lowestoft, where immigrants were very few in number, yet the pattern of prejudice in Islington, London, reflected the pattern of ethnic groupings in the catchment area of the comprehensive school in which his study was undertaken and in which fifteen per cent of the pupils were immigrants. Here the Cypriots, who were seen as culturally more different from the English than the West Indians, were the target for the prejudices of both the other immigrants and the British.[6]

In work carried out in the West Midlands with 1,747 British, Indian and West Indian children of between seven and fifteen years of age Rowley found that 'at least 90 per cent of British children of all ages in the sample preferred to choose British friends' in the three social situations about which they were asked; '75 per cent of Indians chose their own nationality and 60 per cent of West Indians likewise.' There was, as has been found elsewhere, a slight tendency for in-group choices to increase with age.[7] Yet the situation may be more complex than this. From work done in Sparkbrook, Birmingham, it seems that what happens is that children, even in early adolescence, make friends and mix with each other across ethnic divisions whilst in school, but that they do not carry these friendships out of the school into their leisure activities. An easy mixing takes place at school, but segregation at home. In this context, as in many others, familial sanctions seem to overcome behaviour learnt in the schools which are in the eyes of parents of all groups, white or black, seen to be undermining both the accepted pattern of culture and parental authority by sanctioning such friendships.[8]

D. The Power of the Peer Group

We have, finally, to ask what is the relative power of the three agents of socialization so far considered. There are some studies which compare the peer group and the school, or the peer group and the family, but there seem to be no sophisticated studies of a statistical nature that help us to come to any balanced answer as a result of comparing all these agents.

1. *The Peer Group and the School*
The very famous study of the American high school by Coleman (1961) has shown a situation where the system of peer groups almost dominates the school. In the sample of ten high schools that he investigated there were four sub-cultures named by Coleman, namely the fun, the academic, the vocational and the delinquent sub-cultures. The names largely explain the characteristics of each.

The majority of pupils were members of the first culture, which was based on their participation through peer groups in the wide range of extracurricular facilities available at the American high school, and in the many leisure-time activities outside school hours that were arranged whilst at school. The pupils came to school mainly to meet their friends and to arrange future fun at parties or on dates in the evenings or at weekends rather than to participate in academic or vocationally relevant learning. All this activity was closely related to peer groups of one kind or another, though this was less the case in country areas, where adolescents had not so clearly broken away from parental control, than in the urban high schools. The school had not been established with this aim in mind, nor did the teachers see this as either the purpose for which they were employed or the result of their daily teaching. But for the pupils the school was a place where one went to participate in groups dedicated to fun. These adolescents had imported the youth culture of the peer group into the school and it had largely taken the place of the official academic or vocational cultures.

These findings must, however, be set against the British evidence from studies of a grammar school (King, 1969) and a secondary modern school (Hargreaves, 1967). In each case the schools that they studied were partially successful in that they either transmitted some of their values to some of their pupils or else supported and reinforced the values of the families from which some of their pupils came. In the former case, even those who left the grammar school early did gain some academic success at 'O' level, presumably an achievement that the teachers wished for their pupils. In the latter case, the boys in the 'A' stream of the secondary modern school behaved and studied largely as the staff wished, even though those in the 'D' stream were apparently little influenced in the direction in which the school hoped. Yet for many adolescents in the same position as those in the 'D' stream, what the school sees as failure in a non-differentiated way, those involved often see 'as failure at school, and as not particularly important in the broader view that they have of life'.[9]

The examples so far quoted relate to the secondary age range and it is clear that the peer group is more influential amongst older children. Furthermore, in general most attention has been given in the research so far carried out to those peer groups that are opposed to the values of the school. Little attention has been given to those that must exist that are neutral, neither helping nor hindering the school, or that reinforce the lessons which the school is trying to transmit. Since we have seen that whether or not the school is successful in its aims is much dependent upon the family background of the pupils concerned we may suspect that the type of peer group that an adolescent joins and how much it influences him for or against the school will also largely be rooted in his family circumstances.

2. *The Family*

According to Musgrove (1966) the family is so powerful a social influence that the school can avail little. Indeed almost the only way in which the school could succeed in its aims would be for the child to be removed from the family and entrusted totally to the school. There is a less strong version of the thesis that the family is all-powerful which claims that despite the immense power of the youth culture and the peer group the family as a social institution ultimately reasserts itself (Hoggart, 1956). The argument runs this way. At adolescence children, particularly amongst the working class, move away from their families and come under the influence of the youth culture, especially within the peer groups of which they are members, for the reasons and with the consequences outlined earlier in this chapter. There follows a period aptly named by Klein as 'the splash',[10] when the adolescent or young adult is freer of what may be termed primary social responsibilities than he was before or ever will be again. This freedom ends possibly with marriage, but certainly with the birth of a first child, by which time the young adult has completed the socially essential move from his family of origin to his own family of procreation. The constraints of building a new home and family are such that young parents are compelled because of shortage of both money and spare time to leave the constantly changing peer culture and to submit to the timeless and relatively unchanging demands of the roles implicit in membership of a family. In this way behaviour associated with the youth culture and expected of the peer group is replaced by the behaviour traditionally expected of young adults and parents in the social class and region concerned.

Even when the period of 'the splash' is considered more closely, Musgrove (1966) has provided evidence that seems to make the revolt of adolescents against parents something of a myth.[11] He administered a sentence completion test on the expectations and the satisfactions gained in the home to a sample of 250 young persons aged fourteen to eighteen, who were members of youth clubs in the northeast of England and were of mixed IQ and social class. Both expectations and satisfactions were categorized as either instrumental, that is relating to the completion of tasks, or expressive, that is concerned with the emotions. 77·2 per cent of expectations and 72·3 per cent of satisfactions were found to be expressive. These young people did, however, put some important instrumental demands upon their families. For example, they felt that moral training, character development, some social skills and some forms of intellectual enlightenment should rightly be in the hands of their parents. Boys had a higher proportion of instrumental expectations and satisfactions than had girls. In some of the detailed categories of expectations and satisfactions the situation was not so clearcut. Thus demands for emotional security were largely met, but those for freedom and self-satisfaction less so. Though we do not know how the sample rated the importance of the various expectations and satisfactions, it seems that their hopes of their homes were largely satisfied. As Willmott noted, home was home till you married. Few, certainly of the working class, moved away to flats or bed-sitters, though this sample were out on four of the seven evenings of each week, and when they were in, television was the focus of family activity.

Elsewhere, Musgrove (1964) examined the relationship between adults and teenagers. In various samples drawn from adults and from boys and girls, aged between eleven and fifteen, in the Midlands he found that hostility towards adults was highest amongst boys at fifteen and girls at fourteen, but was apparently not so high in England as in the USA. However, adults expressed greater disapproval of adolescents than did adolescents of adults, though the adolescents were aged only up to fifteen whereas the adults were asked to comment on 'teenagers' in general. Yet, there is a real possibility that parents may wrongly perceive the views of their teenage children about their families and themselves. Apparently, despite the power of, and indeed necessity for, the contemporary peer group, the family may still influence adolescents more than their parents feel or know, though one would want much more evidence upon which to build such a judgement with certainty.

E. Conclusion

Peer groups clearly play a definite part in the socialization process, but where a powerful youth culture supported by commercial interests exists, sanctions seem to be so strong for the adolescent to conform that the peer group can become a vehicle for teaching behavioural expectations that go against the aims of the family and the school. Yet there is evidence that contemporary adults wrongly perceive the opinions of adolescents who themselves may have more use for and satisfaction in their families than their parents think to be the case. After 'the splash' the responsibilities of marriage and parenthood seem to constrain former teenagers to take the tradition-al roles associated with the family much as their parents did before them, and much of the ability to do so was learnt previously in the peer groups of which they were members during childhood and adolescence.

BIBLIOGRAPHY

W. A. L. Blyth, 'The Sociometric Study of Children's Groups in English Schools', *British Journal of Educational Studies*, May 1960.

S. Cohen, *Folk Devils and Moral Panics*, 1972.

J. S. Coleman, *The Adolescent Society*, New York, 1961.

D. C. Dunphy, *Cliques, Crowds and Gangs*, Melbourne, 1969.

S. N. Eisenstadt, *From Generation to Generation*, 1956.

S. Hall and T. Jefferson (eds), *Resistance through Rituals*, 1976.

D. Hargreaves, *Social Relations in a Secondary School*, 1967.

R. Hoggart, *The Uses of Literacy*, 1956.

R. King, *Values and Involvement in a Grammar School*, 1969.

K. Mannheim, 'The Sociological Problem of Generations', in *Essays in the Sociology of Knowledge*, 1952.

F. Musgrove, *Youth and the Social Order*, 1964.

F. Musgrove, *The Family, Education and Society*, 1966.

P. Willmott, *Adolescent Boys of East London*, 1966.

NOTES

1 J. W. B. Douglas, J. M. Ross and H. R. Simpson, *All Our Future*, 1968, p. 101.

2 B. Sugarman, 'Social Norms in Teenage Boys' Peer Groups', *Human Relations*, February 1968, especially pp. 54–5.

3 B. Sugarman, 'Youth Culture, Academic Achievement and Conformity in School', *British Journal of Sociology*, June 1967.

4 Douglas, Ross and Simpson, *All Our Future, op. cit.*, p. 102

5 W. Labov, 'The Linguistic Consequences of Being a Lame', *Language in Society*, April 1973.

6 T. Kawwa, 'A Survey of Ethnic Attitudes of Some British Secondary School Pupils', *British Journal of Social and Clinical Psychology*, September 1968.

7 K. A. Rowley, 'Social Relations between British and Immigrant Children', *Educational Research*, February 1968; also T. S. Robertson and T. Kawwa, 'Ethnic Relations in a Girls' Comprehensive School', *Educational Research*, June 1971.

8 J. Williams, 'The Younger Generation', in J. Rex and R. Moore, *Race, Community and Conflict*, Oxford, 1967.

9 I. K. Birkstead, 'School Performance Viewed from the Boys', *Sociological Review*, February 1976.

10 J. Klein, *Samples from English Cultures*, Vol. I, 1965, pp. 193–6.

11 This position is supported by recent US work. See, for example, M. Thurmer, D. Spence and M. F. Lowenthal, 'Value Confluence and Behavioral Conflict in Intergenerational Relations', *Journal of Marriage and the Family*, May 1974; V. L. Bengtson, 'Generation and Family Effects in Value Socialization', *American Sociological Review*, June, 1976.

6

Children and the Mass Media

The nature of mass communications is seen by some as determined purely by their technical characteristics, for instance their dependence upon certain electronic developments or upon their ability to reach all groups in a population uniformly. This is not an incorrect, but an incomplete, view. In this chapter some brief attention will be paid to the technical differences of the various media, but the main focus will be upon 'mass', not upon 'media'. The mass may be seen as a national audience that can be described as heterogeneous, anonymous, spatially separate and unorganized, but it can also be divided into local audiences, which consist of groups of individuals organized by norms that, amongst other things, govern how they view the so-called mass media.[1]

There has been much research done in the field of mass communications by psychologists, but the area has not been a popular one for work by sociologists, especially in Britain (Chaney, 1972). Recently, however, a growing concern about how television affects children has brought about an increase in British research on this medium. The focus here will be on what part the media, especially television, play in the socialization of children. We shall, first of all, examine certain structural aspects of the problem before looking more closely at some of the interpersonal processes involved.

There is, however, one point which is worth making and which is often forgotten in the often critical remarks that are made about the influence of the media on children. Despite the easy availability of the media to contemporary children there continues to exist a culture of childhood that has changed but little within living memory and seems in the main untouched by the media. This exists amongst groups of young children and is made up of games, songs often of a robustly profane nature, rhymes and riddles.[2] Children, urban more so than rural, have a wide knowledge of this folklore of childhood, which clearly is transmitted to them by other children rather than by their parents, many of whom would have felt much of it to be vulgar. Here there seems to exist an underground culture of childhood, located in peer groups of pre-school and primary-aged children, into which our children are socialized despite family, school and media. Indeed, the media pay tribute to the existence of this culture by making frequent use of it.

A. The Structural Perspective

In the late 1940s the American political scientist, Lasswell, asked the following question about communications and the media: 'Who says What in Which Channel to Whom with What Effect?' In the way in which he phrased his question Lasswell drew attention to the existence of socially structured channels through which messages pass to various groups or to individual recipients. Here we shall examine the main ways in which media messages move to their various destinations.

1. The Various Media

The various media each have their own technical characteristics. These may, however, be divided into two main categories, those that depend upon print and those that do not. In the latter group are included film and the media of radio and television. These two electronic media are nearly always available for direct reception in the home and, in addition, television has great visual appeal. Film has something of the same characteristics, but to view it one must leave the home. The printed mass media differ in the reliance that they put upon the visual, with books giving least and comics most space to pictures.

In addition to technical differences each medium has certain norms that are peculiar to it and which must be learnt. An obvious example is the use of bubbles containing speech in comics. A more complex case is that of the Westerns originally shown on film, but now common on television. The convention is such that the shooting of the bad man, usually after an exciting hunt, is expected. Relevant evidence comes from a large-scale survey in London and other large English cities undertaken by Himmelweit, Oppenheim and Vince (1958), using samples of children aged ten to eleven and thirteen to fourteen. They found that those watching Westerns did not see shootings as violent or disturbing incidents, but certain other violence, such as rolling on the floor when fighting, did cause anxiety in children. In Westerns, anxiety diminishes as the conventions are learnt, and one wonders if a similar process is now at work to lessen amongst children the anxiety that adults perceive them to feel when viewing programmes about aggressive heroes. In all media, children must learn what has been called *adult discount*.[3] Through experience the young gradually become able to see plots as a whole so that they are more able to predict or anticipate what is to come, thereby reducing the possibility of anxiety occasioned by seeing the unexpected. Again, they grow used to distinguishing between dramatic experience and reality so that they can remain aloof from what they are watching or reading with the result that less anxiety is created.

Because of its visual attractiveness, television competes strongly with other media. Murdock and Phelps (1973) carried out a major study of the use of mass media by boys and girls in the first and third years in English grammar, modern and comprehensive schools. Some indication of the comparative use of the various media and other leisure-time activities can be found in their findings. Over 40 per cent of the third-year pupils claimed that they had been out dancing in the month prior to answering the questionnaire; over 30 per cent had bought at least one record; over 60 per cent listened to pop radio for more than two hours over a weekend and over 30 per cent for more than two hours on an average weekday evening. Furthermore, on an average weekday evening 60 per cent of the third-year pupils in two inner-urban modern schools claimed to watch television for more than four hours as against 17 per cent for the similar age group at a suburban grammar school. Himmelweit found that after the introduction of television, children initially read less, especially in the cases of boys and those with a low IQ. After a few years' experience of television the amount of reading returned to its original level, though the lower level of reading in the case of comics became permanent. New interests also seemed to have developed in the area of non-fiction. The comics and television, though one is in the print and the other in the non-print category, were both apparently visual enough in character to gratify similar interests in children, whereas books to a great extent competed with television.

Media are clearly in competition with one another for a restricted period of leisure time, though there is one exception to this generalization. Because radios, especially small transistors, have the specific characteristic that they can be used as a background to other activities the specialist provision of music apt for this purpose has been developed as a major function, though short news bulletins and sports commentaries provide other uses to which it may be put. Clearly, the different media, largely because of technical characteristics, are used in different ways by children, and hence different types of message are passed through each medium.

2. *The Two-Step Flow*

The route of any message from a medium to its reception is frequently influenced by the suggestion of someone in the recipient's social circle. Katz and Lazarsfeld (1955) discovered, in an influential study carried out in the USA in the early 1950s, that in any community there appears to be a number of specialized leaders of opinion who have such personal influence over the direction that messages from the media flow in any local community. These leaders are found at a quite specific local level amongst small groups of acquaintances. In their study, if individuals wished to discover what film was good, what new book to read or what fashion to wear, they knew in each particular case whom to consult amongst their friends and on each topic there was a specialist leader of opinion in that field.

An opinion leader can serve as the initiator of ideas, as when by chance or design a leader in the local fashion field wears some garment in a slightly different manner from formerly; or he may diffuse an idea culled from outside the circle within which he is a leader, as when 'the reader' in a teenage group recommends a new comic to his peers; or, finally, he may sanction the use of a medium, as when a teacher asks his class to watch a play on television so that he may use it in an English lesson. Next to nothing is known from research about the manner in which this process of 'the two-step flow'

operates amongst children, but from observation one would predict that there will be specialized leaders of opinion in each medium
amongst children in much the same way as Katz and Lazarsfeld
found was the case amongst adults. This would seem to be par-
larly likely amongst adolescents, who grant high status to those
who are up-to-date in the rapidly changing teenage world.

3. The Individual View of Structure

From the individual's viewpoint the accessibility of the media is
influenced by his personal social circumstances. Thus, the wealthier
he is, and to some extent this depends upon age, the more he can
afford to buy records, magazines and books or to go to dances. But
the use of radio and especially perhaps of television can be profitably examined from another perspective.

The relationship between a listener or a spectator and a performer
on the radio or television can be seen as akin to an actual interpersonal relationship; this seeming face-to-face situation has been
called a *para-social relationship*. Performers of a new type have
evolved – personalities dependent upon the existence of the media
themselves, supported by studio audiences and by the casual approach of their studio support staff. It is easy for an individual, seated
before his television screen, to relate vicariously, almost as a friend,
to such national personalities. 'For the great majority of the
audience, the para-social is complementary to normal social life.'[4]

Noble (1975) has argued that para-social relationships can per-
form a useful socializing function under contemporary social
circumstances. They yield the wider view of the social structure
that was once provided by interaction with extended kin and with
inhabitants of the local village, but which is now not so easily
available to members of a nuclear family living in an anonymous
urban area. As evidence of the closeness of such para-social relationships Noble cites the not uncommon finding that '40 per cent
of viewers admit that they talk to their TV sets'.

B. The Interpersonal Perspective

Clearly in the last section we were already close to a consideration
of the media at the interpersonal level. The mass media of television,

film and comics offer to contemporary children a great variety of role models who offer styles of life to children and with whom they may experience para-social interaction. In a study made in 1967 in Aberdeen, in character still rather a traditional city, children of twelve were asked in relation to various media: 'If you were not yourself, who would you like to be for a week or so, now?' When asked about persons in television, 81 per cent of the boys and 48 per cent of the girls made a choice, and in connection with film and radio the figures were respectively for boys 70 and 42 per cent and for girls 45 and 13 per cent.[5] Most of these children were choosing role models from amongst the offerings made by the media. What influences govern how such choices are made and what effect may they have upon the process of socialization?

1. *Parental Influences*
In Aberdeen the proportion of mothers who claimed to forbid the watching of any specific television programmes by their children aged about twelve was found to be forty-seven per cent. The proportion who encouraged the watching of any programme amongst their sons and daughters was forty per cent. These figures were to all intents and purposes the same for both boys and girls, and in addition there were very slight differences between the social classes. There are no comparable findings against which these may be judged, but the apparent degree of formal control by parents over the use of this medium seems low. Furthermore, except for a slight tendency for those children who claimed to watch television 'not much at all' to have mothers making the same claim on behalf of themselves and their husbands, there was no tendency for children to follow their parents' example either in the amount that they claimed to watch or in the types of programme that they liked or disliked. Thus these parents also seemed to exercise very little informal control over their children's viewing habits.[6] These results parallel those reported much earlier by Himmelweit, who found that few parents – and this also applied to those parents who were teachers – claimed to direct their children's viewing.

This lack of control seems to be set in a situation which, contrary to many popular views, is characterized by a conscious choice of programmes and between channels. About half of the families surveyed in Aberdeen claimed to be choosing what they viewed rather than watching regardless of what was on. It would seem from evidence gathered in Ottawa that the position occupied in the family is an important determinant of who chooses what is viewed. Parents were more often successful in viewing what they wanted when their choice differed from that of their children, but children gained their choices more often in larger families and where they were adolescent rather than younger. In addition, families only viewed together when they had a common interest in a programme.[7] Such results support neither the myth of whole families unthinkingly watching whatever is offered, nor the view that parents govern the viewing habits of their children.

2. Group Membership

Powerful sanctions operate on adolescents from the peer groups of which they are, or hope to be, members, in support of the various forms of behaviour approved by these groups, whether this relates to, for example, dress or television programmes or moral behaviour. In Aberdeen children of twelve claimed to watch programmes characteristically different from their parents. The children, already apparently influenced by the predominant youth culture, favoured programmes about pop music and aggressive heroes, whilst their parents preferred plays and serials.

In some cases the viewer may *identify* with media personalities; he may experience the viewed character in fantasy. In other cases the viewer may merely *recognize* the personality. The tendency to identify rather than to recognize media personalities and, hence, to some extent the ultimate effect of a para-social relationship is mediated by whether or not the person involved is a member of a social group. Noble found that identification decreased and recognition increased in direct relationship to the number of friends claimed by a child. Those with few friends identified with television heroes half as often again as did children with many friends.

The children who had few friends also maintained that television characters spoke more often just to them. Those who related easily to groups had real others to whom they could express themselves and try out new modes of behaviour, whilst the more socially isolated children had to rely upon para-social relationships to serve as mirrors for their developing selves. Work in the USA by Riley and Flowerman supports this view about isolates. They found that those who were isolates differed in their habits concerning media and in the uses to which they put various media. Adolescents who did not associate closely with their peers interpreted any programme that they saw in a different way from those of their peers who saw it. Furthermore, these isolated children tended to be more adult in there tastes than those who were members of a peer group.[8]

In the last chapter we noted that there were different types of peer groups which displayed different norms. The expectation would therefore be that different peer groups might have different styles of using media. Thus, Hargreaves reported that in the secondary modern school in Lancashire which he studied, the higher streams read more and were more often members of organized youth clubs compared with those in the lower streams, who tended to watch television more, to go to more films, to prefer long-haired pop groups and to be members of unorganized clubs. One American study has shown that for acceptance in the youth culture some degree of conformity to the usage of media by the group to which one aspires is a necessity. Sanctions are used to ensure that the members of any group assent to the norms implicit in membership. Thus, a manner of using the media is implied in becoming a member of a group and the media are intricately tied up with experiences undergone at the hands of various groups within which socialization occurs. Each group in a sense determines the content which must be learnt, and to which sanctions will be applied.

The different types of media used by the adolescents in this American sample could be grouped into two categories. The first covered media that were relatively closely concerned with their own day-to-day experience, for example programmes of pop music, and the second related to material that was not so closely linked with their everyday experience, for instance the news. This latter type of programme was more used by the isolates than by those in groups, whereas the first category was more often watched by those in peer groups, who were, therefore, well-integrated into the youth culture. In other words, specialized tastes in the media function as symbols of status attached to particular positions in adolescent society and hence can be seen as influential points of reference for those who aspire to such positions. Furthermore, this principle is not only applicable at this general level, but applies to specific groups, since individual groups seemed to use different pop stars or styles of music as their focus. All those who wanted to be members of a group had to comply in following the norms of that particular group.[9]

In one way the part that the media play in the life of the peer group may increase the conflict between an adolescent and his family. Today immense efforts are made by advertisers to increase the demand for many consumer goods. Because their financial resources are limited, teenagers are unable to consume as conspicuously as they are encouraged to do by commercial advertisements in all the media, but they are often exposed to strong pressures as members of their families to behave in a more realistic manner. Conversation in the peer groups could, therefore, have a positive effect in directing attention to role models whose imitation could be beyond the means of a younger person, whilst the family is trying to damp down unrealistic material aspirations.

3. Latent Roles

Here we shall examine the ways in which the primary roles of age, sex, intelligence and social class are latent when reacting to the media and, hence intervene between the medium and recipients, thereby influencing how messages are received.

(i) *Age.* In a study made in the USA and Canada that was in many respects a replication of Himmelweit's earlier work, Schramm, Lyle and Parker (1961) asked about the number of hours per day that children in the age range from seven to seventeen watched television. The peak age for watching was around thirteen, but the time given to this activity was higher in the USA than in England. Murdock and Phelps found that amongst their third-year pupils the time spent watching television at home on weekday evenings was as follows: less than an hour boys 8, girls 12 per cent, about an hour 22 and 25 per cent, about two hours 33 and 32, and more than four hours 37 and 31 per cent respectively. However, there is an important point to notice in the way that age influences the pattern of usage of the media. Although television now tends to be the most regularly used medium throughout childhood and adolescence, the other media may be substituted for one another according to the age being considered. Thus, obviously adult programmes will be watched more often as children grow older, but also by the age of about fourteen television is apparently less of an attraction, because of the need to meet friends away from home, and this is a particularly strong need when the adolescent begins to go out with partners of the opposite sex. For this reason, at adolescence the cinema takes over in some respects from television. It should be noted that, though children go to the cinema at an earlier age, they do so to seek entertainment, whereas by adolescence they are using the same medium, the film, to provide an opportunity for dating. Murdock and Phelps also noted a change in the type of pop music preferred as children grew older: between the second and fourth year of secondary school, although the support for black pop remained unchanged, there was some switch from favouring mainstream white pop to underground progressive music, though this was more pronounced amongst middle-class youth. Both the emphasis given to and the uses of any medium can change with children's age.

(ii) *Sex*. Murdock and Phelps found that third-year girls recalled more of the Top Twenty records than boys. Thus the average number remembered by girls was 9·1 and by the boys 6·1, but the range was from 13·7 by middle-class grammar-school girls to 4·7 by working-class modern-school boys. Girls do react to many forms of mass communication in a different way from boys. Their role in our society implies a greater interest in people, dress and social settings, so that they tend to form a more responsive audience for many programmes and in particular seem more disturbed by those plays for adults that are marked by anxiety. Himmelweit suggested that this may be due to the comparative absence on television of positive role models with whom girls can identify. Heroines tend to have an unhappy lot. This view is supported by evidence from the sample of twelve-year-olds in Aberdeen. The boys almost never chose a role model of the opposite sex, whereas about a third of those girls who named a role model on television or film made cross-sex choices.[10] The proportion of girls making cross-sex choices for radio was about twice as high as for the other two media, possibly due to the greater availability of such models as male disc jockeys on the radio.

Though Himmelweit found that adult crime serials were as

popular with girls as boys, there are data, both from Aberdeen and from work done in the Midlands, to show that girls tend to prefer programmes about pop music and pop stars rather than those concerned with aggressive heroes. There is similar evidence from the USA relating to the reading of comics. In a study of fifth- and sixth-grade children carried out in Boston, Mass., boys were found to be more exposed to comics and seemed to favour aggressive heroes more than girls. Amongst the fourth-year pupils that Murdock and Phelps interviewed, 51 per cent of the girls mentioned *Jackie* as their favourite magazine, 16 per cent romance magazines, 9 (boys 7) per cent pop magazines, and 7 (boys 29) per cent did not read any magazines; 19 per cent of the boys also mentioned magazines dealing with football, 17 comics and 7 those about hobbies. The sex role, into which children are socialized very soon in their lives, seems to exercise an early and a powerful influence on the selection of messages from the media by children.

(iii) *Intelligence*. Intelligence has rarely been taken into account in studies of the uses and effects of the media. In Aberdeen differences between the two sexes and even between the social classes were more pronounced than those between intelligence levels. However, this may have been due to the particular topics studied, since Himmelweit noted very definite differences of usage in her sample between levels of intelligence as measured by IQ tests, and these variations remained even when allowances were made for the different educational experiences undergone by children of a similar level of IQ in grammar or modern schools. For example, less-intelligent children tended to view more, yet the differences between the groups with an IQ over 115 and those with an IQ between 100 and 114 were more marked than those between this latter group and the children whose IQ was below 100. In this situation it is not surprising that, in a detailed study of one primary school, there was a rise in the percentage of children choosing figures from television as being the famous figures that they would like to be as one passed from the 'A' to the 'C' stream.[11] Himmelweit suggested that it is a mistake to over-generalize about the effect of intelligence since the mental age at which children are most responsive may vary from topic to topic. For example, the maximum increase attributable to watching television in the field of general knowledge occurred for children who had a mental age of ten and below. It could be that children of different mental ages view each medium and the various areas of interest affected by the media in a somewhat different way. (iv) *Social Class*. In the case of third-year pupils at secondary schools Murdock and Phelps found differences between the social classes in the amount of viewing that was done. Children from the working class viewed more than those from the middle class; thus, 40 per cent of those from the lower working class claimed to watch more than four hours on an average weekday evening compared with 35 per cent from the upper working class and 25 per cent from the middle class. In Aberdeen such a variation did not exist for twelve-year-olds, and in Himmelweit's sample the differences had disappeared by thirteen to fourteen. Seemingly the control exercised by middle-class families grows less close, more particularly in relation to television, by the time of adolescence. From research done by Wilensky (1964) in the USA the following proposition about the effects of social class can be advanced, that certain cultural norms which vary with social class influence the way the media are used. In other words, attention must be given not to the aggregates called social classes, but to the underlying nature of social class differences. A specific example concerns attitudes to education and more particularly the age at which children should cease full-time education. This is higher for those in, or for those aspiring to, the middle class. Thus, those who go to college or university in the USA seem to have a different view of television, radio and books from those with a lower educational aspiration and attainment. Their style of life includes a component governing their use of leisure and, hence, of how they use and feel about the media.

If education influences styles of leisure in this way, social class of destination and, in the case of children, of aspiration may be, particularly by adolescence, as important a determinant of the usage of media as social class of origin. Thus, in a study of adolescents aged fourteen to sixteen in three Leicestershire secondary schools, the ways in which pop music was used suggested that 'involvement in the teen culture [was] more a function of where youngsters are headed in the social structure than where they have come from in terms of parental status'.[12]

However, the research carried out by Murdock and Phelps has

given us more understanding of the processes at work whereby choices that vary by social class are made amongst the numerous alternative styles of media on offer to contemporary young people. There are two major environmentally based cultures upon which young persons can draw to express particularly their disengagment from school and generally their generational individuality. There is, firstly, the street culture of the working-class neighbourhood, within which money is scarce and the available amenities consist mainly of the neighbouring streets, cafés and youth clubs, parks and waste land where scratch football games have traditionally been played. This culture forms a logical extension of childhood and, furthermore, can be an obvious anticipation of the male-oriented adult version of this same culture, based in pubs, clubs and the Saturday match. Middle-class youth lacks this neighbourhood basis and, hence, seeks for both generational meanings and an articulation of its opposition to school in pop music, readily available but in the main dependent upon commercial provision, and, additionally, in the case of girls in dating and fashion clothes.

Historically, as was hinted in the last chapter, youth of the different social classes has created or been associated with different styles of media usage. Whereas the great mass have used the mainstream pop music of the Top Twenty, working-class groups of young persons, successors to 'the Teds', have favoured initially rock-and-roll and recently various styles of black music, whilst the middle-class groups, consisting at various times of beatniks, art students, sixth-formers and political radicals, have chosen jazz, blues or folk music; recently these groups have become associated with underground progressive rock.

Similar cultural influences were seen to be operating on the working class in an English study of the uses of television by delinquents. In this research three groups were compared, consisting respectively of delinquents, a matched sample of non-delinquents and a sample of the lower middle class drawn from the same areas in the Midlands as the other two groups. In the majority of the comparisons it was the third group that stood out as different from the sample of delinquents and the controls, both of which were essentially working-class in character. The similarities in their uses of television could best be understood by remembering that in the working-class culture, amongst other things an emphasis is put upon masculinity, toughness and excitement, so that the stress, particularly by boys, on aggressive heroes may be seen in part as the gratification of working-class cultural norms.[13]

4. Uses and Effects

Finally, we must ask, as Lasswell did in the last part of his question: to what effect? Here we shall first look at some uses to which media have been put before describing some of the effects.

(i) *Uses*. Hoggart (1957) asked what are the uses to which literacy is put in an age when almost everyone out of primary school can read. Prior to this century, and certainly before the industrial revolution, few apart from the ruling élite and the clergy were able to read. This small group, similarly educated, had common standards of what was a good or a bad book. Today almost anyone can buy cheap books, magazines or newspapers, and there are many standards of moral excellence, so that in Hoggart's terms literacy is used to support 'the newer mass art', much of which consists of 'spicy magazines' and 'sex and violence novels'.

The control of the mass communications industry is almost entirely in the hands of adults, so that a picture of youth drawn largely by adults is made available to the young. This picture is available to serve many culturally determined uses, and the same manifestation, a song or a television show, may be used by teenagers as entertainment or for excitement, to supply the opportunity to withdraw for a few moments from a busy social life or to provide the chance to identify with a role model who has been given high status by a peer group. Some films, comics or television serials gratify socially induced wants such as the need to feel male or tough; others provide information on the teenage scene, for example fashion hints or this week's hit tunes. Some media of the non-fiction type may be used for educational purposes. Furthermore, any one item may be used for varying purposes. Thus in Aberdeen, 'the news' was used by some twelve-year-old children as a source of information, but by a very few to gratify a need for excitement aroused by the sight of violence.

The last use to be mentioned here is possibly the most important for adolescents. All the media provide a coin of exchange or a common range of topics about which the young may talk and around which they may form the peer groups that have been shown to play so crucial a part in the process of socialization. In Aberdeen 62·7 per cent of the groups with which the children went around talked 'sometimes' about television, 14·4 per cent 'a lot' and 22·9 per cent 'hardly ever'.

(ii) *Effects*. There do seem to be several effects that can definitely be attributed to the media which are social rather than purely psychological in nature. More particularly the media seem able to influence the stereotypes that children hold. Such mental constructs about others vary culturally and are important in governing how we feel and behave towards such whole categories of others as, for example, blacks, Jews and foreigners. As long ago as 1940 Orwell pointed out how grotesque were the pictures of foreigners that were presented in boys' weeklies The Chinese were always sly or the French were loquacious and gesticulating.[14] In Himmelweit's research, however, the attitudes of the children towards foreigners were influenced by watching television. After being exposed to television for a year the children made more objective and fewer evaluative statements about foreigners and they became less insular in their view of their own country. It would therefore seem that the views of other countries, carefully presented by the BBC, did influence the views held and in particular made them less rigid because television had given the children a wider view of reality, a process that invariably weakens stereotypes.

This effect of 'opening windows' also widened the knowledge the children had about adult occupations so that they knew more of the nature of jobs and also of the ways in which status is given to various occupations. The De Fleurs, working in the USA, clearly illustrated this process. When they tested children's knowledge of occupations they found that it increased with age, but that television proved to be a more potent source of knowledge about occupational status than either personal contact or general community culture and, further, that children learnt earlier from television.[15] In other words this medium was assisting in the economic and probably the political socialization of children.

Some media present a more restricted view of the world which may, therefore, be expected to produce or reinforce stereotypes.

Thus many books, magazines and comics give to children a rather more limited view of social and economic reality than is perhaps defensible. Orwell noted that those who read the typical school story for boys are being offered 'the conviction that the major problems of our times do not exist'. Wars, unemployment and poverty are never mentioned. The reader is possibly being socialized into support for the political *status quo*. In another sphere a somewhat similar process may be seen to be at work. Bailyn was able to show that the boys in her sample, who were much attracted to comics and, particularly, to a diet of aggressive heroes, were consequently affected in that they used stereotyped views in judging people. Apparently the stereotyped modes of thought in the stories that they read were in some measure learnt and influenced their behaviour. [16] It would therefore seem that at the social psychological level the effects of media are largely dependent upon the number of alternatives that are offered to those whom the message reaches.

Certainly many of the stereotypes which children learn are deeply embedded in their national culture. Many manifestations of the mass media are vehicles for the transmission of important national *myths*, which can, in the anthropologist Malinowski's view, be seen as charters for social action. Thus, Westerns show good prevailing over bad, man struggling against nature and displaying his innate aggression, and men creating societies based on law and order. Cartoons display other myths: Popeye, for example, celebrates male strength and beliefs about the worth of certain diets. However, in considering cultural myths and overarching values we are moving back from the interpersonal to the structural perspective.

C. Conclusion

Communications, whether mass or individual, travel through channels which, though to some extent technically determined, are best seen in terms of social relationships. Whenever the nature of influence of one of the mass media is being considered the nature of the social setting must be examined and two tools of analysis will yield vital clues to effect. Firstly, the concept of role model is important, particularly when considering adolescents in peer groups, since sanctions will in all likelihood be applied to members or to those aspiring to membership so that deviants are discouraged. Secondly, latent roles are brought to the situation in which the message is received so that the whole audience does not perceive or use any one message in the same way. Such primary roles as those connected with social class, age or sex intervene, with the result that the same objective reality is experienced in various socially patterned ways by those who often appear objectively alike, but unconsciously think differently.

BIBLIOGRAPHY

D. Chaney, *Processes of Mass Communication*, 1972.
H. T. Himmelweit, A. N. Oppenheim and P. Vince, *Television and the Child*, 1958.
R. Hoggart, *The Uses of Literacy*, 1957.
E. Katz and P. F. Lazarsfeld, *Personal Influence*, Glencoe, Ill., 1955.
G. Murdock and G. Phelps, *Mass Media and the Secondary School*, 1973.
G. Noble, *Children in Front of the Small Screen*, 1975.
W. Schramm, J. Lyle and E. B. Parker, *Television in the Lives of Our Children*, Stanford, 1961.
H. L. Wilensky, 'Mass Society and Mass Culture: Interdependence or Independence', *American Sociological Review*, April 1964.

NOTES

1 E. Friedson, 'Communications Research and the Concept of the Mass', *American Sociological Review*, June 1953.
2 I. and P. Opie, *The Lore and Language of Schoolchildren*, 1959; for Australia see I. A. H. Turner, *Cinderella Dressed in Yella*, Melbourne, 1969.
3 E. Friedson, 'Adult Discount: an Aspect of Children's Changing Taste', *Child Development*, March 1953.
4 D. Horton and R. R. Wohl, 'Mass Communication and Para-social Interaction', *Psychiatry*, August 1956.
5 P. W. Musgrave and G. R. B. Reid, 'Some Measures of Children's Values', *Social Sciences Information*, February 1971.
6 P. W. Musgrave, 'How Children Use Television', *New Society*, 20 February 1969.

7 B. Ward, 'Television Viewing and Family Choice Differences', *Public Opinion Quarterly*, Spring 1968.

8 M. R. Riley and S. H. Flowerman, 'Group Relations as a Variable in Communication Research', *American Sociological Review*, April 1951.

9 J. W. C. Johnson, *Social Structure and Patterns of Mass Media Consumption*, unpublished Ph.D. thesis, Chicago, 1961.

10 Musgrave and Reid, 'Some Measures of Children's Values', *op. cit.*

11 B. Jackson, *Streaming: an Educational System in Miniature*, 1964, p. 69.

12 R. L. Brown and M. O'Leary, 'Pop Music in an English Secondary School System', *American Behavioural Scientists*, January/February 1970, p. 411.

13 J. D. Halloran, R. L. Brown and D. C. Chaney, *Television and Delinquency*, Leicester, 1970, especially pp. 176–7.

14 G. Orwell, 'Boys' Weeklies', in *Selected Essays*, 1957.

15 M. L. and L. B. De Fleur, 'The Relative Contribution of Television as a Source of Learning for Children's Occupational Knowledge', *American Sociological Review*, October 1967.

16 L. Bailyn, 'Mass Media and Children: a Study of Exposure Habits and Cognitive Effects', *Psychological Monographs*, 1959.

PART II

The Sociology of Schooling

Introduction

So far we have been examining the main agencies of socialization that influence a child as he grows towards adulthood. In Britain, between the ages of five and sixteen, by law all children must attend school; many do so because their parents wish it even before the age of five. School, therefore, should also be a powerful agent of socialization. In this part of the book the sociology of schooling will be considered in an attempt to see how effective schools are in this respect. Prior to the mid-1960s very little research had been done in this field since the classic and still very relevant work of W. Waller, *The Sociology of Teaching* (New York, 1932, reprinted 1961), which was undertaken in the USA. Recently, however, a great deal of work has been completed in Britain, to which reference will be made in Chapters 9–11.

Firstly, in Chapter 7 the changing structures and cultures of various types of British schools will be analysed. Next, the nature of teachers must be examined, because learning is, or is supposed to be, largely under their control in schools, and the interaction between teacher and pupil is the essence of schooling. After considering the social forces at work on what is taught, namely on the curriculum, in Chapter 9, the processes resulting from the interaction between teacher and pupil will be analysed as they operate at the school level in Chapter 10, and within the classroom in Chapter 11.

7

School Structures and Cultures

In this chapter the school will first be seen as an organization, recognizably British in its structure but with some, perhaps increasing, links with the world around it. Lastly, the characteristically different cultures of different school types will be described.

A. School Structure

1. *The British Idea of a School*[1]

The range of school types in Britain is immense. On the one hand there is the public school and on the other the primary school. There are also historical differences between the school systems of the constituent countries of Britain, though they are today of less importance than they were even fifty years ago. It seems almost impossible to say that there is one idea of a school in Britain. The position taken here is that the following four assumptions underlie most British people's idea of what a school is: (i) a school should have independence and individuality; (ii) a school should be small enough to have a common purpose and be under one Head; (iii) a school should mould character; and (iv) should, therefore, transmit a definite set of values. Each of these assumptions will be examined in turn.

(i) *Independence and Individuality.* The care given to ensure that all schools have the independence necessary to develop their own individuality can best be seen in the attention paid in legislation to the establishment of governing bodies for schools. During the latter part of the nineteenth century the independent schools felt the need to defend themselves, more particularly by founding professional associations, against the possibility of state intervention. At the time of the 1902 Education Act those who had political power and those who advised them were men reared in this tradition of independence, and they therefore felt that they should write specific provision into the Act that was to found the new maintained grammar school. So as to guarantee a degree of autonomy all secondary schools by statute had to have a board of governors. In the 1944 Act similar arrangements were made and the new primary schools were given boards of managers. These provisions, certainly at secondary level, have ensured the wide diversity of internal organization and curriculum in British schools that is remarkable to any foreigner who examines our educational system. Another sign of the same desire for individuality and independence is that nine different examining bodies organize the General Certificate of Education. In Britain the educational unit tends to be the school, whilst the administrative unit is the local authority. This is not always so clearly the case in other countries, nor need it logically be so. Paradoxically, one common feature of British schools is that they all may be different.

(ii) *A Community that is Small and under one Head.*

(a) *The Community.* Education need not necessarily take place in a community that is set apart. One of the oldest of European educational institutions is the apprenticeship system, whereby individuals are educated and trained not in a school but at their place of work. Similarly, in higher technical education there has been a growth since 1945 in the number of so-called 'sandwich courses' in which the student undertakes part of the course in an educational institution and part in the factory. However, the influence of the British boarding schools has been great in this respect as in others. During the nineteenth century these schools grew by recruiting their pupils from a wide geographical area. This tended to limit their contacts with the immediate locality. More recently, many of these schools have moved somewhat in the other direction and have encouraged their pupils to go out into the community around the school to undertake social services in various forms. Yet the emphasis remains the same; the school, either consciously or unconsciously, is the educative community. This leads to a stress on communal activities. Meals together and school games have a higher importance than, for example, in Germany or France.

(b) *Size*. To most British parents and teachers a school must be small so that each individual child may be well-known to his teachers. It has often been said that no school should be so big that the Head does not know each child as an individual. The claim that large schools would be more economic to run has usually given way in the interests of the individual child. The fact that some of the most famous British boarding and day schools have a thousand or more pupils is conveniently overlooked. These schools have developed the house system so as to guarantee that despite their large size someone is responsible for knowing each child well enough to watch his growth. Many have opposed the development of comprehensive schools on the ground that they are too big to cater for the child as an individual. Invariably these new schools have bowed to the British tradition and have organized elaborate house systems in order to gain the advantages of the small school whilst remaining large.

(c) *The Headmaster* (Baron, 1970). In the mid-nineteenth century the headmasters of the public schools who felt that they must fight for their independence often did so by stressing their own authority. In addition to this the *laissez-faire* economic ideas of the time helped to ensure that interference was rare. By 1909 a famous headmaster, Sir Cyril Norwood of Harrow, could write that the headmaster in this country was 'an autocrat of autocrats'. Between 1828 and 1842 Thomas Arnold of Rugby had built the model that was to be imitated by most later heads. He was the leader of a community and was also a clergyman, and from this the idea evolved easily that the head had a pastoral care for his pupils.[2] Such a headmaster would do all in his power to identify his pupils with the aim of the school as determined by himself. All these characteristics of the British idea of a headmaster as it developed in the late nineteenth century tended to force schools to be small. The shepherd's flock could not be too large if he were to tend them properly. Yet it must not be thought that this was an inevitable result. Even by 1850 the position of the headmaster was not as stable as it came to be. In schools in both England and Scotland it was not unusual for the masters to take turns to act as head. The organizational problem of how to run a school larger than was normal at the start of the last century had still not been solved.

Today a similar problem faces the comprehensive school. The tradition of what a British head should be is opposed to an administrative non-teaching headmaster, to what an American head of a large high school once called 'a four-ulcer man doing an eight-ulcer job'. The Arnold tradition passed into the state secondary system after 1902, since so many of the first heads of the new maintained grammar schools were educated and had taught in public schools. From grammar schools this idea of a head has passed into the other types of secondary school and also into the primary schools. Everywhere the head is thought of as a man with power who often has great control over the appointment of staff and who certainly expects to be allowed to mould his school as he wishes.

(iii) *Character Training*. It follows from the British idea of a head that a school must care for all aspects of the child's development, for his character as well as his academic attainments. In Europe the formation of character is left to the home, the church and the youth organizations. In the USA the school tries to adapt the child to the community's, and not its own, idea of good character. But in Britain the school tends to lay down the way in which children are to behave and it holds itself responsible for enforcing this code. The school also takes a protective attitude towards the effects of the rest of the environment on the child; for example, the school must defend the children against the damage that the mass media may do. Therefore, the school concerns itself with how its pupils spend their leisure time and organizes games and societies in order to inculcate the approved virtues and interests. Again, this is not normal in European schools.

(iv) *Values*. This stress on the formation of character assumes an agreed standard of values by which personality may be evaluated. In fact the teacher in Britain has become an agent by which the attempt is made to transmit the typical middle-class values. Since the educational system did not grow from the community, but was imposed from above, it was the values of those in positions of higher status that were considered, usually unconsciously, as worth inculcating. No moral judgement is here being passed on this set of values, but the result has been that many teachers see the schools as a rescue operation to save the children from their parents and their social class.

Schools in Britain vary enormously and in the last decade attempts have been made to introduce radical alternative schools, but except in relation to the values taught in the latter type of schools these four assumptions are common to the majority. Comparison with other countries shows that such assumptions are not universal. In the future, mass literacy may bring change, but at the moment this is the idea of a school that influences the way in which administrators, teachers and parents see schools and therefore this idea governs much of what a teacher considers he ought to do as he practices his vocation.

2. *The School as an Organization* (Musgrave, 1968)

The term, *formal organization*, is used in sociology to cover relatively bounded interlocking systems of social positions, whose incumbents have expectations of behaviour largely determined by the formal system, though, of course, such informal groups as peer groups inevitably also influence how members of organizations behave. Members' behaviour is mainly governed by the goals for the organization of those with power over it. In an industrial company the board of directors aim to make a profit by manufacturing some product; in a school the aim is to teach the pupils. The resulting social structure is usually hierarchical in that those at the top exercise their power to order those in lower echelons to achieve their chosen goals in the ways that they see as most apt. Finally, formal organizations are more or less bounded from the world around them; much of the behaviour expected of members, managers and workers, or teachers and pupils, only applies to them whilst filling positions within the organization concerned.

Schools clearly can be analysed as organizations, though it must be remembered that this concept is, in Weber's terminology, *an ideal type* – that is, a hypothetically concrete construct with the aim of analysing a particular set of social behaviour. Thus, because schools, like most organizations, are constantly recruiting new members, whether staff or pupils, divergent ideas on what should be done are often brought into them so that conflict ensues over whether or not change shall occur. Those higher in the hierarchy use their power to try to achieve their ends against contrary suggestions from others in the school. For example, heads of departments control funds to buy new books, and allocate teachers to age levels, streams and to responsibility for specific syllabuses. This gives them power to block changes that newcomers or others lower in the hierarchy wish to achieve. In one study Lacey found that sixty-five per cent of the teaching of Years One and Two and eighty-five per cent of the teaching of the bottom stream was done by others than heads and deputy heads of departments.[3]

Schools can clearly be analysed with profit as organizations, but they do show certain characteristic peculiarities of structure when compared with most other types of organization. For example, the hierarchy of staff in schools is much flatter and marked by less social distance than that of a factory or a military unit; there are rarely non-professional staff of similar status to the teachers and all the staff have somewhat the same qualifications and training. This peculiarity in the organization of schools has implications for the relative power of the different levels within a school. Secondly, in schools administrative means have a marked tendency to become ends in themselves. In capitalistic industry the goal is profit; means to this end may often change, but usually remain means. In schools, examinations and school rules are set up as means to encourage the goals of academic or moral learning, but very often to pass some examination or to obey some rule, seen by many to be of eventual insignificance, becomes a goal in itself rather than a means to an educational goal.

The ways in which such organizations as schools operate depends upon a number of factors. Clearly the idea that members have of what a school should be is crucial. Teachers and parents in Britain are socialized so that they take the characteristics outlined in the last section largely for granted, though change does occur and will be examined in Chapter 15. However, despite the fact that the staff of British schools have always tried to draw firm boundaries between themselves and parents or others defined as non-members, they cannot entirely ignore the pressures put upon them from the network of outsiders with whom they are in contact. This network will now be examined.[4]

B. Relationships with the World around the School

1. *The State*

In Britain the finance of education comes from two main sources. The Treasury provides funds through the Department of Education and Science; initially this money has come from national taxation. In addition, local authorities find further money from rates. Since both national and local authorities jointly hold the purse-strings, both are in a position to influence the schools and thereby the teacher.

(i) *The Department of Education and Science.* About fifty-five per cent of the funds for current expenditure on education is supplied by the central government through the Department. The largest part of capital expenditure is financed centrally. Thus the Department is in the position of being able to lay down the regulations that govern how this money is spent. It is a major part of the Inspectorate's work to see that such regulations are observed. The influence of these regulations is far-reaching, since they cover staffing ratios, the dimensions of classrooms, the scale of equipment for laboratories and gymnasiums, and a multitude of minor features that matter much to the practising teacher. The sheer detail is immense but, unless a new school meets the present standards of the Department, expenditure will not be authorized and, if old buildings are not up to present standards, criticism may be expected. This system governs the immediate material surroundings within which the teacher carries out his work.

The financing of British education was organized purposely so that both the central government and the local authorities played a major part. The intention was that local interests should come to bear in a democratic manner on the provision of the local educational system (Baron and Tropp, 1961). But this seemingly admirable aim has within it the possibility of conflict, since there is always the chance that the two financing authorities may wish to pursue opposite or different policies. Since both government and local council are democratically elected, their respective majorities may represent different political parties. Since the 1950s there have been major differences in the educational policies of the two parties. There is, therefore, the chance of head-on collision. An example may be given; in 1955 the Manchester Council wished to establish two new comprehensive schools in line with the policy of its Labour-dominated council. The Ministry (as it was then called) refused permission, since Conservative policy was only to allow expenditure on such schools on certain conditions that did not apply in this particular case. The conflict went to the point that the Ministry threatened to withdraw Manchester's financial grant, a step that would have brought the city's school system to a halt. This sanction forced Manchester to abandon its scheme.

This is a very striking case of what is always possible, but rarely happens. The Department has greater power than the local authorities to push through its own policy and is able to prevent local schemes with which it does not agree. Hence its power over the teacher in the school is greater than is often realized. However, the government's power is not absolute, and once again the case of the comprehensive school is relevant.[5] In 1945 the Ministry, in its pamphlet *The Nation's Schools*, indicated that its policy was a tripartite secondary system of grammar, technical and modern schools. During 1946 the local authorities began to submit their development schemes to meet the requirements of the 1944 Act, and the government realized that local feeling demanded a change in policy towards the provision of more comprehensive schools. In 1947 the pamphlet, *The New Secondary Education*, took notice of this and envisaged a greater variety of types of secondary school. Despite the power of the state, democratic pressures, in education as in other fields of government expenditure, can bring change to government policy. To the individual teacher, however, the possibility of his influencing policy seems so remote that the Department remains a powerful, if indirect, external force.

(ii) *The Local Authority*. The local authority both acts as the channel for expenditure of state funds and finances education from its own rates. It therefore stands between the Department and the school, appearing to the teacher to be the main direct external force that influences his work. Though the whole council is responsible for all local government, there are committees responsible for each major field of expenditure. The Education Committee consists of democratically elected members – councillors, members coopted to this committee, and paid officials of the council, such as the

Director of Education – who give advice as experts on the matters under discussion.

The political complexion of the council will normally decide the composition of this committee and, as local politics have become more a party matter, so policies on education have tended to be judged on national political, rather than local educational, criteria. However, the position of the Director of Education can be very influential. He is a former teacher and in close touch with his teachers in the schools. In theory he may be purely an expert who tenders his advice, but often because he alone has the necessary knowledge amongst a committee mainly consisting of laymen he has great power. Major policy decisions may stem from his advice. Thus, the Cambridgeshire Village College system owes its existence to Henry Morris, the pre-war Director for that area.

There are few studies of the forces at work when local education authorities make decisions about the systems that they control. In one recent study of the manner in which Corby made plans to re-organize secondary provision in that area, there seemed to be a number of groups that influenced the ultimate decision. The local head-teachers exercised some power and local branches of more than one professional association expressed views that affected the outcome, although the National Union of Teachers (NUT) carried more weight than the smaller associations. Yet these latter groups had more influence than might have been expected because of the presence of a few very active members. The final report of the authority's Chief Education Officer, which had the support of the NUT, carried the day. Yet in this area issues on the local council were not decided along party political lines, so that an administrator giving what was ostensibly technical advice that had the backing of the majority of teachers would wield much power. Local political conditions must always be taken into account when considering both how a local education authority will operate and also how much power the Director of Education may have over decisions. Thus where councillors are not subservient to their expert advisers, the Director of Education and his staff, they may be more aware of such other local interests as parents or a locally powerful religious denomination. This was the case in the 1950s in Middlesex where middle-class Roman Catholic parents were able, through members of council who pushed their case, to preserve their right to free places in local fee-paying schools.[6]

Local authorities have great power over their schools and the teachers within them. Often teachers are appointed to the authority rather than to the individual school. But the power of the local authority varies according to the type of school. The authority has most influence on fully maintained schools, since it provides either directly from rates or indirectly from the Treasury the whole of the finance needed to run such schools. In addition there are the various types of voluntary schools – the aided, the controlled and the special agreement schools. The factor that differentiates these three school types is the amount of state finance received in each case. The more money given to the school, the greater influence the local authority can claim over it. This control is symbolized in the proportion of the governors or managers that the local authority may nominate to the school's governing body. The more finance the authority finds, the more governors it appoints and hence the more power it can exercise over the workings of the school. This will affect the appointment of the head and staff, and to some extent the activities of the teachers in the school. The intention of this complicated system is to safeguard the interests of the mainly religious bodies who since the nineteenth century have provided so many British schools.

(iii) *Independent Schools*. There are a substantial number of schools that are independent of the Department. They may be run on a profit-making basis or as charitable foundations. These schools include the famous public schools, the so-called 'progressive' schools and many privately run kindergartens. By Part III of the 1944 Act, which came into operation in 1957, all independent schools must apply for registration by the Department and must on the whole conform to the Department's regulations. These regulations are not rigorously imposed. If they were, the experiments of progressive schools might be curbed, but the philosophy of the 1944 Act is that, although parents should be permitted to choose their children's school, the state should safeguard the public by preventing the setting up of poor schools.

Since the independent schools are liable to inspection, they must be influenced by the regulations that set the Department's standards. However, in many respects, especially in the case of the public schools, standards are higher than in maintained schools. The strongest influence on the teacher will be either the proprietor or the governing body of the school. Teachers in these schools need rarely worry about the influence of the Department or any local authority.

2. *Governing Bodies*

As has already been indicated, since the 1944 Act all maintained schools by law are supposed to have some form of governing body, though the Education Act for Scotland does not carry a similar clause. In fact it is only in the last few years that much has come to be known about what these boards do or even to what extent or in what form they exist. It seems that, though throughout the 1970s local authorities have increasingly developed effective governing and managing bodies, these still do not exist everywhere, and that the types of board and method of recruiting their members vary greatly from place to place.[7]

Secondary schools seem to have governing bodies more often than primary schools. In some local authorities – especially, but not always, in county boroughs where the population is dense – boards of governors or managers frequently have minimal powers in systems that are strong and run by highly centralized bureaucracies. Under these circumstances schools may be grouped under one governing body, the membership of which is restricted closely to members of the local council and of the Education Committee. Here little lay influence can be brought to bear on decisions about the schools. In other areas, especially in the counties where population is scattered, each school has its own board of governors or managers to whom more responsibility is given. Here, particularly at the secondary level, members of boards play a large part in appointing senior staff and especially in choosing a new head, a decision that is always crucial for the future development of their school; their advice also carries weight in financial matters. Members of these boards are drawn in varying proportions from three main sources. Firstly, there are the political nominees to whom reference has already been made, many of whom may change with political fortunes. Secondly, since the religious bodies still play so large a part in English education, there are clergymen or nominees of denominations, perhaps watching the interests of a major local denomination or of the sect that originally founded the school concerned. Lastly, there are now more often representatives of parents and of teachers, and in recent years pupils over eighteen and members of the non-teaching staff have sat on these bodies. In general, despite these new sources of recruitment the majority of governors are still drawn from sources which ensure that they will tend to be conservative and wary of educational change.

The governing bodies of the independent schools, originally the model for the system adopted in the state schools, are extremely influential and provide a strong and continuing influence. Headmasters may come and go, but the governing body remains, though its membership slowly changes. It is the guardian of the schools' traditions. In many schools and also in, for example, some colleges of education, a legal trust lays down what interests shall be represented on the governing body and thereby perpetuates the intention of the institution's founder. Many independent schools have religious foundations, and provisions of this nature ensure that the school continues in the spirit in which it was started. The governors guard their trust in two main ways. They personally appoint the headmaster, choosing, as far as they can, the man who seems best fitted to continue the tradition entrusted to their keeping. They also control the financial affairs of the school. Since the school finds all its own funds and none come from the state, the governing body has a big influence on the life of the school. Decisions concerning changes to the fabric of the school, such as a new laboratory or gymnasium, are ultimately in their hands.

In maintained schools the governing bodies are much less powerful, since they are not in a position of financial independence. They can play a part in choosing the head and can watch the interests of the school in local affairs. Governors have been known to fight for their school's survival when the local authority wished to close it down. On the whole, these boards of managers or of governors function in a rather paradoxical manner to link their schools to the local community and education authority whilst simultaneously going some way to ensure their independence *vis-à-vis* the local authority and parents.

3. Parents

Parents can influence a teacher indirectly through their children, but here we are thinking of their direct influence. In a small village or town the teacher may well live in or near to the school. Most of the parents of the children that he teaches will meet him in the street and can easily talk to him about the school and their children. In the contemporary large urban area this is not often the case. Teachers do not want to live in the middle of a slum area or sometimes even in a city. They prefer to travel long distances to their schools. Under these conditions, that are typical for the majority of schools, relations between parents and teachers must be structured. It is because of this that in many schools today Parent–Teacher Associations have been established.

Teachers and parents alike are dedicated to the interests of the children, though they may define these interests somewhat differently. In practice in this country the parents' wishes are usually held to be subordinate to the teacher's idea of what is good for the child. The teacher assumes that he knows better than the parent, and thus heads in this country sometimes oppose the establishment of any form of parents' association, since this would allow the parents a direct influence on the running of their schools (Young and McGeeney, 1968). In the large sample of primary schools studied for the Plowden Report, seventeen per cent had Parent–Teacher Associations, though over sixty per cent arranged meetings for educational or social purposes with parents.

However, in the Australian state of Victoria schools are by law required to organize some form of Parent–Teacher Association. Yet an investigation of how this system operated at the secondary level revealed a situation not dissimilar to that in England. Teachers, despite their desire to improve relationships between school and home, were unwilling to give up power over the curriculum or teaching method to parents, who in their turn saw themselves as too inexpert to claim what the law defined as their rights.[8] The issues involved were shown vividly in London in the mid-1970s when the board of managers, some parents and others became concerned with the, to them radical, way in which the teachers of the William Tyndale School, a primary school, were developing it. After much difficulty they eventually were instrumental in closing the school (Gretton and Jackson, 1976).

The contact between parents and teachers is closest with younger children. This may be exemplified if one calls to mind the picture of parents clustered about the doors of an infant school around 3.30 p.m. during term-time; the junior school next door has a much smaller group. In secondary schools far less contact is observed; in grammar schools fear or shyness may prevent visits by parents, particularly those who did not themselves attend such schools.[9] But at any age the chance of conflict between parents and teacher is great. Values may differ between the middle-class teacher and the working-class parent, or methods have changed since father was at school. Yet there is usually no machinery to resolve these differences.

In the case of the independent schools the position appears simple. The parent is a customer who is buying education for his child. If he ceases to be satisfied with the service provided, he may withdraw his custom. In fact, though organized ways in which parents may approach the school are rare, there is a long tradition that the headmaster or the housemaster is in close touch with the parents of his pupils.

The relationship between parents and teachers in Britain is summed up by the feeling so often expressed in staffrooms that 'we could do so much better a job if only the parents would not interfere'. The contact that is necessary at the infant stage, because the child is young, can create a partnership between parent and teacher in the education of the child. But the teacher of the older children will rarely meet their parents unless there is an organized channel for this purpose. It seems odd that 'the office', the symbol of the state and the local authority, should have so much more influence on a teacher than the parents of the children that he teaches.

C. British Schools and their Cultures

The way in which the British educational system[10] is organized is very largely determined by its historical growth (Musgrave, 1968). There is, firstly, an important division between independent schools and those provided by the state. In January 1976, 4·3 per cent of all children were in independent schools, but the existence of these schools has political and economic consequences out of all proportion to the numbers attending them because of their connections with the higher ranks of the social class system. In addition, the ethos of these schools, especially those secondary boarding schools known as public schools, has had a powerful impact upon the way in which the state secondary schools have developed.

In terms of social structure by 1939 there were two main pathways through the educational system. These were formed by the elementary schools which led in the main to the lower levels of the social hierarchy and by the system of independent and state-provided grammar schools that 'sponsored' their pupils to social positions of high status.[11] For the working class there was a narrow track connecting the two pathways through a scholarship examination at the age of about eleven or twelve.[12] But by this same date there was a strong feeling that the educational provision of the state should be reconstructed to meet the growing demands for a more egalitarian system. This view was strengthened by the idealism engendered in the war, which supported such attempts to plan a fairer society as the Beveridge Report of 1942 that formed the basis of much of the post-war legislation concerning social welfare, and in the field of education the 1944 Education Act.

This Act had two important results for the structure of British education. Firstly, the Elementary Code was abolished so that the state schools were now divided into two sections by age rather than by status. There now exist primary schools for children between five and eleven (twelve in Scotland) and secondary schools for those over eleven (or twelve). The position has been somewhat complicated by the recent introduction of middle schools for the eight to nine and twelve to thirteen age range. Before the 1944 Act the division was between the low-status elementary schools and the high-status secondary schools; in the higher age levels of both systems of schools the same curriculum was taught, but facilities were worse in the former than in the latter. However, secondly, though the Act itself laid down nothing about the structure of secondary education, the newly established (then) Ministry of Education indicated in 1945 that three types of school with 'parity of esteem' were envisaged, namely the secondary grammar, technical and modern schools. Strong criticisms of this structure, which came to be called the tripartite system, led by 1947 to the official recognition of the comprehensive school, a common school for all the children in a given catchment area apart from those whose parents sent them to private schools. Despite the changing policies of various governments, this last type of school has grown so important that in January 1976, out of 4,982 secondary schools, 3,387 (68 per cent) were comprehensive and 75·6 per cent of all secondary pupils were in such schools.

In recent years research into the cultures of British schools has begun and results are now available, but very often reliance has to be put on one or two studies so that this analysis must be largely in terms of ideal types. In all likelihood any one ideal typical account may be shown by future work to be incomplete or even biased, owing to our current ideological blinkers or to contemporary sociological ignorance. However, the construction of such ideal types does enable us to give some account of contemporary social reality in the different types of British school. Two types will be omitted from any consideration here: firstly, the nursery school, because it lies outside the age of compulsory schooling and, secondly, the technical school, because it never held a great proportion of secondary pupils and is now rapidly disappearing from the secondary scene.

1. *The Primary School*

Here three main cultures may be specified (Blyth, 1965). Within the British primary schools there are two main traditions at work, which may be called in the terms of common usage the traditional and the progressive, each of which generates very different school cultures. In addition, there is the rather different culture specific to the independent preparatory schools that cater for a somewhat similar age group.

(i) *The Traditional Culture.* The primary school is in some ways a direct descendant of the former elementary school since it is based on the age range from five to eleven whose education formed the major responsibility of the older type of school. Therefore it is reasonable to expect some historical residues in the new primary school. However, it is not often that a contemporary primary school exhibits the worst features of the old type, those associated with cheapness and nastiness – cheap inasmuch as it provided minimal facilities for teachers and children, and nasty inasmuch as the discipline was repressive, and such was largely the case because of the feeling that this was good enough for the working class. The great changes that have taken place may be seen in a study by Jackson that describes a good example of the traditional culture in a contemporary primary school.[13] The school buildings were new, modern in architectural style and brightly decorated; the teachers had excellent materials and used some up-to-date methods. Yet the characteristics of the traditional culture predominated over the trappings of modern education. Success in the academic field was all-important, not as in the nineteenth-century elementary school in the sound learning of the 3 Rs, but in achieving success in the eleven-plus examination for selection to grammar school. Though corporal punishment was rarely used, very powerful sanctions, often of a punitive nature, were brought to bear by the staff and by the parents of the pupils to achieve the desired academic results. Furthermore, though the children seemed bright and full of ideas, there was an underlying trend of conformity to those behavioural and academic patterns that were perceived by the children as right for future members of the élite. These tendencies influenced the whole school and not only the 'A' stream, most of whom could expect to go to grammar school. In the primary schools, to use the terms of the structural perspective, teachers often create such permanent positions as 'members of number one, two or three group', or 'form captain', which imply behaviour, whether intellectual or social, of a hierarchical nature. In short, the culture of these schools is centred on academic learning, conceived in a rather formal manner and usually achieved in a competitive way, on status along various dimensions and on negative sanctions or punishment.

(ii) *The Progressive Culture.* Very different are those primary schools whose aim is to create a culture based on the child learning rather more of what interests him than what the teacher feels is right for him, on an interpretation of equality that implies each child shall have as many experiences as possible, and, finally, on a pattern of sanctions based upon using reward rather than punishment.

There may well be a degree of double-thinking in the attempt to focus on children's interests, since learning at any age, but especially in the primary school, is fundamentally a situation based on authority and the teacher may well use children's interests as a means of motivation to teach what he has already planned that the child shall learn. But the progressive culture is rooted in the writing of such educational theorists as Froebel and Montessori, and such educational psychologists as Piaget. There is, therefore, a strong tendency to see education in developmental terms. The stress is put on the child's step-by-step progression under his own motivation, rather than upon the class learning given chunks of knowledge under threat of punishment from the teacher with strong support from home.[14]

Structurally a classroom organized in this tradition will have many positions offering varied types of experience through most of which many, but not all, of the children will pass. Furthermore, the positions will probably all carry similar status. This week a child will be book monitor, the next week in charge of the flowers and the following week look after the blackboard. The children – in such a situation one can hardly call them 'pupils' – will be grouped in a number of different ways for their various experiences and these groups will be so arranged that all the class will work with each other and so that no special status is attached to any one group. Such primary schools will attend to individual differences. The teacher will be open to pupils' suggestions and the curriculum will be broadly based, reaching out into the environment around the school and the children's homes. The culture could be described as egalitarian, non-repressive, developmental and non-competitive in comparison with the traditional classroom.

(iii) *The Preparatory Tradition.* Entry to the major independent schools has for a long time been at the age of thirteen or fourteen. Because of this, during the early part of the nineteenth century special schools evolved in answer to a demand from those who wanted and could afford to send their children to the public schools, which were then becoming more popular. Today these preparatory schools take pupils usually at about eight and prepare them to take the Common Entrance Examination which is the hurdle that those wishing to go to public school must pass. Thus, the curriculum of the preparatory schools is largely governed by the fact that their pupils must have reached by the age of about thirteen certain academic standards in, for example, Latin, mathematics and science. Again, the public schools have a very strong sporting tradition. Thus, though not strictly necessarily, pupils will suffer less discontinuity if they can play such games as rugby football or fives before going to their public school. Many of the preparatory schools are boarding schools and can, therefore, have a much fuller control over the life of their pupils than the normal day primary school. In addition, their pupils are homogeneous in nature in that they are drawn from middle-class homes with a very similar set of values which will support the school in term-time and will not seriously undermine its efforts during the holidays. The pupils come from families with high social status where notions of hierarchy and duty are strong; they are going to schools of which the same may be said. Therefore, prefect systems with formal sanctions under the control of the pupils themselves and permanent captains of games teams are common. Under such circumstances the preparatory schools have a rather extreme version of the traditional culture, in which academic learning and status in a hierarchy are given high priority and in both cases are achieved through competition of one sort or another. A major additional element in comparison to the traditional primary school is that there is a strong emphasis on the playing of competitive games.

2. Secondary Schools

(i) *Independent Schools.* The essential features of the independent schools are seen in their fullest form in those public schools whose tradition is firmly based in the past and in the historical connection between such private education and the upper middle class. For over a century now these schools have been popular with those of high social status who have delegated a large part of the socialization of their sons, and less often of their daughters, to teachers who, though usually themselves of somewhat lower social status, were yet experts at teaching 'élite role behaviour' (Weinberg, 1967).

The schools themselves were rigidly hierarchical. New boys joined the ranks of fags and passed gradually upwards through a series of such junior offices with minor responsibilities as head of a bedroom for a few younger boys to the top of the scale of status when they filled the positions of prefects. This progression was seen by all concerned as an apt preparation for a career in the professions, the civil service, the armed forces or, as times changed, even in industry. In all of these occupations organization was based on the readiness of the majority, even in the junior managerial ranks, to obey and of the few to command. The sanctions available in such schools were many, but the means of physical coercion were commonly available to both staff and senior boys. The lessons that the schools had to teach were easily learnt in a boarding school largely closed to outside influence.

Competition was encouraged especially on the games field both with other schools and between the houses into which the schools were usually organized. Though there were always a minority who were keenly interested in things academic and the teaching, especially of the classics, was at the higher levels often inspired, yet it was very largely in the playing of games that those responsible thought that many of the qualities of the gentleman could best be learnt. Such qualities were the easy bearing of authority, loyalty to one's peers and the display of courage, physical and moral, in adversity, and of easy good manners on all occasions.[15]

Under contemporary conditions, those running the public schools have made serious attempts to offset their social isolation, so that they attempt to have their pupils move into the local community and also almost perforce allow them to import many outside influences into the schools. Yet much of their traditional culture remains, like many British institutions, subtly unaltered by changes made to meet today's world. Fagging may either be abolished or exist in a more humane form, but there is still a marked pattern of hierarchy and authority, often reinforced by such traditional elements of ritual as house assemblies, ceremonies associated with awarding colours, or rules about, for example, who may wear certain jacket buttons undone. Academic results may be given more emphasis in an age where success in examinations seems important, but the main lessons of the public schools are still seen to be the learning of those rather intangible qualities of the gentleman that are imparted outside the classroom. The educational world at large may be more democratic, but the public schools remain closely linked to the élite, both because the parents of their pupils are drawn from the upper middle class and because most of their pupils will ultimately achieve that level during their careers. The culture that these schools appear to transmit to the majority of their pupils is, as has been the case for many years, one based on duty, responsibility, loyalty, self-reliance, and one which aims to translate these characteristics into actions with the minimum of intended publicity.

(ii) *The Grammar School*. There were grammar schools in England and burgh schools in Scotland before the public schools ever achieved their great popularity in the nineteenth century, but, as already indicated, the state grammar schools grew up in the twentieth century as an imitation of the nineteenth-century version of the public school. In a recent study King (1969) examined one such school in the London area. The teachers aimed to create a specific culture in the school and to transmit this to their pupils. In many respects they wished to create an atmosphere similar to that in the public schools. They put a high emphasis on the development of personality or, to use their evaluative term, character. They expected the boys to aim for positions of leadership in the professions rather than in industry and not necessarily to go for a job that was well-paid, since the intrinsic worth of work was more important in their view than the monetary reward. Academic work was given great emphasis, partly because examinations must be passed to enter the occupations which today carry high status, but also because much knowledge was seen by the staff as good in itself.

However, the majority of the boys in the school did not subscribe to the values of their teachers and certainly those who left before entering the sixth form did not learn the values that their teachers hoped to impart. They saw themselves as an intellectual élite by virtue of their success in the eleven-plus examination and hence considered that they ought ultimately to earn more than those who had not been selected for a place in a grammar school. Furthermore, they were more attracted than the school hoped to the teenage culture which was examined in Chapter 5. The boys who entered the sixth form were largely those from middle-class homes that had the same values as the teachers and that supported the school in its efforts. Thus, in the sixth form the school did succeed in some measure in creating the intended culture in which a feeling of responsibility for what went on in the lower school, academic excellence in a few subjects oriented towards the universities and the intellectual discipleship involved in intensive work in small classes with a specialist teacher, were highly valued by the pupils.[16]

The study by King, when taken in the context of this analysis, poses a number of questions. For example, which culture was that of the school – that of the staff or that of the boys who left early? Can we then speak of a school having one culture? What about girls' grammar schools? And are coeducational schools very different? Clearly in this school, as is probably the case in most grammar schools, there was an intended official culture in which high priority was given to many values found in the public schools. But there was also a culture that was outside the control of the staff, being that of many of the boys and of their world beyond the walls of the school to which they returned each evening and at weekends. This second culture was in many ways less akin to that of the public school than to that of the secondary modern school to which we now turn.

(iii) *The Secondary Modern School.* The secondary modern school is directly descended from the upper age levels of the old elementary school, but, since it was born at a time of high idealism during and just after the second world war, it was given the aim of parity of esteem. As Taylor (1963) has shown, the hope of many teachers was to recreate at the secondary level the progressive type of education found in many primary schools. This intention was frustrated by the social forces that constrained the way in which the secondary modern school developed during the late 1940s and throughout the 1950s. Parity of esteem was not granted to these schools, which typically occupied the premises of a former elementary school but had been given a new name, because most of their pupils came from the working class and left school to enter jobs that had low social status. Therefore, the schools set out to earn esteem by imitating the grammar schools and in many areas were supported by parents who had hoped that their children would gain places in selective secondary schools. In many such schools the children who were thought to be the abler pupils were entered for external examinations. In this way traditional academic aims and curricula came to take the place of progressive intentions. Heads established school uniforms, systems of houses and prefects, prize days and many of the rituals associated with schools of higher status.

Though forces outside the secondary modern schools gave strong support to these developments, yet for many children school was a place at best to be borne and to worst to be hated or attacked. Hargreaves (1967) studied a typical mixed secondary modern school in urban Lancashire in which there were four streams. The range of reactions to school among its pupils was great and may best be seen by a brief account of the findings concerning the children in 4A and 4D. The children in 4A wore uniform, behaved largely as expected by their teachers both at work and at play, and aimed to do well in external examinations at sixteen. A modified version of the culture of the grammar school existed here. However, in 4D things were very different. The children did not wear the school uniform, did not meet the behavioural expectations of their teachers and did little or no work. Indeed, for them the system of sanctions used in the school had no avail. To offer a pupil who did a good piece of work the reward of praise or of possible promotion resulted in bad work in future as the child did not wish to be normatively or physically isolated from his friends. To censure bad work or behaviour led to further bad behaviour, since censure indicated that the teacher was annoyed and this was the intention of the original action. Here again there were two cultures in the school. One was the official one, valued and sanctioned by the staff and in turn valued by a few pupils, most of whom were successful by the criteria of the school. The other was a culture generated, valued and sanctioned by the pupils and opposed to that of the staff. The proportions of the pupils who learn either of the cultures will vary from school to school and depend upon such factors as the nature of the catchment area, the predominant social class of the children, the aims and qualities of the staff and the leadership exercised by the headmaster.[17]

(iv) *The Comprehensive School.* Increasingly over the years, but especially since the 1930s, there have been criticisms of the existence of the strong connection in Britain between the schools and the system of stratification. One constant target for criticism in this respect has been the continuing popularity of the public schools, though this has so far had little apparent effect. Initially the main drive for reform of the state schools was directed towards widening the social class composition of the entry to grammar school. More scholarships were granted to defray the costs of secondary education for able children from the working class and eventually all secondary education in state schools was declared free by the 1944 Act. However, despite the initial trust in psychological testing there was growing realization after 1945 that such means of selection as the eleven-plus examination in its various forms, though relatively accurate, were not absolutely reliable and, furthermore, that the determinants of IQ were in many ways as much social as genetic. In addition there was growing political criticism of the tripartite system and this soon settled into a demand for some form of common or comprehensive school for all the children in a given catchment area, including those who went to independent schools if the latter were ever abolished (Bellaby, 1977).

Though the comprehensive school came to be seen as the answer to the faults of the tripartite system, the argument for a common school was rarely put in an articulated or testable form. However, there seem to have been two main strings to the case. The first intention seems to have been to create a school in which the children could learn a unified and integrated culture which would overcome those divisions of social class that separate schools linked to specific social classes seemed to perpetuate. Especially where the catchment areas of large schools covered very different types of housing there was a hope that mixing between the social classes in school would help to dissolve differences. This argument was tacitly assumed in the claim made that these schools would lead to social cohesion. The second main argument for the creation of a system of comprehensive secondary schools concerned the wastage of talent in the secondary modern schools, since it was hoped that more of the able children from the working class who now left school early would be encouraged to stay on longer and attain the jobs for which their talent made them capable. In addition, this claim drew attention to the way in which the secondary modern school tended to become a school for failures in which the children, by virtue of not achieving selection to a grammar school, lowered their aspirations and aimed almost entirely for occupations of low status regardless of what their actual capabilities might be. In other words, the argument was that the schools in the tripartite system were closely linked to and perpetuated a social class system divisive in nature, and that in one common school the children could learn a less divided culture and aspire to positions that matched their capabilities. The vision of 'one nation', which was the dream of Disraeli, the nineteenth-century politician and founder of the modern Conservative Party, was to be translated into reality by a reorganization of the secondary schools, largely supported by the Labour Party.

A number of studies have now been made upon which the success to date of the comprehensive school may be judged. One of the most complete is that by Ford (1969), who compared a coeducational comprehensive school in the inner London area, chosen to be representative of such schools in general, with a grammar and a modern school in the same area, having, as far as was possible, characteristics similar to those of the comprehensive school. In the matter of reducing the wastage of talented children, Ford reported that on the evidence of these three schools there was still a persistence of class bias in educational attainment within the comprehensive system. This finding is in some respects perhaps over-pessimistic in the light of Eggleston's large survey of a number of local education areas in the Midlands, where the rate of staying on beyond the minimum leaving age of fifteen was higher in comprehensive schools than in the tripartite system. Yet even in this survey the increase in the proportions of children staying on was greater amongst children from the middle class than from working-class families.[18] As has so often been the case in Britain, the middle classs seems more able and more willing to take advantage of all the increased facilities offered by the various branches of the welfare state.

In the matter of social cohesion Ford found that the children in the comprehensive school showed the same tendency to mix with children of their own social class that was found in the grammar school and the modern school that she investigated. Furthermore, the pupils at the comprehensive school did not appear to learn occupational aspirations that were very different from those learnt in the tripartite schools; the large group of children from the working class expected to enter occupations of low social status, while a small group of children largely from the middle class hoped for careers in the higher reaches of the occupational structure. With continuing divisions of this nature it is hardly surprising that the children in the comprehensive school did not hold a more flexible view of the social class system than those in the grammar school and the modern school.

These findings would perhaps be expected in view of the way in which comprehensive schools are usually organized. Classes are still largely streamed by academic capability, which varies directly with social class. Thus, the cultures of the middle class and the grammar school tend to be recreated in the upper streams of the comprehensive school, whilst those of the working class and the secondary modern school are found in the lower streams. Furthermore, to use the structural perspective, such positions of responsibility as that of prefect, which should ideally in such a school be open to children of all social classes, seem to be filled largely by those from the middle class,[19] so that the hierarchy of social status outside the school is still in some measure reinforced within the school.

In general, those running the comprehensive schools do not seem to have created one common culture to pass on to all their pupils. As these schools are now usually organized they have tended to recreate the grammar and the modern cultures, inasmuch as these are identifiable, within the one school. The social background of the children, particularly in relation to sub-cultures of the various social classes, has largely overcome the influence of the school, which has not acted as an agent of social change as was intended.

D. Conclusion

As a result of the ways in which the British idea of a school has evolved, schools have come to be organized in particular ways and around rarely questioned assumptions. Those running British schools have, therefore, been relatively successful in keeping the boundaries between themselves and the world defined as outside the school sharply differentiated from one another, but they cannot exclude some influence from the powerful members of the social networks within which the school is set. Even parents are coming to be seen as a group who can claim a larger part in decisions about the schooling of their children.

The educational system has come to be structured in such a way that children may pass through a number of possible pathways. In the positions in the various types of schools there are differing expectations of behaviour for the pupils. These patterns may be seen as cultures clustered around certain central values. This analysis is nearer to reality in the public schools and the primary schools, though in the latter case there are three main versions of the culture. In the tripartite system each type of school seems to contain more than one culture, largely because of the power of the roles connected with social class into which the pupils have been socialized at home, but which they play in a latent fashion at school. Although its aim is to overcome these divisions, the comprehensive school does not seem to have achieved one common culture that is learnt by all its pupils, and this seems once again to be due to the power of the family in the process of socialization.

A question may be asked at this point, to which no research worker has yet been able to give an answer, namely how much of what a child learns during his socialization may be attributed to the influence of the family, and how much to the school. However, in a recent report of a longitudinal study, Himmelweit and Swift have begun to show us one way of answering such questions. They studied a group of children at the age of fourteen in four grammar schools and five secondary modern schools in the London area and interviewed this sample again at the age of twenty-five when their education was complete and they had settled into a job. The aim was to examine the nature of the pathways through which various categories of persons had passed and to judge the influence of these routes on the groups of individuals. Their main finding to which we shall refer again in Chapter 10 was that the school was a powerful socializing agency which overcame external influences under certain specific conditions, but the irony of their work in the contemporary ideological setting is that these conditions were in a real sense parallel to those provided by the tripartite system. Thus, the schools that could select, rather than merely accept, pupils had the greatest socializing effect. Again, the use of such organizational strategies as streaming could 'offset the poor motivation generated by a family that is little interested in education'.[20] In our present state of knowledge the school, it seems, can cause some, but not all, of those that believe in different values and hold different patterns of behaviour, to change, but only when given favourable conditions.

BIBLIOGRAPHY

G. Baron, 'Some Aspects of the Headmaster Tradition', in P. W. Musgrave (ed.), *Sociology, History and Education*, 1970.

G. Baron and A. Tropp, 'Teachers in England and America', in A. H. Halsey, J. Floud and C. A. Anderson (eds.), *Education, Economy and Society*, New York, 1961.

P. Bellaby, *The Sociology of Comprehensive Schooling*, 1977.

W. A. L. Blyth, *English Primary Education*, Vols. I and II, 1965.

J. Ford, *Social Class and the Comprehensive School*, 1969.

J. Gretton and M. Jackson, *William Tyndale: Collapse of a School – or a System?*, 1976.

D. Hargreaves, *Social Relations in a Secondary School*, 1967.

R. King, *Values and Involvement in a Grammar School*, 1969.

P. W. Musgrave, *The School as an Organisation*, 1968.

P. W. Musgrave, *Society and Education in England since 1800*, 1968.

W. Taylor, *The Secondary Modern School*, 1963.

I. Weinberg, *The English Public Schools*, New York, 1967.

M. Young and P. J. McGeeney, *Learning Begins at Home: a Study of a Junior School and its Parents*, 1968.

NOTES

1 This section owes much to Professor G. Baron, formerly of the Institute of Education, University of London.

2 Matthew Arnold's poem 'Rugby Chapel' (1857) can be read as a gloss on this sentence.

3 C. Lacey, *The Socialisation of Teachers*, 1977, p. 144.

4 For an examination of this topic see P. W. Musgrave, 'The Relationship between School and Community', *Community Development Journal*, October 1973.

5 See D. Rubinstein and B. Simon, *The Evolution of the Comprehensive School: 1926–1966*, 1969.

6 For Corby see S. J. Eggleston, 'Going Comprehensive – a Case Study

of Secondary Reorganisation', in S. J. Eggleston (ed.), *Contemporary Research in the Sociology of Education*, 1974; and for Middlesex, R. Saran, 'Decision-Making by a Local Education Authority', *Public Administration*, Winter 1967. For studies of Darlington and Gateshead see R. Batley, O. O'Brien and H. Parris, *Going Comprehensive*, 1971.

7 See D. A. Howell, 'The Management of Primary Schools', Appendix 13, *Children and their Primary Schools* (Plowden Report), Vol. II, HMSO, 1967; G. Baron and D. A. Howell, 'School Management and Government', Research Studies No. 6, *Royal Commission on Local Government in England*, HMSO, 1968; *A New Partnership for our Schools* (Taylor Report), HMSO, 1977, pp. 10–11.

8 R. T. Fitzgerald, P. W. Musgrave and D. W. Pettit, *Participation in Schools?*, Melbourne, 1976. Somewhat similar conclusions were reached in a pilot study in Southampton; see J. Lynch and J. Pimlott, *Parents and Teachers*, 1976.

9 B. Jackson and D. Marsden, *Education and the Working Class*, 1962, pp. 205–9.

10 Throughout this book, except where otherwise mentioned, the position is taken that there is a fairly uniform British educational system. For some of the differences between English and Scottish schools, see Musgrave, 1968, Chapter 2.

11 R. H. Turner, 'Sponsored and Context Mobility in the School System', *American Sociological Review*, December 1960 (also in A. H. Halsey, J. E. Floud and C. A. Anderson (eds.), *Education, Economy and Society*,

12 For the way in which this age became the most common see J. D. Nisbet and N. J. Entwistle, *The Age of Transfer to Secondary Education*, 1966.

13 B. Jackson, *Streaming: an Educational System in Miniature*, 1964.

14 For a provocative analysis of 'progressive' education see B. Bernstein, 'Class and Pedagogic: Visible and Invisible', in B. Bernstein, *Class, Codes and Control*, Vol. III, 1975.

15 R. H. Wilkinson, 'The Gentleman Elite and the Maintenance of a Political Elite', *Sociology of Education*, Fall 1963 (also in P. W. Musgrave (ed.), *Sociology, History and Education*, 1970).

16 For a brief account of the culture of the sixth form see *15 to 18* (Crowther Report), Vol. I, HMSO, 1959, Chapter 21, 'The Marks of a Sixth Form'.

17 For an analysis of the influence of these factors on the development of one secondary modern school see C. M. Turner, 'An Organisational Analysis of a Secondary Modern School', *Sociological Review*, March 1969.

18 S. J. Eggleston, 'Some Invironmental Correlates of Extended Secondary Education in England', in S. J. Eggleston (ed.), *Contemporary Research in the Sociology of Education*, 1974.

19 D. N. Holly, 'Profiting from a Comprehensive School: Class, Sex and Ability', *British Journal of Sociology*, June 1965.

20 H. T. Himmelweit and B. Swift, 'A Model for the Understanding of the School as a Socializing Agency', in P. H. Mussen, J. Langer and M. Covington (eds.), *Trends and Issues in Developmental Psychology*, New York, 1969, p. 178.

8

The Occupation of Teaching

There is a group of occupations which the general public usually refers to as the professions. In the nineteenth century doctors, lawyers and the clergy were generally agreed to be in this category. During the last hundred years there has been an increase in the numbers of those claiming to be members of a profession. In the main this has been a result of the rising proportion of occupations that have required a high standard of education. Many members of these newer occupations, for example engineers and accountants, have aspired to professional status. In addition, over the same period a substantial group of occupations of slightly lower social standing has emerged which has come to be referred to as the lesser or quasi-professions; examples are surveyors and estate agents or, and in some ways more directly comparable with teaching, social workers and nurses. This tendency is seen in the Census returns. The categories of Higher Professionals and of Lower Professionals/ Technicians formed respectively the following percentages of the total occupied population at the specified dates: 1901, 1·0 and 3·1; 1951, 1·9 and 4·7; and 1966, 3·4 and 6·5. The numbers in teaching rose less proportionately than those in either the major or the other professions.

About five per cent of occupied males are, therefore, classified as members of professions. This is a large proportion of the labour force, and it forms an important group in view of the responsible nature of the work undertaken. Is this group of occupations merely a statistical category? Or has the term 'profession' entered modern usage because it proved a useful analytical tool to nineteenth-century social historians? Or is there some underlying social relationship which can be revealed by a careful sociological analysis? In this chapter an attempt will be made to answer these questions with particular reference to teaching. The topic is important in itself and, as will be appreciated in the course of the analysis, certain aspects of the behaviour that any teacher will exhibit depends upon the stance he takes up in this matter. However, in addition a consideration of the question of whether teaching is a profession or an occupation does lay bare some of the contemporary constraints upon the teacher as he goes about his work in schools.

A. Occupation or Profession?

T. H. Marshall (1950) in a well-known paper claimed that the practice of the professions that were recognized as such in the last century is based on the close personal relationship between the practitioner and his client. The layman who is sick consults his doctor because he is ignorant of the nature of his illness, whilst the doctor is assumed to know how to cure it. In the same way the lawyer can help his clients because of his knowledge of the complexities of the law. Therefore, the professional situation is characterized by the expert practitioner in consultation with the ignorant client who has absolute trust in the advice tendered to him. The practitioner does not use his knowledge except to benefit his clients. According to this analysis the social fact of 'the professions' rests upon the implications of the social situation involved. Following from the essential nature of this relationship there are, it is said, a number of characteristics that are common to all 'true' professions. These characteristics concern the type of knowledge required to practise, the way in which entry to the profession is controlled, the formulation of an ethical code governing professional behaviour and, finally, the freedom of the professional to practise without lay interference. Though not strictly a consequence of the nature of the interrelationship between practitioner and layman one extension of these implications is usually made, namely that professions tend to found organizations to watch over the codification of the four characteristics identified above.

In a recent reconsideration of those occupations traditionally known as professions Johnson (1972) has focused upon 'the producer–consumer relationship'. By emphasizing this side of the interpersonal relationship he is able both to throw more direct light upon how much power so-called professionals really have and to relate these special occupations in a meaningful comparative way to all other occupations in the labour force. Johnson has presented three ideal typical relationships: the *collegiate*, where 'the producer defines the needs of the consumer and the manner in which these needs are catered for', an important sub-type of which is the traditional profession; *patronage*, where the consumer himself defines his needs and the manner in which they will be supported; and the *mediative*, where a third party stands between producer and consumer. Here these ideal types will be used to see whether the occupation of teaching fits Johnson's collegiate pattern. To do this each of the characteristics implied in Marshall's analysis will be examined in turn.

1. *Knowledge*

The ignorance of the client is fundamental to the need to consult the practitioner. Therefore a member of any of those occupations that are normally called professional must have a command over a very definite field of knowledge, much of which will be particular to one profession. The mastery of such a core of relevant knowledge requires high intelligence and some training. Law and medicine provide clear examples, since considerable training is necessary and in both cases the nature and the complexity of the knowledge demands a high level of intelligence.

Under modern conditions the mass media and advertising have shown that they can sometimes teach better than many teachers. In the schools children have for some time now learnt from the radio and films. Teaching grows to be less of an art and more of a science as research reveals more about the process of learning and the best way to communicate information. Yet it is still true that to practise as a teacher assumes a core of specialized knowledge and skills, and that a relatively high level of intelligence is needed to be a teacher. Exactly who defines this basis of knowledge and skills is difficult to say. Very rarely does the consumer, whether he is defined directly as the pupil or indirectly as his future employer or his parent, have much influence. In another sense the state, as the main employer through the local education authorities and, hence the main consumer of teaching labour, is interested in specifying the minimum standards of knowledge and skill that teachers shall have. But in England today, though as will be seen, not in Scotland, power is usually delegated to the colleges and universities responsible for the initial and further training of teachers.

2. Control of Entry

The knowledge and training essential for any profession can be specified so that control of entry to the profession is possible. The medical profession was the first to achieve control of entry in its modern form. In 1858 the Medical Act established the General Medical Council, whose members were largely representative of the medical profession and whose main function is to keep a register of practitioners and to make certain that only those fit to practise are on this register. The academic qualifications and length of training necessary for admission to the register are laid down in detail. This ensures that all medical practitioners are professionally qualified and thereby guarantees to the general public that professional advice is sound.

The struggle by the teachers to establish a similar register has been a long one.[1] Though a system of registration over which serving teachers have a large measure of control was inaugurated in Scotland in 1966 when the General Teaching Council for Scotland was established, so far teachers in England have been unsuccessful in their attempts to obtain similar machinery. Unqualified teachers are still permitted to teach for short periods under certain regulations of the Department of Education and Science. Furthermore, any graduate, at least in England and Wales, until recently could claim the status of qualified teacher regardless of whether he had any training in teaching or not, though this loophole whereby the profession might be entered by those without training was, except in the case of teachers of mathematics and science, closed in 1974. That untrained teachers might still practise may have been due to the shortage of teachers, but their continued existence made very clear that control of entry to the occupation of teaching had been lax compared with the medical and most other professions, old and new. In addition, except in the limited example of Scotland mentioned above, teachers or their representatives are not themselves responsible for control of entry, since the system is operated by the Department through administrative regulations. The Department can both grant and withdraw the teacher's certificate.

Thus, although in Scotland the producers, that is the teachers have, perhaps, achieved some influence over control of entry to the occupation and, hence, may be said on this count to be partially operating in a collegiate manner, this is certainly not the case elsewhere in Britain. Even in Scotland the state as the employer, that is the main consumer of teaching labour, has considerable influence in the General Teaching Council. Therefore, particularly in England, in respect of control of entry the market situation of teachers is best seen, in Johnson's terms, as one of patronage rather than as collegiate in nature.

3. Code of Professional Conduct

A professional man must not only be of proved competence, but he must be trustworthy. The client assumes that his ignorance will not be exploited and that the practitioner is of a good character. We usually judge personality by behaviour or by what others tell us of a man. In the case of the professions we can rarely know the practitioner well and must refer to others to gain knowledge of his personality. Written references are commonly used as a means of guaranteeing a person's character. Teachers usually cannot apply for posts without supplying some references of their character. Many questions of fairness are raised by this system which is certainly less objective than most formal examinations.

The client trusts the practitioner to behave in a well-defined way. The older professions have ethical codes of long standing. There is the tradition of the Hippocratic oath for the doctors, the inviolability of the confessional for the priest, the devotion of the lawyer to his clients' interests. Some of the teachers' associations have published codes to govern the behaviour of their members in relation to their clients – the children, to outsiders – the parents, and to their colleagues. One of the most important ideas implicit in the ethical codes of all professions is that the work is a thing of importance in itself. It has been said that the professional man does not work in order to be paid, but is paid in order that he may work. One of the most difficult questions of all for teachers has always been whether they ought to strike. This is more than a moral issue. It has sociological importance. Teachers have a calling to help their clients, the children. A strike was thought to damage the children's interest and would, therefore, be seen by the general public as unprofessional conduct, contravening the ethical code expected in any profession. Despite their relatively low earnings, teachers until recent years have not often struck in Britain.

The occupation of teaching is not really controlled by any generally accepted, published professional code. The producer has the power to determine much of a teacher's behaviour towards his pupils but, unlike in the medical or legal professions, the policing of the code is not in the hands of members of the occupation itself. The consumer, or more exactly the employer on his behalf, exercises this function and has the responsibility to terminate the employment of teachers who offend against the ethical conventions governing teaching.

4. *Freedom to Practise the Profession*

There are sanctions on the actions of any profession. An ethical code controls behaviour and only suitably qualified persons may call themselves practitioners. In return for these restrictions the profession expects absolute freedom to practise its calling as the members think fit. We assume that the doctor is competent and of good character; he in his turn assumes that we shall permit him to advise his patient in the way that he feels best and that we shall not interfere with his practice. There is a tension in this position, since where the state gives protection it may also wish to interfere either as a patron or as a mediator.

Under modern conditions the state is coming to employ more and more professional people. In some cases almost all the members of a profession work for the state; examples are the doctors and the teachers. Very few professions are totally outside state employment; acting is perhaps one instance. Two dangers stem from this tendency. Firstly, professional men often find themselves subject to laymen as they do their work. In addition, once the state has decided that it wants a job done, it can lay down the necessary qualifications and conditions of service. Ironically the professions as a whole, and particularly the teachers, have helped this process of increasing dependence to come about. When a group employed in one occupation has made a bid for professional status, the members have put great stress on formal educational qualifications and thereby on longer education. Since the state now pays for much of this extra education, it has naturally felt that it has the right to a greater control of the use of such education. In the case of teaching, the state pays for the greatest part of the education provided in this country. It therefore wishes to exercise some control over educational expenditure. This entails inspecting the work of teachers. In this respect there are few other occupations which are in the same position as teaching. An HMI can walk into a classroom and criticize a teacher's work at any time. Certainly doctors and lawyers, even when employed by the state, are not subject to such very direct interference.

One of the main problems of the professions today is how to maintain their right to practise as they think best, although the contemporary tendency is for a larger proportion of their members to be employed by the state. When the majority of professional men were in private practice, the private practitioner set the standard for those who were employed elsewhere. The fewer there are in private practice, the less influence they can have, although there may be a timelag before the state assumes major or complete control. When the state employs the whole of any profession, it can call the tune, and there is an arguable case that the profession then has ceased to be a profession and become a body of experts employed by a patron.

The teachers have a difficult position to hold. Very few of their number are privately employed and therefore interference could be easy. Furthermore the very nature of their work raises difficult questions of principle. The case of whether known Communists should be allowed to teach children in Britain illustrates the problem. On the one hand there is a strong argument that where this is prevented the local authority is guarding the children from a probable source of propaganda; yet on the other this interference is preventing the absolutely free practice of the calling. But, by and large, teachers do have great freedom to practise as they wish within the contemporary norms relating to curricula and pedagogy, though once they try to move outside the relevant behavioural boundaries the state tends to bring deviants to heel by insisting on its role, always latent, of patron.

5. *Professional Organizations*

We have already seen that the traditional professions have formed associations to which they have delegated some important functions. It is usual, for example, for an association to control the register of practitioners. Professional associations are, therefore, normally in a monopoly position and could use their power over control of entry to raise the educational threshold of membership. Such a course would lower the supply of qualified practitioners and tend to increase the level of remuneration to those in the profession. This has often been the policy of the trade unions with regard to apprentices. An association that follows such a course may endanger the public image of an occupation, because there has been an assumption that professional men do not seek their own selfish ends. The profession is seen as a vocation with a duty to its clients. Whereas a trade union acts out of self-interest, a professional association in the past was believed to work for the advancement of the profession only so that it might more completely fufil its social duty.

The association helps to build the framework within which its members practise. It provides the sanctions so that members undertake their obligations and responsibilities to society. Thus, in essence, it is disciplinary. The association ensures that its new members are able to provide the best possible service to their clients. When a practitioner fails in his obligations by acting in an incompetent or unethical way, that is unprofessionally, the association guards the public by withdrawing the right to practise from that member. The General Medical Council and the Law Society are responsible for both admitting members to and striking them off their respective registers.

Associations cannot call strikes in the way that trade unions do, though associations for *industrial* as opposed to professional purposes, for example of hospital registrars, can and have done so. In recent years there has often been great pressure on the NUT to strike over salaries, but a feeling of duty towards the children has overcome the desire to use industrial action. In the early part of this century the NUT did organize strikes on a local basis, mainly with the aim of gaining a national salary structure and uniform conditions of service. More recently in 1970 a series of rolling strikes, area following area, was organized. The clash of interests here is difficult to resolve. The NUT can claim that without a higher salary scale recruits to the occupation will not be attracted to do the job. Yet the strike is undoubtedly seen by many, amongst both the general public and teachers alike, to be unprofessional in that it harms the children.

The NUT, like other associations, takes as one of its most important functions political action of another type (Manzer, 1970). It carefully watches the professional interests of teachers in Parliament at question time and during the passage of any major legislation that has even a remote connection with education. There has been a series of famous teacher Members of Parliament. An example was Chuter Ede, who was Parliamentary Secretary to the President of the Board of Education, during the passing of the 1944 Education Act. There is some danger in activity, particularly of a political nature, by professional associations, since the image that the public has of the profession may be changed by such action. The NUT followed a very forceful policy between 1870 and 1895. At the beginning of this period the school teacher was seen as a docile, lower middle-class, useful citizen; by 1895 many thought him to be a politically minded, ambitious pusher (Tropp, 1957). An association that aims to assist its members may wish to avoid appearing to follow self-interest. Once the public thinks that the occupation is behaving in a selfish way, the nature of the relationship between the occupation and its clients may be changed.

On the whole since 1945 the NUT has followed what may be called high professional standards in its activities. In one particular instance between 1950 and 1952 it set the very highest example possible. The local authority in County Durham tried to impose a 'closed shop' on all the teachers whom it employed; all had to belong to one union. The NUT, despite obvious advantages to itself, successfully opposed the authority on grounds of professional freedom. During the period 1954–5, however, the NUT was pressed by many of its members to follow a policy of militancy in a fight with the government over changes in the statutory superannuation scheme that were disadvantageous to teachers. In this struggle the NUT acted more like a trade union, though actual strike action was avoided.[2] Yet, until quite recently the NUT has largely retained the image of a professional, rather than an industrial, association, and this is clearly symbolized in the fact that only in 1970, its centennial year, did the NUT join the Labour-oriented Trades Union Congress. Such a move would have political connotations unwelcome to most professional associations. The basic aim, however, of this move was industrial, namely to strengthen the NUT's position in representing the interests of teachers in negotiating with their patron, the state. A near-monopsonist, the state, must face a near-monopolist, the NUT, now with the tacit support of the organized trade union movement.

6. Conditions of Service

Nowhere is this countervailing power against the only, or about the only, employer more obvious than in struggles over conditions of service. This is especially true of those professions whose members are employed by the state or industry rather than in private practice, since by controlling conditions of service the state may interfere with the freedom of a profession to practise its calling.

The teachers' associations, especially the NUT, have paid considerable attention to conditions of service since their foundation. This has been so for two main reasons. Firstly, conditions were very bad for teachers in the early and mid-nineteenth century, and this reflected the low status of teachers. Secondly, the associations wanted to raise the status of their members and saw that by gaining adequate conditions they were promoting respectability. They hoped that in time this would lead to higher status. The battle for adequate pensions has been waged since 1846, and Fisher's Superannuation Act in 1918 was a landmark in the struggle, since it founded a scheme of pensions backed by the state. Security of tenure was gained by 1902, although dismissal is still not in the hands of teachers themselves but under the control of the state or its representatives; this is very different from the position in the old professions, where a court of one's peers strikes one off the register.

A major problem for teachers has always been the demand that they carry out duties extraneous to teaching. In the middle of the last century many teachers knew that they would only be appointed if, for example, they played the church organ on Sundays. The nature of these duties have changed considerably. The growth of what may be called welfare services in the schools has led to the need for teachers to collect dinner money. Many teachers regard such tasks as unprofessional. The achieving of a satisfactory position with regard to conditions of service gives stability and respectability to an occupation. Yet it is true to say that for a member of the old professions in private practice, the problem did not arise. The new concern with conditions of service is due to the greater proportion of professionals who are not in private practice and to the increased number of occupations now considered to be professions of a rather different nature from the old professions.

Undoubtedly there was some truth in Marshall's claim that the occupations traditionally known as professions had a special relationship with their clients and that this situation had specific implications for their social organization. But the changed conditions under which the majority of these persons work and the great extension in the numbers of those claiming to be, or seen by the public as, professionals has undercut the basis of this analysis. Neither the relationship between practitioners and clients nor the consequent implications are the same for 'the new professions' as for the old. It seems, therefore, more worthwhile to see teaching as an occupation, albeit one of some status, and to apply some such framework as Johnson's to enable us to discover the social influences at work upon the occupation of teaching. We may then focus upon the powerful position of the state as a patron or sometimes a mediator and the increasingly industrial activities of the occupational association rather than upon the less predominant collegiate aspects of teaching under contemporary conditions.

B. Recognition of the Occupation

The case has sometimes been made that the existence of any profession merely depends upon recognition by the public. If the majority of teachers consider themselves to be members of a profession, and on the whole the public and the authorities treat them as having that status, then the principle of the self-fulfilling prophecy will operate in the case of the teaching profession. Is this true?

In the first place do teachers see themselves as professionals? In one Australian study teachers were asked in an open-ended interview whether they saw themselves as professionals; the majority said that they did not do so, but went on to display attitudes indicating their feeling that they were members of a high-status, expert group of the type to which traditionally the term, profession, has been applied. In another Australian study which measured the degree of professional awareness amongst samples of Australian and British teachers in government schools some interesting differences were found. Professional awareness, defined as awareness of membership of, and of the issues of concern to, a profession, was higher amongst Australian than British teachers and amongst those with longer service. Being a male and having higher qualifications also had some influence on the degree of awareness shown. Furthermore, one specific attitude seemed to be an influential variable; professional awareness was more pronounced amongst teachers holding reformist rather than conservative attitudes on educational questions. One other conclusion of this study is particularly relevant: 'Adverse reaction to the less attractive aspects of *profession* was weaker than had been anticipated.'[3]

It would, therefore, seem that in Australia and Britain teachers are divided in their minds about whether or not they are members of a profession, and tend nowadays to feel themselves to be members of an occupation of some status who can act in industrial negotiations in the same way as blue-collar workers do. How, then, are they seen by the general public?

Historically teachers have had a status somewhat lower than those occupations defined as professions. As noted above, much of the work done by their associations has been much more akin to that done by trade unions than that of professional associations. Typical of such work were the strikes to ensure uniform conditions of service referred to above. By the 1970s the status of teaching has risen. This was most probably a result of the fact that education has come to have a higher status in Britain; certainly teaching is now often included, as in the Census, amongst those occupations called professions. Many of the other new professions are comparable with teaching in that they are not of the 'pure' nineteenth-century type, since so many of their members are employed by the state in one capacity or another. For the most part these new professions stick to the standards of conduct implicit in the personal relationship fundamental to the 'pure' profession. This is also the case for teaching. Furthermore, although the state as patron has much power over many of these new professions, yet it has in many cases delegated its power to 'the college', thereby confusing the reality in that the occupation sees itself as a self-governing profession. There is something of this misleading situation in the case of the Scottish teachers and the General Teaching Council of Scotland.

So far the evidence concerning public recognition has largely related to the present situation, but an attempt has been made to outline a natural history of becoming a profession. The development of eighteen occupations recognized in the USA as professions was analysed, and on the whole each seemed to pass through an identical series of stages.[4] First, the occupation must have become a full-time job, as teaching had become in Britain well before 1800. Next, a training system must be established; this took place after 1839 for elementary teachers, though its development for graduates has only recently become complete. Thirdly, a professional association is founded, as occurred in Britain in the case of element-ary teachers in the 1870s and of secondary teachers around the turn of the century. In some professions these associations achieved legal recognition, but this does not appear to be an integral part of the process of becoming a profession. Finally, a code of ethics is evolved; this also has taken place in the case of teaching in Britain. This reinforces the conclusion already reached that there is an arguable case for saying that teaching has become one of the higher-status occupations that are often recognized in Britain as lesser professions. This conclusion concerning public recognition taken together with the earlier conclusion about the doubts teachers have about being professionals strengthens the view expressed at the end of the last section that for most purposes it is best to regard teaching as a high-status occupation rather than as a profession.

There is one final point. Who should be included in this occupation? Should all those employed in the field of education be considered? Those administering education are in a very different social position from teachers, since they are far removed from the teachers' clients, the children, and, furthermore, they are in a very different market situation from the teachers whom they often tell what to do. There are also teachers in other educational situations, for example in universities or colleges. Their position is harder to assess until we have examined what determines the status of individual teachers within the occupation as a whole.

C. The Status of the Individual Teacher

A recent High Master of Manchester Grammar School was created a life peer. Headteachers of primary schools who appear in the Honours Lists are awarded the MBE. This is one indication of the very wide range of status that exists within the occupation of teaching. We shall here consider four main determinants of the status of individual teachers.

1. Sex

In the nineteenth century there was no doubt that women had a lower status than men in the world of teaching. The struggle for emancipation for women and the subsequent fight for equal pay for women in many occupations affected the position of women teachers. In the years since the war women teachers have been granted equal pay, so that today there is the same salary scale for both sexes in teaching. But, since there are more men in the more highly paid posts of headteacher or of head of department, the average earnings of women teachers are lower than in the case of men.

This is a common situation throughout the labour market and has a real basis in the fact that few women today expect to follow a career unbroken by motherhood. They therefore in effect lose their position on the scale of seniority and normally expect to forfeit their chances of promotion. In recent years the position has been complicated by the growing number of part-time married women teachers whose status appears to be considered lower than full-time married teachers.[5] Women teachers may be on the same salary as men, but they do not seem, despite recent feminist claims and the Equal Opportunity Act, to have the same status in the schools.

2. The Status and Age of the Pupils Taught

There is an immense range of status of schools from independent schools such as Eton to maintained schools in slum areas. The status of the pupils attending these schools covers an equally wide range and to a great extent the status of the pupils affects the status of those who teach them. Up till 1944 this difference was enshrined in two terms in common usage – 'the teacher' and 'the schoolmaster'. The latter was applied to those who taught in grammar or private schools, whilst the former was given to the lower-status elementary school. The schoolmaster was usually a graduate of a university, whilst the teacher had been to a training college. A degree has always had a higher status than the teacher's certificate. As late as 1949, when the term 'elementary' had officially been abolished, those running the London School of Economics survey of social mobility found that 'elementary teacher' was the term that the general public most readily understood when considering teachers. The sample ranked the elementary teacher as having equal socio-economic status with a news reporter, a commercial traveller and a jobbing master builder, and of higher status than an insurance agent, but of lower status than a Nonconformist minister.[6]

Since the 1944 Act we can speak of primary and secondary teachers. It is doubtful whether the general public can or does distinguish amongst teachers in general. The only differentiation seems to be that they still use the term 'schoolmaster' in the case of those who teach in grammar and private schools. However, a group of 178 students, training for the Postgraduate Diploma of Education at an English provincial university, were asked in the late 1960s to rate teachers in various types of school in two ways. They first indicated how they perceived the general public would rank these teachers and, secondly, how they themselves would do so. The order that they attributed to the general public was as follows: teachers in independent schools, maintained grammar schools, comprehensive schools, secondary modern schools and, lastly, those in primary schools. They themselves both saw far less difference in status between the various types of teacher than they considered the general public to do and also rearranged the order of the first three cases in the following way: teachers in maintained grammar schools, comprehensive schools and independent schools.[7] Though the rising number of comprehensive schools is changing the picture the differences in status between schools is reflected in the average earnings of those who teach in them, those in grammar schools earning most.

Despite the common salary scale, such differences occur not only between those teaching pupils of different status, but also between those teaching children of different ages. Those who teach the younger children in the primary schools earn less on average than those in secondary schools. This seems to be a measure of a difference in status, which is partly connected with two other facts. There are far more women than men teaching in the primary schools. In 1974–5 out of 235,097 full-time teachers in these schools 183,761 (or 78·1 per cent) were women. Furthermore, only 9·1 per cent of all full-time teachers (5·5 per cent of women) in primary schools were graduates.

Such internal differences in status are important, since they may act to prevent structural change in the educational system. Some teachers realize that they cannot claim individual status from the profession as a whole; they therefore cling to the status of the institutions to which they belong. Today grammar school teachers may, at least unconsciously, oppose the change to a comprehensive system of secondary education because they believe that this will lower their own status.

3. Subject Taught

In the nineteenth century the place given to science in the public schools was very low and those who taught science were often considered to be of a lower status than those who taught the classics. Today the situation has changed radically. There is still, however, an academic pecking order in some universities, with classics and the pure sciences high, whilst the social sciences, especially education, and applied science are put low. For example, in one small study in the Midlands, where teachers ranked those teaching certain special subjects by prestige, they put sixth-form mathematics teachers higher than modern language teachers, both of whom were rated considerably higher than teachers of religious education, commercial subjects, woodwork, domestic science or physical education.[8]

To some extent qualifications have come to be tied up with the status of subjects. In primary schools, though sometimes not in middle schools, teachers tend to be general practitioners, most of whom have the same qualification, the teacher's certificate, and therefore status cannot be accorded by the subject taught. But in secondary schools specialists are the rule. The growth in the number of graduates in the old elementary schools did help to raise the status of these schools. Graduates are not uncommon in secondary modern schools today and this may have made the modern school more acceptable to many.

But there are some subjects in which graduates are almost unknown. The clearest examples are handwork and physical education in the case of both boys and girls. Despite the important part played by games in British schools the PE teacher seems not to have the same status as other teachers, and this is particularly true in the grammar school where he is often one of the few non-graduates.[9]

4. The Social Origin of the Teacher

In the last century teaching was a common route for upward mobility. In a sample of 8,516 teachers taken in 1955 Floud and Scott (1956) found that almost half were descended from working-class grandfathers whose sons showed a more than average likelihood of rising up the social scale when compared with the rest of their class. Perhaps rather oddly, six or seven times as many as might be expected were descended from grandfathers who were farmers. However, trends in recruitment since the war seem to indicate that the pull on working-class children to enter teaching is no longer effective. Whether due to the greater security provided by industrial employment today, or because of changes in salary differentials, teaching is no longer so attractive an occupation and proportionally more middle-class young people are entering teaching.

If this trend continues, there will be a slow change in the social background of teachers. In a fairly representative study of teachers carried out in the mid-1960s, 24·8 per cent were children of fathers in managerial, executive or professional work and 26·3 per cent of fathers in administrative or clerical jobs. Thus over half the sample came from 'homes with the pattern of "white-collar work", implying middle class status'.[10] During the last century very many teachers came from a lower social class than was usually associated with the old professions. This rubbed off on the status of the occupation as a whole. Hence they often aspired to high status. Today the status of teaching and the social background of teachers appear to have risen and teachers are on the whole on a par with the new professions. There is no longer the same need to aspire to professional status. Though this may be true of the profession as a whole, circumstances may be different for given individuals.

The proportions of teachers from various social classes do vary by type of school. The position in the case of men in grant-earning schools in 1955 was as shown in the following table.

Father's occupation when teacher left school	Primary	Modern	Technical	Maintained grammar	Direct-grant grammar
	%	%	%	%	%
Professional, administrative	6·0	7·5	6·0	12·5	19·8
Intermediate	48·3	45·9	51·0	55·1	61·5
Manual	45·7	46·6	43·0	32·4	18·6

Source: Floud and Scott (1961), p. 540.

The trend in the case of women was much the same. The proportions of teachers from working-class homes were higher where the status of the school was lower and, conversely, the proportions of teachers with parents of higher social status rose as one went from the lower- to the higher-status schools.

This pattern matches what we should expect from our discussion on the relationship between the status and age of pupils and the status of their teachers. The differing status of these schools is much more likely to be a result of the age and status of the pupils in the schools than the social origins of the teachers concerned. In a society that has a relatively high rate of social mobility the social status of any occupational group tends to be given to all its members whatever their social origins. This is the more likely where geographical mobility is high, since in most cases no one will know the kin of any individual and status will be given according to the socio-economic position that is achieved. Many teachers move to obtain new posts and this may be an additional force in obscuring the influence of social origins on the status of the individual teacher.

D. Becoming a Teacher

In Part I the concept of socialization was used in its broadest sense to cover learning to be a member of any one particular society or of the groups within that society, but sociologists also use the term to cover the more specific learning of the values, attitudes and behaviour associated with a given social position. We can, therefore, speak of the process of becoming a teacher as occupational socialization of a particular type. During initial training courses in colleges or in universities students learn the motivation and behaviour currently acceptable in teachers in the various types of British school. Recently research has been undertaken in an attempt to discover what happens during this process, but much is still not known. Thus, it is not clear what proportion of teachers enter the occupation wishing to be teachers and what proportion as a result of a second choice because they are not able to enter the occupation of their first choice. One would expect these two categories to exhibit a different motivation and to undergo a different process of adaptation to teaching. Furthermore, the values and competences to be learnt are very different according to the type of school for which the student is training. For example, primary teachers must be academic generalists and approach children as whole persons, whilst secondary teachers must usually have specialist knowledge and take a less diffuse approach to their pupils.

As in the case of children being socialized within the family students are subject to sanctions at the hands of those who are responsible for their training. Lecturers have the power to pass or fail students and to praise or criticize their work, whether this is related to their theoretical studies or to their practical teaching in schools. These sanctions can lead to conflict between student and lecturer, as a result of which the student may do as he is required with the full belief in his action or may merely comply because he knows he must to pass the course or, occasionally, may convince his lecturer to change his view of what the student should do.

This process of socialization does seem to operate along a number of different dimensions. For example, Gibson has shown how students change their view of the roles of primary and secondary teachers during their three-year course. He compared 345 women students in their first, second and final years and 68 non-student women matched for education. The students all came to take a more flexible and open view of both roles during the three years of their training, but this effect was more pronounced in their views of primary teachers.[11] The question may be asked whether college courses of this length have a stronger influence on such occupational attitudes than do one-year postgraduate courses. Only one study seems relevant. In a comparative study of the training of teachers in Britain and in the USA there is some relevant material. What is surprising is that although, as may be expected, the graduates scored higher than the students from colleges on an intelligence test and on all but one of the measures of academic achievement in specific subjects, the scores of the two groups on a measure of their attitudes towards various characteristics of teachers were surprisingly similar. There were nine parts to this scale. On four of these parts the scores of the graduates and college students were more or less identical, whilst on two parts, those concerning learning-centredness and verbal understanding, the graduates scored higher, but in the remaining three parts concerning responsibility, methods of stimulation and classroom procedures, the students of the colleges had the higher scores. The impression that college students perhaps had a more professional and less academic attitude is, however, not entirely supported by the fact that on the tests of professional knowledge the graduates scored higher.[12]

During their training most students, certainly on the one-year course, seem to pass through four marked stages (Lacey, 1977). Initially they undergo a honeymoon period, when all seems right with their progress towards becoming a teacher. Then, however, the realization comes to them that they must search for the materials needed and the methods necessary for teaching. Next, and usually associated with their experiences in schools, a crisis occurs, when the student feels that he is not in control of the situation and is clearly failing to teach his pupils. Finally, the student learns to cope on the whole and to accept a measure of failure. Students may adapt to this final stage by retreating into themselves, or by seeking help from the group, or by displacing blame for their form of idealistic adaptation either on to the way in which educational system operates or on to their pupils. Lacey found that students oriented to progressive ideals tended to blame the current system, whereas those with more traditional attitudes tended to blame their pupils.

Most studies show some definite shift towards greater idealism in beliefs and attitudes during training. One study examined the ways in which 268 women students in each of the three years of training at an English college of education defined certain important sectors of their future role. These related to the organization of the classroom, the general aims of the teacher, the manner of motivating children and the type of behaviour that teachers would tolerate in their pupils. The same instrument was administered to 183 head-teachers and there were found to be no major differences in role conceptions held by those in primary and in secondary schools. The students moved consistently towards a less authoritarian pattern of attitudes during the early part of their training. This process reached a peak in their second year, but during their final year they reverted to a more traditional stance, coming to hold views nearer to those of the headteachers in this study. One suggested explanation that seemed to match the data is that the frames of reference used by college lecturers and by headteachers differ so that professional socialization is a two-phased process. In the first and preparatory stage the college students learn from their lecturers an ideal conception of their role as teacher, but in the second stage, that of organizational reality, students come to see themselves more as practising teachers, and taking the advice of those in the schools where they do teaching practice they begin to discount theory and emphasize practice.[13]

There is some American evidence that suggests that those entering such service occupations as teaching may have formed during their training an image of the ideal client with whom they will deal. When their expectations are not met in the real work situation, problems occur that demand some adjustment. Such a process may perhaps be seen at work in a recent study of 157 postgraduate students who were doing the one-year course for the Certificate of Education in an English university as a preparation for teaching in secondary schools. A far larger number wanted to go into comprehensive schools early in their training than ultimately took up first appointments in this type of school. The discrepancy was apparently not due to a shortage of such posts but rather caused by a change of view during the remainder of their course. The explanation seemed to be that student teachers had an ideal concept of their ability to interest their pupils in their own academic subjects and that this was disappointed when on teaching practice. They were fundamentally men of knowledge and the easiest adjustment to their misconception of classroom work was to take up a post in a selective secondary school.[14] Here again, as in the case of the students in the college of education, there was a gradual adjustment during training to the shock of reality, though they changed more quickly than the students in the college because their course was shorter.

By the end of the one-year postgraduate course the commitment to teaching exhibited by the students studied by Lacey seemed to fall into two very general patterns. There was, firstly, a group definitely committed to teaching and to schools but, secondly, there was a considerable number who were committed to education in its broadest sense and to ideals realizable through education, seen as a means to their ends. This second group was, therefore, less tied to teaching as such. If those concerned could not achieve their goals in schools they were willing to move out of teaching into, for example, journalism to try to fulfil their aims in life. Slightly less than forty per cent of the students expected to be in schools in whatever capacity fifteen years after completing their course of initial training.

Taking up their first post was, as already hinted, a shock for many. After one year many of Lacey's sample had reverted in attitude to the positions shown at the start of their training. Indeed, over this period of two years big changes were rare and were usually associated with very difficult teaching situations. Yet the power of schools to socialize teachers after their initial training must not be overemphasized since even in a stable period with few changes of staff or of internal organization the teachers in any school are not in total agreement and hence do not show a united front to newcomers. There is, therefore, considerable room for manoeuvre for young teachers as they start to work out their own futures and either to adapt themselves and their goals to the contemporary school structure or to try to reconstruct that reality to fit more easily to their ideals. The process of socialization will continue throughout their occupational career and where chances to fulfil ambitions do not occur within the school system some will move, where this is possible, into administration or into teacher education in an attempt to achieve their goals more fully. The biography of a teacher, like that of any person, will give a picture of what has influenced him as well as what he has been able to influence.

E. Conclusion

By the nineteenth century a few occupations of high status had come to be known as professions and, as the numbers of those in similar occupations requiring long education prior to qualification grew, many of these new specialists claimed or were given the title of professionals. During the twentieth century this process has continued, but in such a way that occupations of lesser status and requiring lesser education have also come to be called professions or lesser professions. Sociological analysis, however, shows that the market position of these occupations, and teaching is an excellent example, is very different from that of doctors or lawyers in the nineteenth century. Teachers are much in the power of the state which is indirectly their main employer. Even though, in Johnson's terminology, their patron may to a degree treat them in a collegiate or mediative way teachers have still felt the need to act in the matter of conditions of service through their associations, more particularly the NUT, in an industrial rather than professional manner.

Furthermore, there is a range of types of teachers with rather different status so that both the teachers themselves and the general public are in some doubt how to define the membership of any grouping. Because of this there is no one set of behavioural expectations into which all teachers are socialized. The range of behaviour acceptable as a teacher is wide and probably wider than the range into which doctors or lawyers are socialized. Within this range available to teachers those with different motives for teaching are able to create very different biographies and still be known as teachers. A few will wish to behave in a manner beyond this range. It is these teachers who may ultimately be seen by other teachers and the public at large, on the one hand, as creative and innovative or, on the other hand, as deviants who must be sanctioned and forced to behave in an acceptable way.

BIBLIOGRAPHY

J. E. Floud and W. Scott, 'Recruitment to Teaching in England and Wales, 1956', in A. H. Halsey, J. E. Floud and C. A. Anderson (eds.), *Education, Economy and Society*, New York, 1961.

T. J. Johnson, *Professions and Power*, 1972.

C. Lacey, *The Socialization of Teachers*, 1977.

R. A. Manzer, *Teachers and Politics*, Manchester, 1970.

T. H. Marshall, 'The Recent History of Professionalism in Relation to Social Structure and Social Policy', in *Citizenship and Social Class*, 1950.

A. Tropp, *The Sociology of Teaching*, New York, 1957.

NOTES

1 G. Baron, 'The Teachers' Registration Movement', *British Journal of Educational Studies*, May 1954.

2 N. N. Roy, 'Membership Participation in the NUT', *British Journal of Industrial Relations*, July 1964.

3 A. Duckers, 'Professional Awareness among Australian and British School Teachers', unpublished Ph.D. thesis, La Trobe University, 1978; R. T. Fitzgerald, P. W. Musgrave and D. W. Pettit, *Participation in Schools?*, Melbourne, 1976.

4 H. L. Wilensky, 'The Professionalization of Everyone?', *American Journal of Sociology*, September 1964, pp. 148–9.

5 M. Collins, *Women Graduates and the Teaching Profession*, Manchester, 1964, p. 52.

6 D. V. Glass (ed.), *Social Mobility in Britain*, 1954, p. 34.

7 G. Bernbaum, G. Noble and M. T. Whiteside, 'Intra-Occupational Prestige-Differentiation in Teaching', *Europaea Paedagogica*, 1969, p. 49.

8 F. Musgrove and P. H. Taylor, *Society and the Teacher's Role*, 1969, pp. 74–6.

9 See C. Cannon, 'Some Variations on the Teacher's Role', *Education for Teaching*, May 1964, especially pp. 32–6, for the role of the PE teacher in girls' selective secondary schools (also in P. W. Musgrave (ed.), *Sociology, History and Education*, 1970).

10 E. P. Duggan and W. A. C. Stewart, 'The Choice of Work Area of Teachers', *Sociological Review Monograph No. 15*, February 1970, p. 54.

11 D. R. Gibson, 'The Role of the Primary and Secondary School Teacher', *Educational Research*, November 1970.

12 G. E. Dickson *et al.*, *The Characteristics of Teacher Education Students in the British Isles and the United States* (mimeographed), University of Toledo, 1965, pp. 126–8.

13 D. S. Finlayson and L. Cohen, 'The Teacher's Role: a Comparative study of the Conceptions of College of Education Students and Head Teachers', *British Journal of Educational Psychology*, February 1967.

14 M. T. Whiteside, G. Bernbaum and G. Noble, 'Aspirations, Reality Shock and Entry into Teaching', *Sociological Review*, November 1969.

9

The School Curriculum

So far in Part II we have examined some important aspects of the structure of schools and of the occupation of teaching. Teachers are employed in schools primarily either to teach or to enable pupils to learn various types of knowledge, which are often subsumed under the general heading of *the curriculum*. The curriculum will here be defined as those learning experiences that are purposefully organized by such formal educational agents as schools. Such experiences may or may not take place within the educational organization that plans them.

Until very recently sociologists of education have tended to put more emphasis in their writings and research on the results of formal schooling than on its content. Thus, the process of selection and its relation to social class was given more attention than the structure and determinants of the curriculum. However, since about 1970 (Young, 1971) the curriculum has become one of the central foci of the sociology of education. Symbolically this chapter stands at the centre of this book. In it we shall examine the social nature of systems of knowledge, the ways in which they are controlled and, finally, stability and change in the school curriculum.

A. Systems of Knowledge

1. *The Social Nature of Knowledge*

Since Durkheim wrote *The Division of Labour* in 1893, one important way of categorizing societies has been by the degree of complexity in their role structure. Modern societies have a very complicated structure of positions and roles. Hence the distribution of knowledge is very different from that found in less developed societies. Under contemporary conditions there is an increase of knowledge, specific to particular social positions. Today, for example, surgeons, specialists, general practitioners, pharmacists, matrons, sisters and nurses, in each case often practising a particular specialism, have replaced the barbers of our own society three or four hundred years ago or the witch-doctors in other societies. Knowledge with a wide relevance becomes relatively less important, so that in modern societies universally meaningful propositions apply to much narrower ranges of common experience than in less complex societies. This important generalization is clearly seen to be the case in relation to academic disciplines where, for example, laws in science or findings in history are only relevant to one subject, but it also applies to norms governing social behaviour which are found to cover such special sub-cultures as social classes, members of a profession, or even the old boys of a school.

This extension of the generalization to norms of social behaviour is obviously of relevance to what is included in a school's extra-curricular activities and, since such activities have been shown to have such importance to the British idea of a school, they must be included in any consideration of the curriculum as it has here been defined. This latter part of what is taught will be called the *moral curriculum*, referring as it does to the ways in which members of a society should behave towards each other (Musgrave, 1978). The former part will here be termed the *academic curriculum* and includes all that knowledge related to the learned disciplines, usually in written form (Musgrave, 1973).

One further point must be made about the definition of the curriculum given at the start of this chapter. It could be said to cover the manifest curriculum, namely that part which either is declared openly as determined by the aims of the school concerned or is at least intended by those in charge even if their whole intention is not admitted to the general public. The first alternative covers the usual subjects taught in an academically oriented secondary school, whilst the second alternative allows for many of the moral aims that have been commonly emphasized, but usually not publicized, in British schools, such as that of teaching pupils how to behave in the social status which they are expected to achieve in their lives. Recently much of this latter type of teaching has been referred to as the *hidden curriculum*, although the term has been used somewhat inconsistently. Here, the concept of the hidden curriculum will only be used to cover material, academic or moral, that is taught to pupils without this being intended by those running the school concerned. Thus, for example, the award of marks for exercises may be intended to indicate academic standards and to act as a reward or punishment to pupils, but may unintentionally teach them the moral lesson of competitiveness.

One of the major contemporary difficulties in analysing academic knowledge is epistemological; that is, it relates to the very nature of knowledge itself. The problem may be expressed very simply by asking one question: can any particular example of knowledge be said to be true or not? Clearly by this criterion moral knowledge can be seen to be of a different nature from scientific knowledge. Elias (1971) has taken the position that in considering the latter type of knowledge 'the concept of "truth" is an anachronism'. We should be using the criteria of advance which, though not yet highly conceptualized, are widely used in the physical sciences. The most important of these criteria concerns the balance in any science between the emphasis on subjects or objects. The physical sciences, though created by and viewed through the eyes of social beings, focus on objects of some obduracy, whilst the social sciences and the humanities in the main deal with human subjects. Elias is interested to trace how branches of knowledge change, moving towards more emphasis upon objects. Thus, rather than using the concept of truth, the emphasis must be put upon varying degrees of 'relative autonomy' of any knowledge from the social structure. 'No type of knowledge can ever be in its structure and development totally autonomous in relation to the structure of the groups of human beings who use and produce it, but it can be independent of it in a higher or lower degree.'

One important implication of this position is that the social structure is constantly changing for reasons totally out of the control of men of knowledge. Hence scientists and other academics will find the relative autonomy of their subjects constantly changing. This can be seen very clearly in societies where political ideologies have a strong influence over the use of knowledge. Thus, in the USSR for a time the official version of biology was based on Lysenko's view that acquired characteristics could be genetically transmitted. Again, what is to be believed about certain aspects of physics now often depends upon how keen those in control in a society are to generate power by nuclear means.

2. The Academic Curriculum

(i) *Subjects*. At any one time the stock of knowledge is divided up according to agreed definitions of what each subject should include. Likewise each subject is organized by more or less universally agreed theories using accepted concepts. It is, therefore, possible to speak of the normal version of a subject (Kuhn, 1970). Subjects in the humanities that do not have a high degree of relative autonomy from the social structure may have more than one competing version and even in the physical sciences this may be the case, though perhaps only in relation to parts of the whole science. These *normal sciences* are based on *paradigms* which cover what types of questions are answerable within the subject and what methods are acceptable in answering problems. The results of practising normal science to date can be found in university textbooks which indicate the latest version of the subject concerned.

These views of what the subject is are taught to future teachers in their training. This is one part of the process of occupational socialization. Hence, school subjects must be strongly influenced by the relevant normal science as taught in a university or other places of higher learning. But the school curriculum is made up of a selection of all available knowledge and questions can be raised about how this selection is made.

Bernstein has indicated a way of categorizing curricula that provides some useful directions for analysing this problem.[1] He uses the terms *classification* and *framing* in relation to curricula. The former refers to the degree of permeability of the boundaries of subjects included, whereas the latter covers the power exercised by staff and pupils over *pedagogy*, that is over the content, timing and methods used in teaching. The usual selection of subjects in contemporary British secondary schools can be seen to form a collection of subjects with high classification and high framing; the roots of this situation may clearly be studied in historical terms, and particularly in the powerful past position of the classics. Some current developments, however, are characterized by attempts to break down the boundaries between subjects and to give choice to all concerned about what shall be learned and how this is to be done. In such integrated curricula both classification and framing are low. An analysis of the reactions of those in control when faced with efforts to replace the collection curriculum with an integrated one will indicate the sources of power and the ideologies of all involved. When we examine stability and change later in this chapter we shall consider such issues.

As an example of the development of a crucial part of the curriculum the case of English may be cited. Learning to read and write was always an important part of childhood schooling, but for centuries the classics formed the main part of the curriculum. By the nineteenth century this predominance was challenged and as schooling became more common for the working class the question could be raised of what curriculum was suitable for mass education, a question not yet really answered today in any detailed way. Clearly the classics were not suitable, whereas for a variety of reasons, including the needs of the economy, the 3 Rs with a heavy emphasis on literacy were thought to form a sound basis. Once the elements of literacy were learnt the nature of the subject involved, now called English, was developed along lines parallel to the still powerful subject, the classics. Writing, not fluent speech, was the aim. The cultivation of literary taste by the close reading of great works of literature predominated in what became a highly classified and highly framed subject. Interestingly a higher emphasis was put upon such moral elements as disentangling value positions in writings than upon the need for clear expression in writing, for example, letters or simple prose.

Moral elements are implicit in much of the academic curriculum. In many ways the distinction is an analytic rather than a practical one. Textbooks at all levels carry messages other than the academic ones intended. This is most easily seen in the reading books used in early schooling. In one American study of books used in pre-schools the implicit lesson shown to be taught was that women should be invisible and subservient. Eleven pictures of males were shown for every one of a female. The ratio was ninety-five to one if animals were included! The activities portrayed varied systematically by sex; boys were active and girls passive. The adults portrayed, presumably as models for children, also differed by sex; women were mothers, nurses, fairies and fairy-godmothers. Rarely were women seen at work and when they were they worked indoors whereas the men were shown at tough jobs out-of-doors.[2]

At the secondary level similar implicit lessons can be found in textbooks. In history, for example, in a British account of the hundred years war much is made of the victories of Agincourt, Crecy and Poitiers, but little is said of how England lost France except possibly Mary Tudor's loss of Calais. In economics the benefits of *laissez-faire* are compared with the disadvantages of a planned economy. However, somewhat inconsistently in the overall perspective, some textbooks in social studies, when dealing with consumer education, also detail the ways in which consumers are exploited and the environment polluted.

The point to be made is that the content of all school subjects, even when relatively autonomous of the social structure, are based in choices which must be ruled by the values of those, whether in the past or present, who constructed the syllabuses or wrote the textbooks. Furthermore, books and materials are used by teachers with their own sets of values and hence the curriculum is deeply loaded with values which openly or implicitly may be, or even are usually, taught to pupils. The content of the total collection taught also displays values: why physics and not biology? why the former for boys and the latter for girls? why French or German and not Russian or Chinese? why history or geography and not politics or industrial relations? The pedagogy used also betrays values: Who chooses what is to be learnt? Why must pupils work singly and not cooperatively in groups? It is because what are seen to be the basic values of a nation are involved that the content of the curriculum academic or moral, manifest or hidden, is an important focus for analysis and political action.

(ii) *National Intellectual Styles.* There is sufficient evidence for us to believe that there are differences between national intellectual styles. For example, the British academic tradition has often been described as conservative and empirical whereas the European intellectual worker has been portrayed as innovatory and theoretical in his approach. One attempt to analyse the basis of such a style has been made. Bourdieu has shown that the French intellectual displays a fondness for abstraction and worships a cult of brilliance which encourages an emphasis on style and talent at the expense of substance. Fluency and clarity of thought come to be more important in, for example, essays and written answers than precise knowledge. He has traced this national intellectual style back to the nature of secondary schooling and has shown how reports of examiners at both the secondary and tertiary levels have stressed the relevant qualities.[3] Clearly subjects, though international in their basis of knowledge, are filtered through national intellectual styles and those subjects that have a high degree of relative autonomy of the social structure will be less affected.

(iii) *Stratification*. The way in which systems of knowledge develop in any society is closely related to its stratification system. In a hierarchy in the exact sense, that is a society ruled by priests, literacy was a priestly monopoly and knowledge was used for religious ends, though in medieval Europe the situation was complicated by the power held by feudal knights over the church. In a class society power is based on wealth, and those with power wish to preserve the present advantage they have in the distribution not merely of wealth, but also of knowledge. In this way they can ensure their own and their children's future status. It must be remembered that, although much of the recent analysis of the control of knowledge has been in terms of capitalist societies and hence of social class, a somewhat similar analysis could be made of non-capitalist societies in terms of the groups holding power there. Thus, the schools that prepare for positions of high status will teach a curriculum that selects knowledge apt for membership of the ruling class or group. In the mid-twentieth century the way in which knowledge was stratified in Britain could be simply described in the following way: the public schools taught a selection of academic and moral knowledge that prepared those who would fill positions with much power in society; the curriculum of the grammar schools allowed some to move up into the ruling class, but also taught the managers of society; finally, the secondary modern schools taught to the majority of the population a minimal academic curriculum of the 3 Rs and a moral curriculum aimed to ensure obedience and happiness in the lower levels of society.

Selection mechanisms, controlled often unconsciously and with the highest of ideals by the powerful, existed to guard entry to the grammar schools or, in other words, to the opportunity to learn the curriculum needed for upward mobility. More recently, with the development of the comprehensive school and the gradual ending of the eleven-plus examination, these mechanisms have become less obvious, though they are still present in the form of procedures to direct pupils into different streams in the one big school rather than into separate schools. The curriculum in the different streams consists of subjects which carry different status. Thus, subjects associated with the university carry more status than handwork or physical education. Again, academic approaches to music and art, as found in universities, have more status than a study of jazz or the practice of embroidery. Finally, even though certain subjects carry low status, their content is still determined by those with power. There is no attempt to transmit through the school curriculum the culture of the working class, but only that of the dominant class. Knowledge and its representation in the curriculum is stratified in ways deeply dependent upon the power structure.

(iv) *The Moral Curriculum.* The focus so far has been on the academic curriculum, but its close relationship with the moral curriculum has several times been noted. In much the same way as Kuhn spoke of normal sciences we can imagine a 'normal behaviour' of a society upon which the moral curriculum of its schools is based according to decisions by persons who may be called agents of respectability about what is deviant and what is permissible behaviour. In the past the important agents of respectability were judges, clergymen, community leaders and teachers. Today there is less certainty about who these agents are, but, as was noted in discussing youth cultures in Chapter 5, leaders of the entertainment industry who decide, amongst other things, what and how much or how little we wear and what behaviour is allowable by young or old, clearly have considerable power.

There are cultural differences in the emphasis put upon the moral curriculum in schools, but unlike on the continent British schools have always made great efforts to influence moral behaviour. This may be attempted formally through, for example, lessons in religious education, or through physical education, games and the Duke of Edinburgh's Award, or through the head's addresses to morning assembly. In all these cases the aim is that pupils will internalize a specific vocabulary of motives; examples are: 'show respect to your elders and betters', 'play up and play the game', and 'give service to your fellow men'. More often, however, the aim is to teach the moral curriculum informally through the day-to-day operation of the school. In this way it is hoped that the prefect system will teach responsibility to those currently acting as prefects and obedience to those under them.

There are many aspects of school organizations which relate to the moral curriculum. Obvious examples are different entrances and cloakrooms for boys and for girls; the lessons involved here relate to treating the sexes differently. However, of more importance, because often unrealized, is the fact that in all schools there exist with official encouragement many *rituals* which have moral consequences.[4] This term refers to behaviour patterns that are usually unquestioned, but carry a message over and above the obvious actions involved. School assembly is often a highly ritualistic event. First the juniors enter the hall under strict control; seniors follow, trusted to behave, under less control and often permitted to wear freer dress, and to take special seats; next come the staff singly and sometimes gowned; finally the prefects, again perhaps with special marks of dress to indicate their office, precede the head; all stand up and sit once the head has taken his place. The lessons of obedience, deference to authority and to seniority, and of reward for acceptable worth are obvious, but they are made more awesome by being linked with a brief act of religious worship. After this the head associates his authority with all that has gone before and also makes announcements deemed important enough for this occasion. These may concern the results of school matches, problems about school rules, or even more minor administrative matters. This ritual repeated, often daily, throughout a school career may well form the attitudes of many pupils towards, for example, authority or about the place of cooperation in life at school and after.

The importance of such rituals for the moral curriculum can be measured by the extent of the reaction of teachers to rebellions against them. Some of the major recent battles over discipline have related to the ritual elements involved in what is seen as deviant behaviour. For example, in the case of senior boys who will not sing hymns or the national anthem in assembly the problem really is that the whole celebration of authority implicit in morning assembly is being openly challenged in full view of junior pupils. Again, wearing long hair, even when clean and tidy, is seen not merely as the breaking of a somewhat trivial school rule, but as an open challenge to the authority of both the school and the older generation. The present system of authority is in question. If the young succeed here what part of the moral curriculum will be questioned next?

The whole of the analysis so far depends upon the existence of positions carrying the power to decide normal knowledge and normal behaviour. In both cases, but perhaps more clearly in the latter, those who fill these positions have 'the power to *produce* reality'.[5] They manage the social pool of knowledge, determining how much and which specific knowledge shall be available to various categories of persons in that society.

B. The Control of Systems of Knowledge

1. *The Structural Level*

(i) *Power*. In our society an agglomeration of the upper middle class, often without careful definition called 'the Establishment', exercises power in various ways. They form or advise the government. They write leading articles in *The Times*, the *Daily Telegraph* and *The Guardian* to influence their peers in other powerful positions. They man the top rungs of the Civil Service, the universities, industry and even to a minor extent the trade unions. They work more by imposing a common set of ideas than by force, though occasionally the police have to exercise the latter at demonstrations or racial riots to support the approved position. The contemporary French social theorist, Althusser, following Gramsci has spoken in this connection of *cultural hegemony*. He uses this concept to cover a situation where a wide range of values, attitudes and beliefs, particularly, but not entirely, of a moral nature, that support the existing order and the interests of those who dominate it, is accepted as legitimate by those without power (MacDonald, 1977).

The acceptance of cultural hegemony is never total. Certain of the dominated groups may see their situation differently from their rulers and may challenge them. In this way change can emerge. For example, since the middle of the last century demands for political equality have had educational implications that have led to a more diffuse distribution of what was formerly seen as the élite curriculum. Furthermore, those with power often do not realize the way in which they are exercising their power to construct a particular version of reality. Thus, early in this century the doctors who controlled the School Medical Department had complete power to determine not only the extent, content and method of medical inspections, but also the detailed syllabuses in physical education, games, health education and mothercraft throughout the elementary, secondary and technical schools and also in teachers' training colleges. They took for granted the vocabulary of motives that they had learnt in public schools, seeing it as all that was needed for the working class to save the nation from the near-defeat of the Boer War, to see them through the long-drawn-out struggle of the first world war and to weather the depression of the 1920s and 30s.[6] More recently as a result of political change this morality has been challenged and most people now realize that it neither has religious sanction nor is applicable to all.

The crucial point is that such impositions of curricula are a result of those with power acting unconsciously in accordance with their *ideologies*, a term here taken to mean a system of beliefs and values held by a particular group whose members fill similar social positions. Usually we refer to political ideologies, but we can also speak of occupational ideologies, for example relating to teaching. Here we are discussing the ways in which the diffuse ideology of the ruling class, learnt at home and at private school, influences the curricula of state schools and hence the occupational ideology into which teachers are socialized. Many apparently rational justifications will be used in support of actions inspired by this ideology by those with authority. Thus, in the 1920s to have challenged the idea that the classics promoted the intellect and team games the physical and moral health of the nation would have been as heretical as it is today to question the notion that formal studies crush creativity and individual games promote physical and mental health. Yet such challenges make clear both the taken-for-granted assumptions upon which the present curriculum rests and the nature of the power which is exercised to support it.

(ii) *Institutionalization.* The example cited above of the School Medical Department indicates that systems of beliefs and knowledge become institutionalized as patterns of social positions whose incumbents are expected and expect to behave in certain ways, manifesting, often in bureaucratic form, the underlying ideology. The whole of an educational system can be seen in this way though it is perhaps more profitable to conceptualize it as a series of institutionalized examples of different ideologies, for example private or state schools, traditional or progressive schools and so on. Yet underlying all these examples is a general belief that all formal education should be controlled by the state in a minimal way and that some schooling, at least to the age of sixteen, should be provided for all.

In the same way subjects become institutionalized. Departments are founded in universities with professors in charge of a hierarchy of lecturers and others. Promotion is controlled. Teaching is arranged to promote the present version or versions of the normal science. Examinations are set to allow those who pass them to be seen as authorized practitioners of the subject, for example as physicists, linguists, engineers or home economists. At the doctoral level new knowledge is defined as legitimate or deviant; in the first case the candidate is passed, in the latter he fails. Professional journals exist at an international level to diffuse research that is seen as acceptable by those powerful figures who edit them. Similarly, academics act as referees for publishers in relation to possible new textbooks and learned monographs.

This system is closely connected to school curricula mainly through the workings of the examination system that controls entry to the universities and other places of higher learning and also by the fact that teachers learn the contemporary version of their subject whilst undergoing their training either at university or at an institution whose examinations are under the scrutiny of a university. Thus, even where teachers themselves control public examinations they rarely depart from the ruling academic paradigms. Furthermore, if this were to happen, the authority of those supporting the normal science against the deviant version would probably be great enough to cause its condemnation as worthless by inexpert out-siders. Such a situation is rare in Britain, but in the USA there is a range of institutions of higher learning whose degrees carry varying status according to whether they meet the academic standards of those in power in the high-standing institutions.

New teachers joining schools enter departments with names and structures paralleling those in universities, and under the control of departmental heads who usually also have the intention of main-taining in their syllabuses some version of the presently accepted relevant paradigm or paradigms. Even where an integrated curriculum is introduced it is based on the same versions of the normal sciences which underpinned the separate elements in the former traditional collection curriculum. Nevertheless, one source of change in school curricula can be the up-to-date versions of the relevant normal sciences that young teachers bring with them to their first posts.

2. *Organizations*

(i) *Outside Education.* Outside the educational system itself one set of organizations to which reference was made in the last chapter has a strong influence on the curricula of tertiary institutions, namely professional associations. Amongst the issues with which they are concerned one of the most central is the nature and standard of qualifications of those becoming members. Sometimes as in the case of doctors and lawyers in Britain entry to the occupa-tion is under statutory control and the legally constituted body has strong representation from the relevant association. The committee concerned usually also includes representatives from those involved in training new members; these academics are almost always former members of the occupation itself and members of the association involved. Interests inevitably overlap to preserve a somewhat conservative stance towards the curricula taught.

Other associations can achieve similar power in various ways. Thus, contracts may specify that only fully trained persons, for example engineers, may be employed on the project involved, so that the association concerned gains the power to control entry to important jobs and ultimately by convention to all posts in the occupation. Similar controls may also operate at lower levels. Thus, by the Industrial Training Act, 1964, the training of apprentices and other workers can be controlled by boards covering specified industries. These boards lay down the practical and theoretical knowledge needed to enter particular jobs. They, therefore, influence curricula in technical colleges. Once again the usual arrangement is to have representation from both industrial and educational interests on the committees involved in order that apt decisions about curricula are made.

(ii) *Within Education.* Similar institutionalized links exist within education to represent various interests in the control of the distribution of knowledge. Under contemporary conditions the Schools Council, set up in 1964, has a key position because it was established with a responsibility for both curricula and examinations. It is financed equally by the Department of Education and Science and by local authorities, but the Council itself has a majority of teachers and they therefore in theory control it. In fact, the teachers' associations have come to control nominations and, hence, the majority of the membership. This had led to a somewhat conservative policy, particularly in relationship to the present system of examinations, to which, despite admitted very real problems, no major change has recently been made. This system, as noted above, is basically still in the control of the universities whose largely traditional academic viewpoint therefore governs examinations, the majority of the candidates for which have no intention of entering universities. The consequent effects on schools curricula are well known, but the political situation outlined in relation to control makes change difficult.

The Schools Council, however, mainly sponsors developmental work on various aspects of the curriculum. In this field the subject associations of teachers in, for example, English or mathematics have a great interest. These associations act as pressure groups, giving evidence to government committees or publicizing issues; they are often represented on relevant committees, particularly those advising on curricular development. In addition, they organize conferences of a general nature or for the retraining of teachers, often in relation to specific new developments. They run journals and publish new curricular materials. Instances can be quoted of actions taken by such associations that have influenced the development of curricula. In the 1950s the associations of history and geography teachers resisted the development of social studies on the grounds, perhaps then realistic, that the new subject was incoherent and that their own subjects filled the same needs. More recently in several countries subject associations for teachers of home economics have been so keen to raise the status of their own subject that they have sometimes failed to question the perhaps dubious assumptions upon which the present paradigm of their subject is based.

What can be appreciated is that the process of institutionalization tends to preserve the present distribution of knowledge. The process does not necessarily lead to the establishment of formal organizations. At the school level conventions may emerge about what is taught to whom, and by which the teachers invariably act But at the national level the usual result of this process is the formation of formal bureaucratic organizations to which members are recruited on a representative basis. Political battles follow, the outcomes of which tend to be compromises, so that change is slow to come. This certainly has in the main been the case so far for those bodies responsible for selecting the knowledge to form the school curriculum, though some subject associations have a more progressive record. Whence then does curricular change arise?

C. Changes in the Stock of Knowledge

Before looking at the sources of change in curricula we shall summarize the forces for curricular stability. After this three categories of change will be examined: changes in paradigms, ideological change, and, finally and because of its contemporary importance, in more detail, planned curricular change.

1. Stability in the Curriculum

In Bourdieu's terminology the overt and covert effects of the processes outlined so far are to ensure a large measure of 'class reproduction'. Bourdieu sees any agency involved in exercising 'pedagogic action' to be 'the delegated holder of the right to exercise symbolic violence'.[7] In the case of the middle class there is some analytical profit in describing the process of schooling and the choice of the knowledge to include in the curriculum in this way, but for the working class to speak of 'class reproduction' is misleading, because the culture of this class is largely ignored in the process of selecting from the total social stock of knowledge to construct school curricula. 'Arbitrary violence' may be practised, but in the interests of the middle or dominant class. What may be questioned is how successful this curriculum has been in creating an obedient and deferential working class, a point which will be taken up again when examining ideological change. Here we shall examine what effect this attempt at middle-class cultural reproduction has on school curricula.

The selection of knowledge and know-how that is acceptable for curricula consists of material relating to the institutions of the dominant group or class. This is easily seen in the case of the moral curriculum, but is also the case for the academic curriculum. The version of the law, medicine, technology, art and music that forms the basis of school curricula is governed by that of the relevant associations, not by views of the working class. Therefore, much of customary law, home medicine, rule-of-thumb techniques, folk art or craft and music is ignored. 'The hedge-school of the witch and the shepherd' is forgotten.[8] Much of this lore may seem irrational to experts, but the results of the systematic bias in selection can be most easily demonstrated by examining some effects in the medical field. Many women in many different societies are now almost afraid to have a baby without trained doctors and nurses in attendance and in a highly capitalized hospital. They take for granted that they cannot bring a baby through the first year of life without expert help. Yet we know that all this is not and need not be the case. The effects in biology and health education of this questioning of the received medical wisdom could be dramatic. Similarly much other health, and possibly legal, wisdom could be 'demythologized' with implications for school curricula.

Another example, that of music, will be quoted. School music curricula have had the aim of teaching pupils to appreciate the elements of traditional music. In higher streams this was achieved by learning about 'serious' classical music, whilst in the lower streams a wide variety of light music was used, but with the same aim, namely reproducing knowledge of that type of music defined by those with power as worth while. The whole area of jazz and rock was ignored and when it was included in curricula it was used to teach the same middle-class aims. The emphasis was on musical literacy rather than on sounds.[9]

There are a number of effects, apart from the preservation of the *status quo*, of this attempt to impose the dominant group's culture. One, usually ignored, is the creation of a market for the productions of the occupations involved, for example doctors, 'serious' musicians and artists. But from the point of view of the curriculum what matters is that both commonsense knowledge and a valuable part of our culture is devalued by the schools.

2. Change in the Curriculum

(i) *Paradigm Changes*. In the exposition that Kuhn evolved about the way in which an academic subject develops the vast majority of the research that was done was seen to lie within the existing paradigm and to do no more than dot a few i's or cross some t's in the normal science. However, occasionally problems arise that cannot be answered by the science as it exists and a process occurs that leads to a paradigm shift. In physics, the science upon which Kuhn based his work, the revolutions associated with Galileo, Newton and Einstein are examples. In economics the Keynesian revolution, in English the reassessment of methods of literary criticism associated with Leavis, and in art the work of Picasso from similar paradigm shifts. However, increasingly in the examples cited we have moved from subjects with a high degree of relative autonomy from the social structure to those with a much lower degree. In the latter case there are several paradigms competing as the sole organizer of the subject. This situation is even more obvious in the field of morality and it raises difficult problems for the moral curriculum.

In these cases of subjects where multiple paradigms exist the question of who has the power to make their version stick is crucial. In Galileo's case reason was insufficient warrant for his new theory of the universe; the power of the Roman Catholic church was enough to delay the acceptance of the new paradigm. In the USSR for a time the power of the state could enforce as the acceptable basis of biology the theories of Lysenko, though ultimately even the Russian Communist party had to bow before the internationally accepted and basically Darwinian paradigm. Finally, in post-war years the theories of Velikowski concerning the evolution of the universe, whether they are correct or not, have been refused acceptance by the power, rather than by the reasoning, of established scientists.

Educational theories, perhaps owing to their large moral element, very clearly exemplify the way in which subjects having multiple paradigms are prone to competition, marked by ideological support, between contending versions of 'truth'. The never-ending battle between progressive and traditional versions of education or between nature and nurture as determinants of intelligence may be cited as examples. In the former context Bernstein has proposed the following argument. The usual contemporary version of progressive theory is based on an 'invisible pedagogy', whereby pupils are subtly made to do what is required of them without their knowledge and without any visible signs or obvious orders from the teacher. Bernstein sees this pedagogy as particularly appropriate to the needs of members of the new or professional middle class who themselves use similar socialization techniques and tend to be employed in occupations requiring such subtle means of persuasion. He contrasts the traditional middle class, rooted in industrial capitalism, who, to oversimplify, use more a direct or 'visible pedagogy' at home and at work. Unfortunately, the new middle class believes that if its children are to succeed in life they must eventually undergo traditional secondary education.[10] However, the point to be made here is that support for competing educational theories can be located in competing social classes. Once again that social factors may determine subject paradigms is obvious, the more so in the case of subjects with a low degree of relative autonomy from the social structure.

(ii) *Ideological Change.* Clearly where a subject is closely tied to the social structure ideological change will easily cause shifts in the ruling version of that subject. Such change may affect both the content and the distribution of knowledge. Thus, the political activity consequent upon such malfunctions of the industrial capitalist system as high unemployment, poor housing, the very unequal distribution of income and wealth was largely initiated by the working class. One of their more successful demands was for free education, eventually to secondary level, for all, since knowledge was felt to be one key basis for social power. Thus, a demand for fairness, based on a new and increasingly powerful ideology, led to a new distribution of the social stock of knowledge though, because of the middle-class control already referred to, the results did not meet the expectations of many persons. More recently changing ideologies concerning the place of women have affected the content of courses and of textbooks and the distribution of knowledge between boys and girls. Today it seems that those with power, and perhaps even their constituents, the general public, feel that a large enough proportion of the national income has been directed to education to meet current ideas of fairness, but that the returns from the educational system have fallen below their expectations; the result is a political demand, traditional in character, for accountability by the schools to the nation. Thus, an emphasis has been put upon couching curricula in terms of measurable objectives and upon the creation of monitoring systems.

Once again educational ideologies are seen to be linked closely to structural changes. Since 1945 two main stages can be observed. Immediately after the war there was a great demand for trained specialists to serve the embattled economy, but since the mid-1960s educational policies based on this demand have been criticized on the grounds that they lead to one-sided specialists and cultural élitists. In Bernstein's terms they are the expected products of a collection curriculum, which consists of separate, unconnected elements. Therefore, the critics see the cure to be a switch to integrated curricula which will, it is claimed, offset the present detrimental effects of the traditional curriculum by producing persons who are balanced in academic and moral nature and are full members of contemporary society. The arguments developed and the rhetoric used to justify the new educational paradigm clearly owe much to the present social situation.[11]

(iii) *Planned Curriculum Change*. The curricula of schools become obsolete for a number of reasons. Most obviously, the normal science may change in a revolutionary way so that even in the early stages the school curriculum must be redefined. Discoveries made in physics since the war have had such an effect. Secondly, there are the changes brought about because of the way the social institutions that interlock with education alter through time. Thus, there has been a lessening of the salience of religion for education and a rise in the importance of the economy, so that less time is now given to religious instruction and more to science and mathematics than a century ago. Sometimes the effect of the changing salience of an institution interlocking with education works more directly and more quickly. The so-called 'Return to Learning' in the USA during the late 1950s seems to have been due to a sudden realization that national security depended upon the military forces and the industries supplying them, both of which put a high emphasis on scientific skills and knowledge. Thus, although curricula in English, history and foreign languages were reformed, the first moves came in physics and mathematics. Thirdly, autonomous change occurs within the educational system itself. Research, which was always a built-in agent for change, perhaps particularly in the sciences, has now begun to affect the relatively new subject of education. The results are seen particularly clearly in the recently evolved new methods of teaching certain subjects. The teaching of mathematics, science and modern languages, all noteworthy for the possibility of their use in the economy, has been revolutionized.

Some of the indirect ways in which such changes enter the school curriculum were indicated above. Examples are the recruitment of new staff from the universities or colleges and the pressures of subject associations. However, changes could be brought about more directly by *fiat*. In Britain this was often done by examination boards, whose authority is obviously great. More recently a new technique, initially developed in the USA, of planned curricular change has been used, particularly by the Schools Council. When an area of the curriculum has been chosen and publicized so that opinion is receptive of change, a team is established, usually based on a tertiary institution, but consisting largely of practising teachers, to develop and test syllabuses and associated materials. After the results have been commercially published, where relevant, new examinations are negotiated with examining boards. Simultaneously the diffusion of the new curriculum to those responsible for training teachers and the organization of in-service courses is begun (Dale, 1977).

In its first nine years the Schools Council spent more than six million pounds on over one hundred projects; they were also associated with the expenditure of funds for the Nuffield and Ford Foundations. The methods used in this vast attempt at planned curricular change were based on the ideology that controlled gradual change was to be preferred to haphazard alterations or massive upheaval, and that variation in local conditions could be met by this way of creating curricular materials which could be adopted in whole or in part or not at all according to teachers' wishes. Any planned curricular change can be seen as an example of 'administrative processing of the cultural tradition . . . based on the premise that traditional patterns could well be otherwise'.[12] The question, therefore, arises: how successful is this non-compulsory form of curricular planning?

The first results of a study, made by questionnaire, interview and observation, of the impact and take-up of the work of the Schools Council have now been published and relate entirely to projects for the primary school. Heads reported that out of sixteen listed projects between 81 and 85 per cent of the sampled primary schools were using at least one project, 43 to 45 per cent one or two, and 37 per cent three or more. Eight of the sixteen projects were known by over 40 per cent of the headteachers and used in between 15 and 50 per cent of schools. Familiarity with reports, working papers, etc., was much lower, as less than 5 per cent of heads claimed to be well acquainted with any one of the twenty-five listed publications. The heads usually learnt of Schools Council developments from courses or conferences, whilst teachers heard from teachers' centres or educational television, though in their case initial training was also an important source of knowledge. Approximately one-third of teachers had stopped using a project, just under half of whom did so on changing schools.[13]

(iv) *School-based Change.* Some radical educators have criticized such methods of curricular planning on the grounds that they deprive teachers of their freedom and treat children as repositories for knowledge. Those supporting an extreme version of this ideology claim that curricula should emerge from negotiation between pupils and teachers, interacting much more nearly as equals. We shall see in Chapter 11 that to examine the classroom as an arena where what happens is determined by negotiations between those involved is a most profitable way of proceeding. But here a less extreme version of the concept of school-based curricular planning will be examined.

Teachers who see themselves as 'professionals' claim that they know what knowledge and methods are best-suited to their pupils and that, therefore, they should be responsible for making the selection out of the stock of knowledge of what shall form the school's curriculum. In a minor way this is already the case where, for example, the geography syllabus is built on local circumstances. Such curricular variation is, however, more usually justified on the grounds that it will motivate pupils rather than by some ideological argument. However, the danger seen by those with power is that very different local curricula will emerge or be negotiated which will in some way weaken the chances of reproducing the culture of the dominant class or group. An interesting example of this occurred in the mid-nineteenth century when an attempt was made in some English elementary schools to evolve 'a science of common things'. This was rooted in working-class culture and was more meaningful to the pupils concerned. Yet, despite the fact that basic scientific principles could be taught using this material, the dominant class squashed this emergent curriculum because of its implications for cultural and political change.[14] It seems that large variations in curriculum may only emerge within the bounds of the curricular normality accepted by those in power.

(v) *Opposition to Curricular Change*. Because today authority is often distrusted many external attempts to change curricula are defined by teachers as interference and opposed. Thus, much curricular change is negotiated, though often the process is initiated from outside the school as, for example, by the production of a new set of Schools Council materials. In this context Shipman (1974) has shown how the different groups in a Schools Council project on integrated Humanities teaching defined what was happening. Initially the project team invited schools to cooperate in an experiment to develop an integrated humanities curriculum; the teachers supported this effort, but with local perspectives; local administrators were suspicious as they were unwilling for their schools to take on responsibilities that could not be supported in the long term. However, eventually the project team, perceiving time to be short, withdrew power from the teachers and put the emphasis upon integration rather than upon the humanities; the teachers' interest diminished as power moved to the centre; and local administrators breathed a sigh of relief as they felt no major change would result. Differing distribution of power and changing perceptions through time affect the ultimate results of curricular development.

At the school level the views of teachers concerning change vary along different dimensions. In a recent study teachers of economics saw themselves to have a strong influence over both content and method, but to share their influence on content with both examining bodies and the authors of textbooks and on method with their pupils. They felt themselves free of control from many of those who tried to influence them, but not absolutely free. Thus, administrators supported them with advice and expertise; they had to take account of the political system in dealing with contentious issues; and their peers influenced their conduct as teachers.[15]

The opposition of pupils must also be taken into account as they can wreck attempts to introduce curricular innovations. Some fifteen-year-olds in a low stream who were following the Schools Council Mathematics for the Majority Project vandalized the materials and misbehaved badly, because they felt that the course was 'not proper Maths' and hence was 'childish', tending 'to slow us down'. In this case the coercive power of what they saw school learning to be was greater than the power of the school itself.[16] Some attempts to introduce new materials are opposed by pupils because they do not seem to be doing what teachers claim for them. Thus, in an innovatory comprehensive school methods based on individualized learning and on integrated curriculum were criticized because pupils saw the worksheets involved as direction and the themes suggested for projects as restrictions on the choice that teachers claimed to be offering them. Although the teachers had felt that they were moving from a curriculum based on the transmission of knowledge to one based on negotiation, in fact the new pedagogy carried the old message.[17]

Finally, parents may oppose curricular change. This may be done openly as in the case of the Australian rural high school where a conservative parents' association forced the teachers to withdraw a social studies textbook on the family because they felt it was too liberal. More often such opposition is indirect. Thus, in a nursery school in Berkeley, California, no attempts were made to impose the culturally approved behaviour for boys and girls; for example there were no separate toilets. Research based on participant observation, however, revealed the emergence of two groups that showed signs of forming a male and a female sub-culture, apparently based on lessons learnt outside the school.[18] No school is an island and parents clearly exert much influence on the contents that can be included in the moral curriculum, if only because they feel more expert in this area than in academic matters.

D. Conclusion

The curriculum is deeply influenced by the structure of the society, the ideology of those with power and of those who teach, and by the present state of normal sciences and behaviour. These constraints govern the nature of the distribution of the social stock of knowledge. In its turn the curriculum prescribes the academic and social behaviour of pupils and, inasmuch as the aims of those who organize it are successful, the social reality that they perceive will be recreated in those whom they teach. The fact that there are so many very different curricula in any society today would suggest that reality is being variously construed with differing effects on those who learn. For example, those who learn physics through a traditional course have been shown to view physical reality in a different manner from those using a more modern type of curriculum.[19] An increasing amount of research is being done on the curriculum, which is coming to be seen as one, if not the, central focus of the sociology of education. The question that must recur constantly in this work is: whose interests is a particular curriculum serving? Yet the answers must avoid the tendency sometimes apparent of interpreting all such interests as hidden but conscious conspiracies by a capitalist middle class to exploit the working class. Curricula usually result from unconsciously held ideologies which can be challenged, often successfully so that change ensues, by those of other ideological persuasions and they can be imposed by dominant groups in so-called socialist societies as well as by those with power in capitalist societies.

BIBLIOGRAPHY

R. Dale, *The Politics of Curriculum Reform*, Milton Keynes, 1977.

N. Elias, 'Sociology of Knowledge: New Perspectives', *Sociology*, Part One, May 1971; Part Two, September 1971.

T. S. Kuhn, *The Structure of Scientific Revolutions*, 2nd edn, Chicago, 1970.

M. MacDonald, *The Curriculum and Cultural Reproduction*, Milton Keynes, 1977.

P. W. Musgrave, *Knowledge, Curriculum and Change*, 1973.

P. W. Musgrave, *The Moral Curriculum*, 1978.

M. Shipman, B. Bolam and D. R. Jenkins, *Inside a Curriculum Project*, 1974.

M. F. D. Young (ed.), *Knowledge and Control*, 1971.

NOTES

1 B. Bernstein, 'On the Classification and Framing of Knowledge', in Bernstein, *Classes, Codes and Control*, Vol. III, 1975.

2 L. J. Weitzman, D. Eifler, E. Hokada, and C. Ross, 'Sex-Role Socialization in Picture Books for Preschool Children', *American Journal of Sociology*, May 1972.

3 P. Bourdieu, 'Systems of Education and Systems of Thought', *International Social Science Journal*, 1967, No. 3.

4 For a pioneering analysis see B. Bernstein, L. Elvin and R. S. Peters, 'Ritual in Education', in Bernstein, *Class, Codes and Control*, Vol. III, 1975.

5 P. L. Berger and T. Luckmann, *The Social Construction of Reality*, 1967, p. 137.

6 P. W. Musgrave, 'Morality and the Medical Department: 1907–74 *British Journal of Educational Studies*, June 1977.

7 P. Bourdieu and J. C. Passeron, *Reproduction in Education, Society and Culture*, 1977, p. 24.

8 *ibid.*, p. 42.

9 G. Vulliamy, 'Music as a Case Study in the "New Sociology of Education" ', in J. Shepherd, P. Virdan, G. Vulliamy and T. Wishart, *Whose Music? A Sociology of Musical Languages*, 1977.

10 B. Bernstein, 'Class and Pedagogies: Visible and Invisible', in Bernstein, *Class, Codes and Control*, Vol. III, 1975.

11 For a similar argument see B. Bernstein, 'Open School – Open Society?', *ibid.*

12 J. Habermas, *Legitimation Crisis*, 1976, p. 71.

13 S. D. Steadman, C. Parsons and B. G. Salter, *Impact and Take-up Project: a First Interim Report* (mimeographed), Schools Council, 1978, pp. 101–4.

14 D. Layton, *Science for the People*, 1973.

15 P. H. Taylor, B. J. Holley and R. Szreter, 'Influence on Economics Teaching: a Study in Teachers' Perceptions', *Educational Review*, November 1974.

16 J. Spradberry, 'Conservative Pupils? Pupil Resistance to a Curriculum Innovation in Maths', in G. Whitty and M. F. D. Young (eds.), *Explorations in the Politics of School Knowledge*, Driffield, 1976.

17 I. Goodson, 'The Teachers' Curriculum and the New Reformation', *Journal of Curriculum Studies*, November 1975.

18 R. T. Fitzgerald, P. W. Musgrave and D. W. Pettit, *Participation in Schools?*, Hawthorn, Victoria, 1976; C. Joffe, 'Sex Role Socialization and the Nursery School', *Journal of Marriage and the Family*, August 1971.

19 E. Brakken, 'Intellectual Factors in PSSC and Conventional High School Physics', *Journal of Research in Science Teaching*, March 1965.

10

School Processes

The views of academic and moral knowledge held by those running a school will have a great influence upon the nature of the interactions that occur within it. Some of the processes involved can best be studied at the level of the classroom and this will be done in the next chapter, but others can more profitably be examined at the level of the school and such an analysis will be undertaken in this chapter. First, the definitions of certain concepts that have important implications for educational structure will be considered. Views of, for example, intelligence or creativity help to construct the social reality within which choices in school have to be made. Secondly, therefore, the ways in which choice is structured in schools must be analysed. Schools vary in size and, next, some attention will be paid to the ways in which the numbers involved influence school structure. Finally, the social network within which any school is set constrains its operations and the final section of this chapter will examine the processes whereby the social system of a school is related to the parents of its pupils and in the case of secondary schools with the primary schools from which its pupils come.

A. Definitions of the Situation

In Part I a consistent differentiation was made between analysis at the social structural level and at the interpersonal level. This technique, as is invariably the case with such analytical devices, is somewhat unreal in its representation of social reality and one of the major problems in contemporary sociological theory is to find a way of satisfactorily unifying analyses at these two levels. One very profitable attack on this difficulty is through the concept of *the definition of the situation.* Ideas have careers as do persons and their present definition within a society or more often within a given social circle in that society becomes institutionalized.[1] This was clearly seen to be the case for paradigms of academic subjects. Such definitions are passed on to new generations and influence their activities. As already noted this is no guarantee that a definition will be accepted *in toto* by the next generation. The possibility of change in definition is, therefore, always present (Evetts, 1973).

The definitions with which we are here concerned are of two main categories. Firstly, there are a number of concepts related to the academic subject of Education itself. The effect of Education, the subject, upon the educational system is a fascinating socio-logical study in itself and here we shall look at the way in which both differing definitions of education and certain concepts within Education, such as those of ability, intelligence and creativity have affected school structure. The direct effect of these latter concepts is mainly upon the academic structure of the school. In addition, such concepts as that of mental health can influence the moral structure of schools. Finally, systems of sanctions, often very sophisticated, are constructed within schools to support the contemporary definitions of the situation and some examples of this process will be examined.

1. *Definitions of Education*

An important part of the knowledge that is transmitted through the available structure includes the set of definitions and supporting values that govern the very nature of these structures themselves. There are definitions of, for example, primary, secondary and ter-tiary education, of technical and academic education, and of special education, all of which influence the content of the curriculum and the structure of the educational organization through which educa-tion is given. These definitions may be agreed; they may, however, be contested and, even where formalized, hide major differences of opinion which may ultimately become the source of a successful redefinition.

It is extremely difficult for us to examine our own assumptions about the contemporary educational system. Therefore, the examples to be cited here will illustrate definitions of different levels of the nineteenth-century educational system (Musgrave, 1968). In 1861 the Newcastle Commission defined elementary education in terms of the ability to read 'a common narrative', to write 'a letter that shall be both legible and intelligible', and to know 'enough of ciphering to make out, or test the correctness of a common shop bill', together with a little geography and the ability 'to follow the allusions and arguments of a plain Saxon sermon'. This set of definitions was translated into the Code that governed grants to elementary schools and its Christian version of a minimal curriculum in the 3 Rs was influential for the rest of the century. In 1868 the Taunton Commission defined secondary education in stratified terms paralleling the contemporary social hierarchy that was accepted by those with power and also by many of the working class, then comparatively powerless. There were to be three grades of school. The first, for the children of the upper and professional classes, continued to the age of eighteen and taught 'something more than classics and mathematics'; the second stopped at sixteen and served the mercantile and higher commercial classes by giving access to 'knowledge of those subjects which can be turned to practical use in business'; the third was for the upper working classes and, in comparison to elementary education, taught 'very good reading, very good writing, very good arithmetic'. Finally, technical education was defined in terms of general principles so that in the 1860s when *laissez-faire* was at its height, it related to applied scientific education and not to technological processes, and anything else would have been seen as unacceptable assistance to particular firms; by 1910 when the spirit of *laissez-faire* was less powerful and the needs of the economy were more obvious this branch of education could be defined in more specific terms so that teaching about processes was not merely permissible, but encouraged.

The examples of definitions of education given here show how ideological positions can become institutionalized in educational structures. Once established these are difficult to change, but ultimately social structural change, resulting either from uncontrollable external forces or from internal political struggles, overthrows the present definition and establishes a new situation, in which a new definition is based upon consensus or compromise or upon a new power position.

2. *Abilities and Intelligence*

Many abilities are encouraged in schools. These relate to various categories of intellectual, physical and moral behaviour. We tend to use the term 'intelligent' in moral approbation of behaviour that has a strong cognitive content. Thus, pupils can be intelligent in mathematics or in football, but more than brute force is signified by the latter use. Such 'clever' behaviour varies by culture; styles of football vary greatly by nation and we have seen that intellectual styles also do. Therefore, criteria for intelligent behaviour must vary not only between fields of behaviour, but within them cross-culturally and if we want to measure intelligence in any field we have to realize that what is taken for granted varies between cultures.

However, the history of the development of the concept of intelligence is greatly at odds with this perspective. By the early years of this century some educators supported the view of Spearman that there was a general factor in all intelligence, whilst others backed Thorndike and Thomson in their belief that there were a number of special factors relating, for example, to verbal or spatial intelligence. In Paris just before the first world war Binet developed tests to help in the treatment of subnormal children and based his norms of mental age on the proportion, initially sixty-five, but eventually fifty per cent, who could correctly answer a set of apparently relevant questions. When the huge increase in the use of these tests came during the first world war, mainly to ensure the efficient allocation of manpower in the US forces, and subsequently in the 1920s and 30s to allocate grammar school places fairly in Britain, this social basis was forgotten and intelligence tests came to be seen very generally as measures of intrinsic and inborn intellectual ability, a view still held by many people. During the 1950s and 60s for a number of reasons, one of which was that an increasing amount of sociological research threw doubt upon this position, confidence in this view of intelligence was undermined, so that eventually these tests have now come to be viewed by most behavioural scientists as achievement scores in much the same way that reading or arithmetic tests are.[2]

These changing definitions of the nature of intelligence were reflected in a series of famous English educational reports. For example, in 1943 the Norwood Report, basing itself on current psychological theory, saw there to be three types of mind: the academic, who can 'grasp an argument for its own sake'; the technical, 'whose interests and abilities lie markedly in the field of applied science or applied art'; and the practical, who dealt 'more easily with concrete things than ideas'. This stance justified the advocacy by those who wrote this report of three parallel types of school – grammar, technical and modern. It was not until the Plowden Report (1967) that this view of intelligence was fully disavowed by such a national committee. Yet, as can be seen, its influence on school structures and processes has been immense.

Thus, schools have been categorized to meet a hierarchy of intellectual types that were believed to exist. The immediate implication of this system was that intelligence as revealed by tests should be graded so that selection was possible. Much attention will be given to this process of selection in Chapter 14. Curricula also become stratified to meet the supposed needs of those in each type of school or the streams within schools. Finally, testing for diagnostic work has become possible amongst various categories of 'subnormality'; this has related to maladjustment of pupils, especially delinquents, and to mental retardation, amongst both those in special schools and the backward pupils in normal schools. What is obvious is that the implications of one view of intelligence and of ability, or even abilities, are immense and the creation of a complex educational system of a particular character follows on its acceptance.

3. Creativity

Creativity is a particularly interesting case of a quality which schools claim to welcome and to encourage. Much is made in progressive literature of creative writing and work in art. Creativity, however, almost by definition is undefinable; it implies deviance that is evaluated positively and whose nature is not known until it has occurred. Yet one knows that real innovation in any field is not expected in schools. What is implied is that in the particular field to which the term is applied work or behaviour of a specific style should be produced. For example, a piece of comic writing that is rather like an essay from *Punch* in England or The *New Yorker* in the USA or a painting somewhat similar to Picasso would be defined as creative by the teacher. Work by Evans in Melbourne has shown that teachers in pre- and primary schools employ broad definitions of creativity in their teaching and tend to interact differently with boys and girls in this respect. It seems that they interact more and for longer times with the boys than with the girls that they see as most creative and more often dismiss boys than girls as least creative on grounds other than intellectual, for example because they misbehave socially. This work indicates the complexity of behaviour based upon teachers' definitions of the situation, many of which may have similar differential application to each sex.

Different nations give a different priority to creativity. Torrance has shown that when teachers rate pupils on ideal characteristics those from the USA and Germany put more creative traits in the top ten than do those from Greece, India or the Philippines. 'Independent thinking' was rated first in the USA, fourth in Germany, but was not put in the first ten by the other three nations. However, 'obedience' was given second place by India and the Philippines, but not even included in the first ten in the USA. Similar differences exist between schools organized to pursue different ideologies. Progressive schools put more emphasis on a definition of creativity of a certain type than do traditional. The latter type of school is often criticized by the progressives on the grounds that the emphasis given to the one right answer, particularly in examinations, teaches pupils to avoid all creative behaviour. However, Torrance has also shown that in three mid-western high schools the pupils themselves operated sanctions, for example criticism or exclusion, against creative peers, though they in turn developed a repertoire of adaptive techniques, for example persistence or silence.[3]

Creativity is a much desired trait, but criteria for it cannot easily be specified. Usually until creative behaviour is exhibited it cannot be called creative. Innovative behaviour or school work often challenges teachers and hence is not readily positively evaluated. In addition, the presentation of its results demands discipline of one type or another to which the teacher usually gives more weight than the pupil, so that conflict can ensue. Certainly the boundary between creative behaviour and what is seen to be naughty, irrelevant, provocative or unintelligible is often a fine one which the pupil has to learn to negotiate. Since criteria are inevitably vague in defining this term pupils will be in uncertainty about how new forms of behaviour will be received – as creativity or as deviance.

4. *Mental Health* (Wilson, 1969)
British schools, as has been emphasized, make much of the moral curriculum. Therefore, definitions of good and bad interpersonal behaviour are crucial to their operation. These definitions are worked out both through the direct teaching of academic subjects and also indirectly through games and rules about behaviour in school. This intermingling of the academic and the moral can be clearly seen in what today may be seen as an extreme version in the Report of the Chief Medical Officer of the Board of Education for 1919 (p. 171): 'For our business is not only to instruct the child or the adolescent and provide him with information on Hygiene, a body of knowledge, but to teach him actually *how to live*, at the top of his capacity, avoiding evil and choosing the good.'

As Britain has grown more wealthy the incidence of the diseases of poverty has lessened. Rickets has given way to dental caries and to the problems of mental health. In the early years of this century good or bad moral behaviour was easily distinguished from the results of good or bad mental health. More recently these two dimensions, the moral and the medical, have been blurred and problems of the former often reduced to technical problems in the latter; a child who steals does so because of personality problems curable by therapy. Hence, he is no longer responsible for his action, though the application of the correct therapeutic technique will put all to rights.

For a number of reasons (Musgrave, 1978), including the development and increasing influence of psychiatric medicine, a growth of the 'personal service professions' has occurred. Amongst these are counsellors, therapists and other specialists whose skills are largely exercised according to medical models, but are applicable in schools to those with problems of 'maladjustment'. Various systems have been evolved to make their services available to schools. Some are appointed to school staffs as counsellors or guidance teachers; sometimes teams consisting, for example, of a doctor, a psychiatric worker, an educational psychologist and a nurse are allocated to a group of schools; and sometimes individual specialists are on call to heads. In the last system coordination between the specialists may be hard; in the first, pupils in trouble may be in some conflict whether the newcomer is a counsellor or another teacher, as untrustworthy as the others; in the case where teams are available cooperation with teachers may be difficult, but some of the other disadvantages mentioned may be overcome.[4]

Prior to examining some examples of the structures and processes that follow from employing such counsellors in schools the definition of the common term 'maladjustment' must be considered, because assumptions are built into it that govern the ways in which mental health is encouraged in schools. In the Report of the World Health Organization Expert Committee on Health Education (1954, p. 25) the following passage occurred: 'The process of education is the means by which society specifies acceptable outlets for [the] innate needs and capacities of the individual. . . .' What must be noted here, apart from the psychological bias, is that 'society specifies'. In line with this view there has been a tendency for children to be adjusted to society rather than for the social structure to be seen as maladjusted to certain types of children. Deviance, mental or physical, is socially defined and, even where we agree that naughty or sick children are being adjusted to contemporary social norms, it is as well that we realize that this is what is being done by teachers and by those with whom they cooperate in the field of mental health.

5. *Counselling Systems*

Those running a school establish new or maintain existing structures, the main aim of which is to mould pupils into the image of an academically or morally good pupil. Formerly this was done in a very simple way. In a primary school the class teacher acted, as she still largely does, in a pastoral manner, and under the supervision of the head assumed responsibility for all aspects of the child's development. In secondary schools a form master acted in a somewhat similar manner, but occasionally, as schools grew in size, specialists undertook such a role as that of careers teacher. Now the complexity of the definition of the pastoral task is such that complicated systems of interviews with pupils and parents and of record-keeping have been evolved.

There is a study of one US high school that shows the possible hidden outcomes of these systems (Cicourel and Kitsuse, 1963). Lakeshore High School, located in a wealthy suburb, was built in a lavish style and was organized to collect what was defined as talent. Students were routinely categorized as able or not, so that they could be allocated to the various academic paths thought suited to their capabilities. However, this system progressively defined and limited the possible development of students by indicating to them their future educational, occupational and life careers. Counsellors ran a computerized record system that established a self-fulfilling prophecy. Students became what it was predicted they could be. One counsellor when interviewed reported in a puzzled way: 'Once in a great while, I have a student who does not see the situation realistically in school, home etc. They say, "Why work, plan, strive to bet his or that?" . . . They've had misfortunes, with indications of confusion and trouble.' Such individualists, defined as deviant, may even be seen as possible clinical problems and the difficulty is that for some students this may be the reality. The same counsellor admitted that he sometimes had to 'seek' problems. The structure that had been created both maintained the academic *status quo* and strengthened the position of the counsellors, the new bearers of the moral curriculum.

In Britain mechanisms providing labels in this form are rare, though they exist in relation to academic pathways. Often around the age of thirteen pupils have to choose a selection of subjects, aimed towards the natural sciences, the social sciences or the humanities. In the mid-1960s only six, or under certain circumstances sixteen, per cent of those taking eight or more subjects at the Ordinary level of the GCE at sixteen had definitely kept all future options in higher education open, whilst for a further thirty-nine per cent some flexibility was possible, but only if extra work was done in the sixth form.[5] Such a structuring of choices not only narrows the alternatives open later, but also tends either to confirm or to create certain specialized academic frames of mind.

A system of sanctions is also created in schools in order to reward the morally good and punish the bad. Little is known about this. Various actions may be seen as rewards, for example appointment to the position of prefect, verbal praise, the knowledge that a good report or reference will be given; the withholding of such sanctions may also act as punishments. Though corporal punishment still occurs in schools its incidence has diminished during this century; it seems commoner for boys than for girls and to be administered for both academic and for moral offences.[6] The growing influence of progressive education has resulted in more emphasis being put upon rewards than punishments. One problem about the operation of most sanctions systems is that they are worked in a routine manner and, therefore, tend not to create a feeling in the pupils concerned that they have been responsible for their own successes and failures. When children acknowledge this responsibility they have been found to show more persistence and effort in carrying out certainly academic tasks.[7]

B. Choices

Those running schools try to enforce their definitions of the situation, but they also may claim that they want to give their pupils some degree of choice. Often one expressed aim of teachers is to prepare children to make wise choices as adults. Few prescriptions concerning behaviour in schools or elsewhere are total, so that within them an individual has some room for manoeuvre to construct his own version of social reality and to develop his personality in this direction rather than that. Yet very often the so-called opportunity for choice is more structured by the school than teachers know or are prepared to admit.

1. *Choosing*
Choices were categorized in Chapter 2 as either recipe or reflective. Some important choices that will influence their whole life are open to most children, with the advice of parents and teacher, at a comparatively early age. Thus, sometimes they may choose which

secondary school they will attend; usually they can choose some of the subjects they will study, often to enter one specific job that they have already chosen; they can also choose at what age they leave school. To be made wisely these reflective choices should be based on a careful weighing of a number of factors, some of which are by nature nearly imponderable. Such choices must be based on a knowledge of related facts, of the relevant parts of the social structure, of the school, of the personality of those with whom one will be involved and, most difficult of all, especially for a young person, of oneself.

Hudson (1968) has shown that secondary pupils can differentiate between four selves: the actual self – who they feel themselves actually to be; the ideal self – who they would like to be; the perceived self – who their teachers take them to be; and the future self – who they expect to be in, say, ten years time. The weighing of each self when making a major choice is difficult, but is made harder because the four selves are interdependent, mutually influencing each other's development. Thus, to choose one particular future will influence how teachers perceive oneself. Indeed, the more reflective a choice becomes the more difficult it will be, simply because the alternatives and the factors to be balanced and weighed increase in number. It is, therefore, not surprising that some secondary pupils claim to make such difficult choices by methods of chance, for example the toss of a coin. However, in many schools, whether unconsciously or purposefully, great freedom of choice is not allowed. Ethically this raises a problem, since freedom is reduced, but personal security increased.

Much of the process of choice can be seen by considering the process of subject choice. Hudson has described the choice made between arts and science subjects at a public or a grammar school as 'one of the first of the major steps that the able adolescent takes towards his adult identity'. For the first time he can 'select and reject from any of the ways of life that his culture can offer'. He can try to fit 'a chosen style of thinking into some semblance of harmony with his private needs'. He must try to arrange the four selves that he perceives himself to be into some measure of an integrated whole. This may well be a realistic account of what happens for many in the type of schools that Hudson examined or in the top streams of a comprehensive school, but what of other adolescents? How much choice can they exercise?

Woods (1976) examined subject choice in the third year of a three-stream mixed secondary modern school. As a result of their choices pupils were placed for their fourth year in examination or non-examination classes. He interviewed all the pupils concerned and sent questionnaires to all their parents, of whom he also interviewed a quarter; he was a regular observer in the school and spoke often to all the teachers. As a result of his research he wrote a paper with the apt, but challenging title of 'The myth of subject choice'. The process seemed to him to work in the following way. 'Group perspectives' emerged amongst the pupils concerning whether a subject was 'liked' and whether it was 'important'. What 3A liked because it was important 3B often disliked for the very same reason so that for 3C the choice did not matter at all. The group perspectives, except amongst the members of 3A, did not match the rhetoric of the teachers concerning choice and the instrumental use of schooling. Parents were influential in sustaining their children's views through giving or withholding advice and through the nature of what they said. Middle-class parents were more involved than those from the working class in what went on at school and more sympathetic towards arguments based on educational grounds. The teachers, however, were the ringmasters and mediated the choices within the institutional framework. They had in their minds categories of pupil that matched the present framework of the school; there were academic children, drop-outs and so-on. They alerted their pupils to their view of how the child fitted into the system and by a constant process of hints and cues indicated to the child what set of choices was best for what they saw as his future. Direct counselling, though rare, worked in the same direction. The head, for example, in assembly spoke of the needs of the economy and of how ability in subjects that were of use mattered more than interest. The whole process fitted the pupils, whatever their interests and capabilities, into a more or less given number of positions in the school, so that it was kept operating as it was. There was always the need to rechannel some awkward cases, but these, being few in number, could easily be dealt with as special cases.

There was nothing sinister about this system. Those operating it honestly felt that on the whole they were doing their best for their pupils. Yet Woods' account raises some very difficult problems. Firstly, who knows what is best for any young person – his parents, his teachers or himself? And, if cooperation between those concerned in important choices is desired, how may it be achieved to give some equality to each party? Secondly, and more fundamentally, who knows the present nature of the child? And how may he be helped to develop towards those goals that he has for the present chosen? In the case of the choice between the arts and the sciences in a grammar school the young person is able to take a real part in making an informed and balanced choice. Yet almost inevitably the choice is confined to alternatives presented by the school structure; the only alternative for the rebel is to drop out in some way. But in the case of those in the secondary modern school, and they may in some measure represent the majority of young people, the pupils are apparently managed so that they may fit into the subject structure of the school. Thus, when the time of choice comes the young persons do as is expected and the institutional framework is only disturbed a little by the odd difficult case. Those in this last category of young people will be seen either as in some minor way disturbed and hence to be fitted into society or as the failures of the school, the aims of which can be justified by the ideology of the society around it.

2. The Effect of Different School Types

Different schools organized to match the ideologies held by those running them evolve different structures. The content of these structures can be seen as different cultures which their pupils learn to a greater or lesser extent. The question can then be asked: are there any characteristics of school organization which guarantee success in transmitting a school's curriculum? Because there are so many influences at work in the socialization of children, research to isolate the effects of the school demand complex statistical designs, preferably longitudinal in nature. In such studies many variables whose influence may effect outcomes can be taken into account and their changing affect as the child grows older can also be measured.

The longitudinal survey by Himmelweit and Swift to which reference was made at the end of Chapter 7 has begun to answer such questions.[8] In this research a group of London secondary pupils who had been studied at fourteen were interviewed after they had settled into the work force at the age of twenty-five. As noted earlier it was found that the school could have a powerful socializing effect under certain definite conditions. More specifically selective schools had the greatest effect upon their pupils.

The element in school organization that emerges from this study as crucial is the degree of forcefulness with which those running a school convert their goals into structure. One of the main probable reasons for the success of the grammar schools that Himmelweit and Swift demonstrated can be found if we consider King's work reported in Chapter 7. In the grammar school that he studied, the adolescents likely to disrupt it and to fail by its criteria either left or were forced out at the point of entry to the sixth form. As is often the case in formal education success of a school depends upon the early extrusion of its failures. However, another point may be made. Himmelweit and Swift's work was done on a cohort passing through the schools in the 1950s and 60s. Undoubtedly in the years since then the young have become somewhat more certain and vocal about their own rights and aims, some of which oppose those of many of their teachers. This change implies that if the study were replicated the schools might have less effect, but the factor isolated above would probably still be found to be important, so that where a school translated an ideology into structure in a strong manner it will have much impact in the direction desired. It was the force of a closely articulated structure that allowed choice to those in Hudson's study and then ensured that their academic results were good, and also that made choice a myth for those in Woods' secondary modern school. Furthermore, the aim of most progressive schools is to ensure maximum individual development so that, if a study were to be made of such a school, the main criterion for its success could be that the children had been able to express their individuality by choosing many different identities. Once again we see that the nature of the structure and the processes in any school are determined by the ideology of those running it or of those in power over them. This ideology may operate unconsciously, but its success depends upon the detailed way it is worked out in the organization of schools and classrooms.

C. Size of School

The size of a school has effects that have as yet been little investigated apart from those of a strictly economic nature. The larger the school, the more specialization is possible amongst staff and pupils. This has been an argument for establishing comprehensive schools since, it is claimed, in them a larger sixth form would be possible, thereby enabling wider offerings of more specialized courses to be available to economically sized groups of pupils. Lynn produced evidence to support this position when in the late 1950s he found that the award of open scholarships to Oxford and Cambridge correlated highly with the size of those in the sixth form of boys' independent schools (0·67), with the size of grammar schools (0·56). Lower, but substantial correlations existed for results in the GCE at all levels. Though he could not rule out such possibilities as that there were better teachers in the bigger schools he made a case that size of school, whether due to the possibility of better organization or because bigger classes provided a more stimulating and competitive atmosphere, did have some affect on success in the academic curriculum.[9]

However, contrary to expectations, there is work that suggests that the available opportunities do not necessarily imply that all pupils in larger schools have a fuller curriculum than those in smaller schools and this seems true in both the academic and the moral curriculum. In a study of a number of high schools in Kansas, which has been in part replicated in three high schools of differing size in Brisbane, it was found that, although small schools offered a narrower range of both academic and extracurricular experiences, yet the pupils in these schools both filled a larger number and undertook a wider range of such positions than their peers in the bigger schools with supposedly greater opportunities.[10] A richer availability of curricular experiences will not necessarily be used by pupils.

These findings about size can be related to one criticism often made of large schools, namely that pupils do not feel that they belong to or are fully members of the school in the same way that they do in small schools. This lack of rootedness in the social networks of any group or organization is often referred to as *alienation*. Sometimes it is felt that such alienation will result in absenteeism and in bad behaviour in school. However, in one study of thirty large comprehensive schools, made in 1973, Galloway did not find this to be so; rates of persistent absenteeism and suspension from school did not vary with size of school.[11] There do not seem as yet to be any studies that throw light on the effect of size on staff but, if anecdotal evidence can be trusted, staff may be affected more, though differently, than their pupils, especially in large secondary schools where members of staff cannot know all their colleagues and coordination of teaching and extracurricular activities is difficult.

The matter of class, as opposed to school, size is one that has caused considerable controversy. There is no doubt that the average size of classes has dropped considerably compared with the last century, when in urban schools classes of sixty or seventy were not uncommon and were accepted by teachers, parents and politicians. Size of class, and size of school, is perceived as large or small in the light of contemporary definitions of the situation. Today classes in the region of around thirty in primary and between twenty and thirty in secondary schools are seen as reasonable, given contemporary methods, by many teachers and pupils, and as the minimum possible size by most politicians. But many argue that further reductions in size could enable teachers to achieve better academic results. There is little conclusive evidence, but what there is does not support this view. In work done in junior schools in London reading standards in relatively small classes were not very different from those in large classes even after controlling for the social class composition, the proportion of immigrants and the length of education of the pupils. However, these results only relate to reading scores and do not take any account of the skill of the teachers concerned.[12] Furthermore, if the expectations concerning size of any of those involved or the methods used were to be changed the conclusion might no longer hold.

D. Relationship of the School to the Environment

1. *School Catchment Areas*

It has been argued that the school has comparatively little effect on many pupils in competition with such other powerful socializing agents as the family or the mass media. One way of considering the truth of this argument is to examine the effect of the physical environment of the school upon academic outcomes. Eggleston, for example, in a study of 240 schools in eight Midland local authorities found that indices of the age of the buildings of secondary schools and of the facilities for specialist teaching varied positively with staying on beyond the age of fifteen. The effect was significant but less pronounced at sixteen. Eggleston suggested that by this latter age pupils had learnt the goals of the schools.[13] In other words the tone of the school was becoming important.

Some work on the nature of the catchment areas of schools supports this explanation. Two studies are relevant. The first was undertaken in a mainly working-class area in London and discovered marked differences in delinquency rates amongst the pupils of twenty secondary modern schools, but for various reasons further investigation in these schools was impossible. However, a further study followed up these findings by examining the situation in nine secondary modern schools in catchment areas that were similar to each other in social class composition, namely largely working class. In addition, the parents had no choice as to which school their children attended, so that no hidden selection process was at work to distribute children of similar family backgrounds to different schools. Thus, the schools involved were remarkably homogeneous in their clientele. Yet over the period 1966/7 to 1972/3, on three measures there were big and consistent variations between the nine schools. Attendance averaged between 89·1 and 77·2 per cent per year; academic success, as measured by entry to technical college for which four passes in a local examination were needed, varied between 52·7 and 8·4 per cent; finally delinquency, as indicated by being found guilty before a court or officially cautioned before the age of fifteen, varied from 10·8 to 3·8 per cent. There can be problems with all statistics concerning whether they have been collected in a systematically biassed manner, but for the first two indices used here this seems impossible and in the case of the third confidence was expressed that, for example, the catchment areas of none of the schools was policed more rigorously than the others.[14] The only conclusion must be that the schools had a differential effect on their pupils in relation to both the academic and the moral curriculum.

The explanation of these results was again hypothesized to lie in the tone of the schools concerned, and subsequent work supports this view.[15] Two factors seemed crucial: the type of interaction between teachers and pupils and the type of career offered to the pupils. About the first factor more will be said in the next chapter. But in this particular case certain characteristics of the teacher appeared important. Where a relatively high proportion of teachers were either temporary or young and inexperienced, interaction worked against favourable results, but where staff were stable the opposite was the case. The second variable suggests a relationship to the world around the school, because the way in which such knowledgable teachers treat information about local opportunities for delinquency and the sanctions operating in the schools can offset the effects of the environment on pupils. Yet all that is again being said here is that there are very powerful forces at work in the networks within which the school is set, and that under certain conditions it can influence these networks through its pupils. It is to these networks that we now turn.

2. *Relationships with the Family*

The relationships between the school and the families in its catchment area have often been analysed in terms of a clash between the middle-class values that the school is trying to pass on through its curriculum and the mixed, but predominantly working-class, values of the families living locally. In other words there is seen to be a marked cultural discontinuity, for many, especially working-class, children as they move between their social positions as pupils and as members of their families.

A more sophisticated version of this type of structural explanation can be developed from work by Hargreaves and it covers the difficulty that not all members of either social class behave typically. There are many working-class families who, for example, encourage their children to defer immediate gratification. By using Bernstein's concepts of position- and person-oriented families a more realistic account is possible, which can also allow for schools with different ideologies. Children from families of the positional type can move easily to traditional schools where explicit control strategies are used that parallel those to which they are accustomed at home, but will have problems in progressive schools where an invisible pedagogy is found. However, children from person-oriented families will settle easily into progressive schools, since the invisible pedagogy matches their family type well, and also into the traditional school, because they easily identify with the goals of such a school.[16]

Even this version can be further improved. Witkin (1974) has pointed out that two sets of values are involved. Children can hold general views about education, but they also do have views about the particular school in which they and their families are involved. There is, therefore, the possibility that they may be closely involved in the school and greatly enjoy what happens there, but may nevertheless leave at the minimum legal age of sixteen. The middle-class child, or perhaps more accurately the child from a person-oriented family, will tend to hold positive values towards both education in general and his school in particular, whilst the working-class child, or one from a position-oriented family, may have a positive view of the school, but be negative towards wider educational values. Witkin has suggested that as a result, and contrary to predictions based on the culture-clash theory, many middle-class children will have positive views of education that will be disappointed at school, whilst many working-class children, having no great hopes of education, will be pleasantly surprised by their school. To test this hypothesis he examined the attitudes of some 3,400 pupils in their fourth year at thirty-six English secondary schools of various types. He looked particularly at attitudes towards English lessons, because in one version of the culture-clash theory Bernstein had predicted that working-class children would see traditional English teaching as a criticism of their mode of speech and hence of one central basis of their identity.[17] Witkin found that the working-class did evaluate their English lessons more positively than the middle-class pupils. This lends support to his view that we should differentiate between general educational values and those relating to the social system of the particular school in which any group of pupils and their families are involved.

Witkin believes that this finding can be related to the way in which the social system of any school is articulated with the network in which it is set. On this view middle-class families are more closely articulated with school systems than those in the working class. The concept of network is one that allows for interaction between those within it and reminds us that even the most sophisticated of these structural views presented earlier does not cope easily with negotiations between school and family. In these accounts teachers define behaviour and, although pupils may negotiate about how they fulfil expectations, parents do not have any influence upon the way in which teachers construct their definitions of what is to happen in schools. This is clearly not the case, as Witkin's work allows, but the process whereby parents do influence teachers' definitions can be subtle. Even where the teachers amongst themselves claim to work on the principle of 'keep 'em out of the school' parents can still be influential.

In a study of five secondary schools in Victoria (Fitzgerald, Musgrave and Pettit, 1976), undertaken by participant observation, a number of examples were collected that show how this process can operate. Two will be cited. In the first, to which reference has earlier been made, the conservative parents' association of a rural high school managed to have a social studies textbook withdrawn from use in the school but, as a result of this and the many debates about such matters, the teachers of similar subjects upon which the moral curriculum readily impinged constantly had to bear in mind their idea of these parents' views if they were to avoid local political difficulties. Thus, the essays that were set, the topics discussed in class and the books to be used for reading were all chosen with great care. In the second example a highly innovative urban technical school operated on an *à la carte* curriculum, the units of which were largely suggested by the pupils themselves, but attendance at lessons, even for those suggesting any course, was not compulsory. After about two years some parents became anxious about the probability that their children would not gain an apprenticeship, one traditional important outcome of technical schooling. Their criticism at open meetings resulted in the school redefining its ideas of choice so that, although pupils still suggested options, once they had selected any course they had to attend. In the first example pressure was largely latent and from a small organized knowledgable group; in the second it was manifest and from a larger group; in each of these examples parents were working to preserve the *status quo*. In both cases the school's manifest definition of the curriculum and the way in which it put this definition into operation was forced towards the wishes of the families in its environment, though we can say nothing of what the teachers continued to value in their own minds.

3. *Relationships between Schools*

Relationships between schools are less apparently influential upon their operations than are those between schools and families. The examples of sporting fixtures, the joint production of plays or the sharing of specialist teachers come to mind, but in all these cases similar norms are shared. This is also the case when reports are passed from school to school concerning the reputation of individual children. The receiving school only changes its workings in the case of individual pupils. Similarly, teachers, except headteachers, who move between schools, do not often influence their new school in any major way.

The main way in which the mode of operation of one school can be influenced by that of another is through such movement of pupils between them as occurs when children move from primary or from middle school to secondary school. The processes involved are analogous to those described above when children from a positioned family move to a progressive school. Discontinuities occur. Thus, in a study of twenty secondary schools in Victoria and the primary schools that feed them King has shown that pupils moving from progressive primary to traditional secondary or traditional primary to progressive secondary schools carry with them expectations of how their new school will operate that are in the main confounded. The result is that certainly during their first year of secondary schooling their progress, both in academic terms and as measured by certain indices of personality adjustment, is retarded in comparison with those pupils who move between schools with a similar ideology.[18] This is an inevitable consequence of the growth of school-based decisions about curricula, but the imponderable benefit to teachers of such a system can be offset by somewhat more easily measurable costs for the pupils concerned unless very careful countermeasures are instituted.

E. Conclusion

There are a certain number of definitions of the academic and moral situation that have a crucial influence on the structure of formal educational organizations. These definitions change through time for a variety of reasons, but in part under the influence of parents who are the surrogates of pupils. It is hard to know our own definitions, but we need to be wary and to remember that the pupil or parent who asks 'Why teach this?' or 'Why do it that way?' may have a real point. Until questioned in this way teachers rarely examine their own ideological assumptions which are basic to the definitions that they hold.

One common tendency in formal educational organizations is for means to be converted into ends. Structures organized for some, perhaps, justifiable purpose grow to be important in themselves. Thus, counselling systems are operated to keep them going rather than to help pupils make choices. Pupils are fitted to the system when on occasions the system should be changed to fit the pupils or at least individuals among them. Yet, although sociological analysis can uncover such potentially dangerous processes, it cannot tell us what the aims of teachers should ultimately be. Thus, many problems in the sociology of education can be reduced to statements of this type: those in power are ensuring through the system that they maintain or have set up that pupils become persons of a a certain type and this keeps society going as it is now. The implication may or may not be that this situation has an element of conspiracy about it. But the analysis cannot tell us how society or people ought to be. That is a problem for ethical analysis, albeit set in the context of what sociologists have discovered.

BIBLIOGRAPHY

A. V. Cicourel and J. I. Kitsuse, *The Educational Decisionmakers*, Indianapolis, 1963.

J. Evetts, *The Sociology of Educational Ideas*, 1973.

R. T. Fitzgerald, P. W. Musgrave and P. W. Pettit, *Participation in Schools?*, Hawthorn, Victoria, 1976.

L. Hudson, *Frames of Mind*, 1968.

P. W. Musgrave, *Society and Education in England since 1800*, 1968.

P. W. Musgrave, *The Moral Curriculum*, 1978.

R. W. Witkin, 'Social Class Influences on the Amount and Type of Positive Evaluation of School Lessons', in S. J. Eggleston (ed.), *Contemporary Research in the Sociology of Education*, 1974.

P. Woods, 'The Myth of Subject Choice', *British Journal of Sociology*, June 1976.

J. Wilson, *Education and the Concept of Mental Health*, 1969.

NOTES

1 A useful source for many relevant social definitions is R. Williams, *Keywords*, 1976.

2 For an account of this development see P. G. Squibb, 'The Concept of Intelligence – a Sociological Perspective', *Sociological Review*, February 1973.

3 T. D. Evans, 'Creativity, Sex-Role Socialisation and Pupil–Teacher Interactions in Early Schooling', *Sociological Review*, February 1979; E. P. Torrance, *Rewarding Creative Behaviour*, Englewood Cliffs, N.J., 1965.

4 P. W. Musgrave, 'The Place of Social Work in Schools', *Journal of Community Studies*, January 1975.

5 *Enquiry into the Flow of Candidates in Science and Technology into Higher Education*, (Dainton Report), HMSO, 1968, p. 167.

6 P. W. Musgrave, 'Corporal Punishment in Some English Elementary Schools, 1900–1939', *Research in Education*, May 1977.

7 P. E. McGhee and V. C. Crandall, 'Beliefs in Internal–External Control of Reinforcements and Academic Performances', *Child Development*, March 1968.

8 H. T. Himmelweit and B. Swift, 'A Model for the Understanding of the School as a Socializing Agency', in P. H. Mussen, J. Langer and M. Covington (eds.), *Trends and Issues in Developmental Psychology*, New York, 1969, p. 178.

9 R. Lynn, 'The Relation between Educational Achievement and School Size', *British Journal of Sociology*, June 1959.

10 R. G. Barker and P. V. Gump, *Big School, Small School*, Stanford, 1964; W. J. Campbell, 'Some Effects of Size and Organisation of Secondary Schools on the Experience of Pupils in Extracurricular Behaviour Settings', in W. J. Campbell (ed.), *Scholars in Context*, Sydney, 1970.

11 D. Galloway, 'Size of School, Socio-economic Hardship, Suspension Rates and Persistent Unjustified Absence from School', *British Journal of Educational Psychology*, February 1976.

12 A. Little, C. Mabey and J. Russell, 'Do Small Classes Help a Pupil?', *New Society*, 21 October 1971.

13 S. J. Eggleston, 'Some Correlates of Extended Secondary Education in England', in Eggleston (ed.), *Contemporary Research in the Sociology of Education*, 1974.

14 D. Reynolds, D. Jones and S. St Leger, 'Schools Do Make a Difference', *New Society*, 29 July 1976.

15 C. M. Phillipson, 'Juvenile Delinquency and the School', in W. G. Carson and P. Wiles (eds.), *Crime and Delinquency in Britain*, 1971.

16 A. Hargreaves, 'Progressivism and Pupil Autonomy', *Sociological Review*, August 1977; B. Bernstein, 'A Socio-linguistic Approach in Socialization with Some Reference to Educability', in Bernstein, *Class, Codes and Society*, Vol. I, 1971.

17 B. Bernstein, 'Social Class and Linguistic Development: a Theory of Social Learning', in A. H. Halsey, J. E. Floud and C. A. Anderson (eds.), *Education, Economy and Society*, New York, 1951.

18 R. C. King, 'Open Education as an Innovation', in D. E. Edgar (ed.), *Sociology of Education*, Sydney, 1973.

II

Classroom Processes

'The problem for sociology addressed in this [chapter] is the problem of "knowing" school classes' (Robinson, 1974). It is only in the last ten years that many of the difficulties in knowing classrooms have become apparent. Two main traditions of approach have been used: the psychometric and the ethnographic. Until recently the latter, anthropological in its techniques, received little attention despite Waller's still important *Sociology of the School* (1932; reprinted 1961); most work was undertaken by using increasingly complex measurement grids so that trained observers could count the incidence of such events as the types of questioning used. Three problems are now obvious to us about these studies. First, the grids are based on the adults', not upon the pupils', definition of the situation; they are imposed upon the classroom from outside it, often bearing little real relationship to the real culture within. Secondly, the context of what is coded is easily obscured; thus, the question 'What are you doing?' may be a request for information from a pupil, but may equally be a rebuke to him, and coding schedules very often can not make such crucial differentiations. Thirdly, these methods of research rarely allow data to be gathered about interaction patterns between teachers and pupils or pupils and pupils. In order to take more account of the meanings brought into the classroom by pupils, the context, and negotiations within the classroom there has been a switch from psychometric to ethnographic studies. This emphasis will be evident here. Furthermore, in this field of the sociology of education, perhaps because so much thought has been given to it, we are particularly conscious of the primitive state of our knowledge and, therefore, what is presented here must be seen as a set of related concepts that teachers may use in searching for the meaning of what is happening in their own classrooms.

A. Teachers' Perspectives

Teachers bring to their classrooms educational ideologies, often with a high level of abstraction, which they have to apply in a general way in order to develop specific beliefs and practices for use in their day-to-day work. When they are confronted with the everyday problem of teaching they have to convert their higher-level and generalized views into detailed behaviour to meet their present situation. It is to this lower level complex of beliefs and practices that we give the name of *teachers' perspectives*. Very often, as Keddie (1971) has shown, what goes on in the classroom cannot be directly related to the ideology propounded by the teacher outside it. Keddie contrasts the 'educationist' and the 'teacher contexts', but she does not focus on the interaction between these two perspectives, a vital interrelationship for anyone concerned with the sources or the diffusion of educational change. Here we shall examine the way teachers' perspectives relate to the administration and the stratification of classrooms.

1. *Administrative Procedures*

A mass of minor details governing what goes on in any classroom has to be decided either by the teacher or his superiors or by the pupils or by some negotiation between those involved. For example, even if a teacher forbids the posting of pin-ups on the reverse side of desk lids, pupils may still decide how their books will be kept within their desks, although the DES has laid down the number of desks to be placed in that size of classroom and the LEA chosen the type to meet DES recommendations. A teacher will, however, arrange the desks spatially to meet his own perspectives. If he is a progressive he will not want rows, but groups of desks. He will probably give his pupils freedom in the way in which they enter and leave the room; furthermore, interaction during the lesson between pupils will be encouraged, so that what his traditional colleague across the corridor sees as cheating will be encouraged as helping or as cooperation. Finally, he will organize the positions of responsibility in his classroom differently; monitors will change weekly or monthly and not be appointed termly or by the year; everyone must have a chance of experiencing responsibility or authority. One implication of such differing perspectives between teachers within the same school is that pupils have to learn from year to year in primary schools, but sometimes from lesson to lesson in secondary schools, a totally different set of behavioural expectations as they move from classroom to classroom. What is surprising is how well and quickly children cope with this source of possible conflict.

One ethnographic study, made during the first few weeks of children's time in a kindergarten, showed how they learnt the skills and meanings seen as important by their teachers. Much emphasis was given to sharing, listening, putting things away and to following classroom routines. For example, one day a teacher brought two dolls into the classroom and sat them in a chair; later she said to the whole group, 'Raggedy Ann and Raggedy Ann are such good helpers! They haven't said a word all morning.' After two weeks when interviewed the children used a very similar set of meanings concerning things to work and play with. Work was seen as any activity directed by the teacher that was compulsory, started at a designated time, and was completed within school hours. What mattered, it seemed, was that things were 'done', not that they were 'done well'. At the start of the term in September no child used the word 'work', but in interviews during October half of them did so. They talked more of work than of play. The teacher was pleased with their progress and repeatedly used phrases like 'my good workers'. This may be seen as a rather traditional situation. However, in a progressive kindergarten Denzin examined how teachers and children defined what was happening and discovered that what their progressive teachers saw as play was defined by the children as work.[1] It would seem that even where the teachers use different words a similar set of meanings is learnt by the pupils which governs the arrangements made within the classroom, hence reinforcing the process whereby values are transmitted.

Clearly in pre-schools adults assume great importance for the children as they are setting the standards and expressing the meanings which their pupils accept as reality. Even when surrounded by children of their own age pre-school pupils have been found to choose adults when seeking information. However, as they grow older the number of adult–group encounters increases relative to adult–child encounters and by the age of four the teachers begin to make much more use of group instruction and even of Socratic questioning.[2] Clearly the older the child grows the more power he has to negotiate with the teacher how the class is run. The teacher in his turn will apply his ideology to the particular type of pupil he has to teach so as to develop a perspective that comes near to matching his ideology in the specific circumstances concerned.

2. *Stratification of the Classroom*

One recent pioneering ethnographic study is by Sharp and Green (1975) who examined the ways in which three teachers in infant classes in a progressive school negotiated their perspectives with colleagues, pupils and parents. One of the views developed by these teachers that had most practical importance for how they operated in their classrooms related to the way in which they stratified their pupils according to the ability that they seemed to show. There were three strata. First, there were 'normal pupils', who formed a 'bedrock of busyness'; these children worked away busily, giving little bother to their teachers or to the other children around them; they achieved more or less what was expected of them at their age. Secondly, there were 'problem children', whom the teachers labelled as peculiar in some way. These children were difficult to cope with and even a threat, because their parents might feel that the school was not doing what was expected for their children. However, the psychological ethos of the school was such that all believed it was able to deal with these difficult cases; a child could be left to work through his problems and the teacher had the rhetoric to justify his method of dealing with the child to his peers. Thirdly, there were 'ideal clients', who were bright, alive, interested, intelligent and would 'get on' in any school.

The important point made by Sharp and Green is that the very perspective of 'busyness' operated openly to free the teacher to cope with the complex and ever-changing situation in the classroom, but latently to allow them to concentrate upon the ideal clients. Thus, the low status of the problem children was more or less clearly fixed and, though the status of the normal children might have an element of fluidity – some movement up or down was possible – the ideal clients were clearly an élite. The irony of their position was that they were only an élite because the other pupils had not conformed to their teacher's personal ideology.

There has been much criticism of what has usually been seen as the harmful manner in which teachers label their pupils, because there is much evidence that once labels are given they do stick. Some labels can be harmful and there is, therefore, much in the case that as far as possible the actions of children rather than the children themselves should be labelled, so that they do not internalize conceptions that may be detrimental to their self-esteem. Yet the problems of management and control in a classroom where a teacher is isolated for long periods with a group of around thirty pupils are such that some implicit hierarchy is inevitable. It is one way to cope with the problems of discipline and of allocating scarce resources to pupils. Without a hierarchy of pupils the teacher would not legitimately be able to give more time and energy to any type of pupil. The nature of and the flexibility of the hierarchy is, in other words, related to the state of social control within the school and classroom, and to the ways in which the teacher interprets these problems.

A study undertaken by Lacey (1966) amongst the unstreamed first-year pupils of a selective secondary school for boys has shown clearly how this labelling process develops. Amongst the pupils entering, the average number from any one primary school was 3·5, so that no pupil could rely upon a well-supported reputation that he was very clever or ordinarily so – all had passed the eleven-plus. However, the pupils gradually polarized into those who were academically oriented and those who found themselves to be at odds with the school. The process seemed to start because teachers differentiated the successful from the unsuccessful in line with their own teaching perspectives, so that school became a pleasant and rewarding experience to the former, who gained status from the recognition of their good work, whereas status was withdrawn from the latter. Once this process has begun those who are the casualties of the almost inevitable competition for the teacher's attention that operates amongst the pupils become an outgroup who will seek status in a group with its own norms, which will differ, as we saw in Chapter 5, according to the nature of the school. In Lacey's grammar school the focus was on the teenage culture, whilst in

Hargreaves' secondary modern school the fourth-year 'D' stream developed near-delinquent norms.

Another criticism of this labelling process has been that it favours middle-class children because they more easily match the perspectives of their teachers. In Canada Richer studied three middle- and three working-class children in three elementary school classrooms over eighteen sessions, ten of which were categorized as 'open' and eight as 'closed'. He found that in the closed classrooms teachers interacted significantly more with middle- than working-class children, but that the reverse was the case in the open classrooms. The latter situation was usually justified on philosophical or pedagogical, but also on egalitarian grounds.[3] The difficulty is that this study relates to teacher-initiated, and not to pupil-initiated interaction, which, as we have seen earlier, is likely to be less for working-class children. Yet, this study at least shows that some differential labelling that could be harmful to some pupils can be avoided if teachers are careful in developing classroom perspectives that match their egalitarian ideology.

B. Pupils' Perspectives

The perspectives that children bring into the classroom are developed mainly under two influences, home and school. The younger the children are, the less their experience of school and the more influence does their family have on their views of school. The older children, especially in the later years of compulsory schooling, have considerable experience of school and their perspectives are much influenced by whether this has been rewarding or otherwise. In addition, many are also starting to relate their perspectives on school to the world of work and even to their own future marriages, anticipating their coming life beyond the school.

(i) *Primary*. Sharp and Green (1975) were able to isolate a number of characteristic views of those who were successful parents in that their children settled into school and progressed to their teachers' satisfaction. These parents were knowledgeable about the workings of the school; they were interested in their children's schooling and keen for them to succeed; they could understand and accept with ease the system of demands put upon their child by the teacher;

and, finally, they were both willing and able to play the role of a good parent in a way that matched the teacher's definition of this role. Such parents must not hide their light under a bushel, but be recognized by the teacher to be a good parent so that the teacher in her turn can behave towards the child in what she sees to be the apt manner.

The irony of this situation in which the child is still somewhat of a pawn, learning the perspective that is expected of him if he is to succeed in formal schooling, is that if the parents leave all educational influence to the teacher, as they are urged and expected, then their child will be exposed to the competitive accidents of the classroom where the teacher's time and other resources are scarce. The effective parent is one who appears to leave all to the teacher, but in fact can compensate for any possible deprivations at school without the teacher knowing of this.

It is during these early years that the child forms his own perspective on school, basing its development upon the views that he brings from his home and upon his experiences at school with a very few teachers. There is evidence to show that there are many parents who want their children to do well at school, but who have no idea of how to play this role of good parent.[4] Thus, in a major study in Luton there were working-class parents who wanted their sons to go to grammar school to become engineers, but who, when asked to choose subjects that would help towards this aim, chose technical drawing and omitted any pure science subjects; others wanted their daughters to go to a selective school and omitted English or languages, but chose typing and domestic science. Maybe these parents chose correctly by some criteria, but they did not demonstrate the knowledge and attitudes that would help their children to reach a selective secondary school.

The part played by teachers, therefore, in developing children's perspectives on school becomes crucial. One teacher per year, the class teacher, will often be the main channel through which the formal educational system is mediated to a child. Very often by the age of eight or nine, when he is coming to feel his own power to influence the social interaction in which he is involved, his perspective on school will have been almost inflexibly formed as a result of these experiences with a few teachers. In a small study in the top class of a primary and the bottom class of a secondary school in Melbourne pupils were asked to write brief essays about what they saw learning at school to be. What was remarkable was the subtlety of these children's replies. They knew that they as well as their teachers were individually different, both academically and morally, and that this raised problems for group teaching. They had very largely accepted the map and the methods of learning offered to them by their teachers and, therefore, thought in terms of subjects learnt at school, rarely extending this process into the world around the school or into the home, though they palpably learnt from these sources.[5]

(ii) *Secondary*. By the time that children have passed to the secondary school their experience of formal schooling is considerable and they have formed a perspective on school, but, as has been noted, the move from primary to secondary does afford them an opportunity to change their views. This change can either improve their chances of academic success as when, for example, they are placed in an upper stream of a comprehensive school or lessen these chances if they find themselves in the lower streams, though under certain conditions about which we know very little individuals do overcome these disadvantageous circumstances. In either case by this age their peers are beginning to exert considerable influence upon them, sanctioning their pro- or anti-school views.

One major source of pupils' disengagement from school that increases in importance during secondary school is based on the fact that few schools make any attempt to come to terms with the sexual and emotional problems that are becoming central to adolescents' development during these years. Most schools exclude such matters from the curriculum so that their pupils feel school to have little relevance to the issues that in their view are central for their education. In their study, to which reference was made in Chapter 5, Murdock and Phelps found that adolescents very frequently complained about this. Under these conditions it is hardly surprising that they also found that the mean scores on commitment to school of their sample varied by age, school type and social class. Thus, there was no change in the commitment of the middle-class pupils as they moved from years one to three, but the scores of the upper working class fell and those of the lower working class dropped considerably. Furthermore, middle-class adolescents in year three, whether in grammar, comprehensive or modern schools, all had mean scores on commitment to school higher than the working-class respondents, but for both classes scores fell by school type, grammar being highest and secondary modern school being lowest.

There is a process at work here whereby pupils in secondary schools develop perspectives on school under a number of influences, which vary in strength throughout the period. The development differs according to the school setting in which it occurs. Two ideal typical extreme perspectives are the academic 'A' stream pupil from a middle-class home and the anti-school 'D' stream pupil from a lower working-class background. These ideal types can be used to examine the determinants of many perspectives on school intermediate in position between the extremes quoted. The results of such perspectives are usually discussed in terms of the moral rather than the academic curriculum, in terms, that is, of misbehaviour and delinquency. Keddie (1971) has, however, extended the analysis to show how interaction over academic matters is also affected. She noted that pupils in the 'A' stream did not question what counts as learning or as knowledge, whereas those in the 'C' stream did so, because they did not take their teachers' definitions for granted. The latter, therefore, were seen by their teachers to be 'agin school', whilst the former, falling in easily with the teacher's view of the academic curriculum, were much more sure of success. It is to this interaction between teachers' and pupils' perspectives in the learning situation that we now must turn.

C. The Learning Encounter

We have seen that high-level ideologies, claimed to be the basis for a teacher's actions when he is talking outside his classroom, develop into perspectives in his routine day-by-day work of teaching children. Ideologies influence rhetoric used in talk with other teachers and guide a teacher's classroom recipe knowledge, but do not necessarily exactly match the perspectives upon which he operates. However, in much the same way as when a reflective choice has to be made a teacher will consider problems or new situations in the light of his ideology in order to find a solution consistent with his present perspectives on teaching and on life more generally.

Many of the problems faced by teachers concern how to put into operation in the classroom ideologies that relate, for example, to equality of opportunity when the social structure within which the school is set make this well-nigh impossible. Secondary pupils may have perspectives that are opposed to the school; the parents of primary pupils may demand results in the 3 Rs, an easily measurable and traditional criterion, before teachers who have developed a progressive perspective feel these children are ready for such work. How is the teacher to mobilize attention, to communicate his views to his pupils? And where what he offers is refused, what is the nature of the process of negotiation that ensues in which the teacher tries to leave something, if not all, of what he had hoped with his pupils?

1. *Mobilization of Attention* (Hammersley, 1976)

The expected behaviour of teachers and pupils in the classroom has often been conceptualized in terms of roles, that is of the system of mutually expected behaviour amongst those filling the specific positions of teacher and pupil. Although this approach to the problem can tell us much about the boundaries within which those in classrooms are expected to behave along the various dimensions involved, it can explain very little about how those expectations arise, about where actual behaviour in a given classroom may fall within the tolerated bounds, or about the occurrence of deviance in classrooms. It is for this type of reason that sociologists have begun to look more carefully at the processes occurring within the learning encounter itself.

The teacher initially attempts to set up the encounter by enforcing within the classroom his perspectives, often expressed in a series of local rules, upon the use of space, time and resources and upon the permissible interactions between himself and his pupils and amongst the pupils themselves. The pupils, for example, must line up prior to entering the room and enter in a disciplined manner, so that, it is hoped, orderliness will continue. Those who arrive late must account for their rule-breaking, though the teacher himself need not do so if he is late. Permission must be sought to leave the room or even in some classrooms to move about during a lesson. Once the lesson is underway the teacher has the 'task of defending the lesson from disintegration via internal defection'. The pupils must be organized so that they pay attention to the official encounter, and any unofficial encounters between pupils must be prevented. The teacher measures his success by whether or not his pupils are attending or at least appear to be doing so. He will provide frequent opportunities for pupils to participate in the lesson, partly as a check for himself, but partly also to mobilize the attention of his pupils. This he will usually do by asking questions related to the lesson, but also by soliciting relevant questions from the pupils. Some of his questions will be little more than checks on attention; they will do nothing to carry forward the lesson itself.

To display 'intelligence' the pupils must have the cultural resources to work out what their teacher is getting at in his questions, but also to give answers that satisfy him. They must accept the teacher's right to talk for long periods, to ask questions to which he knows the answer – a very odd procedure in any other social setting – and to be the final judge of the worth of all answers. A progressive teacher will organize the encounter to give pupils more freedom than will a traditional teacher, but he will still usually retain the final say concerning what will be seen as knowledge in his classroom

Boydell has examined some aspects of the resulting contact between a teacher and his pupils in a study of six teachers in an informal junior school who were each observed for an hour weekly during mathematics lessons. Their actions were coded every twenty-five seconds. About a quarter of all their activity was directed at individual children, but, although about three-quarters of these teachers' conversations were about the children's activities, only about one-quarter was directly concerned with the substantive content of these activities and only around a tenth with higher-level cognitive contributions involving ideas, explanations and problems. These results may be attributed to the pressure of time in any classroom, but nevertheless they do not represent the usual image of progressive teachers as stimulators of ideas.[6]

The demand for attention in the classroom is also a demand for recognition of authority, because attention structures control in any lesson. Inevitably the reputation of any teacher, particularly amongst his peers, is very dependent upon the success that he achieves in controlling his own classes. In these encounters a teacher has some resources that give him power over his pupils. He will use these resources to gain attention when the legitimacy traditionally granted to him as teacher fails. He can, for example, keep pupils in at break or during the lunch period, thereby depriving them of the chance to play or talk with their friends. He can release them late after 4.0 p.m. He can also vary the nature of his lesson so that he withdraws the opportunity to see a film or gives more written work than his pupils like. One problem about many such sanctions is that their use may inconvenience the teacher as much as those whom he wishes to punish.

2. *Communication*

(i) *Language.* Clearly for most teachers their main strategy will be to impose their definition of the situation upon their classes by talking most of the time. Delamont (1976) has reported that during two-thirds of the time during which teachers and pupils interact someone is talking, and during two-thirds of that time it is the teacher who is talking. In the average secondary lesson that she observed there were about twenty-four pupil contributions, fifteen of which were oriented to lesson content. Thus, there is a very small chance either for the teacher to interact with every one of his pupils during a lesson or for his pupils to earn credit with him by, for example, giving a correct answer to one of his questions.

The characteristic pattern underlying much talk between teachers and pupils has been revealed in work by Bellack in the USA (Stubbs, 1976). He analysed audio-recordings made in some sixty classrooms and used as his starting point the concept of a language game which we owe to the philosopher Wittgenstein. Bellack proposed that four moves were basic to dialogue in any classroom: structuring; soliciting; responding directly; or reacting more generally. The teacher is the most active player in this language game; he normally structures the situation and solicits the pupils to be respondents by various types of question. Slightly more than three-fifths of all moves were found to be of the solicit-response pattern.

In formal classrooms language is used constantly to pass on information or to structure the situation to achieve this aim, whereas in a less formal atmosphere much talk goes on which is related to less general contexts and to such purposes as sustaining those informal social relationships between members of the class or with the teacher that are viewed as crucial in that style of teaching. However, even here there are the same problems of understanding the language used in talk about school subjects. Barnes (1969) has referred to the linguistic 'registers of subjects'. The language used in formal education, particularly at the secondary level, tends to include many technical terms that are used, often unconsciously, as shorthand for a whole series of ideas. The pupil in a science lesson who has not built up the full relevance structure with which the word 'environment' is now endowed will miss much that follows its use. Nor are these technical terms restricted to the natural sciences. Examples from the humanities are: 'irony', 'city-state', 'democracy', 'mass media'. Furthermore, teachers, and not perhaps only in secondary schools, tend to use a style of talk that Barnes has called 'the register of secondary education', which is formal, bland and may best be likened to the style of a government White Paper. This may be thought by teachers to be free of slang, but is often so dense and full of jargon that pupils do not understand, and relax their attention.

Such styles pass messages other than the matter apparently presented. In the case of the register of secondary education the children may understand nothing more than that history is a dull subject. Again, an open-ended question such as 'What could that verse mean?' might be understood as a message that in this class unlike in Mr A's more than one answer is acceptable. But children's understanding is restricted both by their ability to pick up such cues and by their competence with language. In the latter respect Britton (in Barnes, 1969) has shown that the outcome of discussion techniques, often supported as means to discovery learning, is restricted by linguistic competence. In some cases the secondary pupils with whom he was working made a 'group effort at understanding' which enabled them 'to arrive at conclusions that they could not have reached alone and without support'. However, other groups with different perspectives on language and group work reached no such results because they 'had some difficulties in believing others could seriously hold an opinion different from [their] own'; arguments 'were of limited educational value for pupils whose talk was limited in this way'.

(ii) *Paracommunication*. Cues as a means of communication have just been mentioned. All such non-linguistic methods have been termed *paracommunication*. Much work has been done on this topic in education as a result of a now-famous study by Rosenthal and Jacobsen.[7] They chose a random sample of children from several elementary schools in a US city and told their teachers almost *en passant*, that these pupils were 'spurters', although this information bore no relationship to their results on intelligence tests. By the end of the school year many of these children, in some classes a statistically significant number, achieved higher scores on such tests. This research has been severely criticized on methodological grounds, but it did spark off a great deal of research into the possible reasons for such labelling effects.

The most likely explanation is that almost unconsciously teachers indicate to their pupils by non-verbal means how they view their ability, so that these concepts of ability will be passed on without ever being expressed verbally to the pupils concerned. Brookover has shown that such labels not only exist, but are applied to the ability of children in specific school subjects. He found children could hold differing self-concepts of their ability in mathematics, social studies and English which could be changed independently.[8] A teacher may never speak to a child, but may nevertheless encourage him by the manner in which he pats his shoulder as he passes behind his desk when checking what his class is doing; the teacher may refuse a proferred answer from this same child, but indicate by the look on his face that he knows full well that the pupil can easily answer this difficult question; finally, whilst criticizing another pupil severely he may by a brief glance show to the first child that in comparison he is a sensible fellow. A term's warm but unspoken approval of this nature can have a major effect on any pupil's view of his academic and moral worth.

In one study that aimed to investigate such effects Brophy and Good asked the teachers in four classrooms in Texas to rate their pupils on achievement. They then observed the interaction between these pupils and their teachers. In various ways the teachers consistently favoured the high over the low achievers in similar situations. Thus, questions, that is opportunities for reinforcement of a self-concept, tended to be given to the better pupils; they were praised more and criticized less often; they were allowed more second chances and also given more feedback.[9] Very often such situations are considered to be examples of self-fulfilling prophecy, whereby a label is given to a child and then he is, usually unconsciously, treated so that it is almost inevitable that he will become what the label denotes. Sharp and Green (1975) have pointed out that although this may well be so what is important for both practical and theoretical purposes is to discover what are the conditions under which the prophecy both comes to be made and fulfils itself. One set of explanations about the process involved in the self-fulfilling prophecy to which Rosenthal and Jacobsen drew attention would seem to involve the use of paracommunication as Brophy and Good so clearly demonstrated.

Quite subtle gestures may also play a part. Hore investigated physical contact and eye glances between thirty Canadian mothers and their five-year-old children whilst the latter were working on simple verbal tasks. Neither physical closeness nor contact had the predicted effects, but eye glances were important in that the children were more successful where the mothers caught their children's eyes during the tasks.[10] The mothers, though silent, were available to encourage their children. Only words can communicate some information, but there are many non-verbal means open to teachers for passing on certain information and attitudes to children in their classrooms.

3. Negotiation

Teachers, then, holding perspectives on how classrooms should be organized, meet with their pupils, who also hold perspectives on school, in their classrooms and attempt to mobilize their attention by using various means of verbal and non-verbal communication. Quite often some pupils are unwilling to behave as expected and a process of negotiation begins between them. Initially the teacher will treat any infraction of the rules as deviance and use it as a possible basis for making inferences about the character or the academic ability of the pupil or pupils concerned. Since the situation concerning power in any classroom is normally perceived to be asymmetrical there is no expectation that an open process of negotiation will ensue. Neither the teacher nor the pupils expect to bargain as trade unionists do with employers, about how many minutes early the class will be let out if a given quantity of work is successfully performed, though from time to time teachers do try to build up their stock of goodwill with a class in this kind of way. The sanctions available to a teacher are, however, usually sufficient for him to achieve most of his aims.

When a pupil has offended in some way a teacher will give him the opportunity to expatiate his guilt, moral or academic, by being punished or by admitting an academic error ('Oh, I see!') or by apologizing ('Sorry, sir'), whereupon he is allowed, both by the teacher and his peers, to rejoin the moral or the academic community. If the teacher were to degrade any pupil permanently he would lose all leverage over him because whatever the child did he would have no more to lose. What is very obvious is that this whole system depends upon the pupils putting at least some value upon the same norms as the teacher. In the case quoted in Chapter 7 from Hargreaves' work the system of sanctions had become reversed in 4D so that punishments acted as rewards and vice versa. This is often the case amongst adolescents in the low streams of urban schools where pupils do not support the norms held by the teachers. In this situation the teachers are in difficulties because their legitimacy is in question. In extreme situations such pupils may be expelled since the school does not wish to resort to physical violence, but does wish to retain its legitimacy in the eyes of the remaining pupils.

Crucial to the process of negotiation in the classroom is the way in which teachers and pupils construct typifications of each other as a result of which they can make decisions about how to behave towards each other. Early in their experiences of each other, teachers and pupils will speculate about the kind of person the other is. Except on their first introduction to school, pupils all have some idea of a teacher against which they can type their new one and in their turn teachers have ideas built upon their past experience of, say, fourth-form boys against which they can type their new pupils. Soon each will elaborate their hypotheses; pupils will try a teacher out with certain mild kinds of misbehaviour to see if he is 'hard' or 'soft' and the teacher will test each pupil to see how he reacts to academic problems or to moral sanctions, to discover, for example, which pupils are 'intelligent' or 'sensitive'. At this stage each party in the process is trying more subtly differentiated labels as descriptions of the behaviour of the other. These experiments allow the typification of teacher by pupils and of each pupil by the teacher to be extended and clarified. After a time these typifications will become stable and resistant to change. Although we know little about the conditions under which this can occur, a pupil or a teacher may be able to change the way in which others have come to typify him.[11] Probably this can be most easily achieved through some outstanding action, very different from his normal behaviour, being noticed, leading to some such public comment as 'Who'd have thought so-and-so could have done that?'

One of the problems that teachers, particularly in secondary schools where teaching the class as a whole is common, have to face is how to pace their curricular material so that bright pupils are not bored, but so that the less intelligent ones do learn something. Some Swedish work is relevant to the basis upon which teachers negotiate this decision with their classes. Lundgren (1974) found that where teachers were using whole-class methods they pitched their lessons at the level appropriate for a steering group in each class of pupils which was situated between the tenth and twenty-fifth percentile in relation to academic achievement. The standard used in other words was not absolute, but relative to the ability of each class. Thus, in formal classrooms the teacher appears to negotiate a rate of progress with neither the very bright nor the relatively dull, but with the more intelligent of 'the normal pupils'.

The object of the process of negotiation undertaken by teachers is to achieve what is seen as acceptable academic and moral behaviour in the classroom. Furthermore, the hope is that this will be learnt and not merely acted out merely to avoid punishment. The analysis used here has focussed on the normal and the acceptable, and on the means of eliminating deviance. Another, and in some ways a more profitable, way of viewing this same process is to focus, not on normality, but on deviance.

D. Deviance

In the last chapter we saw that delinquency rates vary by school and that this was believed to have some connection with the views of the teachers concerned on standards of behaviour, both inside and outside the school. Such standards vary and within his classroom a teacher will try to lay down the boundaries within which academic and moral behaviour is acceptable to him. Such boundaries may only become stable, particularly in secondary classrooms, after considerable negotiation. In these cases the ultimate truce clearly makes life easier both for teachers, since order of a kind reigns without excessive stress, and to the pupils, since life in an organization whose rewards may mean little to them becomes more bearable.[12] But this analysis tells us little about how deviance arises within the classroom itself.

Stebbins made a study of thirty-six teachers in elementary schools in St John's, Newfoundland to try to find out how they viewed disorderly behaviour. He conceptualized his findings in terms of the teachers' definitions of the situation and saw them as having a 'disorderly behaviour set' which came into operation when deviance arose.[13] This analysis moves us somewhat nearer to the action, but still fails to explain how teachers come to impute deviance to certain acts of certain pupils at certain times in their classrooms. Furthermore, it assumes that all deviance is a function of the pupils concerned, which may explain some deviant acts, but not those that emerge out of the process of negotiation within the classroom. How, for example, does behaviour never exhibited before in a specific classroom come to be seen as deviant? Hargreaves *et al.* (1975) have made a major contribution to our detailed understanding of such processes, basing their work on observations carried out in secondary classrooms.

We are not here considering 'criminal', but routine deviance. All teachers have to process with great speed the multitude of actions that they perceive to be taking place in their classrooms and to act in relation to a host of small apparent breaches of rules. The actual rules in operation involve three main types: those laid down for the whole school, for example about the wearing of uniform; those concerning such specific situations as laboratories or the gymnasium; and, finally, those personal to one teacher – 'Jones, you know you don't do that in *my* classes.' Usually during a class in progress rules are not clearcut or coherently expressed. Hargreaves *et al.* found four categories or 'themes' around which teachers grouped their rules: talk, movement, time, teacher–pupil and pupil–pupil relationships. The actual enunciation of rules might take a number of forms which are not mutually exclusive: descriptions, statements of the rule broken, prohibitions, questions, warnings, threats, sarcasm or attempts to attract a pupil's attention.

However, all such imputations of deviance have to be considered in the context involved. The same words and even intonation may be used both in instruction and in imputing deviance. Jones may be asked to leave the room because he has been naughty or according to some previous arrangement to fetch some teaching materials from next door. Only the context will make clear what is intended by the words, 'Right, Jones, off you go now.' Because of the complexity of contexts and the apparent incoherence of classroom rules pupils have to learn to disentangle the meanings of their different teachers' communications and gestures. To interpret an imputation of deviance they must know the target – names are not always stated by teachers; the rule being broken – often the teacher assumes the pupil knows this; the action seen to be offensive – sometimes assumed to be known to the offender; and, finally, the action seen to conform to the rule. An example where all four pieces of information are made clear would be: 'Jones, you know you're not meant to be talking, so stop it and get on with your work.' No filling-in by the pupil is needed here.

Context governs rules in another way. Lessons can be split into phases within which the rules differ. Hargreaves *et al.* were able to isolate five phases: entry, settling down, the lesson proper, clearing up and exit. Even within the lesson proper a teacher will forbid talking between pupils when he himself is talking, but, particularly when progressive in his ideology, may well permit talk between pupils when they are carrying out experiments or writing up. Teachers use 'switch signals' to indicate to their pupils a change of phase and, hence, a change of rules – 'Right, you can get on writing this up now.' Confusion can result when pupils do not know or hear such cues and believe, or even pretend to do so, that another set of rules is in operation from that claimed by the teacher.

A teacher may interpret an act as breaking some rule because he believes that he has firm evidence; a boy may have hit another pupil in full view of the whole class. On the other hand he may only be suspicious that a rule has been or is being broken; a long, partly hidden glance along the row of desks or a shuffle of papers may make him believe that a pupil is cheating in a test. In this latter case the teacher will have to decide whether or not to attempt to collect 'evidence' to prove the infraction. The very initiation of this process will set off a counter-process by the pupil, who will try to prove his own innocence or cover the tracks of his misdeed. The process of typification outlined in the last section is relevant at this point. The teacher will speculate, and elaborate a view about the pupil and his actions. He will probably have done so often before, especially in the case of a class teacher in a primary school, about many of his pupils and will have constructed more or less stable typification of each of them. These will form the basis of his action when he perceives deviance.

Certain factors seen to be commonly influential in this process of typification as it relates to the imputation of deviance. The following seem to be important: a pupil's appearance, for example of apparent guilt or excess innocence; his usual conformity to academic and moral rules – 'Not you again, Gordon'; his friends – 'Gordon is in with a bad crowd this year'; and some judgement of the pupil's personality – 'He's not a bad lad really.' These factors amongst others will all be scanned mentally with great speed by the teacher when he perceives a rule has been broken, prior to making a decision on what is to be done. Pupils have reputations which they have in part themselves built up amongst staff, though such reputations are often attached by teachers to families – 'Her sister was a horror too!' In a cleverly designed study Seaver was able to isolate two groups of children in Chicago elementary schools. In one group younger siblings were taught by the same teachers as had taught their older brothers or sisters, in the other by different teachers. As predicted, teachers' expectations, based on the achievements of the older siblings, were supported on eight measures of academic achievement, whilst no correlation between results from children of the same family was found in the second group.[14]

A teacher may react to his interpretation of what has occurred or not. He will have to decide whether the act passes his threshold of seriousness, whether to imput deviance will promote so much disturbance in the class that by acting he may escalate the situation, or whether this is an isolated act that may lead to no further bother. With younger children, and even in the early years of secondary schools, he may be in a difficult situation because he is consciously operating on a set of temporary typifications of those in his class, so that not only will his decision be more difficult to make, but also his reaction may seem tentative or even inconsistent to his pupils.

The view of the pupils throughout this process is crucial, although, partly owing to the intrinsic difficulty of gathering sound relevant data, we know little about it. They too have their own rules, one of which, that no 'tales' are told, severely constrains the teacher's ability to gather evidence about rule-breaking in any classroom. Furlong has provided us with some data about the ways in which pupils construct typification of teachers. As a result of observing and interviewing girls in secondary classes he found that they defined classrooms in terms of whether the teachers were 'strict' or 'soft' and of whether they were 'learning a lot'. Lessons were typified as 'successful', or what he termed 'non-learning situations', or as those from which 'bunking it' was possible.[15] Teachers may or may not be conscious of or know the scope and progress of their pupils' typifications of themselves, but certainly in any process of negotiation such knowledge would help them to achieve their aim.

Hargreaves *et al.* (1975, p. 255) summed up their view on the commonsense knowledge of pupils and teachers about the processes operating in a classroom in relation to the imputation of deviance. They made seven points: (i) Certain rules are in play. (ii) Each party knows that the others know these rules to be in play. (iii) Certain acts constitute conformity to or deviance from these rules. (iv) The teacher will act against deviant academic or moral conduct. (v) Therefore, pupils will try to undermine the teacher's ability to recognize deviant acts by resort to strategies of concealment. (vi) Teachers develop rules for recognizing and means for investigating certain acts by pupils. (vii) Where the teacher has no evidence of a deviant act pupils are able to negotiate concerning the imputation of deviance. Through this complex process teachers try to bring bring about so-called normality, though this varies greatly according to context, in their classrooms.

E. Conclusion

The classroom can be seen as a complex social system, an arena within which teachers and pupils exercise various skills and differing power in the service of the hopes and expectations that they bring with them from outside. The perspectives developed in interaction by both parties are never static for long as renegotiation is always possible, perhaps to meet a new curricular aim introduced by the teacher or because pupils, as they grow up, feel more able to assert themselves. To cope with this unceasing flux teachers use various techniques, amongst which is that of applying academic and moral labels to their pupils. This almost inevitable and very common process, supported by an arsenal of linguistic and other more subtle forms of communication, may be harmful to pupils in that those to whom apparently derogatory labels are applied may come to see themselves as they have been described.

Teachers strive to meet the expectations of parents, colleagues and others that their pupils will learn the academic and moral curriculum. Their pupils may be either ordinarily inattentive or downright naughty; indeed, in both cases their teacher's faulty techniques may be the cause. This implies a constant effort by teachers to assert themselves against possible deviance. Their success depends upon the cultivation of a sensitivity to their pupils' views and tactics, an ability to judge motives and to balance many kinds of consideration before making very speedy, but irrevocable and public decisions. Furthermore, there are very few absolute answers, since what is normal and what is deviant depends very much upon context. On some occasions and in some classrooms actions and words are acceptable that would be outlawed at other times in other places. Teachers do have some room for manoeuvre concerning the academic and moral standards that they attempt to assert. But if they go outside present views held by the general public, or by administrators purporting to interpret those views, they will themselves be liable to be seen as deviant and powerful sanctions applied to bring them back into the bounds of educational normality.

BIBLIOGRAPHY

D. Barnes, J. Britton, H. Rosen and L.A.T.E., *Language, the Learner and the School*, 1969.

S. Delamont, *Interaction in the Classroom*, 1976.

M. Hammersley, 'The Mobilisation of Pupil Attention', in M. Hammersley and P. Woods (eds.), *The Process of Schooling*, 1976.

D. H. Hargreaves, S. K. Hestor and F. J. Mellor, *Deviance in Classrooms*, 1975.

N. Keddie, 'Classroom Knowledge', in M. F. D. Young (ed.), *Knowledge and Control*, 1971.

C. Lacey, 'Some Sociological Concomitants of Academic Streaming in a Grammar School', *British Journal of Sociology*, June 1966.

U. P. Lundgren, 'Pedagogical Roles in the Classroom', in S. J. Eggleston (ed.), *Contemporary Research in the Sociology of Education*, 1974.

P. E. D. Robinson, 'An Ethnography of Classrooms', in S. J. Eggleston (ed.), *Contemporary Research in the Sociology of Education*, 1974.

R. Sharp and A. Green, *Education and Social Control: a Study in Progressive Primary Education*, 1975.

M. Stubbs, *Language, Schools and Classrooms*, 1976.

W. Waller, *The Sociology of Teaching*, New York, 1932 (reprinted 1961).

NOTES

1 M. W. Apple and N. R. King, 'What Do Schools Teach?', in A. Molnar and J. H. Zahorik (eds.), *Curriculum Theory*, Washington, D.C., 1977; N. K. Denzin, 'The Work of Little Children', *New Society*, 7 January 1971.

2 A. S. Honig, B. M. Campbell and J. Tannenbaum, 'Patterns of Infor-

mation Processing Used by and with Young Children in a Nursery School Setting', *Child Development*, November 1970.

3 S. Richer, 'Middle Class Bias of Schools – Fact or Fancy?', *Sociology of Education*, Fall 1974.

4 J. H. Goldthorpe, D. Lockwood, F. Bechhofer and J. Platt, *The Affluent Worker in the Class Structure*, 1969, pp. 137–40.

5 P. W. Musgrave, 'Learning: a Sociological Perspective, *Australian College of Education Proceedings*, 1973.

6 D. Boydell, 'Teacher–Pupil Contact in Junior Classrooms', *British Journal of Educational Psychology*, November 1974.

7 R. Rosenthal and L. Jacobsen, *Pygmalion in the Classroom*, New York, 1968.

8 W. B. Brookover, S. Thomas and A. Paterson, 'Self-concept of Ability and School Achievement', *Sociology of Education*, Spring 1964

9 J. E. Brophy and T. L. Good, 'Teacher's Communication of Differential Expectations for Children's Classroom Performance: Some Behavioural Data', *Journal of Educational Psychology*, October 1970.

10 T. Hore, 'Social Class Differences in Some Aspects of the Nonverbal Communication between Mother and Preschool Child', *Australian Journal of Psychology*, April 1970.

11 See D. Hargreaves, 'The Process of Typification in Classroom Interaction: Models and Methods', *British Journal of Educational Psychology*, November 1977.

12 D. Reynolds, 'When Pupils and Teachers Refuse a Truce: the Secondary School and the Creation of Deviance', in G. Mungham and G. Pearson (eds.), *Working Class Youth Cultures*, 1976.

13 R. A. Stebbins, 'The Meaning of Disorderly Behavior: Teacher Definitions of a Classroom Situation', *Sociology of Education*, Spring 1970.

14 W. B. Seaver, 'Effects of Naturally Induced Teacher Expectancies', *Journal of Personal and Social Psychology*, December 1973.

15 V. Furlong, 'Interaction Sets in the Classroom: Towards a Study of Pupil Knowledge', in M. Stubbs and S. Delamont (eds.), *Exploration in Classroom Observation*, Chichester, 1976.

PART III

The Social Functions of Education

Introduction

In an earlier chapter we considered the family and its place in the social structure. It was seen that the family, as an institution, served certain functions. It is possible to analyse most social institutions in this way and to discover in what ways they help to maintain the society in which they exist. These are their social functions. Therefore we may ask the question, what are the social functions of the educational system? Just as we look at a car engine and say what each part of this machine is doing, so we may examine the educational system as a whole or one part of it, for example one individual school, and decide what functions it is performing. Furthermore, in the same way that machines do not always run smoothly, so it may be that social institutions do not fulfil their functions in in efficient manner.

This analysis will not only be of the internal working of the various parts of the educational system from primary school to university, but also of the relations between these parts and between the educational system and other social institutions, such as the family or the economy. It may be found that the way in which education is organized is not meeting the aims assigned to it. The sociological term used to describe this state is *dysfunction* and comes by analogy from the field of medicine. Just as illness brings dysfunction to the body, so there may be dysfunction in the social system. Furthermore, this element of dysfunction may be either *latent* or *manifest*.

When we look for the functions of any social institution, we tend to focus on the way in which that institution helps the rest of the social system at one moment. The picture is static, but we know that society is in flux. Institutions once established begin to have lives and to create values of their own. In consequence we must remember that we are examining a system prone to change. Equilibrium is rare; tensions are common. Often there is a balance between the consequences of contemporary social organization. In some ways it is functional and in others dysfunctional. Where, however, there is no balance, a political decision may be necessary to rearrange the institution so as to meet the nation's present aims.

In functional analysis the aims given to or taken by those operating the educational system or those upon which the teachers in an individual school are working, whether consensually or as a result of some power struggle, are taken as given. It is in their service that the system or school is operating. Imputing functions to a system tells us nothing about how these aims were decided or how the system or school developed to its present state. It is no more than an analytical technique that allows us to concentrate upon a certain number of important social institutions with which education has connections and to try to discover how they are interrelated. Or again it enables us to focus on one type of school and to try to see how it relates to other types. The functions imputed are not explanations, but are hypotheses or the bases for hypotheses that in themselves require explanation.

In the Middle Ages the religious function of education was of great salience; the educational system was controlled by the church and its main aim was to provide priests to ensure the continuance of the church. This is no longer the case, although the various churches still control some schools and colleges in whole or in part. In some societies the military function of education has been important; ancient Sparta is an example. However, in contemporary Britain, and indeed in most developed industrial societies, five functions may usefully be imputed to education, they are listed here in the order in which they will be considered (the last two will be covered in one chapter):

(i) The political function; this may be looked at in two ways. There is firstly the need to provide political leaders at all levels of a democratic society and, secondly, there is the demand that education should help to preserve the present system of government by ensuring loyalty to it.

(ii) The economic function; here the need is that all levels of the labour force should be provided with the quantity and quality of educated manpower required under the current technical conditions.

(iii) The function of social selection; the educational system is central to the process by which the more able are sorted out of the population as a whole.

(iv) The transmission of the culture of the society; here the need is basically the conservative one of passing on the main patterns of society through the schools.

(v) The provision of innovators; someone must initiate the social change that is necessary for a society to survive under modern conditions. Such change may be, for example, technical, political or artistic.

12

The Political Function

A. Political Institutions

In using the term, the polity, sociologists refer to that group of mechanisms which a society develops to deal with the almost universal set of social problems of deciding what is the common good and of ensuring that action follows upon the decision. Different social groups disagree about the form that their society should take, and the ensuing conflict must, at least temporarily, be resolved so that the present arrangements or organized change can prevail. In contemporary Britain, as in many other societies, a form of parliamentary democracy has evolved whereby the election of a national parliament and local councils allows citizens to take part at regular intervals in the political process by choosing between alternative parties and their policies. In theory Parliament has power to make laws and to initiate policies, whilst the judiciary through the courts runs the legal system, and the executive, at the national level through the cabinet and ministries manned by civil servants and at the local level through committees and departments manned by local government officers, administers policy (Rose, 1974).

Two recurring themes in political debate concern who shall have the power to make important decisions and how resources shall be divided amongst citizens. The first question relates to the nature of the élite and the second to the degree of equality. Both themes have been prominent in British political debate over the last century and have therefore, had an impact upon educational policy. At the moment political mechanisms have grown so complex that many individuals feel impotent before them. They have to act politically in a very indirect way – by choosing between rival élites at elections or by working through pressure groups. Today the average citizen rarely has direct access to power; the political system enables rival élites to come to working agreements so that government continues. This process seems so distant that individuals are beginning to demand chances to 'participate' through, for example, reorganized governing bodies of schools.

The nature of the élite that rules a nation is a matter for theoretical dispute. Some conceive of one more or less unified élite which rules the country. The commonly used term, 'the Establishment', covers this idea. Another view, of which Mannheim was a forceful proponent, is that there are a number of élites. Mannheim isolated six main types of élite: the political, the organizing, the intellectual, the artistic, the moral and the religious. He thought great changes were occurring in the ways in which democratic societies were recruiting their élites so that they were becoming less exclusive.[1] This matter of the servicing of élites is seen by many as one of the important links between education and the polity, particularly because the more open the selection is, the less is the distribution of power, wealth and income based upon privilege.

The second major issue to be discussed in this chapter concerns another very important need of those in power in any political system, namely loyalty to the system. This can be achieved with difficulty by the use of force in a police state, but a system is more philosophically acceptable and more economical of resources, and allows for easier administration, if citizens support, certainly the political system, if not the present party in power. Therefore, citizens must in some measure understand the key political concepts upon which the system is based. In Britain this entails an understanding of the nature of parliamentary democracy, including the role of the opposition, and of such political concepts as authority, power and legitimacy, if not under those technical headings. Loyalty is also ensured by the ready adherence to political symbols, for example the Queen or the Mayor, whose presence is usually surrounded with much ritual so that emotion becomes involved in the support of political structures.

When the authority of a political system is accepted as legitimate those in power can lead the citizens in the directions they wish. The Italian Marxist, Gramsci, called this situation, *hegemony*. When hegemony exists the ruling class can exercise total social authority over the subordinate classes; alternatives are ruled out, yet consent is given; legitimacy is apparently spontaneously granted. Such a situation is rare even during a national crisis such as a war. Some political commentators feel that during the 1950s hegemony was granted to the ruling class in Britain, but that this is no longer so in the 1970s. Hegemony is won by gaining unconscious assent to the values, beliefs, rituals and political processes supporting the present political system. Education in family and school is felt to be a major determinant in this process of political socialization which forms the second major theme of this chapter.

B. Education, the Polity and Élites

Structures have been evolved through which those in power exercise political control and leadership. After examining these we shall show how the educational system services the élites at national and local levels. Finally, because the concept of 'leadership' has assumed great importance in Britain and in the public schools, that is those that have been particularly concerned with the preparation of political élites in the past, we shall examine this concept from a sociological perspective.

1. *Education and the Polity* (Kogan, 1978)

The polity can be said to be operating a process of exchange with the educational system. It provides money with which resources of capital and teachers can be bought and it also gives legitimacy to the schools within the system and to those who run them. In return the polity on behalf of the nation receives loyalty and a supply of manpower with various competencies, particularly political and economic. This process is controlled through the DES, the LEAs and the governing bodies of schools.

The political parties involved, not only represent various social class and other interests, but also try to educate citizens to support their present or new policies. Since 1945 both the main parties have been much concerned with expanding the educational system in a way that could achieve greater equality of opportunity. However, each party has come to interpret equality in a different way. The Conservative Party uses what has been called the weak meaning of equality, namely that all should be given an equal chance to be unequal in later life, whilst the Labour Party has eventually come to subscribe to the strong meaning, that compensation for unequal backgrounds is necessary before equality is possible in education. This difference in basic interpretation has led to the pursuit of very different policies towards the reorganization of secondary education – Labour eventually wholeheartedly in favour of a fairly rapid move towards comprehensive secondary schools, the Conservatives holding on to the idea of excellence in education and, hence, tending to support the traditional academic grammar school.

At the level of local government these differences have led to decisions along party political lines so that different patterns of educational provision have developed. In a study of LEAs in the Northeast, Byrne and Williamson (1974) have shown how socio-political pressures, primarily social class in origin, but working through local political organizations, have resulted in differing allocations of resources between schools and other educational expenditure, so that two main patterns of educational systems have emerged. The first, found in areas predominantly working-class in composition and based on an egalitarian policy, is marked by proportionately higher expenditure on primary and lower technical education, whilst the other, more common in areas with a high proportion of middle-class residents and founded upon a more élitist policy, is characterized by greater expenditure on senior secondary schooling and scholarships for tertiary students.

As the proportion of national and local governmental expenditure upon education rose throughout the 1950s and 60s, those lower down the social class hierarchy either felt or were brought by political pressure to feel a sense of *relative deprivation*. They had more educational services available to them than they had ever had, but they now realized how great was their lack despite their present improved situation. However, the consequent political demand for even more resources to be spent on education eventually ran up against the economic troubles of the 1970s – nor was this situation only found in Britain; it was common throughout the democratic world. By this date there was also a growing realization that changes to the educational system could not alone create a more equal society, however that be defined. Thus, the way in which schooling was provided became questioned more commonly by those of all political persuasions. Furthermore, many of the other taken-for-granted assumptions of political thinking were simultaneously under question; the greater demand for individual participation in decisions about education is a relevant example. What, therefore, does become important is to try to discover where political decisions about education are really made.

Kogan believes that MPs 'do less to initiate than react to policies'. Parliament, contrary to belief, is more powerful in 'critique and review' through various select and standing committees. Yet the ministers and the civil servants in the DES do not stand high in the Whitehall political and administrative hierarchies. They are, furthermore, under much pressure from such interest groups as the teachers' unions, the media and, perhaps of increasing importance, the 'social sciences intelligentsia', whose influence upon the struggle for comprehensive secondary schools has been great. Traditionally the teacher has been free to decide much in his own classroom, though he is accountable to the LEA which, as we have seen, can take major political decisions concerning the directions in which its own system develops.

There is, therefore, a very complex process at work in which, over the last thirty years, the centre has decided no more than the broad outlines of what shall be done and within which much power has been exercised locally by LEAs and teachers. However, by the mid-1970s the operation of this system was being strongly challenged from several directions. Parents, as was true at the William Tyndale School, have opposed the right of teachers to follow an ideology that they themselves do not support. Local authorities, as in the case of Tameside, have challenged the views of the DES about how they should organize their secondary schools. Finally, the DES, perhaps in some measure forswearing its policy of non-intervention, formed the Assessment of Performance Unit to monitor curricular performance throughout Britain and, perhaps, to go some way towards establishing some formal measure of the accountability of schools. Yet negotiations between all the interests involved will presumably, as in the past, be the means of making future decisions. The change is not, on the whole, in the system, but in the attitudes and expectations of those involved in it. They are, for one reason or another, more aware of their political rights and responsibilities, and also more likely to want to exercise them.

2. The Education of Élites

(i) *National Élites.* Work by Guttsman (1963) has shown the changing social background of our political leaders over the last century. The Cabinet has become less predominantly aristocratic in its recruitment and is now recruited more from the upper middle and middle classes. By our present constitution a certain number of Cabinet members must sit in the House of Lords, though there is the possibility that these positions could be filled by appointing life peers, rather than hereditary aristocrats. There was a lag of a generation between the changes in the constitution that broadened the social composition of the House of Commons, and the subsequent changes in the social composition of the Cabinet. The lag was not just a question of political connections, but the new political generation had to serve its apprenticeship before reaching high office and positions of leadership. The old political élite had been marked by an aristocratic connection with the more exclusive public schools. The new élite seems to have been drawn principally from the professional classes and more especially from lawyers. Businessmen are under represented, perhaps because of the greater difficulty in their case of combining the earning of a living with Parliamentary duties. The intellectual level of the new élite is high. Some have been to the old public schools, but a fair proportion come from the new public schools that grew up in the nineteenth century in answer to the demand of the new middle class. Oxford and Cambridge are well-represented amongst these new men, whose careers at university indicate more interest in things academic than the old aristocratic élite had shown at these same universities in the nineteenth century.

(a) *The Cabinet.* When Baldwin formed his first government in 1923 he said that one of his first thoughts was that 'it should be a Government of which Harrow should not be ashamed'. Similar sentiments were attributed to Macmillan in the 1950s except that in his case it was Eton and not Harrow that was important. In 1951, 82 per cent of ministers in the new Conservative government had attended public schools; ten years later the proportion was 76 per cent. Labour cabinets have had a somewhat similar source of recruitment. Thus, on appointment in 1964, 43 per cent of Wilson's cabinet had attended public schools and 61 per cent either Oxford or Cambridge universities. The public schools, it seems, are still the main educational source for our political leaders.

(b) *Members of Parliament.* Cabinets are drawn from Parliament and largely from the House of Commons. What types of school have Members of Parliament attended in recent years? In the case of the Conservative Party the position was almost the same in 1955 as between the wars. In 1970, 74·9 per cent had gone to public schools and 24·5 per cent to other secondary schools, whereas the inter-war averages were 78·5 per cent from public schools and 19 per cent from other secondary schools. For the Labour Party the proportion who had been to public schools rose from 9 per cent in between the wars to 21·6 per cent in 1970, and from 15·5 to 57·8 per cent for those attending other secondary schools; these increases were at the expense of those who attended elementary schools only, a very minor source of Conservative members, but one which accounted for 75·5 per cent of Labour members in the inter-war years, but only 20·6 per cent in 1970.[2]

(c) *The Civil Service.* Entry to the administrative grade of the Civil Service is either by some form of examination or by promotion from the executive or clerical grades. Entry by examination would be thought to supply a genuine career open to the talented. However, during the inter-war years more than 80 per cent of the entrants to the senior grades by this method of entry and about 50 per cent of the entrants by other means came from the independent public schools. During the years 1944–52, 56 per cent of entrants by open competition attended independent public schools, 17 per cent direct-grant schools, many of which were in fact Headmasters' Conference schools, and 28 per cent maintained grammar schools. For more recent recruits, namely for those entering by examination between 1960 and 1964, the situation seems little changed.[3] The picture here is similar to that of Parliament. There is a fall in public school representation and a rise in that of maintained grammar schools, but a substantial proportion, about half in both cases, came from the public schools, using a wide definition of the term.

(ii) *Local Élites.* The rise of the Labour Party in local politics has made a considerable change in the educational sources of local leaders. From the few relevant surveys [4] in this field the expected stereotype seems to be true. Most local Conservative leaders, whether on the council or the committee of the local party, are drawn from local managers, small businessmen or shopkeepers, many of whom have been to grammar school and a few of whom have gone to public schools. This seems to be the case in both urban and rural areas. Most local Labour Party leaders come from lower managers, and from clerical and skilled manual workers, few of whom have been to grammar schools, but a greater proportion of whom in the near future will have been to grammar schools or the upper streams in comprehensive schools because of the greater stress on formal educational qualifications at this level. From his own research Rose (1974) has estimated the percentages of the highest educational experience of local councillors as following: university 9, public or direct-grant schools 18; grammar or technical schools 17; elementary or secondary modern schools 45.

The equivalent at local level to the national civil servant is the local government officer. The senior grades, for instance the Director of Education or Town Clerk, must by the nature of their occupation have had a long formal education. In one large Midland City Musgrove found that 76·9 per cent of the senior local government officers had been to grammar or public schools.[5] At the middle levels of the local government service it would seem that many make a career who have left grammar school at sixteen. The grammar and public schools were also found to provide the education of many local leaders, both men and women, in voluntary organizations such as the scouts and guides, and the Red Cross.[6]

3. Education for Leadership

It is very clear that at national level a majority of our political élite is still educated at public schools and at local level at maintained grammar schools. The influence of the public schools on the aims and organization of the grammar schools and on the comprehensive schools where many, especially local, leaders in future will be educated is well known. One of the most important claims of the public schools has been that they can train boys to become leaders. They aim to give our future leaders the sense of duty and responsibility to their country which will ensure that their former pupils will use their talents as leaders, and these schools further believe that they can inculcate the social skills needed by leaders. In other countries, such as the USSR and to a large extent the USA, political leaders are not educated apart. Can the British system be justified?

The early attempts of psychologists to study the nature of leadership concentrated upon the personality traits displayed by those considered to be leaders. The results were inconclusive. In a critique of twenty studies made up to 1936 seventy-nine different traits were reported.[7] Only one trait was common to as many as ten of the studies and that was intelligence.

As a result of the failure of this type of investigation, psychologists have turned their attention away from the concept that the leader is a person who fulfils a special role in a group of people with a shared set of values. The only factor common to all leadership situations is that the other roles in the group are dependent upon the leader's role to fulfil the aim of that particular group. But in different situations a different set of qualities is required to fill the role of leader. For example, the role of the army captain in action demands different traits from that needed by the scientist leading a research team. To a schoolteacher it is clear that the headmaster of a public school must have different qualities from the headmaster of a secondary modern school. The conclusions to be drawn here are that the personality traits demanded in leaders vary from situation to situation, but that the position of the leader is marked by the structural dependence of the roles in the group on his role. Possibly the only personality trait that may be demanded in a leader is that of intelligence.

There are groups that need leaders at all levels of society. We should not be surprised to read that adolescent boys in Liverpool organized a football league with matches every Saturday morning, each team in charge of a boy captain; they did this without any help or encouragement from adults.[8] Again, an investigation compared leadership amongst two school classes of thirteen-year-old boys in Glasgow. The first group was from one of the best fee-paying schools, whilst the other was in one of the toughest non-selective secondary schools in the city. It was found that the general trait of leadership was distributed in each group according to the curve or normal error.[9] At all socio-economic levels men and women fill the role of leader.

The claim of the public schools to train leaders has usually been based upon the fact that they could bring out the qualities essential for leadership in boys. We can now see that this is impossible, since different qualities are required in different situations. It is even difficult to argue the case put by the public schools in their own terms since no one has been able to agree what are the traits that are vital in leaders. What then can the educational system do to educate the potential leaders that exist at all socio-economic levels? It would seem that any policy of educating for leadership must be based on the foregoing analysis.

In the first place at every level of leadership intelligence seems necessary. Any educational system that selects by intelligence, whether between schools or within them, will influence the supply of leaders. A second lesson to be drawn from the analysis of leadership is that no one will take the role of leader unless he feels impelled to do so. The motive is essential. The public schools did give many young men a deep sense of service, particularly of a political nature, and this, rather than any special training in the necessary personality traits, led such men to grasp the role of leader that was offered to them in many different situations.[10] Finally, the prefect system was supposedly an agent in training leaders. Originally, as we have seen, it rested on domination by force, but in its present, less authoritarian form it can have a place in educating leaders. Children who are prefects have the chance to lead others in all the activities in a school. If the many activities in any school could be systematically divided and children given the chance to lead in each sphere, far more children than under the present unitary prefect system would have the chance of acting as leaders.

C. Political Socialization

The general process of political socialization will be examined here first, prior to looking at the part played in it by certain of the agents of socialization. At each stage of the discussion we shall differentiate between political motives, attitudes and knowledge.

1. The Process of Political Socialization

(i) *Motives*. Loyalty to a political system, whether conscious or not, depends upon apt motivation, more especially to accept the authority of those in power. The commonly proposed theory about the source of such motivation states that the acceptance of political authority is learnt in the family. The child early on learns to obey and to accept the authority of his parents. When older he generalizes this learning from familial to political authority figures and eventually to the more abstract concept of the political system.

One of the first authority figures impinging upon the child from outside the family that has a direct relevance for political socialization is often the policeman. The Newsons found that parents used external authority figures to threaten their children. They rarely used teachers or doctors, but the parents of twenty-two per cent (six middle- and thirty-nine lower working-class) of all the four-year-olds in their sample in Nottingham reported using the policeman as a threat. Research in both the USA and Australia (Connell, 1971) has emphasized the way in which early concepts of government are focussed around personal views of characteristic figures; the President and the Queen are other major early links between the child and the political system.

Children tend to see such figures as benevolent and competent, more so in the USA than in Australia. Comparable findings were reported in research into the political development between the ages of twelve and fourteen of 480 children in Aberdeen. Boys and girls had very favourable views of the Prime Minister, a public figure who was found to have great salience for children of this age range, and of the Lord Provost (Lord Mayor), in that at both twelve and fourteen never more than 12 per cent in the first and 22·8 per cent in the latter case thought that these political figures did 'not work as hard as most people'. However, they were, perhaps, more critical of the Queen, since at twelve 42·3 and at fourteen 28·6 per cent placed her in this category.[11] It does, however, seem that this benevolent view depends upon the background in which the children grow up. Thus, in an area of Kentucky characterized by much unemployment, few chances of work for women and much poverty, the authority structure of the family, and particularly the position of the father, was very different from that typical of the USA in the 1960s and the children developed a view of the President as less competent and even somewhat malevolent.[12]

The ascribed role of sex does seem to affect the process of political socialization, though there is some difference of opinion about when this influence operates, in that women are generally found to be less politically active or interested than men. In Aberdeen, by fourteen, girls already displayed this tendency and measures of political interest and knowledge differentiated between the sexes more powerfully than between the social classes. However, in a study of the political attitudes of 627 boys and girls aged eleven to seventeen at grammar and modern schools in Exeter few significant differences between the sexes were found, though those that did exist were all in the expected direction. Few of these differences increased with age, so that the suggestion was made that the main socializing influences operated after leaving school when boys entered work and joined trade unions, whilst for many girls much of the time between the ages of eighteen and thirty-five was spent in the normally non-political environment of the family.[13]

(ii) *Attitudes.* Given that an individual is loyal to the political system, one crucial attitude, particularly in a democracy, concerns whether or not he feels able to influence that system. This attitude is usually referred to as *political efficacy*. The potency of this attitude has been found in the USA to grow between the ages of three and eight. In one large study of political socialization in New Haven, Connecticut, of relevance is Greenstein's (1965) finding that more than two-thirds of his sample of children of elementary school age agreed that it 'makes much difference who wins an election'. However, Connell's data, gathered in Sydney, show that disenchantment with one's political efficacy may begin to grow after thirteen. In Aberdeen, just over half of the children at both twelve and fourteen felt that their families were politically powerful, and during this age range, within which in Scotland the move is made from primary to secondary school, the middle-class boys, namely those of whom more were in grammar schools, moved towards a great belief in political efficacy, whilst the working-class girls became less sure of their efficacy.

Such beliefs about political efficacy are organized around the ideologies of political parties which, as we shall see later, are often learnt in the family. These ideologies are learnt, at least in a primitive way, in late childhood and in early adolescence and structure the way in which political efficacy is directed.

(iii) *Knowledge*. One may be loyal and have a great belief in one's power to influence political events, but yet be ignorant of how to do so or of the nature of the present political structure. One measure of such political knowledge that has been used is whether or not a person knows the names and duties of various political positions. Greenstein found that the name of the President of the USA was known by 97 per cent of his eleven- to thirteen-year-olds, whilst 99 per cent knew the name of the Mayor of New Haven; the very high figure in this latter case may have been due to the then Mayor's high reputation. The President was seen as 'taking care of us' and the Mayor as providing such services as parks and roads. The benevolent view is clear here.

In Aberdeen the name of the Prime Minister, then Harold Wilson, was known by 91 per cent of twelve- and 96 per cent of fourteen-year-olds and of the Lord Provost (Lord Mayor) by 32 and 66 per cent of the two age groups respectively. Though measured intelligence did not seem to be linked with holding more critical or different attitudes, the more intelligent of these children scored higher on political knowledge than those whose IQ was 95 or less.

In the USA children have been found to learn political knowledge that relates to the national and the local levels before they learn that relating to the state level. In Aberdeen the situation was somewhat different since the only possible measure of the middle level was knowing the name of the Secretary of State for Scotland. The sample scored high on this index, probably because of the long and somewhat unpopular term of office of the incumbent. Furthermore, the situation in Britain at present may be complicated by the growth of Scottish and Welsh nationalism.

The important general point that is being made is that much of the content of the process of political socialization must depend upon the local political structure and will, therefore, vary between cultures. Least variation might be expected in the matter of motivation, since all systems demand loyalty, though in the old form of patriotism this motive may be less acceptable today to many young people. Greatest variation may be expected in the learning of political knowledge because its nature and structure relates so obviously to the very different political systems found throughout the world and even by regions within one country. Some variation will occur concerning political attitudes as various political problems, for example equality of opportunity or personal participation, assume importance, though many such issues have become important more or less simultaneously in many different countries.

(iv) *National Differences.* As a result of various research projects undertaken in the late 1960s Adelson was able to make some tentative generalizations about the nature of the political views held by adolescents in Germany, Britain and the USA.[14] In many ways these views appear to be structured around the issues that we might expect from commonsense views of different national characters.

German adolescents feared political confusion. They tended to identify government with a single person. Political authority was seen as parental in nature and the citizen to be childlike in that he would easily follow authority. This easy acceptance of authority, seen by many as dangerous to democracy, must be seen in great part as a product of German history over the last century.

In Britain adolescents saw politics largely in terms of problems of distribution rather than of aggregation. What mattered was not how wealthy the country was, but how this wealth was divided between citizens. There was a deep scepticism concerning authority. In other words the divisiveness over issues of distribution was strongly institutionalized in a dichotomy between 'us' and 'them'. Finally, the focus tended to be upon the individual rather than the social good to such an extent that adolescents, often assumed to be idealistic in their political hopes, displayed selfish views about the nature of future political changes that were sometimes even marked by an element of callousness towards the fate of others. Again, this set of political attitudes must be seen in its historical setting as the result of a long historical process of struggle and negotiation between the social classes.

Lastly, American adolescents held a more benevolent view of the political system, focusing upon social harmony rather than conflict; one should, perhaps, remember that this research was largely completed prior to many of the troubles over Vietnam and over the place of the blacks in the USA. Yet even these conflicts can be seen as expressions of an optimism about the way in which individual rights are represented in the democratic practices of the USA, a feeling that Adelson found to be strong amongst his respondents. They really believed in the equality of citizens and that in the USA the political system was going a long way to put this concept into operation.

Comparative work of this kind is exceptionally difficult to undertake and is marked by formidable conceptual and methodological difficulties, but it not only reminds us of the great cross-cultural differences in the structure of political views, but also forces us to remember that the historical focus of political activity is constantly changing, so that generalizations about many aspects of political socialization are difficult and must be viewed against the history of the societies concerned.

2. *The Agents of Socialization and Political Socialization*

(i) *The Family*. We have seen how important early life in the family is for providing experience of authority to children which they may generalize into acceptance of political authority. The 'good' working-class family is seen as one that produces loyal and patriotic children. Street parties in working-class areas at such times of national celebration as a coronation or jubilee are symbols of the construction and recreation of hegemony. Until recently loyalty to the political *status quo* was assumed almost automatic for the middle class.

However, sometimes the process fails to achieve the result desired by those in power. The work already cited by Jaros *et al.* shows us where to start looking for an explanation. Where there is some discontinuity between the approved authority structure and the family structure experienced in youth a child has to make a choice between the alternatives offered by his family and by the wider social structure. The pressures of family and peers are usually so great that he may opt for what is seen by the majority as the deviant course. Such discontinuity may also occur at an individual, rather than a structural level. In one classic American study Lane carried out depth interviews with fifteen fathers and sons. He focused on fathers because of their dominant role then in the US family. On his evidence a case can be made that sons would follow their fathers' political motivation where mutual relationships were good, but where this relationship was 'damaged' the sons were open to the acceptance of deviant political attitudes.[15]

In recent years there has been a great deal more open disaffiliation from the current political systems in many countries. The traditional brand of working-class politics found in Britain, Australia and New Zealand, where a Labour party and the trade unions work within the present system to better the lot of the subordinate classes, has been forsworn by many as never likely to achieve great changes. This has particularly been the case for some middle-class students in the late 1960s and early 1970s, though how permanent this tendency to disaffiliation is amongst those normally expected to be loyal has become problematic. Many of the former adherents of the political groups involved seem to lose their radicalism as they grow older.

This latter tendency forms the basis for one attempt at a structural explanation of such political deviance. The young, it is claimed, have weaker roots in the social structure, so that they have less to lose by opposing it and working for its overthrow. This is particularly the case of the children of the new professional middle class, since they have no great hopes of inheriting capital invested in the present social system. Many of these young people are tertiary students who are well educated and, hence, are able – indeed, particularly perhaps if taking courses in the social sciences are liable – to criticize the *status quo*. Furthermore, they have been brought up to feel high political efficacy. In other words, the present social structure may be prone to produce a group characterized by a combination of a lack of social roots – certainly during early adult life, a high level of education and critical ability, and a belief in their own political power. At a time when around 1970 contentious political issues either abounded or could be created easily it was not surprising to find that many of this group were alienated from the political *status quo*. Their apparent failure to make major changes and their growing rootedness in the social structure as they started a career and took on family responsibilities may explain the falling away of this radical activity. Competition for jobs may also be a force at work, though severe graduate unemployment might bring a renewal of the demand for changes in the political system.

But students, though important as a major source of the future political élite, are unrepresentative in many ways of the general population and certainly student politics are not representative of general student opinion. What more general effects, then, does the family have on political attitudes? A major comparative study, undertaken by Almond and Verba in five countries, showed that those who remembered being able to influence family decisions at the age of sixteen and to complain about such decisions felt themselves to be highly politically efficacious. Differences in the family structures of the countries concerned influenced this feeling in that the British and American respondents felt this effect more strongly than the Germans or Italians, who in their turn perceived themselves to be more efficacious than the Mexicans. However, in all cases the effect of undertaking higher education was more influential in this respect than participation in family decisions.[16]

Similarly, family background has a strong effect upon voting patterns. Much work has been done over the years on this topic. This shows that a firm and consistent pattern displayed by parents tends to lead to a similar voting pattern in children. Thus, Butler and Stokes found that for the 1963 British General Election, amongst voters both of whose parents had voted Conservative only eleven per cent did not vote Conservative; the equivalent percentage for Labour was eight. Social mobility can lead to changes as new values and beliefs become influential. But the longer a party preference is held the less likely is change to occur; it is not increasing age, but length of adherence to a preference that governs such changes. However, the study in Exeter by Dowse and Hughes to which reference has already been made did not find the family to have so strong an influence on political attitudes. In addition to gathering data from adolescents, just over half the parents of the sample were interviewed. The experiences undergone in their families appeared to have little influence except on those children who perceived their parents' preference of political party, in which case there was some slight, but by no means pronounced, tendency for them to follow their parental example. Two main reasons were suggested as likely to be at the root of this lack of effect by the family. Firstly, politics had a low salience in the interaction between parents and their children, since only sixteen per cent of the parents claimed to be 'very interested' in the subject and twenty-nine per cent were 'not very interested'. Secondly, there was some evidence to show that schools, rather than families, affected the political socialization of children of this age group.[17]

(ii) *The School*. One of the most influential of modern philosophers of education has built his entire philosophy around the need for a full education in a true democracy. John Dewey, particularly in his *Democracy and Education* (1916), argued that, if a democracy was to survive, the educational system must teach certain knowledge about the society and its traditions, and inculcate certain qualities so that citizens would both wish and be able to participate in the ruling of their country. It is hoped that such an education would lead to a greater tolerance of views of others and provide a basis for more rational political choice. There is a suspicion amongst political scientists that less sophisticated people have a simpler view of politics and are, therefore, more likely to fall under the power of extremist political leaders. Lipset has noted that there is a connection between length of education and the degree of tolerance of opposing views.[18] But, more particularly, the fear is that it is the working class, because of their shorter education, who will surrender to extreme political views. This class will not have the same wide general perspective as the more educated middle class, nor will they have the same sense of a past, a present and a future, which is an important element in political continuity. Evidence on the latter point comes from work already reported on early socialization; it will be recalled that working-class children tend to live for the present and are unable to forgo present pleasures for future benefits. Psychologists have found that this kind of limited or fixed frame of reference is one condition for easy suggestibility, which is in itself a major explanation of political extremism.

However, recent work has thrown some doubt on this thesis since rather different results in this field have been reported when different indices are used. More particularly, Lipsitz has shown that members of the working class who have more education tend to have less authoritarian attitudes than those with little education. Furthermore, Zeitlin, working in Cuba since the Castro revolution, indicates that the interest shown in politics seems to be an important influence on authoritarian feelings. Where political interest was found to be high, a lower level of authoritarian feelings has been reported; thus pre-revolutionary Communists and deeply committed revolutionaries, who in both cases came from the working class and by definition showed high political interest, were rated low on authoritarianism.[19]

For many children the school forms a classic double-bind situation; horizontal relationships with peers lead to support for a very different set of beliefs and behaviour from those advanced by the school, the focus of which is often upon the chance of social mobility. How much effect upon political socialization do these, in many ways, opposing influences have on a child's motivation and attitudes?

Little is known about this question. However, in 1966 a comparison was made between some of the political values held by 231 boys aged fifteen and above at Winchester and 238 boys in the sixth form of a nearby grammar school. On most of the measures used, the boys from the public school were surprisingly like those at the grammar school. Both groups saw political decisions as important, personal matters to which their experiences at school were relevant and all felt a definite sense of political efficacy. The outstanding differences were that the boys at Winchester placed a 'much lower moral evaluation ... on the office of politician' and to a lesser extent were more reluctant 'to acknowledge a strong duty to participate in politics'.[20] In the light of the historical position of Winchester and other public schools in supplying political leaders these are surprising findings. The similarities between the schools may be due to a threshold effect; beyond a certain minimum level such values as political efficacy may be little-affected by schooling, particularly amongst children whose families are supportive of education. Possibly this pioneering research did not tap the major dimensions of difference.

In their study in Exeter, Dowse and Hughes found that all ages from eleven to fifteen-plus, scores on their measure of political efficacy were higher amongst pupils at grammar than at modern schools. Furthermore, the range of political knowledge and interest was greater at the grammar schools and those at modern schools were marginally more deferential. The British educational system has been seen as teaching the working class its position early – formerly at the point of failure in the eleven-plus, now perhaps more gradually as pupils come to learn that they are the kind who leave at the minimum school-leaving age of sixteen. Certainly the comparative success in this respect of the senior years of the secondary school must largely be due to the early leaving of those seen by the school as failures, though it must also be remembered that it is from these successes that the possible deviants discussed earlier may be drawn.

The organization of schools can be an important influence on political socialization. In Britain ritual effects provide the obvious examples: prayers for the Queen and her ministers in morning assembly or deference expressed in personal relationships. Such ritual elements are consensual in function, but today dissensual elements are increasingly entering the hidden curriculum. Examples are the support given to teaching about the many ethnic groups now in the population, or the allowing of choice in social studies curricula so that other than the *status quo* or the deferential may be chosen and the making of such choices may be seen as a criticism of the present system. If we consider the more formal elements of school organization, Bronfenbrenner has recently shown how classrooms in the USSR are structured so that the presence of his peers ensures that a child continually grows towards being a good Soviet citizen. Those behaving badly or achieving poor academic results are taken to task by their classmates who, rather than the teacher, punish them or help them to improve their performance. Thus, there are very strong forces at work so that all will learn to cooperate in achieving the kind of socialist behaviour seen as good in the USSR.[21]

There are, however, some differences of opinion concerning the direct teaching of political attitudes and knowledge in formal lessons. Clearly the aim of any syllabus on British politics that focuses on, for example, the Crown, Lords and Commons is to be supportive of the present system. It is difficult to imagine any government tolerating a state educational system that taught anything else. This would even be true for a revolutionary society once the revolution was over. In their study Almond and Verba found that taking school courses in civics correlated with a perception of high political efficacy, though once again a background effect confounded the result. This relationship held for the USA, Britain and Mexico, but not in Germany and Italy, where an anti-democratic ideology was powerful when the sample was young.

It may be thought that it is easiest to build up loyalty to the country in such school subjects as history, geography and the teaching of the mother tongue, and that this process will be more powerful when the child is at the secondary stage. But this is not so. The textbooks of many countries could be quoted. A careful study of anthologies of verse for young children, with their stress on national folk-heroes, would be relevant at this point. But here examples from German textbooks will be given.[22] An elementary reading book dated 1906 will show how the ideal of militarism, then considered a political necessity by the rulers of Germany, was inculcated into the young child:

'We want to play soldiers,' said Albert. 'Yes, soldiers,' cried the others. He divided them into two armies, four boys in each. Charles led his army to a large sand heap. Albert had to storm this with his soldiers. Shouting, 'Hurrah! Hurrah!' they ran up the sand heap, came to grips with the enemy and took them prisoner. Thus Albert won the war with his soldiers.

Or, again, under the Nazis elementary arithmetic was used to teach the young child the political aims of the new regime. The child became familiar with large numbers by reading how 13·5 millions were called up by Germany in the first world war and 11·25 millions by Germany's allies. These men carried on the 'heroic' fight, against the 47·5 millions of the league of Germany's enemies. Language can be used in an emotional way even in elementary arithmetic textbooks.

In an analysis of fourteen studies of the effect of the school upon political socialization Massialas concluded that curricular materials often do not match the complexities and conflicts of political reality – indeed, if they did, many children might not understand them; teaching in this area tends to create an unthinking allegiance – choices become recipe, not reflective, ones; conventional civics lessons have a negligible impact on our present measures of political socialization – a caveat to this conclusion will be made below; but such curricula do have an effect when issues are discussed in a spirit of enquiry.[23]

The caveat concerns a possible threshold effect. Both in the USA and in Jamaica, undertaking a civics course has been found to have no significant effect on the political orientations of the great majority of secondary pupils, but latent roles seem to have been a crucial factor in this finding. Those who already aspired to go to college had different political orientations from those who had no such plans, and when black and white pupils were compared the civics course was found to have had more effect on the former. When the black pupils began the course they knew far less of what was being taught. In each case roles learnt in the family influenced whether or not the version of political reality offered by the teacher was accepted. In other words, there may be a threshold beyond which learning does not take place because of what has already been learnt outside the school.[24] Those with a certain level of value orientation or from homes that are culturally poorly endowed will be more likely to learn something than others.

To sum up the argument, many working-class children come from a poor home background, have an education of a poor standard and leave school as soon as they can. This start in life is followed for many by a job in which they mix with adults from a very similar background. Limited educational experience is followed by low mental stimulation. This restricted frame of reference could well be a breeding ground for extremism. The Communist Party has always seen the leadership of the slumbering masses as one of its historic roles. Education may not be a sufficient condition for democracy, but it certainly is a necessary condition for its survival.

(iii) *The Mass Media.* Surprisingly little work has as yet been done to show the effect of the various mass media upon political socialization. Connell's study, based upon depth interviews with 120 children of varying ages up to sixteen, does provide some evidence. Especially in their earlier years these Australian children did pick up much information about political activity and institutions from the media, and many of their attitudes towards such authority figures as the Queen or the Prime Minister were clearly in large part based upon what they saw on television. The News and regular programmes of comment on contemporary affairs were often specifically mentioned by them in their answers to unstructured questions. Yet we must remember that children put the material picked up from the media to very varied uses. Thus, as noted in Chapter 6, in a study in Aberdeen a very few children, aged about twelve, when asked what programme they watched to see violence answered, 'the News'.[25] It would seem safe to say that the media, especially television, are very influential in providing material with which children can construct their views of political reality, but that this is a complex process, much influenced by the latent roles brought to the media, and a process about which we are as yet not very knowledgable.

D. Conclusion

Rose (1974) has been able to make some judgement about the power of different influences upon the process of political socialization. In an analysis of his data he was able to account for just over 40 per cent of all the variance shown: 13·8 per cent was attributable to father's party preference, 8·8 to father's social class, 7·7 to the respondent's present class and, finally amongst those influences contributing to more than 1 per cent of the variance, 3·7 per cent was attributable to education. Clearly, the family is much more influential than the school, though apart from any independent effect we must remember that the school can have a strong influence in support of the family.

Obviously the educational system has two important functions to play from a political point of view. Firstly, it must be organized so that those with the motivation to lead have the trained intelligence necessary to do so at whatever level or in whatever sphere of society they have the opportunity. At present this is basically part of the selective function of education with which we shall deal in Chapter 14. But what is now clear is that at the moment the social structure is so organized that leaders tend to be drawn largely from one type of educational background and to be educated apart from those whom they will later lead. Furthermore, one of the justifications for this system, namely that it is possible specifically to educate for leadership, is based on an argument that it is difficult to sustain at the theoretical level. Yet, because of the high level of developed intelligence now necessary amongst political élites at various levels this separation is not surprising and, although a common educational experience up to sixteen may be achieved in a comprehensive school, even there streaming may effectively keep the future leaders and the future led, apart.

Secondly, the educational system must ensure that political leaders at each level are followed even by those in loyal opposition. Absolute hegemony may be seen as undesirable and may indeed be a thing of the past since demands for political participation have become more common and forceful. But this new situation has two consequences for political socialization: the motive to take part must be supported by adequate knowledge if wise decisions are to follow and there is, perhaps, an even greater need to ensure loyalty to the political system since increased individual participation at the grassroots can lead to a more atomistic polity.

BIBLIOGRAPHY

D. S. Byrne and W. Williamson, 'Some Intra-regional Variations in Educational Provision and Their Bearing upon Educational Attainment – the Case of the North-east', in John Eggleston (ed.), *Contemporary Research in the Sociology of Education*, 1974.
R. W. Connell, *The Child's Construction of Politics*, Melbourne, 1971.
F. I. Greenstein, *Children and Politics*, New Haven, Conn., 1965.
W. L. Guttsman, *British Political Elites*, 1963.
M. Kogan, *The Politics of Educational Change*, 1978.
R. Rose, *Politics in England Today*, 1974.

NOTES

1 K. Mannheim, *Man and Society in an Age of Reconstruction*, 1940.
2 R. W. Johnson, 'The British Political Elite, 1955–1972', *European Journal of Sociology*, 1973.
3 R. K. Kelsall, *Higher Civil Servants in Britain*, 1955, gives full details of the education of this group (percentages rounded off); C. H. Dodd,

'Recruitment to the Administrative Class, 1960–64', *Public Administration*, Spring 1967.

4 See A. H. Birch, *Small Town Politics*, 1959; T. W. Brennan, E. W. Cooney and H. Pollins, *Social Change in West Wales*, 1954; M. Stacey, *Tradition and Change*, 1960.

5 F. Musgrove, *The Migratory Elite*, 1963.

6 See R. C. Chambers, 'A Study of Three Voluntary Organisations', in D. V. Glass (ed.), *Social Mobility in Britain*, 1954, for a contrary conclusion in the case of voluntary organizations consisting mainly of women.

7 C. Bird, reported in T. H. Newcomb, R. H. Turner and P. M. Converse, *Social Psychology: the Study of Human Interaction*, 2nd edn, 1966, p. 474.

8 J. B. Mays, *Growing up in the City*, Liverpool, 1951, Appendix A, pp. 169–73.

9 J. Kelly, 'A Study of Leadership in Two Contrasting Groups', *Sociological Review*, November 1963.

10 R. H. Wilkinson, 'The Gentleman Ideal and the Maintenance of a Political Elite', *Sociology of Education*, Fall 1963 (also in P. W. Musgrave (ed.), *Sociology, History and Education*, 1970).

11 P. W. Musgrave, 'Aspects of the Political Socialization of some Aberdeen Adolescents and their Educational Implications', *Research in Education*, November 1971.

12 D. Jaros, H. Hirsch and F. J. Fleron, 'The Malevolent Leader: Political Socialization in an American Subculture', *American Political Review*, June 1968.

13 R. E. Dowse and J. Hughes, 'Girls, Boys and Politics', *British Journal of Sociology*, March 1971.

14 J. Adelson, 'The Political Imagination of the Young Adolescent', *Daedalus*, Fall 1971.

15 R. E. Lane, *Political Man*, New York, 1972.

16 A. V. Almond and S. Verba, *The Civic Culture*, Princeton, N.J., 1963.

17 D. Butler and D. Stokes, *Political Change in Britain*, 2nd edn, 1974; R. E. Dowse and J. Hughes, 'The Family, the School and the Political Socialisation Process', *Sociology*, January 1971.

18 S. M. Lipset, *Political Man*, 1960.

19 M. Lipsitz, 'Working Class Authoritarianism; a Re-examination', *American Sociological Review*, February 1965; M. Zeitlin, *Revolutionary Politics and the Cuban Working Class*, Princeton , N.J., 1967, pp. 262–5.

20 D. McQuail, L. O'Sullivan and W. G. Quine, 'Elite Education and Political Values', *Political Studies*, June 1968, especially p. 265.

21 U. Bronfenbrenner, *Two Worlds of Childhood: US and USSR*, 1971.

22 R. H. Thomas and R. H. Samuel, *Education and Society in Modern German*, 1947, *passim*.

23 B. G. Massialas, 'Some Propositions about the Role of the School

and the Formation of Political Behaviour and Political Attitudes of Students: Cross National Perspectives', *Comparative Education Review*, February 1975.

24 K. P. Langton, *Political Socialization*, New York, 1969.

25 P. W. Musgrave, 'How Children Use Television', *New Society*, 20 February 1969.

13

The Economic Function

The British economist, Alfred Marshall, in the late nineteenth century defined economics as 'the study of mankind in the ordinary business of life'. The sociologist, Max Weber, was rather less general and put the emphasis in his definition upon the actions by which men satisfy their wants for goods and services. It is to the complex of values around the activities concerned with production and consumption that sociologists refer when they speak of the economy as a social institution. In this chapter the nature of the British economy will first be examined (Musgrave, 1969) prior to tracing out the important links between it and the educational system.

A. The Economy

The contemporary British economy is marked by three predominant characteristics, each of which will be discussed here in turn. It is capitalist, industrialized and probably undergoing fundamental changes in its nature.

1. *Capitalism*
(i) *Early Capitalism.* In so-called advanced societies, economies based on barter have given way to complex market systems in which money has a vital place. The transactions carried out within the network of markets for various agricultural and manufactured goods give direction to production. However, a capitalist society is marked by a further important characteristic, the private ownership of property of almost all types. Thus, not only consumption goods, but the means of production, whether factories, machinery or agricultural land, are owned privately rather than by the state.

Furthermore, as slavery, that is the ownership of human beings, became less common, men were seen to own and be able to sell freely their own labour to the highest bidder.

In a capitalist system producers themselves make the decision to use their property in this or that way according to their judgement of the priorities of the market. They manufacture this item or grow that product in a given quantity which they hope the market will clear at a price that covers their costs and allows them a profit to reward their enterprise. The first form that capitalism took is usually referred to as commercial capitalism. This was found in late medieval Europe and early modern England. Merchants used their capital to hire the services of craftsmen to whom they usually supplied raw materials. The craftsmen used their own tools or machinery, for example spinning wheels or looms, to make cloth, which the merchant then sold, recouping his costs and hoping for a profit. There were no factories and much of the economy was still under a large measure of control from the government. Thus, restrictions on exports and imports or wage regulations were common. (ii) *Laissez-faire*. Britain was the first country to undergo an industrial revolution. As a result of this social change industrial capitalism was born, a system in which large, privately owned factories became the common source of employment and production. In these factories the owners employed numbers of employees who no longer worked at home with their own tools, but sold their labour to entrepreneurs who often held considerable power over them because, for example, they alone could provide paid work within a given locality.

Simultaneously with this movement of work into factories a new economic ideology, *laissez-faire*, which had immense political implications gained powerful support in Britain and later in many other countries and especially in the USA. The basic belief was that economic transactions should be left alone by the government because, if sellers sought the highest price and buyers the lowest, the satisfaction of both would be maximized and the search for the maximum individual income by consumers and producers would result in the greatest possible income for all and, it was assumed, the greatest possible good for the society. This economic argument logically implied a political consequence: the greatest good in any society would be served by the least possible control by the polity. Adam Smith, whose book *The Wealth of Nations* (1776) was most influential in developing this ideology, wrote that 'every individual ... is ... led by an invisible hand to promote an end which was no part of his intention'.

By the mid-nineteenth century the belief in the power of 'the invisible hand' was so great that when Gladstone was Chancellor of the Exchequer, customs duties had been almost eliminated and there were no income or property taxes. The government needed only a small income to support minimal activities, largely in the fields of the law and foreign policy. Both were important to ensure a stable national and international framework within which capitalists could maintain their property and pursue their enterprises. Thus, a particular type of social structure was supported by *laissez-faire* capitalism. It was characterized by free or almost free markets in land, labour and capital through which private owners sold property or the fruits of their property. Two quintessential markets were those for labour and the Stock Exchange, where stock and shares, that is legal claims to property, much of it relating to industry, were sold.

There were, however, faults in this system, two of which are crucial for any contemporary critique of it. Firstly, a cycle of good and bad trade, of boom and slump, was invariably found in capitalist economies except in times of war, when governments tended to step in and plan for the war effort. Indeed, it was only at such moments, when *laissez-faire* was for the time overruled, that capitalist economies came near fully employing all their workers and other labour. Secondly, the ideal of free bargaining amongst equals upon which *laissez-faire* rested was rarely found; one party tended to be stronger than the other, perhaps because he knew something that the other did not, or more often because buyers or sellers were few in number so that collusion to the detriment of other parties was possible. This latter problem often affected the hiring of labour. In addition, entrepreneurs who were wealthy could force workers who had no machines or capital upon which to fall back to make disadvantageous bargains. Thus it was that trade unions were formed to give greater power to labour in their bargaining with capitalists.

(iii) *Welfare Capitalism*. As the wealth of the country grew, consequent upon the rapid development of industrial capitalism, this inequality in the bargaining power between capital and labour became more obvious. The accompanying table relating to the ownership of capital clearly indicates the scale of this inequality and also shows how growing governmental interference in the form of progressive taxation on income and such taxes on wealth as death duties somewhat reduced inequality, but largely by transferring wealth from the very rich to the ordinarily rich. In the mid-1950s the

Percentage of personal net capital owned by various groups of the population (over 25) in England and Wales, 1911–56

%	1911–13	1924–30	1936	1951–6
1	65·5	59·5	56·0	42·0
5	86·0	82·5	81·0	67·5
10	90·0	89·5	88·0	79·8
20	—	96·0	94·0	89·0

Source: A. H. Halsey (ed.), *Trends in British Society since 1900*, 1972, p. 96.

wealthiest 20 per cent of the population still owned 89 per cent of personal net capital.

The taxes gathered have, in some part, been used to provide services, for example education or health services, to those too poor to buy them through the market. Other measures of intervention have been taken by the government to offset the extreme effects of *laissez-faire* capitalism. Thus, a policy aimed to ensure full employment is now pursued and unemployment benefit is paid to those who are out of work; minimum wage rates are fixed in some industries; the National Health Service exists to provide medical care to all citizens. The general philosophy of what may be called Welfare Capitalism is that a safety net should be stretched below the capitalist system into which the unfortunate – the casualties of capitalism – may fall and from which they may bounce back again into niches in the capitalist system, still basically seen as an efficiently working economic system.

Though Karl Marx was appreciative of the material benefits brought to all, including the workers, by capitalism, he was critical of its working on two main grounds. So far the discussion here has focussed on what he called the exploitation of labour in capitalism. In addition Marx spoke of the alienation of workers caused by the capitalist system. This emotive word refers to a complex of feelings in workers due, as Marx put it, to 'the fact that labour is external to the worker, that is, it does not belong to his essential being'. Because of this feeling the worker 'is at home when he is not working and when he is working he is not at home'. There are a number of dimensions to this concept of alienation: the worker feels that he is powerless in his job; that his work has no meaning for him; that he has no real involvement in what he is doing; and, finally, that his work is set apart from himself.

For Marx, writing in the mid-nineteenth century, capitalism was characterized by factories, and undoubtedly the various dimensions of alienation are commonly felt by factory workers, especially those undertaking seemingly trivial tasks, but today, when factories are also common in non-capitalist societies, we must be careful not to see alienation as a feeling only found in capitalist societies. It could well be a concept applicable in some measure to members of any more or less formal grouping, whether in a factory, a political party or even in some respects in a village community. Clearly, then, we must consider industrialization as a process that is analytically separable from capitalism.

2. Industrialism

(i) *The Labour Force*. Adam Smith began his *The Wealth of Nations* with a chapter on what he called the *division of labour* and he chose the manufacture of pins as one example of this process. One man carrying out the whole process 'could scarcely, perhaps, with his utmost industry, make one pin in a day, and certainly could not make twenty'. But he noted that the job was now divided up into a number of branches, each of which was done by a specialist. In one factory that Adam Smith had visited ten persons in this way 'could make among them upwards of forty-eight thousand pins in a day', or 4,800 each as against 20 made by the one relatively unspecialized man. Thus the division of the job amongst many labourers who each specialized in a small part of it brought a great rise in productivity.

This is the principle upon which most industry is now organized.

Craftsmen do not operate in this way, but a modern economy is characterized by mass production rather than by craft industry. There are, therefore, today a very large number of semi-skilled occupations in our labour force. It is possible to enumerate these occupations under main headings that are usually chosen on an industrial rather than an occupational basis. This gives an indication of how the labour force is employed in any country and provides a rough picture of the occupational structure.

In the United Kingdom in 1974 (mid-June) out of a population of just under 56 million, there were 25·1 million in the labour force, of whom 9·5 million were women. The broad outline of the occupational structure as it relates to civil employment was as below (figures in 000s):

Primary		Secondary		Tertiary	
Agriculture, forestry and fishing	404	Manufacturing industry	7,705	Transport, communications	1,483
		Construction	1,290	Distributive trades	2,707
Mining	347	Gas, electricity, water	337	Professional, commercial, services	6,474
				National and local government	1,551
751		9,332		12,215	
(3·4%)		(41·8%)		(54·8%)	

Source: Annual Abstract of Statistics, 1975, p. 144.

On the basis of these figures a broad comparison can be made with an underdeveloped country and this will indicate a way of analysing the occupational structure. The labour force of an underdeveloped country will contain a far larger proportion than in the United Kingdom in the economic sector that develops first, namely the agricultural and extractive group of occupations. This category has been called the *primary* sector.

(ii) *The Size and Ownership of Units of Production.* The impression given by classical economic analysis is that the size of economic unit, whether for production or distribution of goods, is small. An individual who wanted to set up a new business enterprise could make a start easily since the amount of capital required would be relatively small. An examination of the size of industrial units in the

Size and number of manufacturing establishments in
Great Britain, 1972

Number of employees	Number of establishments	%	% of total employees
11–99	45,942	76·8	20·0
100–499	11,140	18·6	32·2
500–999	1,589	2·7	14.9
1,000+	1,121	1·9	33·0
	59,792	100·0	100·1

Source: Annual Abstract of Statistics, 1974, p. 153.

above table will show the contemporary trend. The usual criterion for measuring size of units is the number of employees, though this is not equally applicable to all types of economic activity.

Clearly most people work in establishments with more than 100 employees, but the majority of manufacturing units employ fewer than 100 workers. Yet even in 1961 a large but unknown number of factories employed fewer than eleven employees. The total of these small units was believed to be around 140,000. These are the small units of the modern economic system. They still exist, but there is a definite tendency for the amount of capital needed to enter most industries today to be so high that the private individual cannot start a manufacturing business on his own out of his personal resources. This must modify the traditional analysis of capitalism and poses the question of who today owns and controls these large enterprises.

The question has become quite crucial because in the 1960s mergers reduced the number of manufacturing companies in Britain by about one-third. This increase in corporate size has meant that, whereas in 1909 the share of the largest 100 companies in net manufacturing output was ten per cent, by 1970 it had become forty-five per cent.[1] Clearly fewer persons, as directors of large companies, are controlling a much larger sector of the economy. In a major study of ownership of British companies, Sargent Florence investigated a representative sample of 1,700 joint stock companies of varying size. He found that in 1951 the average shareholding was about £500. In the fifty-three largest companies there were approximately 10,000 shareholders, but in many cases there was a concentration of ownership which enabled small groups to control the policies of some companies. Furthermore, since there is an increasing flow of savings into pensions schemes a larger proportion of shares is now held by such large institutional investors as insurance companies. Thus, Sargent Florence concludes that 'two-thirds of the large companies in 1951 were probably not owner controlled'.[2] One may then ask, who are the directors of the large companies who control the economic behaviour of a large part of the labour force? One survey made in 1951 of 1,173 directors of large public companies showed that between fifty and sixty per cent started their careers with the advantage of a business connection in the family. Nineteen per cent were directors of firms of which their fathers were directors before them, though only eight per cent were leaders of firms that had been in the same family for more than three generations.[3] Even allowing for this fifty or sixty per cent, many of whom may not have had a large financial stake in the companies that they were controlling, there still remains a large number of directors who can be regarded as professional managers. Particularly at a slightly lower level there are many managers who have made their careers in such companies, who have much power and a relatively high income, but own no shares in the companies for which they work.

(iii) *The Direction of Change*. The Classification of Occupations used for the decennial Census contains approximately 35,500 different occupations. The subdivision of labour is now very great. One Midlands manufacturer of men's clothing has broken down the making of a waistcoat into sixty five separate units of work. The further this process goes, the more specialized, but the less skilled, does the work become. The production line becomes the standard method of large-scale manufacture; a line of highly specialized workers is stationed before a slowly moving conveyer-belt along which the product passes, gradually assuming recognizable shape as each worker adds the piece for which he or she is responsible. Little knowledge of the materials used is necessary. Speed, precision and dexterity are the qualities demanded.

From this it may be imagined that the ratio between the skilled part of the labour force and the unskilled is falling. However, there are two forces at work in the opposite direction. Firstly, there is the great growth in the tertiary sector of the labour force. Many of those employed in these occupations are in work of an administrative or clerical nature. This is true within manufacturing industry itself. Large production lines working on a mass-production basis require careful control and present complex problems of management. Nothing must be allowed to stop production, since idle machinery makes no profit. There is a second force working to preserve the ratio of skill. Production lines are complicated trains of machinery. Some very skilled men are necessary to maintain the machines essential to modern industry. Thus the percentage of maintenance men is rising. Many of these men are craftsmen who not only need the skills to repair complex machines, but also must be able to diagnose just what has caused the breakdown.

The result of these various opposing forces does, however, seem to be a shift of skill off the shop floor into the office, though, as the following table shows, at a somewhat slower rate than many perhaps imagine. The decline in the number of privately owned companies is also indicated in this table.

Occupied population in Great Britain by major occupational groups, 1911 and 1966

	1911	1966
Employers, proprietors	6·7	3·4
White-collar workers	18·7	38·3
Skilled workers	30·5	23·7
Semi-skilled workers	34·4	26·1
Unskilled workers	9·6	8·5

Source: Halsey (ed.), *Trends in British Society Since 1900*, 1972, p. 113.

Behind these tendencies are three changes which affect the very nature of British industry. Firstly, the industries based on science are growing more predominant. This encourages a second but logically separate trend, the move towards a greater use of research and science throughout industry. Lastly, connected with this but again partly autonomous, is the application of new techniques to industry, exemplified particularly by automation (Dunning and Thomas, 1966).

(a) *Science-based industries*. The old staple industries upon which Britain's prosperity in the nineteenth century was founded were not renowned for the application of science to their processes. It may have been that at that time their nature and the state of scientific knowledge were such that it was not possible to apply science to the textile, coal and heavy engineering industries, though this is doubtful. But by the mid-twentieth century other industries were basic to our survival as an industrial power with a high standard of life. The chemical industry has become important both in itself and as a supplier of raw materials to other industries; many of the industries using and producing the new synthetics, such as plastics, clothing fibres and detergents, are based on raw materials provided by the chemical industry. The survival of old as well as the welfare of new industries has come to depend on an industry of a highly scientific nature. These tendencies are vividly represented by examining the growth of the employment of certain types of scientific manpower in recent years. Thus, during the years 1921 to 1966 the indices of growth of employment for some relevant categories were as follows: scientists and engineers, 994; draughtsmen, 450; laboratory technicians, 2,260.[4]

(b) *Research and science*. In 1867 Marx pointed out in *Das Kapital* that capitalism, unlike earlier systems of production, does not regard existing technical methods as definitive. Competition forces the search for new products and methods. This process has been accelerated by the coming of full employment. Change is more worth while in surer markets where sales seem more likely. At the high British standard of life many consumers have to be persuaded by advertising that they need a new product or that it is essentially different from what it replaces and so must be bought. Rapid obsolescence and replacement by the new but slightly different article become integral processes in a fully employed advanced economy. Change is now built into our economic system.

Behind this search for new and 'better' products is the science-based activity of research. The decision to commit manpower and resources to research is an economic one largely dependent upon the search for profits, though whether industry's attitude towards science is favourable or not will also be seen later to be important. Recently there has been a rise in expenditure on research and development; whereas in the late 1950s the proportion of the gross national product spent in this way was less than 2 per cent, by 1966/7 the figure was 2·3. Though about two-fifths (44 per cent) of the funds were supplied by private industry as opposed to the government (50 per cent), over two-thirds of the actual work was carried out by private industry. The amount spent varied considerably from industry to industry, but those referred to above as the science-based industries were the ones with the highest expenditure per employee.[5]

(c) *Methods.* The stress on science in industry has extended beyond an increasing application of the results of pure scientific research to industry. There has been a growing application of scientific methods of management. This had begun early in the century in the USA when F. W. Taylor had introduced what came to be known as the Scientific Management Movement. The aim was a realistic assessment of economic efficiency at every level of industry. Initially the application of Taylor's ideas was often inhumane. Since 1945 much of British industry has begun to use more scientific but humane techniques of management. The rational layout of the management structure, particularly in large companies, is now given more attention. It is more common to find emphasis put on accurate methods of cost accountancy and on the application of systems of wage rates to individual jobs, so that the worker is given maximum incentive. These new techniques of management require complex calculations, as do the increasingly difficult problems posed by stock control in large organizations, and the use of computers may, and often has, become necessary.

(d) *Automation.* Almost a symbol of these changes is automation, the product of a new and scientific industry that implies up-to-date management techniques. The term *automation* is usually applied to an industrial plant that has a very high ratio of capital equipment to labour employed and is in addition characterized by transfer mechanisms. Firstly, the plant is a chain of machines that were formerly separate, but are now linked by transfer mechanisms that pass the semi-finished product from one process to the next without the use of any manpower. Secondly, throughout the train of machines there is a succession of feedback mechanisms, often but not always controlled by computers, that automatically send corrective information to other stages of the process.

3. The Changing Nature of Contemporary Industrial Capitalism

In the nineteenth century *laissez-faire* industrial capitalism was seen by many, particularly by those with power, in Britain and elsewhere as the normal form for any economic system and was felt to set the standard against which other types of economic systems should be measured. During the early years of this century, and particularly in the early 1930s, when in Britain over twenty per cent of the labour force was unemployed, there was a dawning realization that all was not well with this economic system. The development of mechanisms to cope with the welfare of the unfortunate seemed to take care of some of the problems visible to critics. More significantly, the publication in 1936 by J. M. (later Lord) Keynes of his book, *The General Theory of Employment, Interest and Money*, inaugurated the apparent possibility of a system in which the government by central management of the economy ensured full, or almost so, employment, but with which detailed decisions concerning manufacturing and commercial priorities were still determined by a system of *laissez-faire*.

Until the mid-1960s a managed capitalism of this type became the norm. However, in the last decade many have begun to use such phrases as post-industrial society to describe the direction in which contemporary capitalist societies, and even some advanced societies of a more planned type, are moving. Questions are beginning to be asked about the exact nature of contemporary capitalism and industrialism and about the nature and the timing of their various stages of each of these systems. More particularly, a view is gaining ground that *laissez-faire* industrial capitalism as seen in the nineteenth century was nothing more than a temporary economic system that owed its form and its undoubted success by some criteria to a perhaps lucky concatenation of circumstances (Kumar, 1978). On this view the system is not an exemplar, but an historical stage which may greatly influence our present, but whose principles and practices need not be extrapolated into our future.

Industrial capitalism was marked by high population growth in urban areas in which the sense of community became lost, by specialization in large concerns controlled rationally and impersonally by small groups of directors, and by the rhetoric of *laissez-faire* at a time when in fact centralized control in the economy and a return to the power of the polity, partly to support democratic principles, were occurring in practice. The need for a wide diffusion of quite specialized knowledge, often supplied through the educational system, seems to have become vital as a result of the recent changes in this economic system. Furthermore, as industrial capitalism has developed, the need to rely upon scientific rationality based on extensive knowledge in order to control the system seems to have grown more pronounced. But we may ask what new forces have today to be controlled. Two foci seem crucial: one is normative and the other more strictly economic in nature.

A number of norms, central to the working of our present economic system, seem to be changing. One of the foundations upon which *laissez-faire* capitalism rested was the Protestant work ethic. Individuals were to be ambitious and to hope for material achievement from effort; they recognized that they were responsible for their own success; especially important was asceticism in worldly matters and control of one's visible aggressive tendencies. This ethic was above all put to work within the framework of a great respect for property. In the last decade many young persons, who a generation ago would have been well-started on a career motivated by ambitions of a material success, have stood back from the world and by their actions denied the qualities, formerly seen as virtuous, connected with this Protestant ethic. Consumption has come to mean more than production; accumulation of material wealth has been accorded much less priority; and self-discipline has given way to what to many seems permissiveness.

Furthermore, the attitudes that characterized the traditional nineteenth-century professional and the managers whom he deeply influenced, namely those of duty, dedication and service, have become attenuated today for many amongst both the old and the new 'professions'. The growth of professional associations that give more attention to industrial than to other issues exemplifies this process. Economic success for many now comes from seniority, not from striving. These normative changes have begun to lead to a new view of the concept of career. In an already wealthy society in which unemployment benefits are easily available there is the possibility that a growing proportion of the labour force may opt for a 'non-career', that is for the chance to move in and out of work without any long-term plans for moving up the hierarchical steps of one's chosen vocation. There is another, opportunity, possibly becoming more common, that is to opt for an 'uncareer' by rejecting the economic race altogether, since a minimal existence on the edges of a barely tolerated society is possible as long as that society has some welfare provisions.[6]

These normative challenges to the *laissez-faire* ideology, which is still the driving force of capitalism even in its modern welfare version, are supported by a number of developments of a more economic character. Symbolic of these changes is the realization that the very basis of advanced industrial systems, namely the supply of fossil fuels that form the main source of power, is limited and may be nearly exhausted. Control of use, rather than *laissez-faire* exploitation, is demanded, but seems difficult to achieve. Recent attempts have resulted in inflation and the results to date of trying to cure this have been the rebirth of continuing high rates of unemployment. Furthermore, unrestrained industrial, and particularly capitalist, use of many natural resources has done much environmental damage. Thus, water supplies have been polluted; fishing grounds have been destroyed and chemical fertilizers and sprays have disturbed the ecological balance. We are even often unsure of the ultimate effects of many commercially produced clinical drugs upon human beings.

The present position is, therefore, a very difficult one for those who must decide upon any policy issue that is in some way influenced by the economy. So far, in this chapter, the implications of the present form of the economy for education have not been spelt out in detail, but some are obvious, especially those related to the increasingly scientific bases of production. Yet, when one tries to balance the needs of the contemporary industrial capitalist system, albeit tempered by welfare provision, against the future directions in which, in the view of many, the economy may move, any decision about the most suitable educational structure or curriculum is difficult in the extreme.

B. The Educational System and the Economy

For some years sociologists have traced the interrelationships between the economy and education by pointing that education has a function for the economy and proceeding to analyse this in detail. A recent and influential work by Bowles and Gintis (1976), which is Marxist in method and tone and which develops a very critical account of the interrelationships now existing between education and the economy in the USA in particular and under capitalism in general, is in this tradition. The authors base their work upon what they call the *correspondence principle*. There is, they claim to show, 'a close correspondence between the social relationships which govern personal interaction in the work place and the social relationships of the educational system', as a result of which schools 'replicate the hierarchical division of labour which dominates the work place' (pp. 11–12). Such analyses have many problems, not the least of which is that to demonstrate correspondence says nothing about causation. Thus, in wartime Britain the rate of increase in divorces and the rate of fall in the import of bananas were closely correlated inversely, but no one really believes these two changes were in any real sense connected. Bowles and Gintis confirm former analyses that schooling services the economy in four main ways in a capitalist society: it teaches needed technical and cognitive skills; it inculcates appropriate personality traits; it encourages the acceptance of inequalities; and it fulfils this last function particularly in relation to the social class system (p. 54).

It is worth noting that Bowles and Gintis do not put great emphasis, except in passing within their first function, upon what is very often seen as the prime demand of the economy from the educational system, namely to provide a flow of more or less the needed size, category by category, of highly educated and trained manpower. This demand is usually stated in terms of numbers of the various qualifications passed by those leaving education and entering the work force. It is expressed in terms of credentials held, that is in such phrases as 'There's a shortage of B.Sc.s in geology' or 'There aren't enough SRNs around.' Questions relating to the flow of skilled manpower from education to the economy, though receiving mention here, will be dealt with more fully when considering the selection function in the next chapter. It is to the analysis of the type suggested by Boles and Gintis that we will now turn, firstly at the societal level, but finally at the interpersonal level.

1. *The Societal Level*
(i) *The Rate of Return to Education.* It is impossible for an advanced economy to operate without a substantial flow of highly educated persons to the labour force. At all levels, except the most unskilled where even literacy and numeracy may not be required by the nature of the work done, cognitive skills and knowledge, often of a high level, are necessary. Yet to provide this flow the economy must yield a surplus that can be invested in educational capital – in schools, colleges, universities, in classrooms and laboratories, and in administrative services. How great should this investment be? And, furthermore, how much of any increase in a country's national income can be attributed to such educational investment?

Economists have attempted to answer these questions by calculating the probable rate of return to educational expenditure and comparing it with the annual costs of such investment including notional interest payments upon the sums involved. Thus, rates of return for primary, secondary and various branches of tertiary education have been calculated, but there are many problems involved in such exercises. There is, firstly, a major conceptual difficulty because many of the most highly prized returns to education cannot be measured in monetary terms at all. Such are the learnt abilities to make a moral decision or to feel aesthetic enjoyment in the presence of great pictures, music or literature. In addition, there are major technical problems. Sometimes calculations relating to all identifiable factors except education are made and the remaining returns, namely a residual, are attributed to education – not a very sound or necessarily an accurate way of dealing with such a major issue. There are also always doubtful assumptions to be made concerning the allocation of, for example, such overhead costs as the administrative services of the DES or an LEA. How much of each should be set against a primary pupil? (Balogh and Streeten, 1968).

The concept of economic accountability cannot be avoided, particularly in the present circumstances when, because of rapidly falling school rolls due to demographic change, the demand for educational services is dropping and when, because of unemployment and inflation, the supply of resources for a service whose outcomes can only be measured in an approximate fashion must be open to political questioning. Some of the concepts involved, for example the idea of investment in human capital, are unwelcome to many educators, but they are economically sound, even if difficult to put into operation, and will certainly influence the way in which those involved in the political debate about the future scale of our educational effort conceive of the relationship between education and the economy.

(ii) *Flow of Manpower*. In an advanced industrial society such as Britain we tend to take for granted the fact that we have an efficient labour force. We forget that in the eighteenth and nineteenth centuries men and women had to be recruited to industry and we overlook that in many countries this process had to be achieved by force. Once in industrial employment workers must be committed to this way of life and perhaps to one occupation or even one employer for a period of time. The 'here today, gone tomorrow' attitude found among workers in some underdeveloped countries is a considerable handicap to efficiency in industry. Workers at all levels of the labour force must have the skills, attitudes and knowledge appropriate to contemporary techniques, and they must be willing to use these attributes to the utmost if the economy is to prosper. This willingness can come only from a strong desire to work hard and to produce. Such a desire is fostered by the conscious or unconscious attachment to a set of commonly held assumptions. The labour force of an industrial country must be both skilled and 'committed'.

In the first place, then, the educational system must play its part in laying the foundations upon which industrial skills can be built. The sheer factual knowledge needed to do most of the highly specialized jobs that many workers do today is very small. If the worker can read instructions, carry out easy calculations so that he will produce only the required number of articles and fill in a simple report form or work ticket, this will be sufficient. The 3 Rs at a relatively low level are enough. To master such jobs may take only a day or two, and after this brief training period is over little thought is required to do one's daily work. In pre-industrial days the life of a peasant or craftsman, though far from idyllic, was in some measure an education in itself. Life today is not built round work as was then the case. Nor do jobs today allow the exercise of the faculties of judgement and initiative that most humans need for psychological health. Work no longer provides either satisfaction or the feeling of being someone that matters. The worker must look elsewhere, perhaps to his family or friends, for the fulfilment of these needs.

In the field of technical education the industrial skills themselves will sometimes be taught. An example is typewriting. Can we go so far as to say that the connections between the economy and the educational system must be so arranged that what is taught at school matches what industry requires? There is no conflict between the present needs of the economy and the broader aims of education over much of the curriculum. Both demand the thorough teaching of the elementary techniques of the 3 Rs together with some knowledge of the social subjects such as history and geography. When work may be trivial and leisure long, the place of the aesthetic subjects is important in answering the need for men to live a richer life (Bantock, 1963). Without any attempt at cynicism it may be observed that, if such an education forms the basis for future happiness, then contented men will make better workmen.

Changes within school subjects themselves can be of importance. Obvious examples are the revolution in the teaching of mathematics and science in both primary and secondary schools. Any improvement in mathematical competency has a direct relevance for future members of a modern labour force, though there are employers who feel some contemporary methods of teaching mathematics are not beneficial in this respect. It should be noted that so far we have been considering the implications of education for production and not for consumption.

We can, however, isolate a part of the curriculum which we can call education for consumption. This attempts to teach children to discriminate between the many choices open to them.

Discrimination in consumption ensures that the economy uses resources efficiently. The schools have come to play an important part in fulfilling the need for education for consumption. A seminal work was published as long ago as 1933, *Culture and Environment* by F. R. Leavis and D. Thompson. The authors aimed to apply the methods developed in the practical criticism of English literature to a criticism of the whole environment surrounding the individual.[7] The influence of this book has been great, and today secondary schools run courses that aim to teach children to examine advertisements for the use of emotive language and question-begging statements Leavis and Thompson wrote mainly for sixth forms, but teachers now are giving lessons with the same aim to fifteen-year-olds who are about to leave school. Syllabuses for the CSE in Commerce are often relevant, containing, for example, a section on 'Buying Wisely' – which includes 'The Comparison of Price, Quality and Value'. 'The Use of Advertisement' – and on 'Protection of the Consumer'. This is an example of teaching that is often pursued with a frankly moral aim, but which has economic consequences. Inasmuch as children become more discriminating consumers, the schools are contributing to the efficient running of a *laissez-faire* economy.

The economic function of the educational system is not restricted, however, to teaching skills and to matters of the curriculum, though these are perhaps easiest to understand and, providing the means of communication between education and the economy are good, problems in this field should be easily solved. Of far more importance are the attitudes of commitment to the labour force of a capitalist economy which family and school often transmit unconsciously and to which much attention will be given when we analyse the interpersonal level.

(iii) *Forecasting*. One possible answer to the problem of ensuring that the supply of educated, newly trained and retrained manpower leaving the educational system comes near matching the expressed demands of the economy has been seen by some to be the operation of a forecasting system. The data provided by this would allow, it is felt, supply and demand to be adjusted, particularly for future years, with more chance of success. At the national level the government has issued several White Papers attempting to forecast the future needs of such specialized labour as scientists, engineers or teachers. Some large firms make estimates of their future needs for managers and craftsmen, in which case analysis will be purely at a local level, though the same difficulties underlie forecasts by companies as those by the government. The government's estimates have been carefully compiled with the help of the industries concerned. Yet they have gone awry within the brief period of three years.

The reasons for these failures are both economic and educational. At a time of rapid technical change the educational system takes time to answer to the new needs of the economy even where its institutions are very adaptable. But apart from any educational consideration, assumptions of an economic nature underlie any attempt to foresee the needs for trained manpower. An industry that expresses a demand for a particular type of educated and skilled man may find that by the time the educational system has trained him he is no longer required. This may be due to the introduction of a new technique or to a change in the competitive strength of the industry in overseas markets. Again a basic assumption is that the wage structure will remain unaltered. An industry may offer a salary that influences a school-leaver to begin a sandwich course at a college of higher education but by the time he qualifies some four years later the salary in another industry may tempt the graduate away from the industry that he originally intended to enter. Lastly, it is not possible to say whether or not the forecast will affect the future supply of labour. Probably the most valuable effect of forecasts so far has been to give publicity to the shortage of trained manpower in certain fields, thereby influencing the direction of recruitment to the labour force. The need for scientists has been stimulated in industry and the knowledge of openings has been transmitted to the educational system. Despite this result forecasts do not yet appear to have been very successful tools of economic planning.[8] It must be made clear that a fully planned economy will have much the same economic and educational problems in matching the supply of and the demand for labour. There is one major difference, namely that in many planned economies direction of labour replaces free choice of occupations.

The achievement of an equilibrium position between the supply of and the demand for labour is made more difficult by the growing realization of the educational needs of the economy. Over the last century in Britain an escalator effect has been at work; when plans for educational expansion have been made to meet one level of needs, a deeper level has been discovered leading to further needs. There seem to be two influences apart from that of technical change at work here to raise the demand for education. There is the tendency for education to create a desire for more education. Thus, a number of studies in the USA (Berg, 1973) have shown that the huge rise in the supply of highly educated manpower since 1945 does not on the whole depend upon a rise in the educational threshold of the economy except at the topmost levels, where, for example, physicists or mathematicians have come to be in greater demand. In other words, as interviews with employers have shown, the existence of many more persons with higher qualifications, however caused initially, is now used by those hiring labour as a device for selecting between the many applicants for given positions which often have relatively low educational requirements. When this tendency is taken in conjunction with the technical problems of forecasting, except in the broadest of terms we are forced to take up the position that education can best help the economy not by attending to the exact numbers that are following a specific type of education, but by concentrating on giving a broad general curriculum that meets the needs of a technological age.

(iv) *Structure of the Educational System.* The success of the educational system in meeting these needs of the economy can be constrained by the way in which it is administratively structured and by the attitudes underpinning this structure. The link between primary and secondary schools is an important consideration in this respect. It has been said that the British child, particularly from the working class, was early conditioned to failure when he sat the eleven-plus examination, the results of which were used to allocate him either to an academic or to a non-academic type of secondary school. With the reorganization of the secondary system on comprehensive lines this tendency should be eliminated, but we have seen that more subtle selection mechanisms are now at work.

Secondary schools can be thought of as a graded series of take-off ramps into the labour force. Although there is some overlapping each type of secondary school tends to lead into a definite level of occupations. This can be seen very clearly from the existence of predominant leaving ages for each school type. This age implies a level of education and very often the possession or otherwise of a formal qualification. Children tend to leave the secondary modern school where it still exists at the legal minimum age of sixteen – often with no formal qualification, and the grammar or public school at sixteen or eighteen after a higher level of examination. Where there are comprehensive schools, the levels indicated by the separate schools are usually replicated by a hierarchy of streams within the school.

The public school historically has served the professions and the needs of the government at home and overseas. Particularly since 1945 it has come to have stronger connections with top management in commerce and industry; perhaps this new emphasis offsets the lack of openings in the former Empire to which young men from these schools might have expected to go. The grammar school has come to feed the lower levels of management; almost never do grammar school boys become foremen, which in Britain, unlike the USA, is not a career grade, but the highest level to which a capable and ambitious operative can aspire. The secondary modern school is strongly associated with the operative and craftsmen level. Since in 1975 over four-fifths of the pupils left comprehensive schools at sixteen it would seem that, though some of their pupils are entering occupations of the same status as those from grammar schools, this new type of secondary school is providing a take-off point into the labour force similar to those formerly supplied mainly by the modern and technical schools.

Prior to the 1944 Education Act many children of less wealthy parents could hope to rise up the labour force, certainly to the level of foreman, if not beyond, although they had left school at the legal minimum age. Now these more capable young people either are selected at eleven-plus for a grammar school education or eventually enter a comparable stream in a comprehensive school; in either case they tend to enter the higher levels of the labour force. This process ensures a fuller use of the nation's talent, but raises questions about the intellectual quality of the lower levels of the labour force. One important issue is what will be the future source from which foremen are to be recruited. Management may have to re-define the role of foreman and start to feed back ex-grammar or comprehensive school boys into the labour force at this level as junior supervisors with the chance of promotion.

If there is a shortage of educated manpower at any level of the labour force, then clearly the structure of the educational system must be arranged so that it gives the maximum of help or the mini-mum of hindrance to the economy. The schools must be organized so that they do all they can to develop capability and so that no one shall have his aspirations limited, as far as they are realistic. One problem is that parent and teachers may encourage children to be so ambitious that many more aim for occupations with high status than can be accommodated in the existing labour force. In some states in the USA this has resulted in junior colleges setting up special counselling systems to 'cool out' students, so that, for example, a student who wishes to become a surgeon but is incapable of this will come to review his aspirations and perhaps see himself as a potential butcher. In many societies today, however, there is graduate unemployment and if one views education purely from an instrumental viewpoint one might say that the educational system was dysfunctioning in relation to the economy in that it was allow-ing too many to be educated to levels unrequired by the labour force.

In addition to the administrative structure constraining supply, some of the attitudes encouraged within the educational system can limit the ways in which young persons do their work when they leave school. The need for men and women at all levels of the labour force who have some knowledge and training in science must by now be very clear. The nature of the most rapidly expanding in-dustries and their dependence on research, particularly under con-ditions of full employment, has been described. The labour force must therefore not only have scientific knowledge but must exhibit attitudes that are favourable towards science, change and education (Musgrave, 1967).

(a) *Science*. The conversion of British schools and universities to the teaching of science in the nineteenth century was a slow and difficult process (Ashby, 1958) and largely as a result a negative approach to science has much hindered many British industries.

The modern economy, as has been seen, is based on science and development depends upon research in the field of pure science to lay bare the theoretical principles relevant to its working. This research is usually undertaken in a university, namely in an institution that is within the educational, and not the economic, system. Upon the principles that are discovered can be built a technology round which will grow the whole structure of technical education backed by curricula, textbooks and examinations. Therefore the work of pure scientists is the source upon which applied science is built, but a fair proportion of intellectually bright young men and women ready and able to use the results of contemporary research must go into industry. The important point is that of balance. If we examine the way that the UK and the USA employed their stock of qualified scientists in 1956, we find the percentages were as follows: in industry, USA 60, UK 38; in government, USA 20, UK 12; in education, USA 20, UK 50. Allowing for the difficulties of international statistical comparisons we may say that Britain employed twice as many of her pure scientists in schools, colleges and universities as the USA, whilst the USA employed half as many more of her scientists in industry than the UK did.[9] The determinants of these comparative differences must to some extent be rooted in the attitudes to pure and applied science passed on in the schools, to which reference has just been made.

The world of science in Britain is very inbred and attitudes are easily passed from one generation to the next. However, few of the scientists are in the community outside education to spread a knowledge and understanding of modern science throughout industry and commerce, and those within education may well, albeit unconsciously, be transmitting unhelpful attitudes. The early specialization encouraged by the English, but possibly not the Scottish examination system is often seen as culpable here. Those who were not science specialists at school must not lack the knowledge that they need as producers and consumers. In addition all must have attitudes favourable to the application of science to industry and commerce.

(b) *Change.* Innovation in any field, whether artistic or scientific, depends on existing knowledge. The wider this is spread, the more easily can additions to knowledge be made and the easier will be applications of new knowledge. The scientific knowledge necessary for the invention of the Bessemer Converter, which ushered in the age of cheap steel in 1856, was known at the start of the nineteenth century, but it was not known widely or in the right places, so that application was not easy. When the invention was eventually made, there was enough understanding for the new process to be taken up by the industry quite quickly, though lack of scientific knowledge was one reason that prevented the new product from being accepted in some quarters as rapidly as should have been the case. For both consumption and production a high level of literacy and numeracy is even more essential in the late twentieth century, when change is apparently more rapid than was the case a century ago.

Since the educational requirements of most occupations are constantly altering, there is difficulty in specifying the academic content of a curriculum to meet change. The most serviceable education would appear to be a general one out of which specialization can grow. The deeper the specialization the further the general education must be carried. The specialist requirements of a metallurgist need a longer general education, especially in general science, than is necessary for a first-hand melter on a steel furnace. A broad general education will assist adaptability since a worker will be more able to understand future changes in his field and to relate them to his own particular job. If the job is changed, the worker can return to the basis provided by his general education to start out afresh. If the steel industry switches to a new process, the metallurgist with a broad education can more easily cope with this change, as can the operative on the furnace at his own level of education.

Very little is known about how schools affect attitudes towards change. Adaptability is a factor of personality whose source has not been deeply explored. The willingness to accept change is a necessity for young workers who are just entering industry and for older workers who may have to move to new jobs because of technical innovation. In Western European countries since 1945 younger workers have tended to receive higher pay than older men. The benefits of technical change seem to go to the younger men with the formal qualifications. We must, therefore, consider how to teach the present generation in school to meet change, but in addition we must give older workers every chance of retraining themselves to meet new techniques. The revolution demanded in the views of operatives and managers is great if a worker or a manager aged forty-plus is to go back to school to relearn his job or to learn a totally new one. The educational techniques involved in teaching such pupils would seem to be very different from those at present often used in technical education.

(c) *Education.* Unless education is given a high priority, the proportion of the national income spent on education will not be large enough to create an educational system adequate for the type of demand that the economy puts upon it. Thus, during the nineteenth century when education had a low place on the national agenda, the schools did not educate enough men at any level, but particularly at managerial level, who understood the scientific advances of the time. Furthermore, during the same period the schools and universities gave their pupils an attitude towards industry such that able young men of the upper middle class were very unwilling to enter industry.

The educational system and the economy are two social institutions that are closely linked in any society, though many do not realize the nature of their mutual relationship. Industry in Britain has tended to put its faith in the practical man and in effect to say to the schools: 'You teach the 3 Rs and we'll do the rest.' In the schools there has been little knowledge of or sympathy with the industrial and commercial life of the nation. Any social institution can oppose the general direction of the development of the society that contains it. The contemporary situation is complicated in that, although there is agreement that the economy should continue to be used to ensure a high standard of life and to allow the poor to become wealthier, yet there is a growing feeling that as far as possible this must not be achieved in a way that endangers the long-term economic position. The place of the educational system is a difficult one. The schools must teach and shape personality in a way that recognizes economic development. But if children, particularly, though not entirely, of a low socio-economic status, are to cope with greater leisure, the increasing triviality of work, rapid technical change and for some perhaps even unemployment, and if this is to be done in a spirit of constructive social criticism, there is scope for research and for much thought of a more sociological nature in the schools concerning the topics discussed in this section.

2. *The Interpersonal Level*

Many of the values and attitudes, and even some of the knowledge that is relevant to the working of the economy, is taught in interpersonal situations in both the family and the school.

(i) *Commitment to Industrial Capitalism.* Any consideration of the values that the members of the labour force of a country must hold if they are to be wholly committed to industry must take into account the type of the economic system and the stage of its development. In a traditional society such as medieval Europe or Japan before the 1860s a conservative approach to the economy was necessary; an apprentice or a peasant in the fifteenth century learnt how to conserve tradition, not how to forge it anew. In all probability a capitalist country in the early stages of industrialization needs a different set of values from one that is more fully developed. Britain today has an economy of a mixed nature characterized by rather more *laissez-faire* than government intervention, but also marked by large productive units. There seem to be three important sets of values that, when held by the labour force, smooth the working of a semi-capitalist economy (Ginzberg, 1956). These are the value attributed to a successful life, more particularly as measured by whether or not high wages or salary are earned, the value given to equality of opportunity so that the able can 'get on' and, finally, the value put on change. We have just given some consideration to the question of how change is viewed and shall now turn to an examination of the part that the educational system plays in transmitting the first and second of these values.

(a) *Success in life.* Theoretically the mainspring of a *laissez-faire* economy is the attempt by all to buy as cheaply as possible and to sell as dearly as possible. It is assumed that a man will try to earn as high a wage or salary as he can, though allowance must be made for any advantageous conditions of work such as great security in the job or good chances of promotion. In theory the various wage rates direct labour to the highest return and ensure efficiency, since the employer will only pay what a man is worth to him. In fact the wage system does not work as smoothly as this, but what matters here is whether the labour force strives primarily after monetary rewards or gives the wage a low priority as part of its total reward.

In the USA children are imbued with the money-making spirit from an early age. The family plays a large part in the child's early years in encouraging him to work for money on every possible occasion. In the school each generation is inspired with the model of the self-made man. It is not without significance that many Americans work their way through university, whilst British undergraduates receive grants at one of the highest rates in the world. About sixty per cent of graduates in the USA come from what the British would call the working classes, a much higher proportion than in Britain. Much of this educated manpower goes into industry, where rewards are high. The economy of the USA may base its efficiency on great natural advantages, but its industry makes the most of this competitive position by ensuring that its management is capable and committed to its economic assumptions.

European management has different attitudes towards money-making. Financial achievement is seen as only a part of the satisfactions yielded by the job; the true essence is considered to be doing the job itself. The place of the school in the initial formation of such values can be vital. To most teachers in grammar schools an emphasis on money-seeking is unpleasant and conflicts with many of the ideals that they wish to impart, particularly that of service. There is a tradition in the public schools, which can be traced back to Arnold of Rugby, that the occupation into which a young man ought to go should be marked by the giving of service to the community. Such a choice of occupation was truly a vocation and often did not lead to the highest monetary reward consonant with the capability of the man entering the vocation. The connection established by these schools with the learned professions rather than with industry pays tribute to this tradition. The grammar school inherited this ideal in some measure, though, as we saw from King's work quoted in Chapter 7, a spirit of competition and thrust may replace the ideal of service as the modern grammar school comes to be seen more as a way into the higher levels of industry. Until very recently the grammar school educated the majority of secondary modern teachers and hence transmitted some of the same tradition of service into this new form of school and also into the comprehensive school. A recent development in these schools has been the growth of schemes such as the Duke of Edinburgh's Award; here again unpaid service to the community is rated highly.

In the upper levels of the labour force the ideal of service has directed many capable men from industry into the Colonial and Civil Services, and into the professions and politics. A case can be made that until recently industry has been somewhat starved of capable men. Service and security of employment were put before money and risk. As well as an ideal of service the public schools inculcated a strong corporate spirit that continues into adult life and is symbolized by 'the old school tie'. The connections encouraged by this spirit are used for finding jobs and placing business deals. There also exists a strong corporate feeling in the British working class. This is not a consequence of education but was born in the industrial struggles of the last hundred years and is symbolized by loyalty to the trade unions.

There are some signs that the entrepreneurial spirit is no longer taught by the US family quite so fiercely as was once the case. Thus, Miller and Swanson found that in families where the fathers were employed in settings marked by risk, by few hierarchical levels and by income dependent upon enterprise and judgement parents brought up their children to hold orientations appropriate to entrepreneurial positions. However, in families in which the fathers worked in jobs characterized by security, by specialization and by routine, the children were taught an orientation more suited to bureaucratic organizations.[10] Since, as we have seen, there is a tendency for the proportion of workers employed in bureaucratic positions to rise there could be, in Britain as well as in the USA, a built-in tendency in the contemporary social structure that works to lower the level of ambition for entrepreneurial economic achievement.

More recently, work by another American researcher has tied a similar tendency to the mode of operation of some nursery schools. In doing this Kanter (1972) has also shown how the correspondence principle, though not named by her, may be used in analysis with care and with effect at the level of interpersonal interaction in one school, a level almost totally ignored in the work of Bowles and

Gintis (1976) to which reference was made earlier. As a result of participant observation in a Mid-Western nursery school Kanter was able to show how the experiences made available to the children emphasized rationality, security, routine and a lack of individual accountability. All these are characteristics of contemporary bureaucratic organizations. Kanter showed that although 'the organization child' developed some adaptive techniques to maintain his self-esteem, he nevertheless by and large accepted the organizational reality offered to him. The correspondence between this nursery school and most bureaucracies was obvious. We do not know, though we may guess, how its former pupils, and those of schools like it, will settle into their work in an increasingly bureaucratic economy when they join the labour force.

The ideals taught at home and at school can influence both the choice of vocation and the spirit in which a man will do his life work. It would seem that money-making is not rated highly in Britain and that economic ambition may be squashed, especially by allocation to a particular type of secondary school or to some streams within a comprehensive school. Whether this is morally right or wrong is not here in question, but it is clear that the higher the value put on making money and 'getting on', the more efficiently will a *laissez-faire* economy run, if that is what is now needed. What the home or the school now teaches may or may not match the contemporary moral ethos of the country and in view of the changing and probable requirements of the economy, it is even doubtful how much stress should be put upon a value that was once crucial to the running of the *laissez-faire* system.

(b) *Equality of opportunity.* Very closely allied with much of what has just been said is the value given to equality of opportunity. Again a comparison can be made between the USA and Britain. In the USA there is a belief that anyone can improve himself by his own efforts. There is difference of opinion as to whether there is in fact, more upward social mobility in the USA than in Britain. A major comparative study (Lipset and Bendix, 1959) found the rates to be about the same in the two countries. But the really important thing is that men believe that they can rise easily up the social ladder. It is probably true to say that this belief is more strongly held in the USA than in Britain, though more now see a chance to rise in Britain as a result of the reforms implicit in the 1944 Education Act.

In the large public companies that are coming to be typical of British industry today nepotism would seem to be less important than it was, though it must be common in smaller firms, and in some industries, such as the woollen textile industry, there are still many family firms. In a survey of the managers of twenty-eight firms, made in the Manchester area in 1954–5, Clements found only twenty-eight (or four per cent) out of a total of 646 managers who were what he called 'crown princes'.[11] These were men whose start in a firm could be ascribed to close family links with the ownership or management of the firm. It must be noted that this was not nepotism in its crudest sense since these men appeared to deserve their successful careers. They may have had an advantageous start to their lives in industry, but very often they had been educated and trained almost from childhood so that they would want and be able to run the family firm with success. The proportion of these instances seems small and on balance does not invalidate the statement that the incidence of nepotism has probably declined in British industry.

Formal educational qualifications, then, provide the entrée to the various levels of the labour force, and therefore the educational system has come to be seen as the key to equality of economic opportunity. Formerly the way to improve one's social position was by founding a small business and making a success of it, often with the help of one's family. Now that the size of economic unit has grown this is less often seen as the way. Today the ambitious youth enters a large corporation with the hope of working his way up the hierarchy of management. Large companies must, therefore, select their potential managers with care, and the stress has come to be laid on education as well as on qualities of personality. The chance to rise is still there, but has come to be centred on education. From which schools do our economic leaders come?

In the mid-1950s Rosemary Stewart (1956)[12] carried out a survey of the managers of fifty-one of the sixty-five British companies that had 10,000 or more employees and were not nationalized. Managers were defined as all those above the rank of foreman. Half of all managers had been educated at either a grammar or a public school. However, a greater proportion of senior managers had been at these secondary schools; a third went to public schools and a third to grammar schools. It seems that boys from such schools had more chance of achieving high positions in management than those who came up through the ranks. In fact, the trend seems to be moving further in this direction, as might be expected in view of the greater stress on selecting recruits to management who have formal qualifications. More than a fifth of those aged from thirty-five to thirty-nine, that is the more recent recruits, went to public schools as compared with only a tenth of those between fifty-five and fifty-nine. For the same age groups one in four of the younger group had university degrees, whereas only one in ten of the older men had. In Britain those below managerial rank rarely have formal qualifications.[13] In smaller companies there is less stress on educational qualifications, but even here at technician level emphasis is growing. It is by founding such companies that self-made men can make their start, and among such men formal educational qualifications may be rarer. We saw that in these smaller companies nepotism can perhaps occur more easily than in large public limited companies. Both these factors work against stress on educational qualifications in the management of many small companies. Nevertheless the trend is towards an emphasis on education by industry and commerce. Equality of educational opportunity has, therefore, become linked with equality of economic opportunity.

The hypothesis examined here was that two values, largely learnt in interpersonal interaction, were influential in the way in which the labour force was committed to the economy. Earlier we saw that the attitude to change in Britain has in the past been unfavourable. From the discussion in this section it is clear that, though there has been some improvement in the provision of opportunities for education so that entry to the middle levels of the labour force may be more open, yet there are many who are not as motivated by monetary reward as, for example, in the USA. The balance of these forces is difficult to determine, particularly with our present scanty knowledge, but in each case what the educational system is doing has clear consequences for the economy.

(ii) *Vocational Choice and Guidance* (Williams, 1974). The actual transition from school to job is vital, since it is at this point that the new recruits, as opposed to retrained adults, enter the labour force (Carter, 1966). Changes in the direction of recruitment in answer to new techniques can be made here. It is important to consider at what stage and by what means children are shown the occupational opportunities open to them. Vocational guidance now exists at all levels. In the universities there are appointments boards that link higher education to the economy. The public and grammar schools frequently have careers masters who specialize in giving advice on jobs. Finally, there is the Youth Employment Service, a government-sponsored organization, that operates particularly for secondary modern, but also for grammar school leavers.

In the mid-1960s Youth Employment Officers only placed about forty per cent of the younger leavers and about thirty per cent of the older leavers in their first jobs.[14] In Sheffield, Carter found that in 1959 just under two-thirds of the boys in his sample entered the jobs recommended by the Youth Employment Officers; as a result of job changes the proportion fell in a year to a half. In the case of girls the proportion was still about three-quarters, probably because of the rather narrower range of occupations available. Contact with the youths starts during their last year at school. However the majority of young people have decided on an occupation before the Youth Employment Officer speaks to them and these choices are respected, although these decisions seem to be made in a very haphazard fashion. There is no guarantee that the chosen job suits the youth concerned, since many are influenced by parents, relations or school friends, whose detailed knowledge about occupations in general has been found to be scanty and unreliable.

The common use of the word 'choice' in this context is perhaps an unfortunate one, since the opportunities available to the majority of persons who are seeking work at any age are largely constrained by the locally available positions, which cover a very narrow range in, for example, a mining area. In addition, possible first choices are restricted by the pathways through which the young reach the age at which they leave school. By and large a child from a working-class background is fitted for a different range of occupations from a child from the middle class, and an education in a grammar school or the upper streams of a comprehensive school leads to a different level of the labour force from that gained in a secondary modern school or the lower streams of a comprehensive school.[15] In passing, it should be noted that there is some evidence to show that immigrants, certainly Asians in London, may have higher occupational aspirations than their British peers.[16]

As children grow older they gradually build up a knowledge of the occupational structure, in part learnt during, for example, geography lessons. We have already seen that the pictures and material provided in pre-school and primary reading books seem to predispose boys and girls to different sets of occupations. In addition to the influence of educational media at school, children are affected by television, which, as we saw earlier, can be conceived of as a form of interpersonal situation at home. In one study made in the USA, 237 boys and girls between six and thirteen were questioned about various characteristics of three categories of occupations. Both boys and girls knew most about such occupations as postmen or teachers, with whom they had personal contact, but they knew almost as much about occupations which they rarely met in real life, but which were often shown on television, for example lawyers or reporters. Finally, they knew least, and this was more marked amongst girls, about occupations seen neither in real life nor on television, for example electrical engineers or skilled printers.[17] Television apparently does make the labour force more visible to children.

Gradually children come to anticipate their future occupational role. The self-concept of their own ability and personality, gained certainly in the first case very largely at school, is an important determinant of the level and type of occupation to which they begin to commit themselves. Sometimes a child may come to see himself as less capable than he might have been if, for example, he had not been placed in a low stream or in a secondary modern school. In such cases children in some senses make their first choice of occupation under the influence of a partly fictitious handicap.

Some of the ways in which this process works have been traced in a very detailed study of a group of adolescent boys of low social status (Willis, 1977). Whilst at school these 'lads' are exposed to, indeed they help to develop and sustain, a counter-culture in which there are a number of themes, specifically working-class in nature and appropriate for the manual labour to which the 'lads' are seen and gradually are coming to see themselves to be heading. They distrust authority – teachers now and bosses in the future; they are 'practical' and 'havet heir heads screwed on' – theory is distrusted on the shop floor and formal educational qualifications have no meaning for them; they are not going to choose a career, but will commit that part of themselves that is at all involved in work to a life of generalized wage labour – their present involvement in school is as minimal as their future involvement will be in the productive part of the economy. This latter mode of life will supply them with what matters most to the 'lads' even at school, namely the means to consumption – they will have the money to be real men amongst their peers and in the presence of women, just as at school they gain esteem before the other 'lads' and girls by disobedience and by avoiding such effeminate activities as academic 'work'. This dedication to generalized labour contrasts with the range of specific occupations and particular jobs recommended by teachers and offered by careers advisers. The tragedy is that many of these 'lads' ultimately come to see the shop floor as a prison and to regret that they failed to use the opportunity to escape that the school might have provided. However, the point to be made here is that para-doxically, in the case of the 'lads', the counter-culture eases the transition to work, where they are accepted in a way that gives them a self-esteem which they lacked at school.

Once the point of actual choice is reached, a process of exchange takes place in which the young person, with more or less rationality, balances the tangible and intangible rewards judged to flow from the various jobs then on offer against the tangible and intangible costs seen to be involved in doing each job. There are great varia-tions in the age at which the decision must be made and in its irrevocability. The extremes are exemplified, on the one hand, by the temporary choice of such unskilled seasonal labour as hop-picking which requires little training and is known to be a short-term job and, on the other hand, by a medical career, which necessi-tates a decision early in secondary school to do a course biassed towards science subjects. This latter example also shows the increas-ing finality of many choices of managerial and professional careers since the further the young person goes along the pathway towards his ultimate goal, the more irrevocable his choice becomes. At each stage he narrows his chance for manoeuvre. At fourteen he has the chance of becoming a doctor, dentist or a pure or applied scientist. Ten years later his options have narrowed to becoming, perhaps, either an eye surgeon or an ear, nose and throat specialist.

It must be added that in Britain most workers are placed in jobs at all levels of the labour force by interview and without the help of any psychological testing. In these interviews personality as well as educational attainment is assessed. The interview is known to be a fickle tool and social background and unconsciously influence decisions. The aim of many interviewers is consciously to assess social factors. A public school education may be considered important for an industrial appointment, on social rather than educational grounds. Social background can influence the work of the Youth Employment Officer in that he may consciously place secondary modern school-leavers in jobs that match their family backgrounds. In both these cases the placings can be defended as matching the needs of the workers and the companies. However, it is clear that there is need for the closer integration of this service into the educational system, so that children can be helped to a wise choice by learning accurate details about themselves and possible jobs as early as possible.

C. Conclusion

In its economic function the educational system has to observe both quantitative and qualitative criteria: the latter have been covered very fully here, the former will be given more attention in the next chapter. Schools inculcate ideals that can help or hinder the economy, but the curriculum best-suited to the rapidly changing needs of a modern economy seems to be that preferred by most teachers on strictly educational grounds, namely a broad general education ensuring both literacy and numeracy pursued to as late an age as possible. To organize schooling in this way would also seem to assist the economy by inculcating qualities favourable to change. The fundamental difficulties in accurately forecasting the needs of the labour force leads to the same conclusion. Therefore on the criteria of both quality and quantity the same type of curriculum is needed. However, the actual structure of the educational system has also to be considered. This may be dysfunctional in that the pool of capability may not be developed in the way that matches the needs of the economy, as mediated by the labour force. The situation can be made worse by institutions which are ancillary to the educational system, but which are not usually considered in Britain as a part of it; the rigidities of the apprenticeship system or the methods of giving vocational guidance are relevant at this point.

It is apparent that there may be conflict between the ideals needed for a smoothly working economy and those inculcated by the ethos of the schools. A *laissez-faire* economy requires on the production side a positive attitude towards money-making and 'getting on', and on the consumption side there must be an eagerness to 'keep up with the Joneses'. These attitudes have not been greatly favoured by British teachers. Such conflicts may be due, as is probably true in this case, to autonomous developments rather than to policy decision. However, in today's changing economic climate less entrepreneurial attitudes may be more appropriate to the economy of the future than is often realized. There are, however, very real difficulties in ensuring the continuing operation of what, in many ways, is still a highly complex *laissez-faire* capitalist, industrialized economy at the level needed for the present standard of life during a time of transition when Britain could well be moving towards an economy of a character that will, in all likelihood, demand more intervention by the polity, force more leisure upon most workers and require the personal attributes associated today with zero production growth rather than with inevitable and endless development.

BIBLIOGRAPHY

E. Ashby, *Technology and the Academics*, 1958.
T. Balogh and P. P. Streeten, 'The Planning of Education in Poor Countries', in M. Blang (ed.), *Economics of Education*, Vol. I, 1968.
G. H. Bantock, *Education in an Industrial Society*, 1963.
I. Berg, *Education and Jobs. The Great Training Robbery*, 1973.

B. Bowles and H. Gintis, *Schooling in Capitalist America*, 1976.

M. P. Carter, *Into Work*, 1966.

J. H. Dunning and C. J. Thomas, *British Industry*, 2nd edn, 1966.

E. Ginzberg, 'Education and National Efficiency in the U.S.A.', *The Yearbook of Education*, 1956.

R. M. Kanter, 'The Organization Child: Experience Management in a Nursery School', *Sociology of Education*, Spring 1972.

K. Kumar, *Prophecy and Progress*, 1978.

S. M. Lipset and R. Bendix, *Social Mobility in an Industrial Society*, 1959.

P. W. Musgrave, *Technical Change, the Labour Force and Education*, Oxford, 1967.

P. W. Musgrave, *The Economic Structure*, 1969.

R. Stewart, *Management Succession*, 1956.

W. M. Williams (ed.), *Occupational Choice*, 1974.

P. E. Willis, *Learning to Labour*, 1977.

NOTES

1 L. Hannah, *The Rise of the Corporate Economy*, 1976.

2 P. Sargent Florence, *Ownership, Control and Success of Large Companies*, 1961.

3 G. H. Copeman, *Leaders of British Industry*, 1954, pp. 95–6 and 98.

4 A. H. Halsey (ed.), *Trends in British Society Since 1900*, 1972, p. 114.

5 L. Sklair, *Organized Knowledge*, 1973, especially pp. 18 and 22; C. Freeman, *The Economics of Industrial Innovation*, 1974, pp. 34–6.

6 J. Hearn, 'Toward a Concept of Non-Career', *Sociological Review*, May 1977.

7 For some more recent comments on education in this context see R. Williams, *Communications*, 1962, pp. 100–11.

8 See, for instance, the triennial reports of the Committee of Scientific Manpower, set up by the Advisory Council on Scientific Policy, and also the series of Manpower Studies begun in 1964 by the then Ministry of Labour.

9 G. L. Payne, *Britain's Scientific and Technological Manpower*, 1960.

10 D. R. Miller and G. E. Swanson, *The Changing American Parent*, New York, 1958.

11 R. V. Clements, *Managers: a Study of their Careers in Industry*, 1958, especially Chapter III.

12 An abridgement of this book has been published as *Managers for To-morrow* (DSIR) 1957.

13 In a survey (P. W. Musgrave, 'The Educational Profile of Two British

Iron and Steel Companies with some Comparisons National and International', *British Journal of Industrial Relations*, July 1966) carried out in two large British iron and steel companies in 1961, the author found that only one out of 365 foremen had the equivalent of a degree, 4 had NHC, 6 ONC and 9 City & Guilds.

14 *The Future Development of the Youth Employment Service*, HMSO, 1965, p. 14.

15 For the literature on the influences on a child prior to choosing an occupation see P. W. Musgrave, 'Family, School, Friends and Work: a Sociological Perspective', *Educational Research*, June 1967.

16 Y. P. Gupta, 'The Educational and Vocational Aspirations of Asian Immigrants and English School Leavers – a Comparative Study', *British Journal of Sociology*, June 1977.

17 M. L. and L. B. De Fleur, 'The Relative Contribution of Television as a Learning Source of Children's Occupational Knowledge', *American Sociological Review*, October 1967.

14

The Selection Function

In the last two chapters we have already briefly mentioned the selection function when we noted the way in which political and economic leaders tended to be drawn from certain parts of the social structure through such specific educational routes as the public schools or the universities and, in particular, Oxford and Cambridge. In this chapter the main focus will be upon the selection function itself. Firstly, the place of selection in a class society will be examined, prior to looking at the part education plays in this process and the situation in contemporary Britain.

A. Selection in a Class Society

When the nature of social class was discussed in Chapter 4 the point was made that one of the main characteristics of class as a type of social stratification is that mobility between the various strata is possible. The more social mobility there is, the more open the society is said to be in this particular respect. The measurement of social mobility is very difficult to undertake, largely because of the degree of change that the social structure itself can undergo in the time during which a generation, say, takes to move up and down between social strata. Thus, because of the direction in which the economy is known to be changing the number of bureaucratic positions with relatively high status should increase over the next decade or so, providing more positions into which upward social mobility is possible.

Despite these difficulties in measurement the concept of social mobility is one which can be used with great power in analysis. Furthermore, at least in logical terms there is the possibility of conceiving a state of *perfect mobility* or absolute openness. In this situation every member of a generation, into whatever social stratum he is born, has from birth the same opportunity as every other member of reaching positions in any other strata. The child of a road sweeper, whether boy or girl, has as much chance as that of a barrister, of becoming either a road sweeper or a barrister. It is such a situation of perfect mobility that those who are politically dedicated to equality often hold as their ideal.

The methods of achieving social mobility differ from society to society. In medieval society the main avenue between the social strata of a rather closed society was to move up the hierarchy of the church. In other societies, for example ancient Rome, the army served a similar selective function. But in a capitalist society, because of its very nature, social mobility is usually achieved through economic advancement. Thus, during the industrial revolution men of humble origin rose by making a success of their commercial or manufacturing businesses. Today, such entre-preneurial mobility, as opposed to what may be termed bureaucratic mobility, is still possible, but is much more difficult because of the growth in size of many concerns so that the amount of capital often required to start a business has become very great. However, particularly in the growing tertiary sector of the labour force, new ways of achieving social mobility have become possible. For example, jockeys can become trainers, and young amateurs can become famous pop singers or fashion designers. In different societies, therefore, the drive for achievement and other relevant traits of personality become attached to different types of social position so as to provide the motor for the selection function as organized in that social system. But what we have to examine here is how formal education is related to social mobility under con-temporary industrial capitalism.

B. Education and Selection

1. *The Centrality of the Economy*
In advanced industrial societies, as we saw in the last chapter, there is said to be an increasing need that those in the higher levels of the labour force should have undergone considerable formal education. Those filling these positions have high social status so that success

in formal education becomes a prerequisite for attaining high economic position. Therefore, in an industrial capitalist society such as Britain, social mobility has been thought to be very dependent upon the educational system. Technical needs seem to force an even tighter bond between formal education and the stratification system. Clearly, therefore, any consideration of the selection function of education is bound to be very much concerned with the debates concerning educational inequality (Tyler, 1977).[1] Most crucially, the argument just outlined, which has been called the technical functional case, has, as was noted briefly in the last chapter, come to be questioned.[2] We must, therefore, ask: has the bond between education and the labour force been growing tighter so that mobility depends more strongly upon formal qualifications, or not?

Undoubtedly there is a connection between success in formal education and movement into many positions of high status, but a very careful study by Folger and Nam has shown that only about fifteen per cent of the higher demand for formal educational qualifications in the US labour force between 1940 and 1960 was due to technical upgrading of jobs. The remaining upgrading occurred within occupational groupings.[3] There is absolutely no doubt that during the same period in the USA and in Britain and other industrial societies there was a considerable rise in the formal educational standards of the labour force. The situation has become one in which most persons have more formal education, and therefore struggle for upward social mobility under much the same terms of competition as before. Two questions then become important in any discussion of the selection function of education. What connection is there now between formal educational qualifications and occupational attainment? And between education and social mobility?

Work by Ridge in Britain gives an answer to the first question. Ridge re-analysed data collected by Glass in 1949 in the course of his major study of social mobility in Britain during the first half of this century. Ridge found, and similar results has been reported for several other European countries, that an index measuring inheritance of occupational status between fathers and sons showed little change over the last three generations. He concluded: 'The evidence supports only a weak hypothesis on the "tightening links" between education and occupation in the period.' The level of occupation attained as an adult has, it is true, grown very dependent upon success at Ordinary level in GCE and a similar tendency can be seen for formal qualifications gained after leaving school. But the overall effect of these changes has been to strengthen the measure of the link between father's and son's social status, thereby indicating a reduction of mobility between generations. This result seems due to the higher dependence of success in formal education upon a child's original social status. Thus, on the whole success in education does lead to a better job, but just because higher status leads to a better chance of success in formal education.[4]

Although Ridge's work touched upon the link between education and social mobility a major study by Treiman and Terrell that re-analysed data from very representative samples in both the USA and Britain, is more relevant to our second question. This research is interesting in that it directly compares the situation in the USA and Britain. Their conclusions in brief are as follows. There is somewhat less mobility between recent generations in Britain than in the USA. This difference seems to be due to the stronger direct effect of father's occupational status upon son's occupational status in Britain, that is upon a social class rather than an educational link. The effects of father's occupation upon son's education and of son's education upon son's occupation are equally strong in both countries. Finally, incomes are more dependent in Britain upon occupational attainment than in the USA. From our point of view the important points to note are that Britain has a somewhat more closely stratified social system than the USA, but that 'opportunities for social mobility through education are no more and no less restricted in Britain than the United States'.[5]

The situation, therefore, seems to be one where, certainly in Britain and the USA, but probably in most advanced capitalist countries, there is a link, perhaps weaker than generally thought, between education and the labour force, and hence with social mobility, but that its relative strength, except in the case of some high-status occupations, has changed little in recent years. What has happened is that there has been, for mainly non-economic reasons, a rise in the supply of persons with formal educational qualifications, and employers have used these credentials to allocate jobs between applicants. For this and a number of other reasons Jencks and others in their famous book *Inequality* (1972) attributed much inequality to 'luck'. However, Boudon has shown how such randomness can be an outcome of the very way in which capitalist societies are organized, more especially in respect of their class bias in attainment and their reliance upon formal qualifications for allocating jobs in the labour force. The competition engendered in such a social structure ensures that some children of high-status homes do not attain occupations of as high status as those of their fathers and similarly some from low-status homes do move up the social scale. Boudon constructed a model of a fictitious society on quite realistic assumptions in which he found that the numbers of such downwardly and upwardly socially mobile persons were considerable. A fair degree of social mobility is, therefore, possible and explainable in terms of a two-stage competition. The first stage is governed by the differential outcomes of the process of social class learning and the second by the way in which credentials are sought in the labour force.[6] The education system, then, has a selective function, but it works in a somewhat different way from that specified by the popular technical functional explanation.

2. *Changing Definitions of Equality*

Several major attempts have been made in Britain since the turn of the century to structure the way in which the educational system fulfils its selective function so that it operates in a more egalitarian fashion, though their efforts to-date seem slight. Many more working-class children have, it is true, reached grammar schools and universities, but these greater numbers have been due to a widening of the whole educational system. The result of this has been that because all social classes have benefited absolutely, the ultimate proportional changes in the social class composition of those in selective schools have been small. Even though research in the 1950s appeared to show that equality as measured by the chances of reaching grammar school for those with the same IQ had been achieved,[7] the differential distribution of IQ by social classes, largely dependent upon the early learning experiences available to the different social classes in their families, still ensured that the chances against working-class children of achieving the same educational outcomes as middle-class children were great.

The various administrative changes that have been made were dependent upon shifts in ideological positions. These in their turn have largely taken the form of reactions to the failure of former administrative changes which were seen to have been ineffective in producing a more egalitarian educational system. The major changes in the relevant educational ideologies can be traced by examining the way in which definitions of educational equality have changed during this century since it is these definitions that have largely governed the nature of the educational reforms that have occurred (Evetts, 1973).

Equality in education was originally seen to be a situation in which all children had the same access to future educational experiences. The main problem implicit in converting this definition into an educational system is that powerful forces that are related to other parts of the social structure intervene between children and success at school. For example, as we see again and again, the power of a child's upbringing in his family setting is such that whatever chances are ostensibly offered at school he may be unable to make any use of them either because he or his parents put no value upon education or because his parents do not believe that they can afford to lose his wages by keeping him out of the labour force beyond the minimum legal leaving age. This was the position around 1900 when what was known as 'the scholarship ladder' existed as the mechanism to provide educational opportunity to needy children. A few achieved social mobility through the educational system, but clearly many more were capable of it.

The development of psychology as a behavioural science encouraged the use of various tests in selecting candidates for academic secondary schooling. In this climate of opinion educational equality came to be redefined after about 1930 so that all with the same IQ should be treated educationally in the same way. However, this definition also was seen to be inadequate when during the 1950s the efficiency and the nature of these tests came into question. Furthermore, a total reliance upon intelligence as the sole criterion governing entry to such opportunities as selective secondary schooling clearly ignored other educationally valuable qualities; average intelligence coupled with great persistence can probably ensure a higher level of formal educational attainment than high intelligence linked to an unpredictable temperament.

Both the definitions discussed so far have been termed 'weak' definitions, because they assume, somewhat unrealistically, that all children have the capacity to compete in the educational competition once it has been made fair. By the 1960s, largely due to wider knowledge of work done on social class learning there was a growing realization that this assumption was totally unrealistic. The necessity to compensate for inappropriate backgrounds had become clear. As a result a 'strong' definition of educational equality was born. This was based on the belief that the educational performance of the different social classes should be equal. The philosophical position embodied in this belief is best understood by examining Rawls' 'difference principle'. This relates to the way in which socially valued goods and services, such as liberty and education, should be distributed and states that they 'are to be distributed equally unless an unequal distribution . . . is to the advantage of the least favoured'.[8] Thus, outcomes, rather than inputs, became important as the criterion of equality and since the aim must be to equalize prior environmental factors to ensure equality of outcome, compensatory education is seen to be one administrative mechanism whereby inequality can be reduced.

This definition informed the various attempts to discriminate positively in favour of those seen to be too poorly endowed, materially or cognitively, to take advantage of educational opportunities. In Britain research was undertaken in five Educational Priority Area (EPAs) following the recommendations of the Plowden Report (1967) on primary schools. The aim was to try out a wide range of compensatory methods in areas marked by great need so that a policy on a wider scale could ultimately be evolved (Halsey, 1972). Simultaneously the work of reorganizing secondary schools on a comprehensive basis was stepped up. Both policies were seen as administrative means towards a more egalitarian educational system in which selection was less influenced by the social class of origin of any child. The hope was by educational policy to move the social structure in the direction of perfect mobility.

We have seen that the educational methods associated with the tripartite system were to a great extent reproduced within comprehensive schools in that academic streaming within one school often replaced the former channels provided by three types of school. Other compensatory devices developed in Britain and the USA have also come to be seen as less powerful in their ultimate effects than was originally expected, largely because most of these treatments took place early in a child's schooling and the further he moved from the compensatory treatment the more powerfully did the factors which they were intended to affect, namely those associated with the social class of origin, reassert themselves. The provision of educational resources rather than the way in which they were used has been the focus of most compensatory schemes. As a result of the relative failure of this policy more and more educationists and social theorists have begun to take the position that, although one should continue to attempt to create an educational system that operates in as egalitarian a way as is possible, nevertheless major support must also be given to this traditional policy by somewhat more radical measures that aim to reduce the very strong extra-educational factors influencing the child, particularly those connected with his family and social class of origin.

Bernstein aptly entitled one of his most influential papers, 'Education Cannot Compensate for Society'.[9] Here he made the point very strongly that many compensatory policies are based on the assumption that one particular style of life, usually some version of that found in the middle class, is much superior to other existing or possible ways of living, especially if the aim is to ensure success in formal schooling as it is now organized. This view may be seen as 'cultural imperialism' but, as long as attempts are made to establish a more egalitarian educational system within a society which is basically still capitalist, parents and children will want to 'get on' and in advanced industrial societies today this ambition does entail, as far as any individual is concerned, the achieving of a relatively high standard of formal educational attainment. Therefore, a set of capabilities, relating both to the academic and the moral curriculum, must be learnt that are not necessarily middle-class in their nature, but that are generally, though by no means always, under contemporary conditions valued more highly by middle- than by working-class parents.

If, then, education does act selectively, particularly at the individual level, by social class and is likely in the near future to continue to do so, how unfair is the present situation?

3. Selection in Contemporary British Education

One simple way of measuring the manner in which the contemporary educational system is fulfilling the selection function is to examine the destinations of those leaving the various categories of schools, since to a very great extent these types have class biases in their composition.

Destination of School Leavers (Boys) by Type of School, England and Wales, 1974–5 (percentages)

	Universities	Colleges of education	Polytechnics	Other full-time further education	Employment
Independent recognized	30·4	0·6	3·0	21·8	44·2
Direct grant	41·5	0·3	3·6	14·2	39·3
Grammar	24·5	2·8	4·0	13·1	55·7
Comprehensive	4·3	0·8	0·9	7·5	86·6
Other maintained secondary	2·8	0·8	0·9	8·3	87·2
Modern	0·2	0·1	0·1	9·3	90·4

Source: Social Trends, HMSO, 1977, p. 76.

The table reiterates the point made in the last chapter that types of schools can be seen as take-off ramps into various levels of the labour force, but does so in relation to the selection, rather than the economic, function. Those leaving the higher-status secondary schools in which the social class composition is biassed towards the upper middle class, more often enter tertiary institutions which lead to occupations of high social status. The recent elimination of the direct grant system has resulted in many of the schools formerly depending upon that method of funding becoming independent, so that figures relating to the present situation would probably indicate the selective position of the independent schools even more forcibly. If the statistics for girls were to be presented they would be somewhat similar to the table except in one respect, that fewer girls from all types of school go to universities or polytechnics, but very many more to colleges of education; for example 11·5 and 8·9 per cent of girl leavers from grammar and direct grant schools respectively went to these colleges. Teaching, as was seen in Chapter 8, is, especially at the primary level, largely a women's occupation and does not carry high status. It is, therefore, not surprising that the proportion of those leaving independent schools to enter teaching is so low. A similar, but less strong, comment could be made concerning entry to polytechnics from boys' independent schools.

The ultimate effect of this selective process as it relates to success at university can be seen in the following table, drawn from research based on a large sample of graduates who completed their first degree in 1960.

Social class	*1* *Class distribution* *England & Wales* *1961* *(%)*	*2* *Expected number* *of fathers in* *each class in a* *situation of* *perfect* *mobility*	*3* *Actual* *number of* *fathers*	*4* *Index of* *opportunity* *(3 ÷ 2)*
Professional	2·4	268	1,669	6·23
Intermediate non-manual	22·9	2,556	4,567	1·79
Routine non-manual	9·8	1,094	1,789	1·64
Skilled manual	29·4	3,282	2,245	0·68
Semi-skilled manual	20·9	2,333	772	0·33
Unskilled manual	14.6	1,631	122	0·07
All classes	100·0	11,164	11,164	1·00

Source: R. K. Kelsall, A. Poole and A. Kuhn, *Graduates: the Sociology of an Elite*, 1972, p. 180.

This set of data shows very clearly the different social class chances of negotiating the various routes through the educational system to reach a university and, having succeeded, of ultimately becoming a graduate. Most children of manual workers leave at sixteen and, therefore, never really enter the competition. However, the children of the professional classes make excellent use of the advantages of their upbringing. The process of self-recruitment of the social classes at each end of the social hierarchy is particularly clearly demonstrated in this table.

The reorganization of secondary education along comprehensive lines has been one of the major administrative changes made to the British educational system since 1945. This reform is aimed to offset the selective effects that have been demonstrated here. Therefore, the question must arise: how successful has this new system of secondary schooling, now more than half completed, been in increasing the educational opportunities of the working class? In considering this question we must remember that until compensatory mechanisms can eliminate differences in social class learning, some, perhaps considerable, selective effects must inevitably remain.

Neave (1975) studied the 1968 intake into the universities who came from comprehensive schools. He gathered a representative sample of 969 such leavers and his research showed that this new type of secondary school did seem to be having some success in changing the nature of the selective effect. About one-eighth of these entrants had been originally categorized as failures in the eleven-plus examination. Therefore, under the tripartite system they would have been allocated to technical or modern schools from which the chances of entering tertiary education are low, probably, as we shall see when we consider the interpersonal perspective, because pupils' aspirations are lowered in such schools. However, since these pupils were in comprehensive schools there was somewhat less chance of this occurring; their development through adolescence was eased so that they were able to enter the sixth form and move on to the university. The fact that the proportion in the sample going to university was much the same as that from maintained grammar schools provides further evidence to indicate that the all-in school does seem to be lessening social class differences. Indeed the proportion of working-class entrants to university in this sample was higher than amongst those coming from grammar schools.

There does, therefore, seem to be some change in the direction demanded by a social policy supported, at least in some measure, by both the main political parties in Britain, but the problem to be solved is an immense one. We can see both its size and its main causes if we study what has been called 'the pool of capability'.

D. The Pool of Capability

At any time the population of a country contains children who have different abilities and personalities. In this context we can conceive the educational system to be acting as a sorting mechanism: children with many individual differences are helped to the starting places for their adult lives that are seen as most suited to the present stage of development of their own particular qualities. It is the sum of these qualities that is sometimes called the pool of talent or the pool of ability. For reasons that will become clear the *pool of capability* is perhaps a more apt term.

Around 1960 much thought was given to the more exact analysis of the pool of capability (Vernon, 1963). Interest had been stimulated for two main reasons. There was a political interest, based on the growing desire that able children of all social classes should be given the fullest education of which they were capable. There was also a strong economic interest, stimulated by the widely held belief that Britain could best provide for its economic survival against increasingly fierce foreign competition by ensuring a steady and numerous supply of highly educated technicians and technologists from her tertiary institutions.

In this climate of opinion much research was undertaken that directly related to the pool of capability and hence to the selective function of education. We have seen that the economic argument is now a less certainly based one and that research into the flow of such categories as whole classes through the educational system tends to overlook important interpersonal effects which, especially in the last decade, have come to be seen as more worthwhile fields for research and to which much attention has been given in the first two parts of this book. Yet the large-scale studies undertaken in that period, and particularly those carried out on behalf of two major government enquiries, still provide the fullest picture of the way in which the selection function works in Britain today, since, as we have seen, the situation is only now beginning to change, and probably only marginally, as a result of the introduction of comprehensive schooling. The reports upon which much reliance will be put are *15 to 18* (1959 and 1960), usually known as the Crowther Report, and *Higher Education* (1963), usually called the Robbins Report.

The initial attempts to measure reserves of ability were based on the use of tests, usually of IQ, which were considered to have a value for predicting future academic success. A typical method was to calculate the proportion of the population of a given IQ that was thought to be the minimum requisite for a given level of education, for example to achieve success in a grammar school course as measured by passing five 'O' levels, or for university entry. This proportion was then compared with the proportion that was in fact undergoing that level of education at that particular time. Any shortfall would indicate the order of the reserves of ability. Such a calculation has been called an assessment of reserves in the narrow sense. Usually the sole criterion is IQ, whereas it is well known that many other considerations are important for the progress of children at school or of undergraduates at university. Apart from the influence of the home and the rest of the environment there is the whole complex of personality factors. It is for such reasons that Vernon wishes to talk of 'the pool of capability' rather than 'the pool of talent'. The statistical measurement of reserves of capability must obviously be a much more complex task.

Although no adequate allowance has yet been made for personality factors, measurements or reserves in the broad sense have been made. The population has been divided into strata, usually by social class, and the distribution in these strata of measured intelligence or some such measure of school success as passing a given examination has been calculated. If it is assumed that the highest stratum covers the optimal conditions for all the possible variables, then the shortfall in the lower strata can be calculated. Some calculations have attempted to allow for the effect of removing the economic hindrances to success at school. It is hoped that such methods can be extended to the measurement of the reserves of special abilities such as those needed by mathematicians and scientists. This is partly dependent on further improvements in the psychological tests used to measure such special aptitudes. When thinking about these methods it is worth while reminding ourselves constantly that it is usually ability and not capability that is being used as the criterion. In this connection we should remember that 'merit' has been defined as 'IQ plus Effort'.[10]

Some indications can be given of the quantity of capability that now appears to be wasted in Britain. The very framework of the analysis used will show some of the causes of this waste, since it will make clear the way in which this country fails to allow many individuals to develop and use their capabilities to the full. It is possible in this context to make comparisons between countries, the sexes, geographical regions within the same country, social classes and between types of school.

1. *International Comparisons*

There is immense difficulty in international comparisons of educational statistics, mainly because of differences in standards. Yet the fact that in 1970 40·9 per cent of nineteen-year-olds in the USA were enrolled in full-time education compared with 14·3 per cent in the UK cannot be attributed entirely to the somewhat lower standards of some American tertiary institutions. Again it is known that in 1972 68·1 per cent of those between fifteen and eighteen in Sweden were enrolled in full-time education compared with 39·4 per cent of those in the UK in the same age range.[11] These differences can hardly be attributed to a higher level of innate intelligence amongst the Americans and Swedes than amongst the British.

2. *Inter-Sex Comparisons*

It is generally held that there are no significant differences in the innate intellectual potential of men and women. Differences in kind may exist, but not of level. Yet a recent re-analysis of the data gathered by Douglas in his longitudinal survey has shown that in comparison with the disadvantage consequent upon being working class, attendance at a non-selective secondary school or low ability, the disadvantage consequent solely upon being a girl increases after obtaining 'O' levels though 'A' levels to entry to university. One main conclusion of this research was that 'Sex plays an increasingly important determining role as pupils progress through the system.'[12]

Any attempts to calculate reserves of capability are complicated when comparing the sexes by the fact that girls often study a different curriculum from boys even in coeducational schools. This can be seen clearly in the table below. This table shows the proportions of boys and girls taking certain subjects at 'A' level in the sixth form of a large sample of English and Welsh secondary schools in Autumn 1973. This tendency is as pronounced in the universities where the proportions of young men come near

	All boys	All girls	Boys Single-sex schools	Boys Mixed schools	Girls Single-sex schools	Girls Mixed schools
Mathematics	41	15	37	41	19	12
Physics	9	3	9	9	5	2
Chemistry	41	9	36	43	12	7
Biology	30	13	27	31	15	11
English literature	23	53	28	21	48	55
French	8	24	11	5	23	25
History	23	28	26	20	28	28

Source: Curricular Differences for Boys and Girls, HMSO, 1975, p. 15.

matching the occupational structure, whereas a much higher proportion of women are in arts rather than science or technology faculties. Though there is no doubt that this matches the structure in women's occupations, the swing to the arts appears to have gone further than economic needs would demand. There is, therefore, a tendency built into the school system to divert young women into one particular educational avenue which may be dysfunctional, if one is considering the optimum use of available capability. Marriage and consequent withdrawal from the labour force also complicate the issue and make calculations, for instance, of the reserves of women teachers a very difficult task. However, these complications should in no way be allowed to obscure the fact that in Britain, and indeed in many other countries, women do not receive an equal chance compared with men to be educated beyond the minimum school-leaving age. It is, therefore, amongst women that one of the largely untapped pools of capability lies.

3. Geographical Comparisons

In view of the very different social characteristics of the areas for which the local education authorities in Britain are responsible, it is not surprising that the proportion continuing school beyond the minimum school-leaving age of sixteen varies through the country. Explanations for this might be sought in the fact that there is difficulty in matching the rate of change of the population in any area to such a 'lumpy' piece of capital investment as a new school. Each local authority has reached its present pattern of provision by a different historical route. The problems of educational provision are not the same in rural and urban areas. Social class differences in measured intelligence exist and often characterize a local authority's catchment area; thus, different patterns of the distribution of measured intelligence will be found in Southport and in Salford. Yet after allowing for all such considerations the recorded variations between areas in Britain seem unduly high. Investigations made on behalf of the Robbins Committee showed that in 1960 amongst counties Cardiganshire had the highest proportion of seventeen-year-olds at school with 27·9 per cent, Lincolnshire (Holland) the lowest with 5·5 per cent; the highest county borough was Merthyr Tydfil with 15·2 per cent and the lowest Bury with 2·5 per cent.[13] Such large regional variations, which on the whole mirrored the provision of grammar school places, can in no way match differences in the distribution of capability or even of measured intelligence, nor for that matter do they bear any relation to the availability of fee-paying schools. Political pressure for greater educational opportunity and the greater number of comprehensive schools has helped to lessen some of these inequalities. Yet in 1975 there were still substantial interregional differences in England in the percentages of those aged sixteen and over in maintained schools; the highest percentage was 42·29 in the Greater London region and the lowest 37·01 in Yorkshire and Humberside.[14]

If we contrast the performance of pupils in local education authorities that provide many places in selective secondary schools with those where there are few places, we can see some of the effects of these regional inequalities of opportunity. In Douglas' (1968) study of children in secondary schools he compared areas providing places in selective schools for between 13 and 23 per cent of pupils, with areas where between 26 and 36 per cent of children were found such places. In the areas of low provision the percentages completing fifth form were 38 for boys and 32 for girls compared with 43 and 44 respectively in the areas of high provision, whilst the percentages gaining General Certificates were 25 for boys and 21 for girls in those areas with low provision against 27 per cent for both boys and girls in those areas with the higher rate of provision of selective places. Thus, the girls seemed to be at a greater disadvantage than the boys as a result of lower provision, though both sexes were influenced to some extent, particularly before entry to the sixth form.[15]

These differences are often founded on local attitudes towards education. An analysis of similar regional inequalities in France has shown that the southern third has on average higher attendance rates in secondary education than the rest of France (Ferez in Halsey (ed.), 1961). This was attributed partly to the strong cultural tradition left by the Roman civilization in this area and partly to the fact that the small-scale vineyard owners of this area see in education an escape from their own economic uncertainty, whilst the industrial areas of northern France have provided a more certain demand for labour amongst those who could leave school at the minimum age. A further comparison was made between the dispersed rural areas and the concentrated urban and suburban areas. In the latter the provision of secondary schooling does not demand boarding facilities or long journeys, both of which are needed in rural areas and demand exceptionally favourable attitudes towards education.

In the USA place of residence has been found to influence the desire for university education.[16] In Wisconsin the intelligent sons of prosperous farmers were less liable to want to go to university than were equally intelligent urban boys, since higher education was regarded by the farmers' sons as irrelevant to their chosen career of farming. Their sisters, however, could not easily find an occupation at home and chose a career, such as teaching or social work, for which higher education was necessary.

Little is known of this nature with regard to Britain. Yet similar forces must be at work. It is in an analysis of this kind that we must seek the answer to the question why it is that both the five counties with the highest proportion of children staying at school until seventeen and the five counties with the highest proportion entering higher education were found in the Robbins Committee's survey to be Welsh. When the proportions vary between local education authorities as much as those given above, it can be clearly seen that here is another source of inequality and of unused capability.

4. Social Class Comparisons

The argument about the reserves of ability is often stated in terms of social class. Sometimes crude comparisons are made between the proportions from various social classes at different stages of the educational system, for example the percentage of children of manual workers at university. Apart from the by-now familiar warning against confusing ability with capability, there are two other considerations to be taken into account. Comparisons between the measured intelligence of the various social classes may for many purposes need to be corrected to allow for the skewed distribution of IQ by social class. But perhaps of more importance is the influence of social class learning as described in Chapter 4, which works so that many able children from working-class homes cannot gain the experience necessary for the full development of their intelligence.

It is possible to quote statistics that show clearly the differences between measured intelligence and academic attainments in each social class. For example, during the course of its enquiry the Crowther Committee examined a representative sample of 5,940 National Service recruits to the army. It found that in the top 11 per cent of measured intelligence the proportion who gained the entry qualifications necessary for higher education, namely two or more 'A' levels or an Ordinary National Certificate, was 68 per cent in the case of children of fathers in professional or managerial jobs, compared with 52 per cent for those whose fathers were in clerical employment, 45 per cent for the children of skilled manual workers and 31 per cent in the case of children of semi-skilled and unskilled workers. It is not so much amongst the very able that these differences are so apparent. Thus, in the second level of ability 69·1 per cent of the children of fathers in professional and managerial occupations were in independent, grammar or technical secondary schools, whilst only 26·3 per cent of the children of fathers in unskilled manual work were; at the first level of ability the respective percentages were 96·2 and 77·2.[17]

Using this type of statistic it is possible to calculate the reserves of ability 'in the broad sense', but such a figure would be very artificial, since the academic achievements of children in the upper social classes have improved greatly in recent years, but there has been only a small reduction in the differential rate of achievement between the social classes. All classes have been affected more or less equally by the recent expansion in education. Therefore, any calculation of the reserves of ability made in the future may well yield a higher estimate than at present, assuming that this differential rate of achievement diminishes. It is clear, however, that there is a dysfunction in the British educational system so that it is not playing its proper part in sorting out the capability available in all the social classes of the population.

5. *Type of School*

The four comparisons made so far have all relied on factors external to the educational system. It is possible to tackle the problem in a different way. This examines the educational achievements of children who have the same apparent capacity as measured by intelligence tests or by some form of teacher's report, but who have taken different routes through the secondary school system or have left before taking certain examinations. The difficulty inherent in this type of estimate can be seen from the fact that in the report on *Early Leaving* (1954) heads of a sample of grammar schools in England and Wales thought that 33 per cent of their entry were capable of a course leading to two or more 'A' levels, but for 1962 well over 40 per cent of their pupils had begun such a course. In fact in 1960–1 26 per cent of all grammar school leavers had obtained two or more 'A' levels.

At the moment little is known of the effect of different types of secondary education on children of equal measured intelligence at the time of entry. In one study of 5,362 children it was shown that there is a considerable overlap in the IQ scores of children in different types of secondary school. The ranges within which 90 per cent of the children's IQ scores fell were: grammar schools 106–127, technical schools 100–122·5, independent schools 85–124, secondary modern schools 76–107·5.[18] It is known that in some independent schools children attain much higher academic results than might be expected from their IQ scores. There is also the possibility that children may lose points of IQ through the experience of being placed in the lower streams of a primary school (Douglas, 1964). The possibility will be discussed later in this chapter that the very act of putting a child in a certain type of school may provide him with the experience that can help to develop or hinder the growth of his intelligence.

6. Conclusion

The problem of the pool of capability viewed from an educational standpoint is whether the schools and other educational institutions are so organized that they help to bring about the full development of the capability potentially available to the country. Perhaps the best way to epitomize what has been said is to take an imaginary, but not atypical case. What is lost to the country when the daughter of an unskilled labourer just fails the selection test for the grammar school at the age of eleven and becomes a member of the top stream of a single-sex secondary modern school in an urban area with a ready demand for unskilled young women in the local labour force?

E. The Interpersonal Level

1. The Family

Much of the work already reported on social class learning is relevant at this point. It is through the interpersonal interaction experienced within the family that many of the attributes are learnt that make for success or otherwise at school. Very rarely have compensating mechanisms been established to work on parents in order to improve the educational chances of their children. One such British attempt was undertaken in an EPA in a Yorkshire mining village, where a Community Education Centre, the Red House, was established. Here, amongst several innovatory projects, mothers, who also helped their children at pre-school, were given informal instruction so that they knew both what was happening to their children at school and how they might set about assisting them at home. As far as the results were measurable the children involved improved greatly in their language skills. Furthermore, unusually for such intervention programmes, the initial advantage seemed to last beyond the immediate time when the special treatment was given.[19] In this case not just the children were influenced, but also apparently their mothers and, hence, their home environment.

Parents have a very real influence on whether or not their children are selected for educational success, in that their own values in relation to education can affect the behaviour of their children. Swift has shown the very subtle nature of the relevant socialization processes at work. In a detailed study by interview of 132 boys and girls who had taken the eleven-plus in two LEAs in the North of England he found that the parents of successful working-class children saw further up the social ladder than the working class in general. Though these parents in this respect held views nearer to the middle class, yet they did not see very much further than other members of the working class – their choice of occupations for their children tended to be for one of the lower middle-class 'professions', for example draughtsman or librarian. These parents of successful working-class children had no delusions about their own social class position. They saw themselves as 'respectable' members of their class; in other words their style of life was on some counts, especially in relation to their values, qualitatively akin to the middle class, but their status was still definitely working class. Perhaps the most important finding of Swift's study was that he showed that the nature of the achievement motivation learnt in the families of the working-class children who passed the eleven-plus was of a different kind from that learnt in middle-class families with successful children. In the former the motivation was built around the emphasis of the parents upon gaining certificates, whilst in the latter the focus was upon education as a socially liberating process.[20] Social class learning, an interpersonal process *par excellence*, has crucial implications for education, but successful working-class children must not be seen as having the same social attributes as either all or even only successful middle-class children.

In the past working-class children who passed the eleven-plus examination were referred to as 'scholarship boys and girls'. This success was usually the first step for the child from the working-l class home who achieved social mobility through the educationa system. This has been the way of social advancement for many teachers and therefore has an especial interest in this context. Jackson and Marsden (1962) made a pioneer study of their problems in a large industrial community in the North of England. They concluded that on the whole such children transferred their loyalty, sometimes in an exaggerated fashion, to their new and higher class. This did not happen without soul-searching and often was accompanied by emotional difficulties. But it is clear that the grammar-school education which is so necessary for achieving upward social mobility not only gives the child the factual knowledge that he must have, but has as well a stereotyping effect on many children. It tends to select children, often but not always, from families well-disposed towards education, and to turn them into young adults who have middle-class values, whatever the social class from which they originally came.[21]

2. *The School*

One organizational pattern about which there has been much controversy at both the expert and lay levels, namely streaming, has great implications for the selective function of education. This is because it is alleged that to allocate children to streams, or for that matter to different types of secondary school supposedly catering for different levels of potential ability, has effects on the level of actual ability at which children come to operate as well as upon the level of their aspirations. The work on classroom interaction reported in Chapter 11, particularly such studies as that by Brophy and Good, has shown the importance of non-verbal communication between teachers and their pupils in these respects. But what size of a problem are these interpersonal factors being asked to explain?

When children first go to school at five years of age they enter classes that are not divided by ability level. There may be parallel classes in the larger schools in order to divide the children into groups of a teachable size. The children remain in such unstreamed classes until about the age of seven. In many of these schools the children are divided into streams by ability some time between the ages of seven and nine. This is the first selection process in our educational system. The arguments used to justify organization of the school in this way are that the brighter children will be given the chance to develop more fully and more quickly, whilst the less able children will have the advantage of proceeding at a rate most suited to their ability. Admittedly there may be innate differences in the potential capability of children that can sometimes be discovered by this age, and certainly by eight many of the effects of social class learning have influenced the development of children's intelligence. But if it can be shown that the IQ scores of the children in the upper streams improve whilst those in the lower streams deteriorate between the ages of eight and eleven, the period when the children are in the junior school streams, some of the basis for streaming would be removed. In fact, it could then be said that streaming acts as a self-fulfilling prophecy, bringing about what it predicts.

It is just this that seems to be shown by the work of Douglas (1964). He found that there was a big overlap between the IQ scores of the children in his sample who were in the upper and in the lower streams of junior schools. Yet at all levels of measured intelligence children in the upper streams gained points of IQ between the ages of eight and eleven, whilst children in the lower streams lost IQ points. To give examples, children in upper streams with IQs between 87·5 and 92·5 gained 8·6 points, whilst children of the same measured ability in lower streams lost 1·5 IQ points. For the IQ range 98·5 to 101·5 the upper stream gained 6·7 points against a loss of 2·4 points by the children in the lower streams. In the range from 107·5 to 110·5 the upper stream gained 3·4 points compared with a loss of 2·9 points by the children in the lower stream. It must be noted in addition that it is the less able children in the upper streams who at every level improve more than the abler children in the same streams, whilst in the lower streams the range of ability remains more or less the same throughout the time spent in the junior school.

There is great difficulty in interpreting statistics of this type. There are problems both of a theoretical nature inherent in the comparability through time of the measures used,[22] and also of a more practical nature because, for instance, many of the unstreamed schools are in rural areas or are schools with poor records of past academic success. The Plowden Committee set up a large-scale project using two samples of fifty carefully matched schools to investigate the effects of streaming in the junior school. This study was cross-sectional rather than longitudinal in design, and hence comparison between the various age groups is dangerous. However, although there were some differences between streamed and unstreamed schools amongst the eight- and nine-year-old children in scores on a test of verbal ability, there were no such differences amongst the ten-year-olds, nor did the latter age groups show any marked differences on a verbal/non-verbal test of ability. The children in streamed schools did score more highly on attainment tests relating to the subject of mechanical arithmetic, usually taught in a more traditional manner, whilst those in unstreamed schools did as well as their peers in the streamed classes on tests of reading attainment, often associated with more progressive methods of teaching. Furthermore, as has been found before by other workers in investigations of activity methods of teaching, there was some evidence to show that the children in the less-structured unstreamed schools were catching up with the children in the streamed schools where more traditional methods were probably more often used. Even within each category of schools it seems that the attitudes of the teachers towards the method of teaching employed has some effect on attainments and on a measure of anxiety shown by the children.[23] It can therefore be seen that contradictory evidence about the effects of streaming exists and that more research is needed before a reasonably definite judgement can be passed, but certainly we should bear in mind that merely to change the structure of a school may not have the desired effect if the teachers concerned do not favour the structure within which they are working.

In the past, when the tripartite system was the administrative norm, similar forces may well have been at work within and between the three types of secondary school and any evidence of this would reinforce the suspicion that this process of selective differentiation could well be operating within the streams of contemporary comprehensive schools. Thus, it is relevant that Douglas (1964) found that, whereas 40·1 per cent of upper middle-class children with an IQ of 106 or less were in grammar schools, only 7·9 per cent of lower working-class children of the same measured intelligence gained entry to these schools. What is more, once children reached the grammar school, their average IQ score seemed to change as compared with that of those children in the secondary modern school, in much the same way as happened in the streams of the junior school. The average scores of those who went to a grammar school rose, and the average scores of those at the secondary modern school fell. The decline was most pronounced for children from the manual working class with the highest test scores; those in the range 112–115 IQ points lost about 6 IQ points by the age of fifteen (Douglas, 1968).

Some children are, therefore, placed in secondary modern schools whose achievement could be higher in the ethos of a different type of school. It may well be that it is not only the development of intelligence that is crucial in this selection process, but that different levels of aspiration are internalized in the different types of schools. Studies of the vocational aspirations of children in modern schools show them to be realistic and to accord well with the measured intelligence of the children concerned. An investigation made in 1956 (Veness, 1962) found that boys and girls in secondary modern schools were less preoccupied with their future work than were children in other types of school. Such motivation or lack of it could partly govern the academic attainments of a child and thereby determine whether or not the child had the experience necessary to develop his intelligence fully. If the children of slightly above-average or average intelligence are educated apart from other children of their intelligence, but together with children of below-average intelligence, they may well come to hold the lower aspirations of those who form the majority of their school fellows. These 'more realistic' hopes may be inappropriate to the more able pupils in a secondary modern school or to children of a slightly higher level of ability in those areas where provision of grammar school places is low.

Another way of considering this problem of the effects of streaming is to examine what could happen if the system were abolished in a school where it had formerly existed. Lacey (1974) has reported the effects of such a change in a four-stream grammar school. A new headmaster, soon after his appointment, abolished an existing express stream which allowed the ablest pupils to sit 'O' level a year early and destreamed the remaining three forms. Lengthening the course for those who would have been the express stream improved their results at 'O' level, whilst the effect of destreaming the remainder of the entry was to produce a marked improvement in the performance of those who would have been in the bottom stream, an overall decrease in differentiation between the achievements of all pupils and an all-round increase in the number of 'O'-level passes achieved. Lacey believes that the evidence shows that this result was due to the fact that the 'C' stream no longer saw themselves as failures. He does, however, issue a warning: this result was achieved in a grammar school and the efforts of destreaming might not be so dramatic in a school where IQs were lower and initial motivation was less favourable.

Education may not be as influential in this process of social selection as was until recently felt to be the case. Yet it still fulfils a powerful supportive social role and for individuals its effects can be utterly decisive. If both the social and individual functions are to be lessened in their impact, then much attention has to be given to influencing the workings of the interpersonal factors examined in this section, particularly as they operate within the family, since they lie at the heart of the statistics that portray the educational fate of the various social categories usually considered at the societal level.

E. Conclusion

We have been examining the function of selection and to do this is to view education in its social context. It is clear that the position in Britain is complicated by the private system. However, a consideration of the way the educational system undertakes selection shows firstly that, looked at in various ways, there is a pool of capability which is not at the moment fully used. Secondly, given the present structure of education, which is still much influenced by the tripartite system, we may ask, are the most capable children selected? It seems that the often rigid form of organization makes it difficult to meet demographic change and hence brings about a loss of capability. Within the system children of lower social class still appear to be at a disadvantage, though this is not so gross as formerly. But one can ask a deeper question. Once the children are segregated, even assuming absolutely 'fair' initial selection, is such segregation in itself dysfunctional? The answer, based on studies of the results of streaming, seems to be that this could be so. The cumulative nature of both processes may be summed up in one set of statistics: when the sample of children born in 1940-1 investigated by the Robbins Committee had reached the age of twenty-one, those who were children of fathers in non-manual occupations had greater chances of academic achievement than those who were children of fathers in manual occupations at each IQ level and at each stage of the educational system. The one exception was for the most able at the end of their course in the fifth form. The ratios were as in the following table.

Social class chances of academic achievement by IQ at eleven

IQ	Degree-level Courses	At least two 'A' levels	At least five 'O' levels
130+	2·06	1·43	0·97
115-129	2·12	1·64	1·24
100-114	3·00	1·50	1·68

Source: Higher Education (Robbins), Appendix I, p. 43.

Segregation at primary and secondary levels hinders development of capability and leads to low aspirations. The selection process fulfils the prophecy upon which the system is founded, but equally surely it lessens the capability available to this country. However, the best means to change this situation are problematic and depend greatly upon the political ideology that is brought to the data outlined in this chapter. But clearly, whatever the political affiliation, the starting point must be that the problem of educational inequality under present social circumstances is a multi-causal one; it is rooted in various processes in several social institutions – in the family and in the economy as well as in education. Therefore, only a multi-dimensional policy will be likely to have much influence upon the present inequality of educational opportunity. The aim must be not merely to ensure equal *access*, but equal *use* of educational experiences. However, even granted that this can be achieved – and Tyler (1977) has given us new directions for thinking about means to such an end – there remain the problems associated with the direction of development of industrial capitalism to which attention was drawn in the last chapter. How can an educational system both allow access for the able and the ambitious to qualifications which later have a high monetary value, and simultaneously permit others, some able and some not, to opt for an 'uncareer' or a 'non-career'? The ensuring of equality of educational opportunity under the economic circumstances that permit such options to be available must be a more difficult task than it has been at any time over the last hundred years, during which period it has been an object of social policy.

BIBLIOGRAPHY

J. W. B. Douglas, *The Home and The School*, 1964.

J. W. B. Douglas, *All Our Future*, 1968.

J. Evetts, *The Sociology of Educational Ideas*, 1973.

A. H. Halsey (ed.), *Ability and Educational Opportunity*, Paris, 1961, especially Chapters 2, 5 and 6.

A. H. Halsey (ed.), *Educational Priority*, 1972.

B. Jackson and D. Marsden, *Education and the Working Class*, 1962.

C. Jencks *et al.*, *Inequality: a Re-assessment of the Effect of Family and Schooling in America*, New York, 1972.

C. Lacey, 'Destreaming in a "Pressured" Academic Environment', in S. J. Eggleston (ed.), *Contemporary Research in the Sociology of Education*, 1974.

G. Neave, *How They Fared*, 1975.

W. Tyler, *The Sociology of Educational Inequality*, 1977.

T. Veness, *School Leavers*, 1962.

P. E. Vernon, 'The Pool of Ability', *Sociological Studies in British University Education: Sociological Review Monograph No. 7*, Keele, 1963.

15 to 18 (Crowther Report), Vol. I, 1959; Vol. II, 1960.

Higher Education (Robbins Report), Appendix I (especially Part Three), 1963.

NOTES

1 The references in the rest of this section, though each separately cited, are referred to in more detail in Tyler's excellent introduction to this topic.

2 A. M. Collins, 'Functional and Conflict Theories of Educational Stratification', *American Sociological Review*, December 1971.

3 J. K. Folger and C. B. Nam, 'Trends in Education in Relation to Occupational Structure', *Sociology of Education*, Fall 1964.

4 J. M. Ridge, 'Fathers and Sons', in Ridge (ed.), *Mobility in Britain Reconsidered*, Oxford, 1974.

5 D. J. Treiman and K. Terrell, 'The Process of Status Attainment in the United States and Great Britain', *American Journal of Sociology*, May 1976.

6 R. Boudon, *Education, Opportunity and Social Inequality*, New York, 1974.

7 J. E. Floud, A. H. Halsey and F. M. Martin, *Social Class and Educational Opportunity*, 1956.

8 J. Rawls, *A Theory of Justice*, Oxford, 1971, p. 303.

9 B. Bernstein, in *New Society*, 26 February 1970.

10 M. Young, *The Rise of the Meritocracy*, 1958, p. 94. For an attempt to measure the way selection taps the pool of capability differentially, see D. F. Swift, 'Meritocratic and Social Class Selection at Age Eleven', *Educational Research*, November 1965.

11 *The Educational Situation in OECD Countries*, Paris, 1974, pp. 27 and 34.

12 M. G. Tuck, 'The Effect of Different Factors on the Level of Academic Achievement in England and Wales', *Social Science Research*, September 1974.

13 *Higher Education* (Robbins Report), Appendix I, p. 65.

14 Percentages calculated from *Statistics of Education 1976*, Vol. 1, Tables 18 and 27.

15 Douglas, 1968, pp. 80 and 213.

16 W. H. Sewell *et al.*, 'Social Status and Educational and Occupational Aspiration', *American Sociological Review*, February 1957.

17 *15 to 18* (Crowther Report), Vol. II, pp. 120 and 122.

18 Douglas, 1964, p. 21 (T Scores converted to IQ points as on p. 7). S. Wiseman, *Education and Environment*, Manchester, 1964, pp. 21–4 and 132, found a similar overlap in his work in the Manchester area.

19 Halsey, *Educational Priority*, HMSO, Vol. I, 1972, especially Chapters 8 and 9.

20 D. F. Swift, 'Social Class Mobility, Ideology and 11+ Success', *British Journal of Sociology*, June 1967.

21 For a novelist's picture of this process, based on personal experience, see R. Williams, *Border Country*, 1960.

22 For some problems of interpreting Douglas' results see G. Horobin, D. Oldman and W. Bytheway, 'The Social Differentiation of Ability', *Sociology*, May 1967.

23 *Children and their Primary Schools* (Plowden Report), Vol. 2, pp. 573–6 and 581.

15

Stability and Change

The influential contemporary German sociologist, Habermas, has written: 'The level of development of a society is determined by [its] institutionally permitted learning capacity. . . . Not *learning*, but *not-learning* is the phenomenon that calls for explanation. . . .'[1] Clearly, the educational system plays some part in helping or hindering social change of all types by the way in which it encourages learning or not-learning. Paradoxically in this respect the educational system has two relevant, but contradictory functions. As we have seen, it both transmits the existing culture and assists in or even produces change.

Any consideration of stability tends to raise the problem of change and vice versa. Certainly the educational system of a modern community has a function in respect of both. It is because they are so closely connected, though opposites, that these two functions, that of producing stability and that of producing change, are considered together in this chapter. Firstly, we shall look at the manner in which education plays a part in transmitting culture. Next, we shall examine how the educational system produces and mediates ideas that might bring about change. Finally, the ways in which schools both react to change and produce innovators will be considered.

A. Culture Transmission

1. *Conserving the Culture*

When looking at primitive cultures which are very different from our own, it is relatively simple to appreciate their particular customs and see how their children learn these patterns of behaviour. It is more difficult to examine our own culture and discover which parts are passed on by the family and which by the school. The extent and nature of culture transmission through the school can perhaps best be shown by a series of examples. Some of these will be extreme cases, since these throw a very clear light on just what is happening.

Let us take the case of a five-year-old British child who comes from an agnostic home. When he first goes to school, this child will spend much of the latter part of each autumn term preparing the classroom for Christmas. It is almost impossible that the child will not learn something of the Christmas story from a Christian viewpoint and this learning will be reinforced yearly till the child leaves school. It is difficult to imagine this process not taking place. By law, state-aided schools must give religious instruction, and the religion taught is almost always Christianity. A child may be withdrawn from religious instruction if his parents demand it. But even in such a case this aspect of our culture will almost inevitably be transmitted to the child. The classroom walls will be covered with pictures or decorations, many of which his classmates have made. His friends will eagerly talk of what they have done and this may include the making of a nativity scene in the corner of the classroom. The new songs learnt will be carols. The theme of Christmas will recur throughout all his work and play. How can he escape learning about it?

A second example of the same extreme type is the case of the British school in a foreign land, such as the Argentine, or even in a Commonwealth country, such as Malaysia. In this school a British child will not only learn the English language which, as will be seen later, is an important vehicle for transmitting the culture and which he will be accustomed to using in his own family circle, but he will learn much that will make him a Briton and which his family's restricted pattern of experience cannot provide. Perhaps the most obvious example is seen in the games that he will play; cricket overseas is a well-worn joke. Less obvious is the particular way in which the British of the social class to which the child belongs mix with others of their own age and sex. The triumph of the British school abroad is that the British at home shall say of its old scholars: 'You would never have thought that he was brought up abroad.'

As a child grows older he is constantly learning new patterns of behaviour and at the same time expanding his vocabulary. These two processes bear a unique relation to each other in any single culture. Under modern conditions much of both types of learning occurs at school or under its influence. In this way what is considered polite, whether in actions or in words, is often 'picked up' at school and may well be considered wrong in the family. Much of the work that is done in the classroom under the heading of 'English' is of the nature of moral education and therefore attempts to transmit cultural values.

Our language is full of metaphors and, particularly in poetry, of images that are peculiar to us as a nation. Children undertake many comprehension exercises during which these cultural images are attached to words and analogies are explained. One has only to try to read contemporary American or Australian poetry to children to realize that what is ostensibly the same language carries very different meanings, references and values, all of which are part of an alien culture. Or again, one should note the difficulty of using American children's books, even when illustrated, in English schools. In Scotland and in Wales some schools play an important part in preserving the national cultures by teaching the national tongue and emphasizing the national literature so that, for example, the poetry of Burns is given more attention in Scottish than in English schools. The young child is of an age at which he is unable to appreciate that culture transmission is taking place during an English lesson, whilst the parents are either unaware or in some respect wish the process to occur.

From the examples given it is clear that, on the whole, culture transmission is conservative. The teachers in the schools tend to pass on what they have been given. Conformity to what went before is stressed. The schools help the family, which plays a more predominant part in infancy, to pass on the national culture, which may be taken to include the national character. This last point is best exemplified from American educational history. The task of the typical American city school, especially on the eastern seaboard, has always tended to be the creation of good American citizens from the children of the most recent immigrants. They have to learn not only a language, but a national character. The symbol of this task is still the Stars and Stripes on the teacher's desk. In passing it is worth commenting that this task has become more common since 1945. For example, immigrants into Australia, the so-called 'New Australians', have had, with more or less success, to be made into Australians, and Jews from all over the world into Israelis; also in Britain the assimilation of white and coloured immigrants has brought problems of an educational nature.

2. *Immigrants*

Immigrants have always formed a substantial minority of our labour force, but during the nineteenth century they were largely Irish, so that, although there were religious problems, assimilation was not complicated by differences in colour or in language. In 1975/6 it was estimated that there were about 1·7 million of New Commonwealth and Pakistani ethnic origin in Great Britain, or 3·3 per cent of the total population. The greatest part of this number were relatively recent immigrants, though it should be noted here that there are increasing numbers of second generation coloured children born in Britain. These migrants have come mainly from the West Indies, especially Jamaica; India, Pakistan, Bangla Desh; and West Africa. This rapid influx of migrants, all coloured, was concentrated in such large cities as London, Birmingham, Liverpool and Leeds, and brought as its consequence a number of social problems, particularly in the fields of housing and education. In some schools more than a third or even a half of classes consisted of immigrant children. Those from the East were Hindus or Muslims by religion and had very different cultural patterns both from their host culture, the British, and from such other immigrant groups as the West Indians, Africans or Cypriots. Furthermore, many of the Christians amongst the West Indians found the practice of their religion in Britain very different from that of their home country. The motives for migrating tended to differ by ethnic group. Thus, many West Indians aimed to assimilate into the host culture and to be seen as British citizens, whilst many Indians aimed to earn more than they could in their home country, but wished to remain a socially distinct grouping (Bowker, 1968).

In this situation the schools have a difficult task in passing on the host culture, if such is their aim. The immigrant child finds that the habits and behaviour learnt from his parents, and hence valued highly by him, are despised sometimes by his teacher and almost always by the community at large. Much of the behaviour that he has learnt at home is totally inapplicable in his new land, and this applies both to migrant children and to the majority of children born of immigrant parents after their arrival in Britain. For example, there are the problems due to language, obvious in the case of Indians, but, though less obvious, no less real for West Indians, whose English is in many ways syntactically different from that spoken in Britain. Minor matters like school dinners cause difficulties, since the children are unused to the food and styles of eating. Many immigrants have names that seem odd to the native British and the large numbers of Singhs and Khans can even cause administrative frustration, though this is more often due to doubt over children's ages because registration of births is either unknown or inefficient in their country of origin. However, perhaps the major problem is the prejudice against the incomers amongst British parents, who feel the hostility to coloured persons, apparently usual in Britain, and also hold the possibly well-founded view that a high proportion of ill-educated children, particularly from a culturally very different group, will lower the quality of education given to their own sons and daughters.

In 1965 the DES issued *The Education of Immigrants*, in which it specified the 'integration' of immigrants as a social aim in the fulfilment of which the schools had a large part to play, though it did not closely define this term. Initially the schools had, on the whole, attempted to fulfil such a policy by trying to help immigrants to become British but, though this course coincided with the motives of many West Indian parents, it clearly conflicted with the desires of most Indians and Pakistanis. However, there have always been a number of schools whose aim has been, on the one hand, to teach migrants enough to enable them to live successfully in Britain, whilst at the same time respecting their ways of life and religion, and, on the other hand, to try to lower the level of prejudice amongst British children against coloured persons. In one school in Huddersfield the religious festivals of the various ethnic groups in the school are respected and used as starting points for the groups to teach each other, with the aim of breaking down stereotyped attitudes based on ignorance and a lack of thought.[2] Inasmuch as teachers succeed in these two aims, their function is to change in some respects both the cultures concerned, since the immigrants become a little more British and the British a little less prejudiced.

Attitudes relating to colour and to ethnicity do seem to be learnt early. In work carried out in 1965 Kawwa compared two large groups of English and immigrant children in a primary and a secondary school, and found ethnic prejudice to exist in children as young as seven. English children held the stereotyped views of immigrants displayed in such comments as 'They're dirty', or 'They take our houses and jobs', which clearly seemed to have been learnt from their parents. Immigrant children in their turn saw native children as unfriendly and inegalitarian. In the secondary school, children chose their friends within their own ethnic groups. Yet the situation may be more complex than this. From work done in Sparkbrook, Birmingham, it seems that what happens is that children, even in early adolescence, make friendships and mix with each other across ethnic divisions whilst in school, but that they do not carry these friendships out of the school into their leisure activities. An easy mixing takes place at school, but segregation at home. In this context, as in many others, familial sanctions seem to overcome behaviour learnt in the schools, which are in the eyes of parents of all groups, white or black, seen to be undermining both the accepted pattern of culture and parental authority by sanctioning such friendships.[3]

In all these instances, the schools are acting either on the one hand to pass on the existing culture in greater or lesser measure to new members who may or may not have been born in the community, or, on the other hand, they are in some small way changing the present pattern of culture. Such innovation may or may not be the policy given to the educational system.

3. *Changing the Culture*
The historian, G. M. Young, writing more specifically of the mid-Victorian era, but in words of more general application, said: 'Culture is not a state but a process. . . . The judgements of parents, nurses, governesses, pastors and masters of all degrees are, on the whole, the voice of society in equilibrium and bent on maintaining its equilibrium. The judgements of the younger generation

are, on the whole, the voice of society dissident and exploratory.'[4] Later in this chapter we shall examine the sources of change and see that the conflict between the younger and the older generations is but one amongst a host of sources of unplanned and autonomous change.

The educational system may, however, be given a much more positive role in transmitting culture. A political decision may be taken that the existing way of life ought not to continue, and the government may want to use a social institution which is as central to this purpose as the educational system in an attempt to change the culture. The Russian schools were in this position in the 1920s, though by today an existing culture is being transmitted. One of the clearest examples of an attempt to alter the culture of a country was that made in Germany by the Nazis after they came to power in 1933. In this case the full extent of the term 'education' can be seen. The Nazis used every type of school for every age range and all the facilities for further education, including universities and technical colleges. They used the existing institutions for adult education and created new ones. Finally, they used the apprenticeship and training system in industry, always considered a part of the educational system in Germany. Though this attempt failed, it is a reminder of how many and varied are the institutions which we lump together under the heading 'the educational system'.

In Britain we may think that what the Russians succeeded in doing and what the Germans attempted to do was morally wrong, but we should remember that a similar role is sometimes suggested for our schools today. The argument runs somewhat as follows: the modern adolescent is not of the type that, according to some, is good for Britain today, or according to others, of whom they approve. He must be changed, and the schools must play a big part in this policy. To put it bluntly, the child must be saved from society. It is a worthwhile exercise for any teacher to examine his role and see whether he is neutral or positive in the way in which he passes on his country's culture. And can he justify either his neutral or his positive position?

The child stands between two powerful influences, the school and the family. Every teacher needs to remind himself constantly that the family is often the stronger of the two influences, especially when the child is young. Yet, paradoxically, teachers of children in primary schools probably have more direct influence on their pupils than teachers at any later stage, more particularly because of the greater influence of the peer group amongst children of the secondary age. But at all stages the influence of the school and later the university or college is great, especially in the introduction of ideas to older pupils. An inspiring teacher can create what the Crowther Report has called 'intellectual discipleship'. The great French sociologist, Durkheim (1956, p. 89), spoke of the teacher as 'the interpreter of the great moral ideas of his time and his country'. It is clear that these ideas may be Marxist or Christian, but the teacher in his role as teacher will pass them on to the next generation.

4. Sub-cultures

(i) *Regional Differences.* So far we have spoken as if it was one culture that was being passed on by the schools. We must now face the question of whether the educational system does or can transmit only one culture. Sub-cultures exist within our society. T. S. Eliot (1948) has argued that the tensions produced by their existence, provided that they do not cause great conflict, bring gain and that, therefore, the resulting whole is greater than its parts, though in view of the demands for devolution for Scotland and Wales and of the present problems in Northern Ireland one might well wonder how Eliot would have viewed the situation in Great Britain today. Hoggart (1957) has traced the way in which the traditional rural English culture was taken by migrants during the nineteenth century to the great northern industrial cities and how by today the traces of this traditional way of life have in some respects disappeared, though in others they remain. A school set in the midst of any sub-culture, be it urban or rural, English or Scottish, Mancunian or Aberdonian, will find it difficult to pass on the culture in any form other than that in which it is interpreted by that sub-culture. This is particularly true when the differentiation is mainly along material lines, as is perhaps the case for rural and urban sub-cultures. It would be hard to teach a rural way of life against a background of tall chimneys.

(ii) *Educational Sub-cultures.* There is another aspect of the passing on of one culture which must be considered. This is the problem known today as 'the two cultures controversy'. In its modern form, which is relevant to all levels of education, including higher education, it was sparked off in 1959 by C. P. Snow (1964). In brief, the argument runs that specialization in education is nowadays so intense that even in the final years at school, but certainly by the time higher education has been reached, it has become impossible for those following arts courses to understand and communicate at any depth with those following science courses, and vice versa. The effect created by specialization goes further than difficulty in understanding the material with which the other side is dealing, but extends to the fact that the two sides are learning totally different modes of thought.[5]

The validity of this argument in such an extreme form can be questioned, but there is an element of truth in it. For perhaps the greater part of the last hundred years the claims of science to a place in the school curriculum have been overlooked despite the fact that the contemporary culture was growing more scientific throughout the period. The influence of this neglect is still with us. It is therefore true to say that in organizing a curriculum which fits children and older students for the modern world the whole of the present culture must be considered. To use the word coined by the Crowther Report, 'numeracy' as well as literacy is important if the schools are to come near passing on the culture in this respect.

(iii) *Social Class Differences*. There is another difficulty, similar in some ways to that of the rural and urban sub-cultures. This problem lies in the fact that social classes may be considered as sub-cultures. This affects the schools in various ways, but one important aspect is found in the relation between teacher and taught. Very often the teacher is middle-class and hence has middle-class values. Even if he has come from a working-class background, the teacher will in all probability aspire to the middle class and hence hold the values of that class more strongly. Since the majority of pupils in schools come from the working class, the teaching situation is normally such that a member of one sub-culture tries to communicate with members of another sub-culture. Very often, as we saw when considering social class learning, the teacher is trying to teach his pupils a way of life and set of values that is alien to them. The process, if successful, could lead to cultural change.

A way to look at the policy begun in Britain in the 1870s by the Elementary Education Acts of mass popular education, certainly as it was conceived in the minds of the gentlemen then in both political and administrative power over the educational system, is to see it as an attempt to 'gentle the masses'. In other words, schools were to be the agents of cultural change on behalf of the rulers and at the expense of the ruled. Some of the details of the changes aimed for may have been justifiable on ethical or social grounds, but today we are a little more tender of conscience about how we treat those who differ from ourselves. Yet, although universal formal schooling now exists administratively, our theory of mass education is still unsettled in some important respects. Thus, education is by definition the passing-on by one set of persons, usually teachers, to another, their pupils, of a selection from the culture. It, therefore, almost inevitably makes some attempt to emphasize the contents of one sub-culture rather than of any others. As schools are now organized in Britain and in most other societies the culture of those who dominate is given emphasis at the expense of that of the ruled. Many theorists, however, reject this apparently inevitable development as cultural imperialism, whereas it can most profitably be seen either from one point of view as one facet of the endless political conflict between the ruling class and the ruled, or from another viewpoint as the continuous process of negotiation whereby a culture comes to change. Perhaps in this context teachers should humbly remember how such sub-cultures have survived in most essential respects despite mass schooling and the spread of the mass media. This survival is a further tribute to the power of the family as an agent of socialization.

(iv) *Differences by Types of School.* In Chapter 7 we saw that there were a number of different types of school at both primary and secondary levels whose styles of operation and whose curricula were so different that each could be seen as transmitting different patterns of culture. It therefore seems likely that the organization of British education, especially at the secondary level, may further complicate the way in which the culture is transmitted. In general, children at first attend a primary school that is common to the majority including, for at least a year or two, many of those who are going to enter the private school system. From about eleven, secondary education is given in several types of school. A brief examination of the main reasons given for reorganizing the secondary schools on a comprehensive basis will indicate the type of dysfunction that is caused by the existence of several types of secondary school, at least in respect of the particular function of the educational system now under consideration.

The main aim is that by including all the children from a given large catchment area in one school, already existing sub-cultural differences amongst them will be broken down and, furthermore, because children destined in their later lives for different types of social position will no longer be educated apart, separate sub-cultures will neither be created nor strengthened. In addition, the different curricula now taught in the existing types of secondary schools will be united in the comprehensive school so that, it is hoped, curricula based on stratified versions of the stock of knowledge will be eliminated.

However, Ford's research indicated that in respect of such a major part of the British culture as the normal views held about social class, different versions of the culture were either still being passed on or not being eliminated within at least one typical comprehensive school, and Miller's older work shows that a stratified version of the stock of knowledge still formed the basis of the curriculum in the comprehensive school in Birmingham in which his research was undertaken.[6] The conclusion must be that the sub-cultures transmitted by the tripartite system are in very large measure learnt, or at least supported, in the various streams of the comprehensive school. Thus, this new type of school, as now organized, functions to perpetuate many of the cultural divisions associated with the system of organization which it is replacing. Nor is it easy to see how the comprehensive school could ever overcome the problem of social class learning, since the fundamental differences in thought processes caused in this way occur long before the child reaches the secondary stage. Further, as long as parents can contract out of the state system and buy their children a different culture in the private system, the transmission of one single culture cannot be achieved. Nor, perhaps, should this be our aim for several reasons, one of the most cogent of which is the need to provide religious education of different types and to respect the ways of life of the various groups of immigrants that we now find settled amongst us.

(v) *Sub-cultures within the School*. There is one final difficulty which must be examined. Within schools themselves it is possible to identify sub-cultures. Often there exists a group whose main aim in school is to play games well, whilst at the other extreme there is a group whose whole aim is academic work. Again, in some schools, particularly in the poorer urban areas, there is a small group whose interests seem centred in activities best described as delinquent. In his work published in 1961 on the US high school Coleman called the sub-cultures associated with these groups the fun, the academic and the delinquent sub-cultures. He also found traces of a fourth subculture, the vocational.[7] It may well be that this sub-culture, with its stress on values relevant to success in one's chosen career, is to be found in Britain in the secondary technical school.

The fun culture in the shape of organized games has for some time been consciously used in British schools with definite objects in view. It had been assumed that games trained character. However, this aspect of the fun culture, games, has often come to have such importance in many British schools as to encroach seriously on the academic sub-culture. Games mattered and work did not. Intellectual pursuits such as poetry and art have not a very high standing in our culture. How much of this is due to the cult of games in our secondary schools?

Coleman found that the delinquent sub-culture was marked by avoidance of and rebellion against the school. This was not mere adolescent negativism, but a conscious total rejection of the school. It was found in Britain that, when the school-leaving age was raised from fourteen to fifteen, the peak age for juvenile delinquency also rose, so that it still occurred in the final year at school.[8] There seems to be a conscious revolt against a system where the adolescent is treated as a child. This rejection is symbolized by the boy who had just left school and was asked by his former headmaster what he thought of the new buildings. 'It could be marble, sir,' he replied, 'but it would still be a bloody school.'[9] If the delinquent sub-culture is strong in a school, the transmission of the present culture becomes very difficult. The children who become members of the deliquent group will learn to reject much or even all that the school stands for, and thereby most of that the majority of adults would think worth while.

The function of transmitting culture is a complex one. Much of this process, and particularly that part relating to the passing on of the stock of knowledge, is now carried out in the educational system, but the creation of institutions has in some cases built in dysfunctions which are often not recognized. Sub-cultures can provide a healthy tension, but this is not always the case. We have to consider whether our educational aims are such that when we recognize dysfunction we should reform the institutional framework which our analysis reveals to have caused it.

B. Sources of Change

I. *External to the Educational System*

Not only does much of the impetus for the social change that affects the schools originate outside the educational system, it often comes from outside the country itself. Thus, wars can bring major disruption to children's schooling, as was the case in the second world war in Britain, when many children were evacuated from danger areas and brought up for years away from their own parents; less dramatically the arrival of US troops in Australia in 1942 resulted in a greater emphasis upon American studies in school curricula. Another example of such a change forced upon a society from outside was the reaction of Western nations to the USSR's putting of Sputnik into orbit in 1957. Certainly in the USA this was perceived as a military crisis in that a probable enemy had caught up or even overtaken a supposed firmly-held technological lead. There followed immediately an attempt to improve the teaching of mathematics and science upon which advanced technology was seen to be founded. In the UK this perception was reinforced by the need to improve the efficiency of our economy so as to gain advantages in the battle for experts upon which our standard of life was felt to depend. The curriculum renewal movement in both countries can be dated from this event.

Crises that are internal to one country can have a similar effect of suddenly jolting assumptions concerning the efficiency or the aims of the educational system. Questions of aim are more often asked after such major internal upheavals as a revolution. Economic problems of the type felt by advanced industrial capitalist societies since the mid-1970s, for example continuing inflation and unemployment, have also led to the asking of questions about how effective the huge resources now invested in education really are and how responsive the educational system is, or ought to be, to changes occurring in other social institutions.

One major source of such change is demographic. The 'baby boom' of the post-war years demanded a huge expansion in the numbers of school places and of teachers to staff them. The problems implicit in this situation were compounded for many societies by the increase in international migration, whether unplanned, as with coloured migration to Britain, or planned, as in the vast migration to Australia of British in the 1950s, or Italians, Greeks and Yugoslavs in the 1960s and of those of near-Eastern stock from the mid-1960s. More recently in most advanced industrial societies, birth and migration rates have declined so that currently the difficult political problem of planning a decrease in the educational effort has to be solved. For example, it is already known that in the period between 1975 and 1988 the numbers of children attending the secondary schools of the Inner London Education Authority will decline from 180,126 to around 109,235. Very detailed questions concerned the closing of schools, the recruitment and distribution of specialist teachers and of preserving the general morale of the school system during the period of change can immediately be raised.

Falls in the birth rate originate within the family, a social institution about whose future any prediction is difficult. We have seen that at the present there are changes built into the social structure that could alter the direction of socialization towards producing bureacratic rather than entrepreneurial traits in children. Furthermore, the norms of family life have changed somewhat, both because of the altered position of women and because of the new views of what a family might be – one-parent families or *de facto* relationships are now more easily accepted. All these changes can affect either the techniques used by teachers in the classroom to meet the changed personalities of their pupils or the curriculum because the altered moral standards outside the school demand new content in the teaching of religious education or social studies.

The changes in the rates of migration are, and the answers to questions about the future scale of the educational system will be, largely determined by decisions ultimately made by politicians. In the great age of educational expansion after 1945 those involved in education in many countries have tended to forget that the public educational system by which they are employed is financed out of taxation and that, therefore, in some sense, the nature of which is at present very unclear, schools are not autonomous, but are responsible to the society around them. The position of all so-called professionals in such a situation is difficult. The amount available to the experts, that is the doctors, in the National Health Service, to cover the cost of prescriptions, operations and the medical care that will save life or ease pain becomes a political decision, made by laymen. Similar political decisions do, and will, determine the scale and the direction of the educational system. Thus, a very large research project was established in the mid-1960s by the government to discover as far as was possible what the effects of reorganizing secondary schools along comprehensive lines might be. In 1967, before any results could be made known, the political decision was made to move more rapidly towards comprehensive reorganization. It is hard for many in the educational service, but it is an inevitable consequence of our social structure, that much of what they do must be determined, at least at the margin, but on occasions much more centrally, by the results of normal democratic political conflict.

The nature of the political struggle, however, depends to a great extent upon ideas, many of which are generated by intellectuals. This is a difficult category to define closely, but within it fall those who by their writing, teaching and conversation produce, develop and spread ideas which later influence action in various spheres. Some intellectuals cover a very wide range in their thinking and may be termed general: for example, Marx and Marcuse have discussed and deeply influenced political, economic and educational ideologies, policies and action. They were certainly deeply influential on the spirit of radical individualism that came to the fore in the late-1960s in the universities and upon which many of the contemporary pleas for non-competitive individual equality in all social spheres and for individual participation at various political levels are founded. At this point the importance of the source of social change that G. M. Young emphasized becomes very clear. The ideas already built into the experience of the younger generation, will in some way or other be carried forward, perhaps somewhat altered, perhaps less utopian in tenor, and will during the lifetime of that generation be present to influence political conflicts about the future direction of social and, hence, of educational change.

Other intellectuals may be called institutional, as they mainly work within one particular institution, though the effects of their thinking may be more general. Economists are obvious examples since the object of their thought inevitably affects us all. Thus, the work of Keynes came to form the basis of policies concerning full employment and that of Beveridge profoundly influenced the way the welfare state developed in Britain. In the last chapter the influence of the writings of the philosopher, Rawls, upon social policy, more particularly upon the policy of positive discrimination in education, was cited. Lastly, the writing of theologians, trying to clarify their views about God, can have a wide impact, as was the case when modern theological thinking was channelled through a paperback, Bishop John Robinson's *Honest to God* (1963), that became a bestseller, so that many people were influenced to rethink their basic moral principles. One thing that becomes obvious as one cites examples is that many of the British intellectuals whose ideas are sources of change are themselves located within the educational system.

2. *Internal to the Educational System*

On the Continent, historically, very many intellectuals have been what Mannheim called 'free-floating', that is not firmly located in any social institution, though they might have earned much of their livelihood, as Marx did in his early life, by diffusing their ideas through the medium of journalism. In Britain this has been a much rarer pattern of life for intellectuals, who have more often been employed in education, particularly in universities. This is obviously the case for such institutional intellectuals as Keynes or Beveridge referred to above, but there is also a long British tradition of general intellectuals being employed within education, many of whom were seen by the public as literary critics, yet concerning themselves with the wider conditions of culture (Johnson, 1979). Matthew Arnold – poet, literary critic and school inspector – wrote *Culture and Anarchy* (1869) in an attempt to influence the direction in which he believed the new middle class was leading the culture. Today, Raymond Williams – university lecturer, critic and novelist – has tried to do much the same, though with a more radical emphasis, in much of his writing.[10]

An influential figure in this tradition was F. R. Leavis – literary critic, editor and university lecturer, whose guiding critical principle was that the reading of any work must uncover the values implicit in it. He openly extended this principle from literary to general education in which he hoped that pupils would be taught to discriminate between the values at work in the environment around them. Furthermore, his idea of education was extensive in that not only did he make recommendations concerning the curriculum at the various stages of the educational system, but he also wrote trenchantly about the role of such para-educational agencies as the BBC and the Arts Council. His influence, both through his own writing and editorial work, especially on *Scrutiny*, and through the diffusion of his ideas by his pupils, has been very wide within formal education on the choice of curriculum and on the preparation of curricular materials, particularly but not entirely within the humanities, but his general ideas have also strengthened the consumers' movement both in relation to general purchasing, for example the journal *Choice*, but also concerning the provision of educational services, for example the journal *Where*.[11] Since such intellectuals are located within education they must to some extent be controlled by the existing structure of power of the organizations within which they work. Leavis made his way within his own university of Cambridge only with extreme difficulty due to intense opposition to his ideas by those with power.

Intellectuals of this type are rarely located within schools, so that change relating to academic ideas infrequently arises from the schools, if only because next to no research is done there. But new methods of teaching or new ways of choosing material from the total culture, that is new types of curricula, are usually born in schools or generated by intellectuals, for example college lecturers, who are in close touch with the schools, that is by education's own institutional intellectuals. Even in this case conflict can occur. Thus, in the mid-nineteenth century a new science curriculum was evolved in the elementary schools; it was based on the idea of teaching the science of everyday things, a choice of material seen as more apt for the working-class pupils of these schools. However, this curriculum met neither the view of science held in the universities nor that of contemporary educational administrators or their political masters, who did not want the teaching of material that they saw as potentially culturally divisive.[12]

Changes to the moral curriculum confront sanctions of a different nature. The growth of games as an instrument of moral education was largely generated in the schools without great public opposition, but changes to the moral curriculum depend for their acceptance upon local agreement or upon their falling within the already generally accepted boundaries of tolerated behaviour. Change is born in deviance and raises the whole issue of social control (Davies, 1976). As was indicated at the start of this chapter one of the main functions entrusted to education is that of ensuring conformity. Thus, when educational organizations develop changes, those around them may not allow behaviour that is seen as deviant. Universities are usually permitted to generate academic deviance, often called creative research. Under some circumstances, for example in restrictive political regimes, this is not the situation and, as in the USSR, some forms of research are either not permitted or their results are not universally published. Moral creativity is harder to establish and those, whether teachers or others, who advocate that, for example, Marxism or homosexuality be discussed in schools, are likely to be seen by the general public or by administrators ostensibly acting in the public interest, as deviants who are suggesting changes that are beyond the bounds of what is now tolerated.

To date, very little important change has emanated from the schools, which have tended to function as agents, not engines, of social change. Universities are different, since for certainly well over a century now, they have been seen as licensed deviants and have acted as the social location from which intellectuals of various types can work for changes to the academic and the moral knowledge upon which social action must ultimately be based. But to have an idea is not to put it into action; change has to be negotiated politically. Even when we feel sure that we can predict change, individuals may successfully oppose it or harness the social forces involved in an unexpected way. Few theologians saw how some of their ideas would be used to help justify the morally more permissive ideas of the 1960s.

C. Change in the Schools

Selleck has shown very clearly how the ideas of education's own institutional intellectuals, in this case those developing ideas about what was necessary for the reform of primary education, become attenuated over time as they are put into action through the educational system.[13] What eventually happens at the chalk-face, rarely matches either the utopian ideals of the intellectual innovator or the hard-nosed aims of the administrator or his political master. In this final section we shall examine why schools are so slow to change, what strategies may be used to overcome this tardiness and whether or not the school's conservatism tends to squash individual creativity.

1. *Changing Schools*

All organizations, once established, tend to become somewhat fixed in their structure. Except in crises their members for various reasons are unwilling to change what seems a workable system. Schools seem especially prone to this conservative stance. Admittedly one of the major aims is to pass on the contemporary culture much as it is, a role that encourages preservation of the *status quo*. Yet this goal could be achieved in various and changing ways. But great diversity and much large-scale change are rare in schools. Why? One reason sometimes given by laymen is that teachers have an easy life and either are or grow lazy. Such explanations are supported by little real evidence. Most studies that compare the personality structures of the members of the different 'professions' show no major differences between them; teachers are not very different in personality from others of professional status. Furthermore, we must try to avoid psychological explanations here and look for social processes at work that cause what we are trying to explain.

Teachers, unlike those working in most similar occupations, have much prior experience of their work milieu. They are socialized into the general ways of schools from childhood. They then, without much or any other occupational experience, undergo a powerful process of occupational socialization, often in the isolated environment of a monotechnic, the college of education, prior to returning for life to schools as teachers. Furthermore, the academic knowledge which they teach is basic in nature and hence rarely subject to much change. In the case of the moral curriculum teachers are often seen as the guardians of traditional behavioural standards to which parents wish their children to conform, but which they themselves tacitly, or even sometimes openly, abjure. On all these counts teachers are not easily going to act as major agents of change.

One recent American study illustrates a number of further common difficulties, social in their nature, in bringing about change in schools. At Cambire School the majority of the teachers were dedicated to the introduction of a new teaching method, open and discovery-based, and described as 'the catalytic role model'. The innovation failed because there was no clear common understanding of what it really was that constituted the change and because the young teachers involved did not have, or were not taught, the necessary new skills. In addition, and this is a common problem, the organization of the school did not match the demands of the new system; in this case the timetable was rigid and was not changed to allow for a more open, flexible, discovery-oriented style of teaching.[14]

This last difficulty points to the importance in this context of viewing schools as micro-political systems in which the present arrangement of sanctions, the rewards to and the punishments of teachers is in a sensitive and negotiated balance. Change disturbs this state; someone always loses or at least perceives themselves to do so. Perhaps Mr X or Miss Y can no longer have the period after lunch free to go to the shops or Mrs Z must teach in a room that she dislikes. It is because there are costs for people in changes that when they are forced on schools the unwilling teachers domesticate the new methods, using such comments as, 'It's what I've always done really', or continue within the acknowledged privacy of their classrooms, whatever they may claim elsewhere, to do much as they did before.

The strategies used to-date when attempting to bring about changes in the schools have generally tended to overlook the political nature of schools. Three general strategies have been identified: the power–coercive, the empirical–rational and the normative–reeducational (Whiteside, 1978). Each will be examined in turn.

The use of power to implement educational innovation was until perhaps 1950 the classic method in most societies. An excellent example when massive change, consequent upon a crisis, was brought about by decree occurred after the defeat of the Prussians by Napoleon at the battle of Jena in 1807. The Prussians believed that the successful development throughout the eighteenth century till then of what was really a poorly endowed country was due to their educational system, and their rulers determined to build it anew; during 1808–10, under von Humboldt, the plans were drawn up and introduced by decree to establish the system which was to support the Prussian drive to unite Germany and to form an educational example at the secondary and tertiary levels that was imitated throughout much of the rest of the world. Rather less massive changes were similarly introduced in Britain in the second third of the nineteenth century each time the elementary code was revised. Today the revision of many examination syllabuses functions in a similar manner for secondary schools. In the days when, to use Beeby's terms, the educational system was still at 'the formal stage', when teachers were poorly trained and ill-educated, worked by rule-of-thumb and were unable to devise a syllabus, the use of informed power to cause changes was justifiable. But in contemporary advanced industrial societies the educational systems have reached 'the stage of meaning', when teachers are well enough educated and trained to match their teaching to local, and even individual, needs.[15] Teachers not only oppose coercive strategies of change because of their greater competence, but because they now feel themselves to be 'professionals' who should be free to decide for themselves rather than be ordered how and what to teach.

Furthermore, since the contemporary professional ideology demands freedom for teachers so that all coercive orders from administrators or even from the headmaster are resented, the use of power is often counter-productive in that it sets teachers against the changes to be introduced.

Because of these difficulties and objections other strategies, based on techniques of persuasion, are now more common. The first of these, the empirical–rational, depends upon one-way communication with teachers by lecturers, authors or educational critics. The teacher is assumed to be a rational man who will appreciate the force of empirical evidence concerning the rights and wrongs of suggested and present methods of teaching or organization. Although this sounds well there are problems, the first of which is that there is usually very little sound evidence available that gives unambiguous support for any one educational position. The case for many educational changes – and the voluminous recent writings on alternative schooling may be taken as an excellent example – usually consists of a little hard data, interpreted in the light of a modicum of common sense, filtered through a great deal of ideology, whilst the contrary position is often supported as strongly by the same data and common sense, but a contrary ideology. Much of this writing, as the teachers at Cambire School found, is unclear in style, so that different, often opposing, interpretations are possible for those who read it, though teachers in both the UK and the USA have been shown to read little professional writing, perhaps viewing most such educational material as too theoretical for busy and practical people to use in their own classrooms. In addition to these social psychological objections the strategy of approaching the teacher as an individual by definition forgets that, however rational he may be about pedagogical matters, he is set in the social system of a school, the changing of which has political implications and costs.

The second strategy that relies on techniques based on persuasion has been termed the normative–reeducational. This method relies on two-way communication between, for example, a consultant and a teacher or a group of teachers. In-service training is often based on this method; a temporary social system is established away from the schools of those involved, but within which great support can be generated for some set of innovatory ideas or techniques. However, as soon as the participants return to their usual social system, namely the school, the permanent existing political pressures overcome the drive for change of the reeducated individuals. This process may to some extent be averted if two or more teachers undergo the same in-service course so that on their return to their school they are able to support each other's innovatory moves against the opposition of those who have never left the permanent social system. Smith has shown how a Schools Council primary science programme lasted longest after its introduction in schools where two teachers were involved in its introduction.[16] Consultants have also been introduced into schools both on a temporary and on a permanent basis. In the former case their influence may last little longer than their presence in the school, but in the latter case they become part of the ongoing social system. Richardson (1973) has analysed how she was accepted in the role of consultant in one comprehensive school for more than a year, serving on committees, attending meetings of various types and always being available for consultancy. Though this method takes time, great skill in interpersonal relationships, and exacts the high costs of any outsider intruding into an existing political system, it does seem to be capable of easing organizational change.

The comments made on all three common strategies used in the past to achieve change return us to the point that was reached at the end of the discussion upon stability in educational organizations. Schools are social systems that can, especially in the context of bringing about change, profitably be seen in political terms. The contemporary reliance upon the school-based development of curricula can be examined in this light. It is an extension of the normative–reeducative strategy. Colleagues do not leave their permanent social system; they renegotiate the present political truce, but do so knowing that they have to live with the decisions made; since they jointly pledge themselves publicly to any future change that is agreed they can not easily back out of a cooperatively accepted innovation. The presence of an outsider may be needed, however, for two reasons: firstly, to break an initial political logjam, though often the head, as legitimate leader, can afford the costs of taking such an initiative; and secondly, to avert the danger that, since the innovation will be totally internally generated, it may not be based on the fullest or the best available information.

One further point needs consideration. Innovation in the past has rarely taken into account the views of a school's clients, whether these are seen as pupils or their parents. The balance of political power, particularly owing to demands for participation in school governance by parents and pupils, has altered so that both groups are now sometimes consulted when changes are being discussed. The part played by parents and pupils must depend upon the age of the pupils and the nature of the school concerned and, indeed, the only wise generalization that can perhaps be made about educational innovation in the contemporary circumstances and in the present shortage of empirical knowledge is that we are best-advised to start by making any analysis of the problems relating to educational change in political terms.

2. *Producing Innovators*

We do not know much about the education of recent innovators. During the industrial revolution many were self-taught, but this is no longer common in industry, if only because of the extensive knowledge needed to understand present-day techniques. Recent research in the field of psychology has, however, revealed a disturbing possibility. Our teaching methods, certainly up to the age of sixteen, tend to demand the one right answer and throughout are characterized by examinations which encourage standard answers. It may be that we turn children who are potentially creative into adults whose only wish is to succeed through conformity. Psychologists now believe that some people have an innate mode of thinking such that they tend to give the expected answer or follow the usual line of thought, whilst others have a mode that enables them to diverge easily from the conventional. It is suspected that the emphasis in our schools may teach the 'diverger' to think in a more conformist manner and thereby crush potential creativity.[17]

One piece of research already mentioned has explored in a more sociological fashion the manner in which the interpersonal inter-action between teacher and pupil seems to encourage or limit the development in children of the mutual perception that they are creative. Evans, working in two pre-schools and two primary schools in Melbourne, found that the teachers involved held ideas of who were the most and the least creative children in their classes. These ideas about what behaviour is perceived to be creative were probably learnt during their training period, though children, unlike those in these schools, who have been in a school for some time may have reputations amongst the teachers concerning their personalities; in such cases teachers may hear and react to the reports of the former teachers of their own pupils. Evans found that these teachers gave more attention and encouragement by word and by other non-verbal ways to those children who were perceived to be creative than to those seen as non-creative, and, as was reported in Chapter 11, there were more creative boys than girls. This process can be conceptualized in terms of deviance theory in that positively evaluated deviant behaviour, called 'being creative', was condoned or rewarded, whilst negatively, or perhaps neutrally, evaluated behaviour, being not creative, went unnoticed or unrewarded.[18] Under these circumstances creativity is seen as a self-perception, learnt in the classroom, whose basis may not be some innate psychological trait, but rather a teacher's either chance or socially patterned observation of some act of behaviour by a child, previously learnt or exhibited randomly, that matches a socially approved perception of what is creativity.

We may not know the educational background of our innovators, but work in the USA has revealed two facts that we may suspect to be true in Britain. Despite the growth of research in large teams, about half of industrial innovations still seems to be made by individuals.[19] This emphasizes that, if the schools do stunt the creative potential of individuals, they are acting in a dysfunctional way in that they are stopping the flow of innovators. Secondly, there seems to be no difference in the quality of the output of American scientists from schools or colleges in which the expenditure per pupil is high and from those where it is low.[20] Anyone with experience in British education might go so far as to say that the correlation in Britain was inverse!

The educational system has itself changed, as we have seen, so as to ease adaptation to continuous technical change. The movement towards staying longer at school and towards less specialized courses at all levels of education is helping to meet change on the side of production. But what little we know of the education of our present innovators leads us to believe that here the educational system, whether for administrative reasons or because of the manner in which teachers and pupils interact, is acting in a dysfunctional way in that it may well be checking the supply of innovators. This would seem a serious fault in a country traditionally as conservative as Britain.

D. Conclusion

As was observed at the beginning of this chapter the consideration of social change and of cultural stability are so closely linked that an analysis of one, being an artificial abstraction from the real world, almost inevitably leads back to some facet of the other. This conclusion to an analysis of two of the functions of education posited for analysis in Part III of this book reminds us that any examination of one function of education on its own is artificial and is a strategy only used to gain greater theoretical purchase on the problems involved in the analysis of the structure of education. All functions are interrelated. This must not be forgotten, and in examining issues of policy we must trace out not only how the educational system is fulfilling the various functions that we have posited *individually*, but also how in its operation the goals relating to the main social institutions that are given to the schools, *taken together* balance or conflict in the way in which they are worked out between teacher and pupils.

The very decision to hand part of the task of socializing the young to an institution other than the family builds in the chance of conflict and, hence, of possible change, though for the last time the comment must be made about the power of the family as an agent of socialization. As more educational organizations are set up, so sub-cultures can be born within them. This can result in healthy tension, but it can also lead to dysfunctions which may be latent until a careful analysis is made. The results of such an examination may drive us to justify a particular sub-culture; this will force us out of the realm of sociological analysis into the field of politics or philosophy, since we must then consider our aims in education. In one particular sphere, namely the position of coloured immigrants, recent developments in Britain force us to think about the social aims that must be settled prior to determining what we do in the schools, since we cannot know how to teach white or coloured children, together or apart, until we know whether our policy is to integrate immigrants to our own way of life, or to aim for a pluralist society in which all cultures are given equal respect. This decision must be taken at a political level and, indeed, the ultimate power over the direction of change must rest with politicians or voters; this is true even when the change under consideration is economic, since our present version of capitalism no longer relies entirely on the self-steering capabilities of a *laissez-faire* system to determine the future directions of change. Our knowledge of the effects and sources of change is very limited, particularly in the field of education. We are still unsure of the most efficient strategies through which innovatory policy, decided by those with political power, may best be converted into the behaviour of teachers and pupils in schools. In a rapidly changing world, the least we can do is to be constantly aware that this is a problem and that it is closely related to whether we go on teaching what, and how we do so.

BIBLIOGRAPHY

G. Bowker, *Education of Coloured Immigrants*, 1968.

B. Davies, *Social Control and Education*, 1976.

E. Durkheim, *Education and Sociology*, Glencoe, Ill., 1956.

T. S. Eliot, *Notes Towards the Definition of Culture*, 1948.

R. Hoggart, *The Uses of Literacy*, 1957.

L. R. Johnson, *The Cultural Critics*, 1979.

E. Richardson, *The Teacher, the School and the Task of Management*, 1973.

C. P. Snow, *The Two Cultures and the Scientific Revolution*, Cambridge, 1964.

T. Whiteside, *The Sociology of Educational Innovation*, 1978.

NOTES

1 J. Habermas, *Legitimation Crisis*, 1976, p. 8.
2 T. Burgin and P. Edson, *Spring Grove*, Oxford, 1967.
3 For Sparkbrook see J. Williams, 'The Younger Generation', Chapter X in J. Rex and R. Moore, *Race, Community and Conflict*, Oxford, 1967. For a general survey see R. J. Goldman and F. M. Taylor, 'Coloured Immigrant Children: a Survey of Research, Studies and Literature on their Educational Problems and Potential – in Britain', *Educational Research*, June 1966. See also T. Kawwa, 'A Survey of Ethnic Attitudes of Some British Secondary School Pupils', *British Journal of Social and Clinical Psychology*, September 1968.
4 G. M. Young, *Portrait of an Age*, 1936.
5 C. P. Snow treats the same problem in his novel *The New Man*, London, 1950, though here he introduces an intermediate sub-culture, that of the engineers.
6 J. Ford, *Social Class and the Comprehensive School*, 1969; T. W. G. Miller, *Values in the Comprehensive School*, Edinburgh, 1961.
7 J. S. Coleman, *The Adolescent Society*, New York, 1961.
8 D. J. West, *The Young Offender*, 1967, p. 15.
9 *Half our Future* (Newsom Report), 1963, p. 2.
10 See, for example, *Culture and Society*, 1958.
11 P. W. Musgrave, ' "Scrutiny" and Education', *British Journal of Educational Studies*, October 1973.
12 D. Layton, *Science for the People*, 1973.
13 R. J. W. Selleck, *English Primary Education and the Progressives, 1914–1939*, 1972.
14 N. Gross, J. B. Giacquinta and M. Bernstein, *Implementing Organizational Innovation: a Sociological Analysis of Planned Educational Change* New York, 1971.
15 C. E. Beeby, *The Quality of Education in Developing Countries*, Cambridge, Mass., 1966.
16 M. P. Smith, 'Curriculum Change at the Local Level', *Journal of Curriculum Studies*, November 1971.
17 For a recent account of work in this field as it relates to education, see H. Lytton, *Creativity and Education*, 1971.
18 T. D. Evans, 'Creativity, Sex Role Socialization and Pupil–Teacher Interactions in Early Schooling', *Sociological Review*, February 1979.
19 J. Jewkes *et al.*, *The Sources of Invention*, 1958.
20 For schools see an unpublished survey in Connecticut in J. S. Coleman, *The Adolescent Society*, New York, 1961, p. 235, and for colleges see R. H. Knapp and H. B. Goodrich, *Origins of American Scientists*, Chicago, 1952, pp. 45–6.

Indexes

Name Index

Subject Index

Aberdeen, 74, 78, 86, 121, 122, 125, 282, 283, 284, 294
academic traditions of different countries, 198, 224
accent: as indicator of social class, 61, 71
achievement, 74, 77, 87
adolescence: definitions of, 94
adolescents, 43, 53, 71, 92: and careers, 331; and colour, 109: crime rate among, 55; and leadership, 280; and mass media, 122–4; and peer groups, 92–115; and politics, 285; and school, 110, 251; and sex, 101, 106–7, 250; and social class, 70, 107
adult discount, 118
age grades, 21
age roles, 103
alienation of workers, 302
Assessment of Performance Unit, 276
authority: in families, 74
authority figures: child's perception of, 282

Belfast, 85
Bethnal Green, 100, 107, 108
Beveridge Report, 152
Boy Scouts, 99, 102, 108
Boys' Own Paper, 94
bricolage, 99
Brisbane, Australia, 233
Bristol, 84

Cambire School, 386, 388
Canada, 248
capability: and family, 356; and

streamlining, 358; and type of school, 355; geographical comparisons, 352; international comparisons, 353, 384; inter-sex comparisons, 353, 354; social class comparisons, 354, 357
capitalism, 298, 309
cartoon films, 131
character training, 141
choice: for pupils, 228
Civil Service: education of, 278
Classics, 197, 203
classrooms: attention in, 253; authority in, 244; communication in, 254; deviance in, 260; interaction in, 243; negotiation in, 257; stratification in, 246; in the USSR, 291
communes, 56
Communists, 174, 293
corporal punishment, 26, 27, 154, 228
counselling, 226
County Durham, 176
creativity, 223, 390
Crowther Report, 349, 354, 364, 374, 375
Cuba, 289
cues, 255
cultural hegemony, 202
culture, 47, 48; changing, 372, 379; conservation of, 367–70; immigrants and, 320; of childhood, 116; transmission of, 367, 373

delinquency, 31, 55, 99, 235, 247, 251, 260, 378